Oracle Fusion Middleware 11*g* Architecture and Management

Oracle Press™

Oracle Fusion Middleware 11*g* Architecture and Management

Reza Shafii
Stephen Lee
Gangadhar Konduri

New York Chicago San Francisco
Lisbon London Madrid Mexico City Milan
New Delhi San Juan Seoul Singapore Sydney Toronto

The McGraw-Hill Companies

Cataloging-in-Publication Data is on file with the Library of Congress

McGraw-Hill books are available at special quantity discounts to use as premiums and sales promotions, or for use in corporate training programs. To contact a representative, please e-mail us at bulksales@mcgraw-hill.com.

Oracle Fusion Middleware 11*g* Architecture and Management

1 2 3 4 5 6 7 8 9 0 DOC DOC 1 0 9 8 7 6 5 4 3 2 1

ISBN 978-0-07-175417-0
MHID 0-07-175417-2

Sponsoring Editor
Meghan Riley Manfre

Editorial Supervisor
Jody McKenzie

Project Manager
Tania Andrabi,
Cenveo Publisher Services

Acquisitions Coordinator
Stephanie Evans

Technical Editor
Jason Aiken

Copy Editor
Bart Reed

Proofreader
Carol Shields

Indexer
James Minkin

Production Supervisor
Jean Bodeaux

Composition
Cenveo Publisher Services

Illustration
Cenveo Publisher Services

Art Director, Cover
Jeff Weeks

Cover Designer
Pattie Lee

To Karine, your hard work and dedication will always be a source of inspiration.
—Reza

To my parents—for everything you have taught me and given me. To my wife, April—for being here.
—Stephen

To my parents.
—Gangadhar

About the Authors

Reza Shafii is a Senior Principal Product Manager within the Oracle Fusion Middleware group. He is a member of the Oracle Coherence product management team and was previously responsible for ensuring that all Oracle Fusion Middleware products are architecturally aligned, optimized for life-cycle management, and tightly integrated.

Prior to his work at Oracle, Reza was a consultant within the BEA Systems Canadian Consulting practice, where he was recognized as the consultant of the year in 2006. As a consultant, Reza worked closely with a number of customers across North America to assist them in their design, delivery, and maintenance of enterprise applications.

Reza has a BS in computer science from the University of British Columbia, where he graduated with honors. He also has an MBA from the University of Ottawa. Reza is a published author of several technical articles.

Stephen Lee spent 12 years at Oracle in various roles within the Oracle Identity Management team. He was a Principal Product Manager for Oracle Identity Analytics and owned the Fusion Middleware Audit Framework component of Oracle Fusion Middleware 11*g*. As a technical lead, he led the design and development of the middleware application security framework for Oracle Application Server 9*i* and 10*g*, holding multiple patents for his work. Prior to that, he was one of the original members of the Oracle Internet Directory team from 1998 to 2001.

Stephen is currently a Senior Product Manager at Okta, Inc., focusing on cloud identity management. He has a B.Math (Double Honors with Distinction) in Computer Science and "Combinatorics and Optimization" from the University of Waterloo, Ontario, Canada.

Gangadhar Konduri is a Senior Director of product management at Oracle and currently leads a product management team responsible for Oracle ADF, JDeveloper, MDS, and Oracle Fusion Middleware extensions for Fusion Applications. He was previously responsible for the architecture, design, and development of Oracle Metadata Services as well as the strategy and design for the integration of Oracle WebCenter Enterprise 2.0 technologies with Oracle Fusion Applications. Gangadhar has been with Oracle since 1999, holding various development, engineering management, and product management positions.

Gangadhar holds a bachelor's degree in Computer Sciences from I.I.T., Kharagpur (India) where he graduated summa cum laude. He holds a master's degree in Electrical Engineering and Computer Science from M.I.T. Gangadhar, has authored several technical articles, and presented at various conferences. Gangadhar has four patents pending in the areas of metadata and customization.

About the Technical Editors

Jason Aiken is an Engineering Manager at Walt Disney Parks and Resorts Online. Jason has over 18 years of software engineering experience. His professional journey has included stints at Corel Corporation, Nortel, Motorola, Sprint, and most recently Disney. He is currently responsible for managing the software development and sustainment of e-commerce websites (utilizing Oracle RAC) for the Walt Disney Company, generating annual revenues in excess of a billion dollars.

James Bayer, Principal Product Manager, WebLogic Server, Oracle Corporation, has worked as a customer-facing Sales Consultant and as a Product Manager with Oracle WebLogic Server for five years and with Java application servers for over ten years. He also maintains a public blog and is a frequent contributor to the WebLogic Server forums on the Oracle Technology Network. He has a bachelor's degree in Mathematics and Computer Science from the University of Nebraska, Lincoln.

Marc Chanliau has been in the software industry for over 35 years. Marc first started as a developer (Assembly language and C in those days), and then managed teams of developers distributed across multiple countries. Over the past ten years, Marc has been substantially involved in industry standards for Java and XML security. In particular, Marc was one of the original designers of the Security Assertion Markup Language (SAML) and a contributor to the WS-Security and WS-Policy standards. Marc is currently employed by Oracle as a director of product management for identity and access control products. Marc has a post-graduate degree in computational linguistics from the University of Paris (France).

Paul Encarnación is a Director in the Oracle WebCenter development team. His responsibilities have included software development and management in the areas of Security, Framework, Portlets, Lifecycle, Install, Upgrade, System Management, and Design-Time Tooling of the Oracle WebCenter Suite. He provides technical guidance and coordination to a broad team of service and framework developers. Paul is also involved in addressing Fusion Application requirements in the WebCenter Suite, including the design and implementation of capabilities in WebCenter to implement software as a service, in line with Oracle's cloud computing initiatives.

Srini Indla is Senior Manager in the Oracle Application Development Framework organization. Srini has more than ten years of experience in building enterprise-class application development frameworks with a focus on building highly scalable and customizable applications declaratively using XML metadata rather than writing code. Areas of expertise include building configuration, management, and customization infrastructures for applications. He has a master's degree in Computer Engineering from the University of Toledo.

Duncan Mills is Senior Director of Product Management for Oracle's Application Development Tools, including Oracle JDeveloper, Oracle Enterprise Pack for Eclipse, NetBeans, Oracle Forms, and the ADF Framework. Duncan is currently responsible for product direction, evangelism, and courseware development around the Development Tools products. He has been working with Oracle in a variety of application development and DBA roles since 1988. For the past 18 years he has been working at Oracle in both support and product development, spending the last eight years in product management. Duncan is the co-author of the Oracle Press books *Oracle JDeveloper 10g for Forms and PL/SQL Developers: A Guide to Web Development with Oracle ADF* and *Oracle JDeveloper 11g Handbook: A Guide to Fusion Web Development.*

Mark Nelson has been designing distributed middleware systems for nearly 20 years. As a Fusion Middleware Platform Architect, he is currently responsible for lending architectural guidance for the Oracle Fusion Middleware product suite in life cycle and related areas such as Install, Upgrade, Patching, and Virtualization. In his 14 years at Oracle, he has been the technical architect for a number of Fusion Middleware products, including Oracle Notification Service (ONS), Oracle HTTP Server (OHS), Oracle Process Manager and Notifications (OPMN), and Oracle Virtual Assembly Builder (OVAB). He holds bachelor's and master's degrees from the University of Illinois at Urbana-Champaign.

Contents at a Glance

Contents

PART II

Deploying and Managing Enterprise Applications on Fusion Middleware

Foreword

I've had a long history with the products that now make up Oracle Fusion Middleware, starting with joining the early WebLogic team, joining BEA via acquisition, leaving BEA to pursue some other ventures, and later joining Oracle just as it was acquiring BEA. During this time, I've watched the products evolve into a market-leading portfolio of middleware.

I now have the pleasure of leading a portion of the Middleware team, including a team that has responsibility for product managing software lifecycle features across the Fusion Middleware and Fusion Applications product lines. In this capacity, I've come to know many of the authors and editors of this book. I can attest to the fact that there is no finer team of technologists to author this book; individually and collectively, they are the masters of the subject area. These are the people who are tasked here at Oracle to lead product improvements and the same experts to whom I frequently turn for answers myself.

The Fusion Middleware product line is both powerful and comprehensive. It forms the backbone of many of our customers' businesses, and it is so pervasive that it's nearly impossible to go a day without interacting somehow with a system that is running on top of Fusion Middleware—be it tracking a package, booking a travel reservation, or even swiping a credit card. Fusion Middleware also forms the technology stack for many of Oracle's business applications, including our newest product line, Fusion Applications, which has been written ground-up to take advantage of the Fusion Middleware portfolio.

The subject matter covered in these pages is both quite complex and expansive. There are a number of interconnected concepts to understand, and the breadth of the topics means that even an experienced technologist will take some time to understand how the different pieces fit together.

All the more reason, then, for an excellent book such as this, which pulls together related topics to explain how they are interconnected. I'm delighted that such a talented group of authors have come together to write a book that I believe will be tremendously useful to both Oracle and our customers.

This book is both an excellent starting point for those just getting started in this area as well as an excellent reference for those with many years of experience. I hope that you will enjoy learning about this fascinating and powerful area as much as I have.

Adam Messinger
Vice President of Development
Oracle Fusion Middleware
Oracle

Acknowledgments

A true and complete acknowledgment of all the people who have contributed to the knowledge and confidence I needed prior to taking on the writing of this book would require more than the couple of paragraphs available to me in this section. With the need for brevity in mind, I must start by acknowledging two important teachers from my childhood: Mr. Albert Grün of Switzerland, and Mr. Ronald Parker of Canada. I am certain that without their encouragement, I would not have been in a position to take on this project.

I would also like to thank my colleagues at Oracle who either directly or indirectly provided valuable input as I was undertaking the writing process: James Bayer, Marc Nelson, and Mike Blevins are among this group of individuals whom I am highly privileged to be working with. A big thanks also to Jason Aiken, who graciously accepted to take on the overall technical editing work and provided much valuable feedback. I must also thank my two co-authors, Gangadhar Konduri and Stephen Lee, for accepting to join me on the journey of writing this book and for their valuable contribution to the content. Thanks also to my executive management, Adam Messinger, Hasan Rizvi, and Thomas Kurian, for their support of this project.

This section would not be complete without the acknowledgement of the courageous choices, and their associated personal sacrifices, that my parents, Behnaz Bahmanighadjar and Ahmad Shafii, have had to face in their life; it is thanks to these choices that the opportunity of writing this book was afforded to me. Finally, a special thanks to Percy and Elsa Skuy, for their mentorship and friendship; we are extremely fortunate to have crossed path with you.

—**Reza Shafii**

Thank you, Marc Chanliau, for spending the time reviewing my material. Merci. Special thanks to Buddhika Kottahachchi, Raymond Leung, Rey Ong, Catherine Wong, Srikant Tirumalai, Sudip Regmi, and Pratik Datta for supporting me throughout the process with technical support and guidance.

—Stephen Lee

First and foremost, I would like to thank my parents for always believing in me, wanting the best for me, and for all the sacrifices they have made for me. I would like to thank my brother, who has always been a role model, inspiration, friend, and guide for me ever since childhood. I want to thank my wife for her encouragement in this effort and for being so understanding and patient about the many late nights, weekends, and holidays spent writing this book while she also took care of our two little daughters, who always bring a smile on my face.

This book could not have happened without the input and thorough feedback of the technical reviewers—Duncan Mills, Paul Encarnación, and Srini Indla—who are the most prominent experts in the field. I thank them for taking the time to help with this book. My sincere thanks to my co-authors—Stephen and Reza—for making this book possible. A special thanks to Reza Shafii for all his efforts on this book, for inviting me to join the team, and for his reviews of the material as well as coordinating all things related to this book. I would like to thank my management team at Oracle for their support. I would also like to thank the teams at Oracle that put in all the hard work behind this great product.

—Gangadhar Konduri

Introduction

The idea behind this book was seeded at a customer advisory board event when one of the attending customers asked an interesting question: Why isn't there a single, definitive book one could read in order to obtain a complete understanding of the Fusion Middleware product's architecture as well as its management best practices? This book addresses the gap identified by this simple question.

Oracle Fusion Middleware

With the release of Oracle Fusion Middleware 11*g*, Oracle introduced a consolidated stack of infrastructure software products designed from the ground up to suit the needs of modern enterprise applications. The components that form this next generation of Oracle's middleware products provide a wide range of services on which enterprises can build the software applications that allow them to optimize their business processes for the sake of efficiency and competitive advantage. In fact, Oracle itself is taking advantage of Fusion Middleware 11*g* as the basis for its next generation of business applications known as Oracle Fusion Applications.

Fusion Middleware 11*g* products take advantage of industry open standards to ensure that the new skills and knowledge needed for their use are minimized. However, a detailed knowledge of the organization of these products, their underlying architecture, and their operations management processes is essential to the successful uptake of the benefits they offer. This book provides, within a single source, the content needed for system administrators, application developers, and software architects to quickly obtain this knowledge.

Objective

A number of resources (books, articles, and so on) are available today that detail the capabilities of the different product suites within Fusion Middleware. However, these resources are typically focused on a particular subset of products and are mainly concerned with the software development aspects of enterprise applications. Resources are scarce that provide a description of the full set of core Fusion Middleware products and their common infrastructure, as well as an understanding of the post-development operations pertaining to enterprise applications built on this platform. However, the need for such content for use by architects, system administrators, and software developers is apparent for two important reasons. First, today's enterprise applications span a wide range of middleware services. Although their development can be organized into different modules assigned to groups with targeted expertise, the administrators who are in charge of their deployment and operational management require a breadth of knowledge crossing all of the middleware products. Second, the software developers and architects who are in charge of the design of Fusion Middleware enterprise applications also benefit from this type of wider knowledge because it allows them to better adapt their application's design to aspects beyond their immediate scope of concern.

The aim of this book is to provide a definitive source of information for the architecture of the core set of Fusion Middleware products and their associated management processes. This aim is achieved in two ways. First, this book contains a detailed description of the architecture and design of the core Fusion Middleware products and their common infrastructure. Second, it contains a set of use cases and step-by-step instructions designed to walk the reader through the end-to-end management of Fusion Middleware–based enterprise applications and to highlight best practices for their operational management.

Organization

This book is organized into two parts. Part I describes the components of the different product categories that make up Fusion Middleware. Each chapter in Part I, except Chapter 1, ends with a use case designed to illustrate a real-life scenario that demonstrates some of the concepts covered in the chapter. The use cases in Part I are incremental in that each chapter develops the same use case further, using concepts introduced within the chapter. Each use case section within the Part I chapters are marked with a gray shaded heading.

Part II outlines a set of hands-on, step-by-step instructions that walk the reader through operational processes for the management of the enterprise application incrementally, described as part of the use cases of the first section. These step-by-step instructions are detailed and designed to be followed along by the reader using the associated Fusion Middleware products. The content covered by this part of the book consists of the deployment of the application to a multinode environment designed for reliability and scalability, securing the application's environment, optimizing the application's performance, and finally an overview of the features that allow for the monitoring and diagnosing of possible problems with the application's environment. In some of the chapters of the second part of the book, download material is also available to allow the reader to create and sample the application's environment and follow the section's step-by-step instructions. Parts of the chapter where such material is available are offset from the text and marked with the heading "Download."

Readers can begin at either the first or second part of the book: Those readers who would like to first build a solid understanding of the fundamental architectural concepts and principles behind the Fusion Middleware components should start with Part I. On the other hand, those readers who would like to start learning through practice can begin with Part II. The idea is that together, the first and the second parts of the book provide an ideal mix of theory and practice to allow the reader to develop a complete understanding of the Fusion Middleware product's architecture and management.

The following table contains a brief chapter-by-chapter description of the content of this book.

Chapter	Description
Part I: Oracle Fusion Middleware Architecture and Management	
Chapter 1: Fusion Middleware Primer	Provides a brief description of the general concepts of enterprise applications and middleware. The chapter then proceeds with an overview of the different categories of products in Fusion Middleware and highlights key products in each category.

Chapter	Description
Chapter 2: Oracle WebLogic Server	Details the architecture of WebLogic Server. The chapter begins with a description of key WebLogic Server concepts, such as domains and servers. It then proceeds with a deep-dive description of the services and management tools provided by WebLogic Server. The chapter use case introduces the pricing application as a simple Java EE application.
Chapter 3: Fusion Middleware Common Infrastructure	Details the architecture of the Fusion Middleware common infrastructure components on which other Fusion Middleware products depend. The components discussed are Metadata Repository Services, Oracle Process Management and Notification, Dynamic Monitoring Service, Oracle Diagnostic Logging, Oracle Web Services Manager, and Enterprise Manager Fusion Middleware Control. The chapter use case extends the pricing application with the Fusion Middleware common infrastructure services to allow for the protection of its web service with Oracle Web Services Manager and the fronting of its web application with a managed Oracle HTTP Server instance.
Chapter 4: Oracle Fusion Middleware Platform Security Services and Identity Management	Details the functionality of Fusion Middleware security services and Identity Management products. The Identity Management products discussed are Oracle Identity Management, Oracle Identity Federation, Oracle Internet Directory, Oracle Virtual Directory, Oracle Access Manager, Oracle Adaptive Access Manager, Oracle Identity Analytics, Oracle Entitlements Server, and Oracle Directory Server Enterprise Edition. The chapter use case involves the configuration of the pricing application with an enterprise LDAP server and the protection of its web interface through Single-Sign-On using the Oracle Access Manager product.

Chapter	Description
Chapter 5: Oracle Service-Oriented Architecture Suite	Details the architecture of key components of the Oracle Service-Oriented Architecture (SOA) Suite of products. The components discussed consist of the SOA Suite Service Component Architecture (SCA) based infrastructure, Oracle Business Activity Monitoring, and User Messaging Service. The chapter use case involves the extension of the pricing application with a fronting SOA infrastructure–based SCA composite integrated with Oracle Business Activity Monitoring.
Chapter 6: Oracle Application Development Framework	Details the architecture of the Oracle Application Development Framework (ADF) infrastructure and key operational aspects for managing ADF-based applications. The chapter use case involves the deployment of a custom ADF-based worklist application for use by the pricing application's SOA Suite composite.
Chapter 7: Oracle WebCenter	Details the architecture of Oracle WebCenter. The WebCenter services covered are Composer, Customization and Personalization, Enterprise 2.0 Services, Portal Services, and Spaces. The chapter use case involves the creation of a WebCenter portal that integrates the pricing application's different web user interfaces.
Part II: Deploying and Managing Enterprise Applications on Fusion Middleware	
Chapter 8: Deploying Fusion Middleware Enterprise Applications	Introduces the pricing application, its functionality, and its use of the Fusion Middleware components. The pricing application is an enterprise application with WebLogic Server, ADF, SOA Suite, and WebCenter components. The chapter describes the steps required for the installation, configuration, and deployment of the pricing application within a simple single-node environment. It then proceeds to describe the steps required to scale out the application to a multinode clustered configuration.

Chapter	Description
Chapter 9: Securing Fusion Middleware Enterprise Applications	Describes the steps for ensuring that the pricing application is properly secured. This includes securing the application's environment through SSL and file system permissions, integrating the application with an enterprise LDAP, configuring the application's policy and credential stores, and configuring the application's web UIs for Single-Sign-On (SSO) authentication.
Chapter 10: Optimizing Fusion Middleware Enterprise Applications	Describes the steps for ensuring that the pricing application is properly optimized. This includes tuning the WebLogic Server and JVM layers, configuring the SOA infrastructure audit settings, and optimizing the ADF- and WebCenter-specific configurations within the environment.
Chapter 11: Monitoring and Diagnosing Fusion Middleware Enterprise Applications	Describes common monitoring and diagnostics concepts through examples applied to the pricing application. The chapter includes an overview of the Fusion Middleware logging infrastructure, a review of the WebLogic Diagnostics Framework, and the step-by-step instructions for the configuration of the WebLogic node manager to allow for the remote management of Fusion Middleware servers.
Chapter 12: Virtualizing Fusion Middleware Enterprise Applications	Using the pricing application as an example, this chapter describes how Oracle virtualization products can be used to create and manage virtual-machine–based enterprise applications and the implications of virtualization on the concepts discussed throughout the book. The chapter provides an overview of the following Oracle products: Oracle Virtual Machine (OVM), Oracle WebLogic Server Virtual Edition (VE), Oracle Virtual Assembly Builder (OVAB), and Oracle Exalogic.

Target Audience

This book has two target audiences. The primary audience consists of architects and administrators responsible for the deployment and management of Fusion Middleware enterprise applications. As such, the book's content is centered on this audience's view of Fusion Middleware enterprise applications and does not address any of the development-specific elements in detail. As an example, the book does not describe how to develop Fusion Middleware web services applications, but it does describe how to provision security for applications that expose web services. The secondary audience of this book consists of application developers and development managers wanting to learn about the architecture of the different Fusion Middleware products. The content of this book should allow this audience to design and develop applications built with optimal system architecture in mind (that is, architecture that decreases operational costs and simplifies an administrator's life).

The book targets introductory- and intermediate-level audiences. The content is introductory from a Fusion Middleware product knowledge perspective, but intermediate from a general Java-based enterprise software development knowledge point of view. As an example, whereas it is assumed that the reader is knowledgeable of Java Enterprise Edition concepts, it is not assumed that the user is familiar with the Oracle SOA Suite product's capabilities.

Oracle Fusion Middleware consists of a large set of components spanning a wide array of features. It is the hope of the authors that readers will find this book to be a useful roadmap in navigating this large set of components and that they gain some valuable insight in doing so.

PART I

Oracle Fusion Middleware Architecture and Management

CHAPTER 1

Fusion Middleware Primer

This chapter serves as a brief primer to Oracle Fusion Middleware. We begin the chapter by introducing the terms "enterprise application" and "middleware," which are the fundamental concepts behind the purpose of all Fusion Middleware products. The chapter then provides a whirlwind tour of all Fusion Middleware products and highlights the ones that are the subject of the architecture and management deep-dive of the remaining chapters of this section.

Enterprise Applications and Middleware

Simply put, an *enterprise application* is a data-processing tool on which an enterprise (business) relies to deliver any part of its core capabilities. Using this definition, one could argue that enterprise applications have existed since the dawn of computing, maybe going back to when merchants started using an abacus to perform the basic accounting required for running their business. Of course, in today's world the term applies specifically to a set of related software services used by an enterprise to conduct its business. Modern-day enterprise applications therefore have their root in the 1960s when companies and government organizations started to establish Information Technology (IT) departments to maintain newly purchased mainframe computers. These computers were in turn used to run software applications for performing such functions as payroll management or census data processing.

As the software and computing world has progressed, so have enterprise applications and IT. The nature of the enterprise applications that today's IT departments are responsible for managing is vastly different from the early mainframe software applications of the 1960s. For starters, enterprise applications are now much more critical to business needs. No longer are software applications used to execute batch jobs with minimal consequence of failure. Instead, businesses rely on their IT departments to deliver real-time capabilities, such as sending automated notifications to the sales force on imminent opportunities or processing orders from their online channels.

Failure of such capabilities, even if only for a few minutes, can have even in the best of scenarios a significant impact to a company's bottom line.

Second, enterprise applications are omnipresent, and modern-day knowledge workers rely on them for almost every aspect of their work. Whether it is for executing operational tasks such as managing accounting processes, facilitating the communication of information among the workforce, or running the company's public website, enterprise applications play a role in almost all aspects of a company's day-to-day work. As a result, the number of software applications present in modern-day IT shops is typically very large.

Finally, enterprise applications have shifted from their initial incarnation, as centralized mainframe processes, to a set of distributed and interdependent processes running on multiple machines. As a result, the boundary of what a single enterprise application consists of is often hard to determine because each application has a large set of dependencies, and therefore integration points, with other enterprise applications.

The shift of enterprise applications to critical, omnipresent, distributed, and interdependent entities has progressively increased the need for software applications that exist not to provide actual business logic for the enterprise but to facilitate and optimize the execution of software that does. Such software is what typically is referred to as "middleware," with the idea being that it resides "in the middle" between the enterprise application software and the machine operating system on which software applications execute. In today's IT organizations, middleware software is used to provide a wide array of capabilities that together allow businesses to more quickly deliver the enterprise applications needed, decrease the cost of ownership in maintaining them, and ensure that they maintain the quality of service required by their users. Figure 1-1 shows—within the boxes highlighted—some of the areas where middleware software can be used within the IT infrastructure.

Oracle Fusion Middleware consists of a wide set of products that cover all areas where middleware software can play a role within an IT organization. In the next section, we go over the set of products that are part of Oracle Fusion Middleware, provide a brief overview of their capabilities, and highlight the set of products covered as part of the scope of this book.

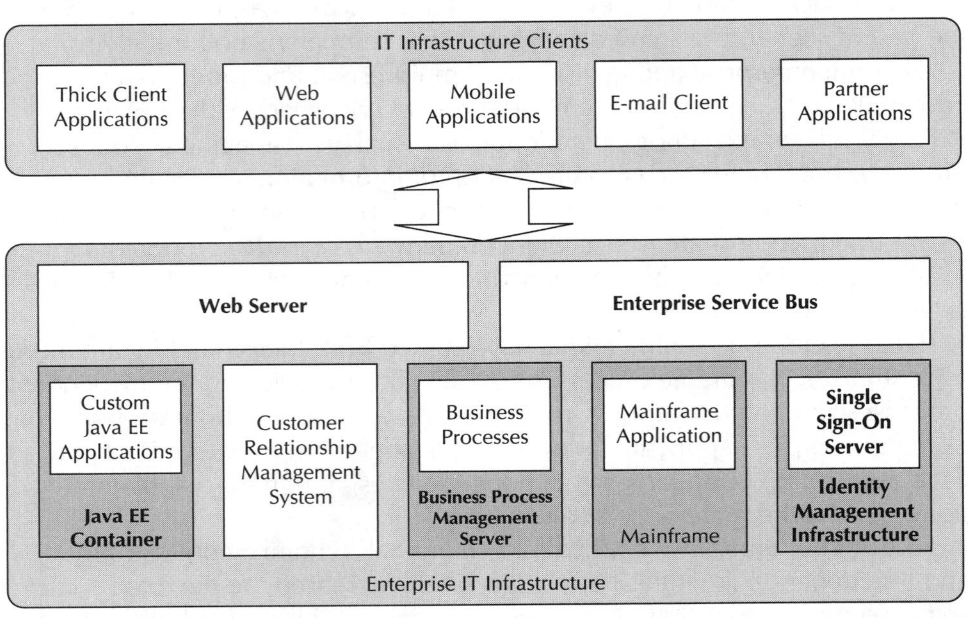

FIGURE 1-1. *Sample areas of Fusion Middleware use*

Oracle Fusion Middleware Products

The full set of Oracle Fusion Middleware products can be grouped into different categories based on the type of problems they are meant to solve. Figure 1-2 shows the different categories of Fusion Middleware products in dark grey. The figure also shows—within the boxes highlighted—the products (or in the case of the Identity Management category, the functional areas) that are covered in detail within the scope of this book in subsequent chapters.

The remainder of this chapter provides an overview of each of the categories shown in Figure 1-2.

Integrated Development Environments and Frameworks

Oracle provides two primary integrated development environments (IDEs) that software application developers can use to build enterprise applications: Oracle JDeveloper and the Oracle Enterprise Pack for Eclipse. The next two

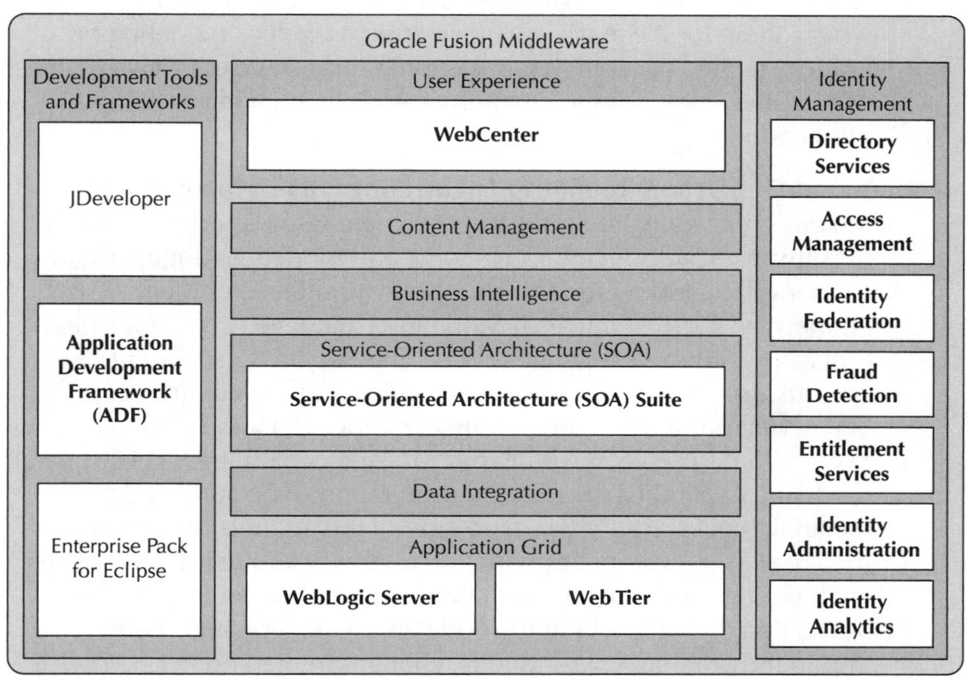

FIGURE 1-2. *Fusion Middleware Products*

sections describe these IDEs, their associated development frameworks, and the Fusion Middleware products they are associated with.

JDeveloper and Application Development Framework (ADF)

JDeveloper is the main integrated development environment for building Fusion Middleware–based enterprise applications. It offers a set of capabilities that span software programming, visual design, and definition of metadata, as follows:

- **Programming** JDeveloper allows for the writing of software programs using the Java, JavaScript, PL/SQL, and PHP programming languages. It provides features such as automatic indentation of code and integration with build scripts, which make the life of software developers writing programs in these languages simpler. Additionally, JDeveloper provides features specific to different software specifications and standards such as Java Enterprise Edition (Java EE) and Java Swing, which allow for the automatic generation as well as modeling of artifacts related to them. As an example, the JDeveloper Java Swing capabilities allow for the creation of Java Swing widgets using a visual editor.

- **Visual Design and Roundtrip Engineering** JDeveloper allows for the design of software applications using a visual model. A number of software development frameworks and modeling languages are supported, including the Oracle Application Development Framework (ADF), Universal Modeling Language (UML), Business Process Execution Language (BPEL), and Service Component Architecture (SCA). In some cases, such as for the creation of Java Server Pages (JSP), JDeveloper also provides WYSIWYG (What You See Is What You Get) user interface design capabilities. These visual modeling capabilities lead to the generation of backing code or metadata necessary for the execution of the artifacts being designed. In all cases, JDeveloper provides a capability known as "roundtrip engineering." This means that changes to the model lead to the associated changes within the code and metadata, and more importantly the opposite—that is, changes to the underlying code or metadata lead to changes within the model.
- **Metadata Definition** JDeveloper allows for the creation of metadata for dependent components used by developers when writing code or modeling their application. These include a connection framework that allows for the definition of connection properties such as databases and application servers that can be used as part of the testing of the applications being developed. Other metadata definition artifacts include the ability to create Ant scripts that can be used to build and package the elements of the application being developed, as appropriate.

The main development framework that is exposed by JDeveloper is known as the Oracle Application Development Framework (ADF). ADF is a set of application programming interfaces (API) and JDeveloper-based modeling tools that allow for the creation of Java EE–based applications with user interfaces that can be exposed through a variety of ways, including thick-client (Java Swing-based) applications, rich Java Server Faces–based web applications, and mobile applications. ADF is an integral part of Fusion Middleware, and its architectural details are the subject of Chapter 6. Other than being the main design tool for ADF applications, JDeveloper is also the primary IDE for a number of Fusion Middleware product categories, including Application Grid, SOA Suite, WebCenter, Data Integration, and Business Intelligence. For these products, special extensions to JDeveloper must be downloaded to enable their capabilities. These capabilities usually include a set of dedicated editors, wizards, and ADF component extensions for the development of custom user interfaces that provide end-user integration with the associated products.

Oracle Enterprise Pack for Eclipse

The Oracle Enterprise Pack for Eclipse (OEPE) is a packaged set of Oracle-certified plugins to the Eclipse open-source IDE. The history of OEPE goes back to Oracle's acquisition of BEA Systems Corporation: BEA was using Eclipse as its main IDE platform. Today, OEPE offers developers who prefer to use Eclipse as their IDE an option for its continued use. OEPE plugins can be grouped into three categories, as follows:

- **Application Grid Development Plugins** A set of plugins that facilitate the development of custom Java EE applications targeted for deployment to the Fusion Middleware application grid set of products. Specifically, these plugins allow for the creation of Java EE artifacts such as servlets, Enterprise Java Beans, and others with a set of wizards and modeling tools to streamline their deployment to the WebLogic Server application server, a core product of Fusion Middleware that we will explore in detail in Chapter 2.
- **Oracle Service Bus Development Plugins** A set of plugins that enable the offline development of Oracle Service Bus (OSB) message flows, the main unit of deployment for this product. A detailed discussion of OSB is beyond the scope of this book, although we briefly discuss the OSB capabilities in Chapter 5.
- **Plugin for Ex-BEA Products** A number of products which Oracle inherited in its acquisition of BEA Systems have their development capabilities rooted in OEPE. These products include WebLogic Integration and Workshop Page Flows. These products now have a different strategic alternative within the Oracle Fusion Middleware

set of products (for example, WebLogic Integration Java process definitions should be replaced with SOA Suite BPEL processes) and as such are not further discussed in this book.

Given the focus of this book on the architecture and post-development management practices for Fusion Middleware products, the two IDEs we discussed in this section are not explored in any further detail within the rest of this book.

Application Grid

The Fusion Middleware products under the Application Grid category provide middleware application execution services on which enterprise applications can be built. The primary product in this category is the WebLogic Server, a Java EE–based application server that provides a set of services that optimize the execution of Java EE–based applications. The services provided by WebLogic Server allow for the separation of concerns between the development of applications and elements such as their database, security, and performance-tuning configurations. We will explore WebLogic Server and its architecture in detail within Chapter 2. Other important products in the Application Grid category are Oracle JRockit, Oracle Coherence, and the Oracle Web Tier set of products. Oracle JRockit is a Java Standard Edition virtual machine that provides advanced capabilities such as the ability to monitor the virtual machine's detailed performance parameters in production environments and the ability to execute Java code with deterministic response times. Oracle Coherence provides a clustered, distributed, and partitioned in-memory data cache—also known as a "data grid"—that can be used by software developers to improve the reliability, availability, scalability, and performance of enterprise applications. Finally, the Web Tier package of products consists of the Oracle HTTP Server (OHS), which is a reverse-proxy based on the open-source Apache HTTP server, and Oracle Web Cache, which, as the name suggests, is used for fronting an HTTP server to allow for the caching of frequently accessed web content.

The application grid set of products, and specially WebLogic Server, form the foundation on which all other Java-based (and that is almost all of them) Fusion Middleware products are founded. As such, Fusion Middleware products that do not fall into this category are sometimes referred to as "layered products," meaning that they introduce another layer of logic on top of the application grid base layer.

Identity Management

The Fusion Middleware products under the Identity Management category provide services that allow IT organizations to establish and manage security across their enterprise applications. The core set of identity management services provided by the products in this category are as follows:

- **Directory Services** Allow for the central storage and management of information about users of enterprise applications.
- **Access Management** Allows for the centralization of authentication services to enable Single Sign-On (SSO).
- **Identity Federation** Allows for federation of access management services across departmental and organizational boundaries.
- **Fraud Detection** Allows for the definition of advanced algorithms for strengthening authentication mechanism and detecting potential fraudulent access attempts.
- **Entitlement Services** Allow for the centralization of enterprise resource access control information.
- **Identity Administration** Allows for the orchestrated management of user information across enterprise applications. These services facilitate the implementation of processes such as provisioning of user access and password management across multiple applications.
- **Identity Analytics** Allow for the analysis of identity access information through audit violations and access review.

Fusion Middleware products in other categories can integrate with the Identity Management set of products to take advantage of the security services they offer. These services are discussed in detail in Chapter 4.

Service-Oriented Architecture

A Service-Oriented Architecture (SOA) is a set of enterprise application architecture principles that allow IT organizations to organize such applications and their environments in a more efficient and cost-effective manner. At a very high level, SOA principles dictate the organization of an enterprise's IT applications into loosely coupled and highly cohesive services with a clear separation of their interface description from their implementation technology. New services are then composed using the existing set of services. SOA thus allows for reuse and facilitates the introduction of enterprise application changes over time. These changes can be holistic in nature, such as implementation rewrites using a new language, or they can be evolutionary, such as the application of defect patches or upgrades of a service.

Products within the SOA category of Fusion Middleware Products enable an enterprise to organize their environments and build applications according to SOA principles. The main products within this category are the Oracle SOA Suite and Oracle Service Bus. Oracle SOA Suite allows for the development and deployment of applications that follow the Service Component Architecture (SCA) specification. SOA Suite allows for the creation and deployment of applications that are made up of components with different implementation technologies. The implementation technologies supported by SOA Suite are as follows:

- **Business Process Execution Language (BPEL) and Business Process Modeling Notation (BPMN) Processes** Used to define end-to-end business processes that involve orchestration of human user tasks, business rules, and invocation of other services
- **Mediations** Used to define transformation and routing logic that maps services with different interfaces, protocols, and implementations
- **Human Tasks** Used to implement interaction points with business users
- **Business Rules** Used to expose application parameters that need to be adjusted over time based on business needs
- **Spring Service Components** Used to create components implemented in Java using the Spring framework

Beside its SCA-based service implementation capabilities, SOA Suite also provides three other core capabilities: Business Activity Monitoring (BAM), User Messaging Services (UMS), and Business-to-Business (B2B). BAM allows for the real-time monitoring of the business parameters associated with enterprise applications. UMS provides a framework that enterprise applications can use to interact with end users through various mechanisms, such as instant messaging, SMS text, and e-mail. Finally, the SOA Suite B2B component allows for enterprise applications to interact with services in other departments or businesses using a standard B2B protocol (for example, ebXML or RosettaNet) and the due diligence (auditing, message integrity check, security requirements, and so on) that might be required for such interactions. The SCA, BAM, and UMS capabilities of SOA Suite are explored in detail in Chapter 5.

The second core product of the SOA category of Fusion Middleware Products is the Oracle Service Bus (OSB). In a similar fashion to the mediations implementation type of SOA Suite, OSB allows for the implementation of message flows that define transformation and routing logic that maps services with different interfaces, protocols, and implementations. The primary differences between OSB and SOA Suite mediations are two-fold: First, OSB is designed for handling more complex and high-volume scenarios. Second, all aspects of OSB message flows can be dynamically defined and modified on the runtime environment itself, without the need for a full develop/deploy cycle.

User Experience

The User Experience category of products contains, as the name suggests, products that are used for the creation of user interfaces for enterprise applications. The two core products that fall into this category are the Oracle Application Development Framework (ADF) and Oracle WebCenter.

ADF is a Java EE–based framework that provides a set of tools and widgets that simplify the creation of web and thick-client user interfaces that can be used through different access points, such as web browser and mobile phones. For web applications, ADF builds on top of the Java Server Faces (JSF) components and controllers to enable the construction of rich AJAX-based applications. ADF also provides other capabilities that are meant to simplify the management of enterprise applications. One of these capabilities is the ability for ADF developers to specify separate customization layers as part of the design of user interfaces in order to expose different customization features to end users, depending on their roles, and to simplify the upgrade of applications after their user interfaces have undergone such customizations.

Oracle WebCenter allows for the creation of applications that bring together services from other enterprise applications and allows for the extension of these applications with collaboration services. WebCenter functionality can be separated into a set of different services. WebCenter framework services provide the capabilities usually associated with traditional portals, such as the ability to create portlet-based user interfaces as well as customization and personalization features. WebCenter Social Computing services provide out-of-the-box collaboration tools—such as instant messaging, discussion forums, and presence detection—that can be integrated with other enterprise applications. WebCenter Composer and Business Directory services allow business users to create enterprise applications on the fly by bringing together content exposed through web services and feeds. Finally, WebCenter Spaces is an out-of-the-box enterprise application that brings together the core capabilities of WebCenter so that they can be used without development effort within the enterprise. The WebCenter Spaces application is composed of a personal area where users can store and manage information such as notes and calendar content, a business roles area that allows the broadcasting of information to end users of specific roles, and finally a group spaces area that allows end users with common interests to collaborate using tools such as blogs and wikis.

The functionality and architecture of ADF and WebCenter are discussed in detail within Chapters 6 and 7, respectively.

Content Management, Data Integration, and Business Intelligence

Fusion Middleware products within the Content Management, Data Integration, and Business Intelligence categories are outside of the scope of this book. However, the following sections provide a brief description of each category and the products they contain.

Content Management

The Oracle Enterprise Content Management suite of products can be used across an organization for the management of heterogeneous documents such as spreadsheets, web pages, e-mails, and digital images (generally referred to as "content"). The products contained in the Enterprise Content Management suite are as follows:

- **Universal Content Management** Provides a central repository for the storage and management of content. It also provides the ability to define and execute life-cycle processes for the content it stores (for example, submission process, publishing process, deletion process, and so on).

- **Universal Records Management** Used for the storage and management of archive data retained for legal, historical, or other use. It provides the ability for end users to specify archiving and disposition rules to be associated with different types of documents.
- **Imaging and Process Management** Used for the storage and management of scanned images of physical documents. The Imaging and Process Management product is often used in the context of business functions that by nature involve the need for scanned images, such as expense and invoice management.
- **Information Rights Management** Enables documents to be secured to ensure that users can only perform the operations (read, write, modify, delete) for which they have proper authorization. Furthermore, the Information and Rights Management product allows for the auditing of all operations performed on documents that are secured. This product is often used for the management of digital content with sensitive information such as corporate financial or legal documents.

The Enterprise Content Management products rely on each other to provide their functionality. As an example, the content server of the Universal Content Management product serves as the content repository for all other products in this category.

Data Integration

The two core products within the Fusion Middleware Data Integration category are Oracle Data Integrator and Oracle Golden Gate. Oracle Data Integrator is used to process data from source repositories and transform it for inclusion in destination repositories of different types. It provides the ability to define and execute Extract, Transform, Load (ETL) functions between heterogeneous sources of data, such as RDBMS schemas, File (in XML and other formats), Web Services, and others. Oracle Golden Gate allows for the bridging of databases between multiple sites in order to ensure that their content stays synchronized according to a set of administrator-configured polices. Golden Gate is often used to facilitate disaster recovery topologies by replicating data in real time between different sites.

Business Intelligence

The Oracle Business Intelligence suite of products allows for the analysis of historical, current, and predictive business data. These products allow for the aggregation of multiple heterogeneous physical data sources into a single logical model that can then be used for analysis and reporting purposes. The core products contained in the Business Intelligence suite are as follows:

- **Business Intelligence Enterprise Edition** Allows for the collection of data from multiple heterogeneous data sources and the organization of this data into a logical data model. The logical data model can then be queried and its content can be used for the creation of dashboards and alerts.
- **Business Intelligence Publisher** Allows for the creation of report templates that can contain data retrieved from multiple data sources. The report templates can then be used to generate reports in multiple formats, such as spreadsheets and HTML. Business Intelligence Publisher also allows for the advanced scheduling of report generation.

The Fusion Middleware products within the Business Intelligence category are tightly integrated. As an example, the Business Intelligence Enterprise Edition and Business Intelligence Publisher products can share a single set of data objects for reporting and dashboards.

Conclusion

In this chapter we reviewed the key concepts of enterprise applications and middleware. We then proceeded with a quick tour of Oracle Fusion Middleware and the different types of products it offers. In the next chapters of Part I, we proceed with a deep dive of some of the key Oracle Fusion Middleware products introduced in this chapter.

CHAPTER 2

Oracle WebLogic Server

e begin our exploration of the Oracle Fusion Middleware architecture with a detailed look at Oracle WebLogic Server. As the foundation on which all Java EE–based Oracle Fusion Middleware components are built, a solid understanding of WebLogic Server for any Fusion Middleware system architect is essential. WebLogic Server has the proud claim of being the first Java EE (at the time called J2EE) application server to achieve full-specification compliance. As such, the product is mature and contains a large array of capabilities that have been developed and hardened through the test of time and a great many business-critical enterprise applications. Our aim in this chapter is not to analyze the entire spectrum of these capabilities but to provide an overview of WebLogic Server and its main subsystems as well as to highlight the key architectural concepts and administrative knobs they expose.

This chapter begins with an introduction of some core administrative concepts and then proceeds to describe WebLogic Server's application containers. These containers provide the main abstraction for the deployment and management of enterprise applications. We then continue with a detailed description of WebLogic Server's management capabilities and tools before turning our attention to WebLogic Server's container services, which allow applications to implement advanced database connection management, messaging, and security capabilities. We conclude the chapter with a discussion of WebLogic Server's threading model and, finally, as with all chapters in this section of the book, a use case that will bring some of the core concepts covered through the chapter together within the context of a practical example.

Introducing Oracle WebLogic Server

The concepts of a server instance, domain, and cluster are fundamental to the understanding of WebLogic Server, and we begin this section with their overview. We then discuss the WebLogic Server installation and domain artifacts and finally end the section with an overview of domain startup options.

Servers, Clusters, and Domains

A WebLogic Server instance is a Java Virtual Machine (VM) process executing the code that provides all of the APIs and services mandated by the Java EE specification as well as WebLogic specific extensions. Java applications created by development teams who are in turn using the Java EE specification and WebLogic-specific APIs are deployed to and executed by a server instance. The main components of a server instance are illustrated in Figure 2-1.

In this chapter, we will be reviewing the core concepts associated with each of the components shown in Figure 2-1.

Each WebLogic Server instance is always part of a WebLogic Server domain, which is an administrative grouping and configuration scoping mechanism for a set of servers. Domains are managed, configured, and monitored through a special server instance called the domain administration (admin) server. The admin server is just like any other server instance within

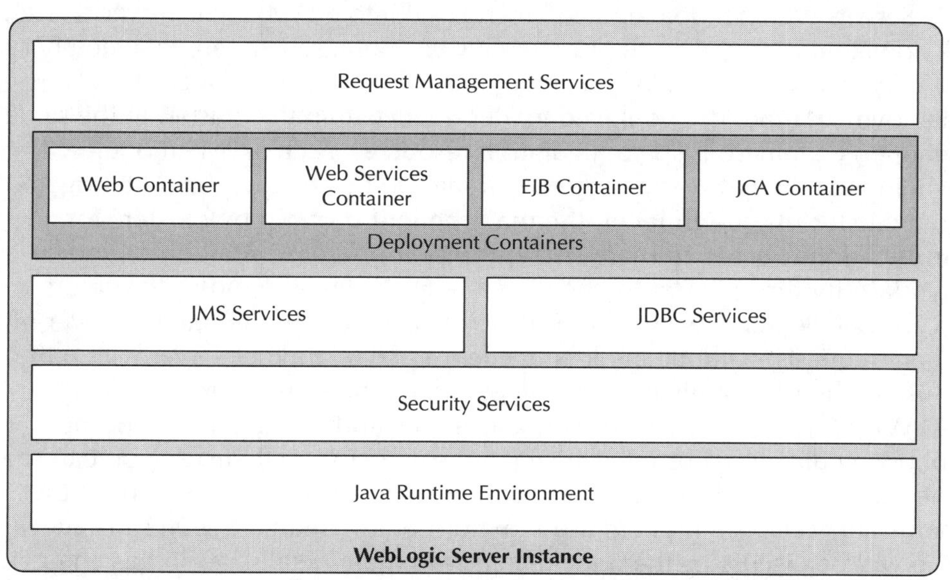

FIGURE 2-1. *WebLogic Server components*

the domain, with the exception that it is configured with a distinctive set of applications that allows it to perform the following functions:

- Manage configuration information for all servers within the domain and act as a central point of synchronization for this information. That is, all managed servers obtain their latest configuration from the administration server.
- Provide a browser-based administrative console (admin console) application used to manage configuration of the domain and its servers.

Other than the single admin server, all other WebLogic Server instances within a domain are known as managed servers. Java EE applications are usually deployed on managed servers that are tuned to their needs, as opposed to the admin server that is left alone for administrative purposes. A domain could, however, consist of a lone admin server (and no managed server) that is used as the target for the deployment of Java EE applications. Such a setup is, however, often used only in development environments for convenience and hardware resource optimization purposes.

Servers within a domain can be grouped into a WebLogic Server cluster. A domain can contain one or more clusters, but a server can be a member of only a single cluster. When an application is targeted to a cluster at deployment time, it is deployed to all servers within the cluster. In the same manner, certain domain configuration resources, such as JMS modules, which we will explore in more detail later in this chapter, can be targeted to a cluster. At a high level, the main benefit brought by clusters for applications hosted to them is the ability to increase scalability and availability through deployment of the application to multiple servers. WebLogic Server clusters also provide capabilities for automatic failover of client requests, without any loss of client state, to another server within the cluster when the original server target of the request is not reachable.

With this overview of servers, domains, and clusters in mind, the following diagram illustrates the relationship between them. As you can see, the diagram also shows an entity called "Node Manager," which, as the name suggests, is a process used to monitor and manage server instances. We will be discussing the node manager in more detail later in this chapter, but we now move on to a discussion of the WebLogic Server installation process and the content of the installation and domain directories.

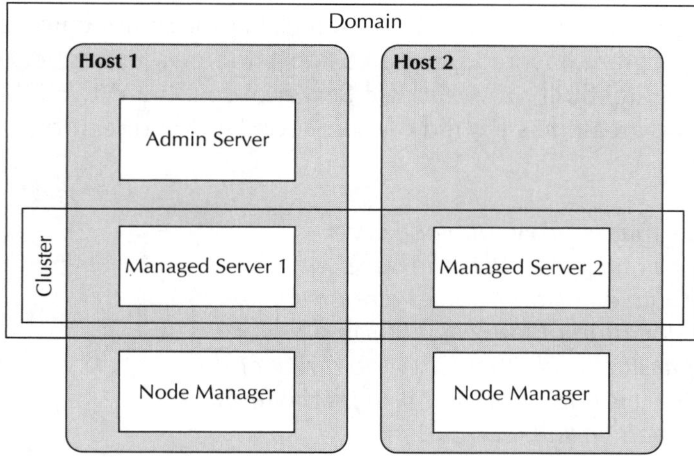

Installation and Domain Artifacts

The WebLogic Server components are installed through the WebLogic installation tool, which allows you to specify the following two directory paths:

- The top-level installation directory into which common WebLogic Server components (JDK, utilities, and so on) are installed. This directory is referred to as the middleware home. From now on we refer to this directory as MW_HOME, which is the environment variable that the path of the directory is assigned to in a WebLogic Server runtime environment. Such environment variables can be initiated by running a domain's setDomainEnv.cmd or .sh command.
- The top-level installation directory into which the WebLogic Server–specific binaries (that is, JAR files, data files, third-party libraries, and all other software that form the product) are installed. This directory is referred to as the WebLogic home. From now on we refer to this directory as WL_HOME, which is the environment variable that the path of the directory is assigned to in a WebLogic Server runtime environment.

The WebLogic Server installation within an MW_HOME acts as the underlying application server to all other Java EE–based Fusion Middleware products, and for this reason such products are sometimes also referred to as layered Oracle Fusion Middleware products. Although not enforced by the installation program, layered Oracle Fusion Middleware products (such as Oracle SOA Suite) built on WebLogic Server expect the WL_HOME directory to be created as a child of their MW_HOME directory.

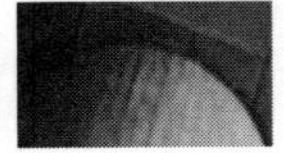

NOTE
To ensure that your WebLogic Server installation can be used as the basis for other layered Oracle Fusion Middleware products, keep the location of the WL_HOME directory as the default choice (that is, as the direct child of the MW_HOME directory) provided within the WebLogic installation program.

Table 2-1 provides a description of the most important paths that are directly under the MW_HOME and WL_HOME directory.

As you might notice by the content of the WebLogic Server directory listed in Table 2-1, the installation of WebLogic Server does not lead to an executable that in turn allows you to "run the installation." This is due to the fact that one of the important aspects of WebLogic Server architecture is the decoupling of a server environment's configuration, abstracted through the concept of a domain, from the WebLogic Server executable binaries. WebLogic Server instances are therefore always run from the context of a domain, which must be created after the installation of the WebLogic Server binaries through the installation tool has been completed. This clear separation between installation binaries and domain configurations has two important implications. First, a WebLogic Server domain directory can be created anywhere on the file system and does not need to be placed in a specific path relative to the installation directories. The only link between a domain directory and its installation binaries are the environment variables that are set at server startup time and point to the installation directory's Java libraries. Second, there can be any number of domains created from a single installation directory. In other words, the cardinality between a WebLogic Server installation and the number of domains that use it is one-to-many. The only criterion for the domain to function is that the installation directory it refers to needs to be accessible by running servers.

Directory/Filename	Description
MW_HOME/jdkNNN and MW_HOME/jrockitNNN	Oracle Java HotSpot JDK and Oracle JRockit JDK, which can both be used as the Java runtime by a WebLogic installation.
MW_HOME/logs	The log directory for the WebLogic Server installation program and configuration wizard. Installation program log files are placed in the file log.txt and contain an inventory of the components that were installed. Each configuration wizard session leads to a separate log file with the following format: wlsconfig_<time_stamp>.
MW_HOME/modules	Contains OSGi modules used by the WebLogic Server runtime. OSGi is a component model that allows for the modularization of Java applications. WebLogic Server uses an OSGi component model to structure its internal modules. A discussion of OSGi and the associated modularization of WebLogic Server is beyond the scope of this book, and it is not required for the understanding of the Oracle Fusion Middleware architecture.
MW_HOME/utils	Contains installation and domain configuration utility tools. The main utility tools contained in this directory are WebLogic Smart Update and Oracle Configuration Manager.

TABLE 2-1. *WebLogic Server Installation Directory Structure*

Directory/Filename	Description
	WebLogic Smart Update is a tool used for patching of the WebLogic Server installation, and Oracle Configuration Manager is an Oracle service that, if configured at installation time, periodically collects configuration information from your installation and configured domains and sends it back to Oracle support in order to allow extended support management capabilities through the My Oracle Support portal. Configuration Framework is used by the domain configuration wizard and other domain management tools that we will cover in more detail later in this chapter.
MW_HOME/domain-registry.xml	The file maintained by the domain configuration tools in order to keep track of the domains created from this installation. The file is used for the simplification of patching processes that might require domain modifications and there is no loss of operations if the configuration wizard is unable to write to it.
MW_HOME/registry.xml	The file maintained by the installation tools in order to record all products installed within a given MW_HOME directory.
WL_HOME/common	Contains the common WebLogic Server components, the most important of which are the WebLogic Server node manager, the WebLogic Server Scripting Tool, and the installation's domain creation and extension templates. We will cover all three of these components in more detail later in this chapter.
WL_HOME/server	Contains the Java libraries and binaries that form the functionality for WebLogic Server components executed from WebLogic Server domains.

TABLE 2-1. *WebLogic Server Installation Directory Structure* (continued)

Once a domain has been created (later in this chapter we analyze in detail the various ways in which this can be done), its top-level directory is referred to as the domain home (from now on referred to as DOMAIN_HOME, which is the environment variable that the path of the directory is assigned to in a WebLogic Server environment). The DOMAIN_HOME is the working area for all the domain's server instances that are executed from it; therefore, it is important to have an understanding of the various subdirectories it contains and their use. Table 2-2 provides a description of the most important paths directly under the DOMAIN_HOME directory.

Server Startup and Node Manager

As we saw in the previous section, WebLogic Server is started from the context of a domain, and starting up a domain means starting up one or more of its configured server instances. WebLogic Server instances are started through the startWebLogic.cmd and startManagedWebLogic.cmd startup scripts (or their .sh equivalent on UNIX systems) found in the domain's bin directory. The first script is used for starting the domain admin server, whereas the second is used for starting any of the domain's managed servers by providing the admin server URL and the name of the managed server to be started as a parameter. These scripts are generated as part of the domain creation process. Each script begins by initializing a number of environment variables that are used as arguments on the Java command line for the execution of the WebLogic Server code, such as the class path, Java options (such as memory arguments), and the Java runtime home directory. It should be noted that the start scripts do not perform the initialization of all environment variables on their own. Instead, both start scripts invoke the DOMAIN_HOME/bin/setDomainEnv.sh|.cmd script, which in turn invokes the WL_HOME/common/bin/commEnv.sh|.cmd script. The setDomainEnv.sh script initializes environment variables that are domain specific, such as DOMAIN_HOME, and indicate whether the servers should be running in development or production mode. The commEnv.sh script initializes variables that apply to all domains, such as the default JAVA_HOME and Java command-line properties that are required by WebLogic Server. The final step within each script is to execute the Java command to start WebLogic Server using the initialized environment variables.

Directory Name	Description
bin	Contains the scripts for starting and stopping a domain's servers as well as node manager.
config	Contains the domain's deployment and configuration information. Configuration information is stored within the config.xml file as well as within component-specific XML files referred to from the config.xml file and located within subdirectories. The config.xml file contains global domain configuration values and refers to configuration elements within the JDBC, JMS, and Diagnostics subdirectories, which contain the configuration of their associated domain-scoped modules. The Deployment subdirectory is used by server instances to manage the applications deployed in staged mode. We cover the server's deployment modes in more detail later in this chapter.
lib	The directory used to extend the server class path. Any JAR file placed in this directory is loaded as part of a direct child class-loader of the system class path, thus achieving the same effect as adding a JAR file to the system class path of the entire domain's running servers. This directory should only be used when the JAR file in question truly needs to be exposed to the server's system class loader (a good example of the use of this directory is for JDBC driver JAR files).
servers	Contains a subdirectory for each server that is part of this domain and is executing on the host using this domain directory. Each server uses this directory to output its logs and store its replicated embedded LDAP server data, which we will discuss in more detail later in this chapter.

TABLE 2-2. *WebLogic Server Domain Directory Structure*

NOTE
It is possible to modify the class path, Java runtime, and Java options used by WebLogic Server through direct modification of a domain's startup scripts location within the domain's /bin directory. The modification of the server class path in this manner is not recommended because WebLogic provides a number of more granular ways for ensuring that the server's class path is appropriately extended.

In order to successfully start, a server instance requires the user name and password for a user with Admin role privileges within the domain's security realm. We will discuss the concept of a security realm and how to manage users and roles in the Authentication and Authorization Services section of this chapter in detail. However, in the context of server startup, it is sufficient to know that the required credentials can be provided to the server in two ways:

- Through the -Dweblogic.management.username=<user name> and -Dweblogic.management.password=<password> Java command-line options.
- Through the boot.properties file within the DOMAIN_HOME/server/<server-name>/security directory, which contains the two properties of "username" and "password". Each server instance reads this file at startup time and if the value of the properties is specified in plain text, the server automatically encrypts the value and rewrites it to the file.

We have now covered how the servers of a WebLogic Server domain are manually started through their startup scripts. However, a complete discussion of server startup requires the introduction of the WebLogic Server node manager, which, among other things, allows for automated and remote startup of domain servers. Node manager is a process that optionally runs on each physical machine that can host one or more WebLogic Server domains. Domains can be configured to allow for automatic startup of their managed servers through the node manager residing on each host. To do this, the Java start command must be sent to the domain's admin server, which in turn sends it to the node manager on which the target managed server is configured to execute. In order for managed servers to be remotely started by the admin server using the remote host's node manager, the admin server needs to be configured with the managed server's startup class path, Java runtime, Java options, and credentials. This information is then passed on by the admin server to node manager for it to execute the managed server's Java command line. It is important to note that when managed servers are started with node manager in this manner, by default their startup scripts, and therefore all startup parameters they might have been customized with, are not used.

NOTE
When node manager is used for starting managed servers, any customizations made to the domain's startup scripts are not used by default. If you have customized start scripts and would like to use node manager, consider using the StartScriptEnabled *parameter of node manager.*

We will be taking a closer look at the detailed steps for the configuration of node manager within a Fusion Middleware environment in Chapter 11.

Managed Server Independence

To close our discussion of server startup capabilities, we must cover one more important element related to the dependency between a domain's managed servers and the admin server. When a managed server starts up, it first tries to connect to the domain's admin server in order to retrieve the latest domain configuration. If the administrative server is not accessible, the managed server starts operating in a state known as managed server independence mode, which is by default enabled on all servers. In this mode, the managed server uses the local config.xml file it has access to instead as a temporary source of the domain's configuration. When the admin server is able to connect to the managed server again, it refreshes the managed server's configuration information.

We have now completed our discussion of the main components that form a WebLogic Server domain. In order to be of any use, however, a domain must be customized for applications that can then be deployed to it. At runtime, deployed applications execute in the context of a different set of domain services and capabilities, which are together referred to as application containers. In the next section, we will analyze WebLogic Server application deployment and application containers in more detail.

Application Containers and Deployment

The behavior and life-cycle operations of a Java EE application are a function of not only its custom developed logic, but also the configuration of its associated runtime containers. In this section we provide an overview of WebLogic Server's application containers as well as their deployment considerations.

WebLogic Server, Oracle Coherence, and ActiveCache

Oracle Coherence is a product that provides an in-memory data cluster. Coherence allows for the partitioning of application data within a clustered in-memory cache. Two of the main benefits that can be achieved through the usage of Oracle Coherence are as follows:

- **Performance Improvements** By allowing for the caching of data from a shared data source (typically an RDBMS) within the application's heap memory space.
- **Linear Scalability** By spreading the data within a clustered data grid. Coherence's distributed cache allows for the amount of data that is stored by each individual application JVM within the cluster to decrease as the size of the cluster increases, while guaranteeing no more than single remote call latency for any application data access across the cluster.

(continued)

WebLogic Server provides tight integration with Coherence through a feature named ActiveCache. ActiveCache allows for the creation and management of Coherence clusters through a domain's management tools. Applications deployed to a WebLogic Server domain can directly access coherence clusters using ActiveCache. ActiveCache also allows integration with a Coherence feature named Coherence*Web that allows web applications deployed to a Java EE application server to replicate their HTTP session data using a Coherence cluster instead of the WebLogic Server default session replication mechanism. Usage of Coherence*Web allows for the more efficient management of session replication for applications with large amounts of session data. Coherence*Web can also be used to achieve enhanced session state reliability as well as to allow for the sharing of HTTP sessions between different web applications. A detailed discussion of Coherence and ActiveCache is beyond the scope of this book. For more information regarding ActiveCache please refer to the Using ActiveCache document within the Fusion Middleware documentation library.

Application Containers

As illustrated in Figure 2-1, at the highest level, WebLogic Server's application containers can be categorized as follows:

- Web container
- Enterprise Java Beans (EJB) container
- Web Services container
- Java Connector Architecture (JCA) container

Application developers build their applications according to the specifications associated with these containers, and when these applications are deployed to WebLogic Server they are executed within their associated runtime services. In this section, we consider the first three application containers listed in terms of their supported interfaces, deployment artifacts life cycle, and transaction management capabilities. We also describe the key deployment-time configuration parameters of each container that should be considered for the architecture and management of its dependent applications. A discussion of WebLogic Server's JCA container, which allows Java EE applications deployed to WebLogic Server to communicate with (usually non-standard-based) external systems, is beyond the scope of this book. Oracle Fusion Middleware Service-Oriented Architecture (SOA) Suite is, however, packaged with its own set of JCA adapters out of the box, and we will be discussing these in more detail within Chapter 5.

Web Container

HTTP servlets and Java Server Pages (JSP) are the main Java EE specifications for the development of applications geared at running within the Web application container. JSPs are designed to make it simpler for web application developers to focus on the view elements of Model-View-Controller (MVC) web-based applications, although they are also in turn compiled into servlets for runtime execution. There is also a variety of frameworks and specifications designed to simplify the development of MVC web-based applications (such as the Oracle Application Development Framework, which we will be looking at in more detail in Chapter 6), but in the end the core resulting artifacts of these frameworks, from a runtime execution point of view, are a set of HTTP servlets that process HTTP-based requests and responses.

Servlets are by themselves stateless, and the way web applications manage client state is through an HTTP session object that is assigned an ID upon initiation and stored on the client through an HTTP cookie, which by default is named JSESSIONID. For all remaining requests the client—which in most cases is a web browser—passes this ID within its requests, which in turn is used by the servlet code to look up the associated session state. HTTP session state is managed by the Web container, and its behavior is controlled by a number of parameters at the domain and deployment descriptor level. WebLogic Server also provides cluster session replication capabilities to increase the availability and reliability of web applications deployed to it. A discussion of the session replication functionality of WebLogic Server is, however, beyond the scope of this book. The key categories of the Web container's HTTP session management configuration are controlled through the weblogic.xml deployment descriptor. The most commonly modified deployment descriptor attributes are those that set the length of time a client session is valid and those that control session persistence capabilities.

The default life cycle of a servlet consists of WebLogic Server creating a single instance of the servlet, which is then used to process all incoming requests in parallel. Although rare, it is possible to develop a web application so that each incoming request leads to the instantiation of a new servlet object. In such cases, WebLogic Server initiates a pool of servlet instances upon startup that it uses to serve the incoming requests and only starts instantiating new servlets if the instances within the pool are all being used. The weblogic.xml <single-threaded-servlet-pool-size> element's value is used to control the initial size of the servlet pool. Finally, we should note that servlets are not transaction aware in that there is no container managed transaction capabilities available for them.

Enterprise Java Bean Container

Enterprise Java Beans (EJB) are the main Java EE specification for the creation of scalable, secure, and transactional business logic within the context of a Java EE application server. WebLogic Server provides both EJB 2.1 and EJB 3 container capabilities. The EJB 2.1 container capabilities are provided for compatibility purposes, and we will therefore not discuss them any further in this book. As a replacement to EJB 2.1, the EJB 3 container capabilities of WebLogic Server are covered through the following means:

- An EJB 3 Stateless/Stateful Session Beans and Message Driven Beans container developed in collaboration with SpringSource as part of project Pitchfork.
- Support for Java object-relational mapping through two different providers of the Java Persistence API (JPA) implementation: Kodo and TopLink, with Kodo being the default JPA provider in WebLogic Server and TopLink being Oracle's strategic JPA implementation and slated for replacement as the WebLogic Server default. In this section, we will discuss only JPA configuration aspects that are standard (and therefore implementation agnostic).

The following two sections provide more detail on each of these capabilities of the WebLogic Server EJB container.

Stateless, Stateful, and Message Driven Beans Stateless Session Beans (SLSB) and Stateful Session Beans (SFSB) expose an interface that can be configured for local as well as remote invocations. Local invocation can only be performed by modules within the same deployment archive (deployment archives and structure are covered in more detail later in this chapter) of the EJB and therefore do not require any system-level or deployment-time configuration considerations. If such EJBs, however, expose any interfaces that are expected to be used by clients outside of the archive—whether that client is itself deployed to the same server/cluster or is completely external to the domain—then the invocation should be considered remote and requires the following two deployment-time considerations:

- Remote invocation of EJB interfaces can be performed using WebLogic's proprietary T3 protocol or through the standard IIOP protocol. WebLogic Server's default protocol is T3, and WebLogic Server is by default configured to handle T3 requests. However, if IIOP clients are expected, then the servers on which the EJBs are deployed need to be configured to manage the incoming IIOP requests as described in the "IIOP Access" row of Table 2-3. Note that as a general rule, the T3 protocol is more efficient, but if interoperability with clients running in other environments than WebLogic Server is needed, then IIOP is the protocol of choice.
- Remote clients access EJBs through a lookup within the server's JNDI tree. The integration of an EJB's services with its clients therefore requires the synchronization of the JNDI lookup name used by the EJB clients and the JNDI name exposed by the EJB. It is therefore important to understand how these parameters are configured, as described by the "JNDI Mapping" and "JNDI Referencing" rows of Table 2-3.

The instantiation of SLSBs is pooled by WebLogic Server in order save the performance costs of instantiating a new object for every instance. The WebLogic deployment descriptors provide a set of parameters for configuring the SLSB pooling behavior. SFSBs, on the other hand, cannot be pooled because each client is associated with a specific instance of an SLSB that stores the client state. Each new request to an SFSB therefore leads to

Configuration Category	Description
IIOP Access	To allow remote client IIOP access, a server's Listen Address attribute must be set to a valid IP address or DNS attribute and cannot be set to the default empty value, which signifies that the server listens to "all configured network interfaces." This restriction does not apply for remote clients accessing the server using the T3 protocol.
JNDI Mapping	EJBs can map to the server JNDI tree either through annotations (within the EJB class code) or through the weblogic-ejb-jar.xml <business-interface-jndi-name> element. The annotation method does not allow for the modification of the JNDI name for different environments, whereas the deployment descriptor method provides such flexibility through the use of deployment plans—a capability we will cover in more detail later in this chapter.
JNDI Referencing	Remote EJB clients should use the <ejb-ref> element in the ejb-jar.xml deployment descriptor and the corresponding <ejb-reference-description> element in the weblogic-ejb-jar.xml deployment descriptor to look up references in the server's JNDI tree. For cases where the client and the EJB are not within the same domain, the configuration of a foreign JNDI provider is necessary. Foreign JNDI providers allow a WebLogic Server instance's JNDI tree to contain references to JNDI servers outside of the local domain. A detailed discussion of foreign JNDI providers is outside the scope of this book. Please refer to the "Programming JNDI for Oracle WebLogic Server" document within the Fusion Middleware documentation library for a thorough discussion of this topic.

TABLE 2-3. *EJB Container Key Configuration Parameters*

Configuration Category	Description
SFSB Caching	The weblogic-ejb-jar.xml <cache-type>, <idle-timeout-seconds>, and < max-beans-in-cache> control the container's SFSB cache management settings.
SLSB Pooling	The weblogic-ejb-jar.xml <initial-beans-in-free-pool> controls the container's SLSB pool management settings.
Transaction Management	The weblogic-ejb-jar.xml <trans-attribute> controls the container's EJB transaction management settings.

TABLE 2-3. *EJB Container Key Configuration Parameters* (continued)

the creation of a new SFSB instance and associated client session. WebLogic Server provides SFSB caching capabilities, which allow SFSB instances to be stored in memory for a certain period of time before passivating the state of the bean out of memory and onto disk. These WebLogic server session bean pooling and caching parameters are described within the "SLSB Pooling" and "SFSB Caching" rows of Table 2-3.

Message Driven Beans (MDB) are the Java EE mechanism for initiating container-managed business logic through the arrival of asynchronous messages on a JMS destination (queue or topic). MDBs can therefore not expose any remote interfaces. The mapping of an MDB and its dependent JMS destination is performed through JNDI, and the same configurations considerations listed within the "JNDI Referencing" row of Table 2-3 apply. MDBs are pooled in a similar fashion as SLSBs.

Finally, all three types of EJBs described in this section can participate in WebLogic Server container-managed transactions. The transaction demarcation points are a bean's interface methods for SLSBs and SFSBs and the receipt of messages from its destination for MDBs. Because MDBs do not expose operations that can be called by clients with an existing transaction context, their transaction model is restricted to the initiation of a new transaction for every new message received (or a set of messages as configured through the WebLogic Server MDB transaction-batching mechanism). The transactional configuration capabilities of EJBs are described within the "Transaction Management" row of Table 2-3.

Java Persistence API Container The Java Persistence API (JPA) specification was designed to serve as the basis for a standard-based model for Java object-relational (OR) mapping frameworks. Prior to JPA, the EJB 2.1 specifications contained their own OR mapping capability through the EJB 2.1 entity beans. Although JPA was drafted by the EJB 3 working group partly as a replacement to EJB 2.1 entity beans, it is a specification that stands on its own and the implementation of which can also be used by standalone Java SE applications. At its core, JPA consists of two categories of APIs. The first is a set of Java annotations used by developers to map the fields of certain Plain Old Java Objects (POJOs)—referred to as JPA entities—to corresponding database tables. The second is a set of control APIs that allow application code to control the management of JPA entities such as the creation and modification of entity instances.

The default JPA implementation used by WebLogic Server is called Kodo, although the product also comes packaged with another implementation called TopLink. Oracle has identified TopLink as its strategic JPA implementation for WebLogic Server. If an application uses only the standard JPA APIs, the switch of the JPA provider from Kodo to TopLink is only a matter of adding the element

```
<provider>org.eclipse.persistence.jpa.PersistenceProvider</provider>
```

to the application's persistence.xml standard deployment descriptor file. Otherwise, the application's Kodo-specific API usage needs to be ported prior to switching the provider to TopLink. Both implementations provide a set of implementation-specific configuration parameters described within the "Programming Enterprise JavaBeans" document within the Fusion Middleware documentation library.

From a deployment-time configuration point of view, the only standard JPA parameters are the data source configurations that are also exposed through a JPA application's persistence.xml deployment descriptor. In cases where the JPA application uses container-managed transactions—and for Java EE JPA applications, this should be the case—two JDBC data sources need to be referred to by this file for each persistence unit used by the application. These data source are identified through the <jta-data source> and <non-jta-data source> elements and must contain the JNDI name of a valid WebLogic Server data source.

The <jta-data source> element must point to a data source that is configured so that it is able to participate in global transactions (we will be covering the architecture of WebLogic JDBC data sources and transaction configurations in more detail later in this chapter) and is used as the data source through which all of the application's queries are passed. The <non-jta-data source> element must point to a data source that does not allow any other resources to participate in the transaction (this is achieved through a non-XA data source that either has its Supports Global-Transactions setting disabled or, if enabled, has its value set to One-Phase Commit) and is used by the JPA implementation to access the database independently from the application's entity management queries.

Other than the few parameters discussed in this section, most of the intricacies of JPA applications lie either in their development or in provider-specific settings.

Web Services Container

Thanks to the standardization of interface definitions through the Web Services Definition Language (WSDL) and the wide array of WS-* specifications designed to provide a common mechanism for implementing distributed integration capabilities, web services have become the preferred choice for the exposure of business logic for remote invocation. The most common transport protocol used by web services is HTTP, although the WebLogic Server container also allows for the implementation of web services that are exposed through a JMS/IIOP transport. The message format of web services is usually defined through the Simple Object Access Protocol (SOAP), although it is also possible to use plain XML messages through the exposure of a REST-style web services.

Web services can be implemented as POJOs (through a Java class referred to as the Java Web Services [JWS] file) or as an SLSB EJB. The life cycle of web services objects upon the receipt of a new HTTP request targeted at them depends on their implementation type. If the web service was implemented as an SLSB EJB, then the EJB container's SLSB life-cycle management and instance pooling capabilities, as described in the "Enterprise Java Bean Container" section of this chapter, apply. If the web service was implemented as a POJO, then the web services container creates a new instance of the Web Services JWS class and invokes the request's operation. The main benefit of implementing the web service as an EJB is the fact that in such cases all of the container's SLSB management capabilities (transaction management, pooling, and container managed security) take effect.

The WebLogic Server web services container is capable of executing both JAX-RPC and JAX-WS-based web services, with the latter being the recommended choice for the development of new web services because it is the replacement of JAX-RPC. The capabilities provided by WebLogic's web services container vary depending on the web service type. Table 2-4 provides a brief description of the capabilities supported by the WebLogic Server web services container for each web service type.

Capability	JAX-RPC Web Services	JAX-WS Web Services
Security	Supports WS-Security-based message-level security for the encryption of SOAP message content as well as the propagation of user name token and SAML-based identity. The enabling of WS-Security on WebLogic Server web services endpoints requires application-level coding, although JAX-WS-based web services can be protected with WS-Security using the Fusion Middleware Oracle Web Services Manager (OWSM). We will examine OWSM in detail in Chapter 3.	
Asynchronous Web Services Invocation	Implemented through a set of WLS features to support web services conversations, buffering, and reliable messaging for SOAP/HTTP. Asynchronous invocation can also be offered by implementing the web service as a SOAP/JMS service. Requires coding.	Not supported.

TABLE 2-4. *JAX-RPC and JAX-WS Web Services Capabilities*

Capability	JAX-RPC Web Services	JAX-WS Web Services
Transaction Management	EJB-based web services can support the initiation of new JTA transactions; however, transaction propagation—that is, the ability to ensure that the client transaction context is carried over to the server—is not supported.	Full integration with container-managed transactions and the propagation of transactions from incoming requests through the WS-Atomic Transaction specification. Transactional behavior does not require development time coding and can be controlled through the <wsat-config> element of weblogic-webservices.xml.
Stateful Web Services	Implemented through proprietary WebLogic Server web services conversation protocol. Requires coding.	Implemented through JAX-WS standard session propagation capabilities, which allow session management using the HTTP session. Requires coding.
RESTFul Web Services	Not supported.	Implemented through the JAX-WS HTTPBinding.HTTP_BINDING binding type. Requires coding.

TABLE 2-4. *JAX-RPC and JAX-WS Web Services Capabilities* (continued)

As is noticeable by the content of Table 2-4, many aspects of the WebLogic Server web services container's behavior are controlled through logic within the web service's code and are not configurable at deployment time; however, the elements that are configurable are specifically called out within the table.

For more information regarding the support for these capabilities and the WebLogic Server web service's container configuration elements related to them, please refer to the JAX-WS and JAX-RPC Advanced Features Guides within the Fusion Middleware documentation library.

Application Deployment

Application functionality is deployed to WebLogic Server through files in Java JAR archive format with specific extension names that imply an associated application type and content structures. The different types of deployment archives that can be deployed to WebLogic Server are the standard Java EE deployment archives with the extension of JAR, WAR, EAR, or RAR. Along with the standard Java EE deployment descriptors associated with these deployment types, WebLogic Server provides a set of its own in order to facilitate proprietary feature extensions. Table 2-5 describes each of these deployment types and their associated WebLogic deployment descriptors.

WebLogic Server web services can be deployed through either a JAR or WAR archive. In cases where web services are developed through annotations on an EJB—effectively exposing the business methods of an EJB as web services—the deployment is done through a JAR file. In cases where web services are developed by starting with a WSDL (top-down development model) or by starting with Plain Old Java Objects (POJOs), the deployment is done through a WAR file.

Archive files can be deployed to a WebLogic Server domain using the admin console or WLST commands, which are further described in the "Management Capabilities" section of this chapter. A number of important variables impact the deployment of an archive to a domain:

- **Deployment Target** Specifies the domain's server instances to which the archive needs to be deployed. The target can be either a set of specific server instances or a cluster, in which case the archive is deployed to all servers within the cluster. There is no default deployment target assumed by WebLogic Server, and the deployment target must always be specified at deployment time.

- **Staging Mode** Specifies the way in which a deployment archive is referenced from the servers to which it has been targeted after deployment. The default deployment mode is "staged," which indicates that a copy of the deployment archives is transferred to each target server by the admin server, which also manages all subsequent changes. The deployment mode of an archive has important implications on its life-cycle management. We will discuss all available WebLogic Server deployment modes in more detail within the "Deployment Modes" section of this chapter.

<table>
<tr><th>Deployment Type</th><th>Description</th></tr>
<tr><td>JAR</td><td>A Java Archive File (JAR) can be deployed to WebLogic Server in two different ways. The first is as an archive that contains a set of Enterprise Java Beans and/or Java Persistence API–based entities. Such an archive must have the following:
■ A root level META-INF directory and optionally:
  ■ A set of persistence.xml and/or application-persistence.xml deployment descriptor files that provide metadata for the JPA entities within the JAR file and also map the entity to a set of JDBC data sources.
  ■ ejb-jar.xml and/or weblogic-ejb-jar.xml deployment descriptor files that identify and provide metadata for the EJBs within the archive.
  ■ If any of the EJBs within the archive are marked for exposure as a web service, this directory may also contain webservices.xml and/or weblogic-webservices.xml deployment descriptor files that identify and provide metadata for the web services interfaces of these EJBs.
■ One or more Java class files within their proper Java package path for each of the EJBs identified within the ejb-jar.xml deployment descriptor.
The use of the ejb-jar.xml file is optional because an EJB could be described entirely through EJB 3 Java annotations, which are then compiled into an ejb-jar.xml by WebLogic Server at deployment time.
The second type of .JAR file that is valid as a deployment is one that contains any set of other .JAR files and/or .class files and is deployed as a shared library. We will discuss shared library deployments in more detail later in this section.</td></tr>
</table>

TABLE 2-5. *WebLogic Server Deployment Units*

Deployment Type	Description
WAR	A Web Archive (WAR) file must contain a root-level META-INF and WEB-INF directory. WEB-INF is used to maintain the following: ■ Optional web.xml and/or weblogic.xml deployment descriptor files that identify and provide metadata for the web application within the archive. ■ Optional webservices.xml and/or weblogic-webservices.xml deployment descriptor files that identify and provide metadata for the web services within the archive. ■ A \classes directory that contains the .class files—within their proper Java package path—that contain the implementation of the web and/or web services applications included in the archive. ■ A \lib directory that can contain any dependent JAR files on which the application's implementation might depend. The content of these JAR files are loaded through a dedicated class loader for the application. Additionally, a WAR file typically includes any number of HTML, JSP, and resource files (such as localization properties files or cascading style sheets) that implement the web application's view logic. Also note that the use of the deployment descriptors is optional because a web application could be described entirely through Java annotations that are then compiled into their associated descriptor files by WebLogic Server at deployment time.
EAR	An Enterprise Archive (EAR) file must contain a root-level META-INF and APP-INF directory. The APP-INF directory has a similar directory structure as a WEB-INF directory in a WAR file, except that the deployment descriptors used for an EAR are the application.xml and/or weblogic-application.xml files. The purpose of an EAR file is to aggregate a set of related EJB/JPA-based JAR or WAR deployment archives and deploy them as a single archive.

TABLE 2-5. *WebLogic Server Deployment Units* (continued)

Deployment Type	Description
RAR	A Resource Adapter Archive (RAR) file contains the logic and description for a JCA-based resource adapter. As mentioned in the introduction of this section, a detailed discussion of the WebLogic Server JCA container and its artifacts is beyond the scope of this book.

TABLE 2-5. *WebLogic Server Deployment Units* (continued)

- **Security Model** Specifies the way in which the roles and policies included within the archive's deployment descriptors are handled by the targeted servers. The default security model is "Deployment Descriptor Only," which indicates that only the roles and policies within the archives deployment descriptor are in effect and that no external authorization policies and role mappings can be defined for the application. We will discuss all available security models in more detail within the "Authentication and Authorization Services" section of this chapter.
- **Deployment Plan** A file that allows for deployment-time changes to an archive's standard and WebLogic Server–specific deployment descriptors. Deployment plans can play an important role in the management of an application's deployment descriptor configurations between different types of environments. We will discuss deployment plans and their use in more detail within the "Deployment Plans" section of this chapter.

To deploy an archive, WebLogic Server uses a two-phase model. In the first phase, the archive binaries are made available to each target server and each server is asked by the admin server to validate its configuration for the deployment of the archive. As part of this phase, the applications contained within the archive are not made available for service requests. If all target servers successfully pass this phase, then the second phase, which is the activation of the applications within the archive on each server, is executed by the admin server. If any of the servers are unable to execute the first phase, then deployment is aborted on all target servers. This method reduces the risk of having an archive only partially deployed to its target server sets.

When the deployment target is a cluster, not all of the cluster members need to be up and running for the deployment to succeed. Instead, the admin server deploys the archive to all accessible cluster servers, and upon recovery each unavailable cluster server resynchronizes itself with any missed deployments. However, this behavior can be overridden through the addition of the -DClusterConstraintsEnabled=true Java option to the command line of the admin server.

In addition to the JAR archive format, applications can also be deployed in exploded archive directory format. In such a case, the exploded archive directory must have the same structure as in its unexploded format. The application can then be deployed by pointing the WebLogic Server deployment tool of choice to its root directory. In general, exploded archive directory deployments are best suited for development environments with a single server in order to facilitate the frequent update of content (for example, JSP or application-specific configuration files) of the archive directory.

The following diagram illustrates the relationship between the WebLogic Server application containers and the deployment archives we have discussed in this section.

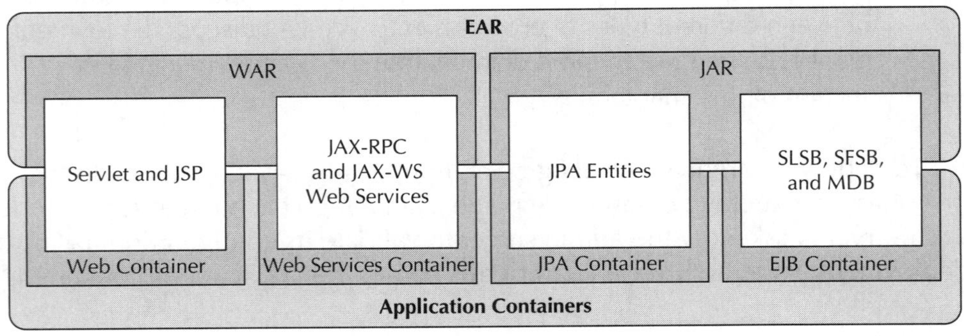

All of the deployment archives we have discussed so far can have dependencies on a specific type of deployment known as a shared library, which we describe next.

Shared Libraries

WebLogic Server allows for the deployment of JAR, WAR, and EAR archive formats described in Table 2-5 as a shared library. Other deployed applications can declare a dependency to shared libraries through their WebLogic proprietary deployment descriptor's <library-ref> element. When such a dependency is declared, the entire content of the referenced shared library is exported into the dependent application's class path and, as such, all Java classes contained within the referenced shared libraries become available to the application. In cases where the shared library itself contains web, web services, or EJB applications, the deployment descriptors of the library are also merged with the importing application's own deployment descriptors.

Shared libraries can be versioned through the content of their META-INF/MANIFEST.MF file, and the referencing applications can in turn specifically reference a particular version of a shared library. An application's referenced shared libraries must be deployed before the deployment of the application itself, and shared libraries cannot be undeployed until all referencing applications have been undeployed.

Deployment Modes

As we briefly discussed in the "Application Deployment" section, when deploying an archive, WebLogic Server allows for three different types of staging modes. This mode determines the way in which the archive content is managed and distributed to its target servers. The three staging modes that WebLogic Server allows for are stage, nostage, and external_stage. The main difference between the stage mode and the two latter modes is that in stage mode, a copy of the archive is made available to the admin server, which then takes care of distributing its content to the DOMAIN_HOME/servers/<server-name>/stage directory of each of the targeted servers as part of the first phase of deployment. In nostage and external_stage mode, the admin server does not distribute the archive to the managed servers. In nostage mode, the path of archive is specified at deployment time and all target servers must have access to the specified path no matter which host they are running on. This can be achieved either by using a shared directory for the staging of the archive or by ensuring that a copy of the archive with the same path is present on each host's file system. Finally, with external_stage, the archive needs to be made available—by the entity doing the deployment rather than the admin server, as is the case with the stage mode—to each server's DOMAIN_HOME/servers/<server-name>/stage directory on each host before the deployment operation is initiated.

Each of the staging modes has its intended use, depending on the specific administrative needs of the application involved. By far the most commonly used deployment modes are the stage and nostage modes. When using stage mode, keep in mind that as the size of the archive being deployed grows, so does the chances of deployment failures due to network file transfers to distributed target managed servers from the admin server. Another implication of using staged mode is that in cases where multiple domains are using a version of the archive and this version requires update on all domains, then an explicit redeployment operation to each domain is required. If, on the other hand, the nostage mode is used with all domains pointing to the same path, then the update of the archive on all domains consists of simply shutting down of all servers within all domains, updating the single archive file, and restarting the servers of all domains. This latter scenario is especially important for cases where the end user's use of the application involves the creation of multiple domains and where the application binaries might require frequent patching.

Deployment Plans

A deployment plan is an XML file that can specify overrides to a deployment archive's standard and WebLogic-specific deployment descriptors. Deployment plans are useful because sometimes the content of a deployment archive's deployment descriptors need to be tweaked based on the needs of the different environment on which the archive is being deployed. As an example, a web application's <page-check-seconds> value defined within its weblogic.xml's <jsp-descriptor> element sets the interval at which the server checks to see if the JSPs within the archive have changed and, if so, need to be compiled. The default value of 1 second might be optimal for a development environment because developers might be making in-place changes to the deployment's JSPs, but it is not a good value for production because the JSPs are not likely to change and therefore will lead to an unnecessary performance hit. The modification of an archive's deployment descriptor elements could be handled through the maintenance of separate deployment descriptors that are used for different environments, but this can lead to tricky build management and content synchronization issues. WebLogic Server provides the ability to manage changes to an archive's deployment descriptors externally through its deployment plans capabilities.

Using our example of <page-check-seconds>, an administrator could create a deployment plan for a production environment to specify that the value of the element should be –1, which indicates that the container should never check for JSP changes. Such a deployment plan would look as follows:

```
<deployment-plan xmlns=" ... "
  <application-name>PricingApp</application-name>
  <variable-definition>
    <variable>
      <name>PageCheckSecondsVar</name>
      <value>-1</value>
    </variable>
  </variable-definition>
  <module-override>
    <module-name>PricingServiceWeb.war</module-name>
    <module-type>war</module-type>
    <module-descriptor external="false">
      <root-element>weblogic-web-app</root-element>
      <uri>WEB-INF/weblogic.xml</uri>
      <variable-assignment>
              <name>PageCheckSecondsVar</name>
              <xpath>/weblogic/jsp-descriptor/page-check-seconds</
xpath>
              <operation>add</operation>
      </variable-assignment>
    </module-descriptor>
  </module-override>
  <config-root>C:\PricingApp\plan</config-root>
</deployment-plan>
```

As you can see, a deployment plan contains metadata with specific override instructions. In the preceding example, we have defined a variable, within the <variable-definition> element, with a name of PageCheckSecondsVar and a value of –1. We subsequently use this variable within the <module-override> element to indicate that the application's weblogic.xml deployment descriptor should be modified to have its <page-check-seconds> element reset. The <operation> child element of the <variable-assignment> segment indicates that page-check-seconds should be added to the deployment descriptor in question. This is the default WebLogic Server behavior and therefore, strictly speaking, it does not need to be specified within the plan. However, the <operation> element can also have a value of "replace" or "delete". The replace operation indicates that the element value should be reset within the deployment descriptor if the element already exists. The delete operation indicates that the element in question should be removed from the deployment descriptor altogether.

All WebLogic Server deployment tools provide the ability to specify a deployment plan at deployment time. Furthermore, if the deployment archive is located within an /app directory along with a /plan directory sibling (as in the following example) and the application is deployed by pointing to the root directory, then all of the changes made through the admin console lead to the generation of a deployment plan (with a name of "Plan.xml") within the plan directory:

```
\PricingApp\app\PricingAppWeb.war
\PricingApp\plan
```

If the /plan directory already contains a Plan.xml file, its contents are honored by the server and the changes made to the admin console are merged into the existing file. Deployment plans can be created from scratch or generated from an archive through the weblogic.PlanGenerator utility. The tool allows for a wide range of options, such as the generation of automatic variables for all of the deployment descriptor elements present within the archive. This tool is usually useful for the creation of an initial deployment plan, which can be further refined for different deployment environments. Finally, it should also be noted that the Oracle Enterprise Pack for Eclipse integrated development environment also provides the ability to visually create and modify WebLogic Server deployment plans.

Management Capabilities

In this section we will take a detailed look at the configuration management capabilities offered by WebLogic Server.

Domain Creation and Templates

WebLogic Server domain creation tooling is built on a common configuration framework that is based on the concept of a domain configuration template. A domain configuration template is a JAR archive that contains information about the structure and content of a domain. WebLogic Server is packaged with a default template (WL_HOME/common/templates/domains/wls.jar) that serves as the seed for the creation of generic domains. As we will see in later chapters, other Fusion Middleware products also use templates to enable the provisioning of their required resources within a WebLogic Server domain. The common configuration framework supports three different types of domain configuration templates:

- **Domain Template** Contains complete information for the creation of a functional domain from scratch. Domain templates are used for the creation of new domains.
- **Extension Template** Contains partial domain information meant to extend an existing domain with new resources or deployments.
- **Managed Server Template** Contains partial domain information for a set of managed servers only. Used for the distribution of a domain's servers on different hosts.

New domain templates can be created from an existing domain by using the WebLogic Server Domain Template Builder Tool. The following is the list of tools that use templates to provide domain management capabilities:

- **WebLogic Server Configuration Wizard** A user interface (UI) that can be run in graphical or console mode. The configuration wizard is often used for the creation of new domains in development and/or test environments. The wizard is pointed to a domain or extension template that is used as the basis for the domain to be created. The tool then navigates through a set of options that allow for the customization of the template domain (such as the number/name of servers and their cluster memberships) and finally creates the domain directory and its content.

- **WebLogic Server Scripting Tool (WLST)** A scripting tool, using the Jython language, with a large set of prepackaged operations for the management of a domain. WLST also provides domain creation and extension capabilities through the use of a domain or extension template. The WLST domain creation and extension capabilities are often used in conjunction with its other domain management capabilities, such as a deployment and online configuration management, to automate the provisioning of a domain through a script. We will be discussing WLST in more detail within the "WebLogic Server Scripting Tool" section later in this chapter.
- **Pack/Unpack Commands** A pair of command-line tools that allow for the packaging of a domain into a domain template (pack) and the re-creation of a domain directory from a template (unpack) in a different location. The pack command can be used to create a managed server template. These commands are often used for the movement of domains from one environment to another and for the distribution of domain artifacts across the file systems of different hosts that the domain's servers span.

WebLogic Java Management Extensions MBeans Servers

The Java Management Extensions (JMX) technology forms the backbone upon which WebLogic Server's configuration infrastructure is built. A domain's configuration is managed at runtime through a set of JMX MBeans servers. The MBeans servers are made available by each WebLogic Server instance through a special port called the administration port. Each server's administration port is, by default, set to its default listen port. JMX clients can connect to the server's administration port to obtain or edit its configuration.

Each managed server can have two MBean servers: the Runtime server and the Platform server. The Runtime server hosts two types of MBeans. The first are configuration MBeans that are initialized by the managed server from the admin server, if it is available, or from the local copy of the domain's config.xml otherwise. Configuration MBeans are organized in a tree hierarchy with a DomainMBean at the root. The configuration MBeans of a managed server are available in read-only mode. The second set of MBeans hosted by the Runtime server are Runtime MBeans and are initiated by the server to provide metrics or status about the runtime state of the server's resources (for example, the health state of the server's subsystem). The server's Platform server hosts the JVM's platform MBeans (referred to as MXBeans), which provide metrics or status about the runtime state of the JVM's resources (for example, the current heap size).

The admin server of a domain also has the same MBean servers as managed servers, with the exception of the fact that the configuration MBeans are available for modifications within the admin server. The admin server also has two additional MBean servers: the Domain Runtime server and the Edit server. The Domain Runtime server hosts MBeans that store domain-wide configurations, metrics, and services. The Edit server is used as a single point of entry for controlling configuration changes, through lock, save, and activate operations to the domain. To execute a domain configuration change, a JMX client would need to connect to the Edit MBeans server to perform a lock operation, then connect to the admin server's Runtime MBean server to modify its target MBean and finally to perform a save and activate operation through the Edit MBeans server.

As previously mentioned, the admin server is the only server within the domain that possesses an editable version of the configuration MBeans. When a configuration change is saved, the admin server sends the changes to the domain's managed servers, which store the change within the DOMAIN_HOME/pending directory. When the change is activated, the admin server then asks each managed server to apply the changes within the pending directory. Each server assesses the changes to verify that they can be accepted, and if all servers accept the changes, the admin server asks them to commit the changes to their configuration MBeans as well as the domain's config.xml file.

JMX Clients

The WebLogic Server JMX infrastructure we have described so far makes it possible for custom JMX clients to connect to the servers of a domain to retrieve information as well as to connect to the admin server to edit configurations. The following code is for a sample JMX client that connects to the admin server to query the list of servers within the domain:

```
public MBeanServerConnection connectToServer(String host, int adminport,
 String JmxServerURI) {
   try {
      JMXServiceURL serviceURL = new JMXServiceURL("t3", host, adminport,
```

```
"/jndi/" + JmxServerURI);
      Hashtable<String, String> context = new Hashtable<String, String>();
      context.put(Context.SECURITY_PRINCIPAL, "weblogic");
      context.put(Context.SECURITY_CREDENTIALS, "welcome1");
      context.put(JMXConnectorFactory.PROTOCOL_PROVIDER_PACKAGES,
            "weblogic.management.remote");
      JMXConnector connector = JMXConnectorFactory.connect(serviceURL,
            context);
      MBeanServerConnection connection = connector
            .getMBeanServerConnection();
      return connection;
   } catch (Exception e) {
      throw new RuntimeException(e);
   }
}
public void displayServers() {
   try {
      MBeanServerConnection runTimeServer = connectToServer("localhost",
            7001, "weblogic.management.mbeanservers.runtime");
      ObjectName runtimeObjectName = new ObjectName(
"com.bea:Name=RuntimeService,Type=weblogic.management.mbeanservers.
runtime.RuntimeServiceMBean");
      ObjectName domain = (ObjectName) runTimeServer.getAttribute(
            runtimeObjectName, "DomainConfiguration");
      ObjectName servers[] = (ObjectName[])runTimeServer.getAttribute(domain,
 "Servers");
      for (ObjectName server : servers) {
         System.out.println(runTimeServer.getAttribute(server, "Name")
               .toString());
      }
      catch (Throwable e) {
         throw new RuntimeException(e);
   }
}
```

In the preceding code, the connectToServer() method establishes a connection to a server with the given host and administration port coordinates to obtain a reference to a specific MBeans server, as indicated by the URI parameter. The displayServers() method uses the connectToServer() method to establish a connection to the admin server's Runtime MBean server. As you can see, to establish such a connection, the client needs to know the specific URI and object name of the target MBean server. The object name—which includes the URI as a prefix within its Type property—of each of the WebLogic MBeans servers is listed in Table 2-6.

Server	Object Name
Runtime MBeans Server	com.bea:Name=RuntimeService, Type=weblogic .management.mbeanservers.runtime.RuntimeServiceM Bean
Domain Runtime MBeans Server	com.bea:Name=DomainRuntimeService, Type= weblogic.management.mbeanservers.domainruntime .DomainRuntimeServiceMBean.
Edit MBeans Server	com.bea:Name=EditService, Type=weblogic .management.mbeanservers.edit.EditServiceMBean

TABLE 2-6. *WebLogic Server MBean Servers URIs*

Although it is possible for anyone to write a JMX client to manage a domain's configuration, WebLogic Server comes packaged with two such clients that make this task much simpler. The first client is the domain admin console—a web application that is deployed to the admin server of any WebLogic Server domain and is accessible through the http://<admin server host IP>:<admin port>/console URL. The admin console not only provides a user-friendly GUI for viewing and managing the domain's MBeans, it also provides other capabilities such as the ability to view the JNDI tree of each domain server. The second prepackaged JMX client application is the WebLogic Server Scripting Tool (WLST), which we cover in detail within the next section.

WebLogic Server Scripting Tool

The WebLogic Server Scripting Tool (WLST) is a Jython-based scripting interface that provides a set of commands to automate domain administration tasks. All Fusion Middleware products provide specific WLST commands that are geared toward their specific administration needs, and we will be covering these product's specific capabilities in more detail in their associated chapters. For WebLogic Server, WLST provides commands for creating, configuring, and monitoring domains, as well as for deploying applications. WLST can be executed in either offline or online mode.

In offline mode, WLST can be used to create and change the configuration of domains without requiring a connection to any of the servers. WLST offline works on a domain's config.xml file, and the modifications made through it to the domain configuration will be overwritten if the domain's servers are running. Therefore, for performing domain configuration changes, WLST offline must be run when the domain servers are shut down.

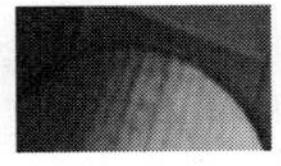

NOTE
Don't use WLST offline to modify domain configuration on manager server hosts or when the admin server is running because your changes could be overwritten.

In online mode, WLST maintains an active connection to the domain admin server and performs its changes by directly modifying the domain's MBeans. WLST online also allows you to browse the runtime status MBeans and to deploy and undeploy applications. Because the WebLogic Server configuration MBeans are organized in a tree hierarchy, it is possible to browse through them very much like a file system directory structure, and that is exactly what WLST allows you to do. As an example, the WLST online script used to achieve the same task as the JMX client code in the previous section is as follows:

```
connect('weblogic','welcome1','t3://localhost:7001');
ls('Servers');
```

By default, WLST online MBeans' browsing hierarchy is set to the runtime MBeans server of the server instance to which you connect. However, the MBeans browsing hierarchy can be switched to the domain runtime server when connected to an admin server through the domainConfig() command. The hierarchy can be switched back to the runtime server through the serverConfig() command. Neither of these hierarchies, however, allows you to modify the MBeans attributes through WLST. For making edits, you need to use the edit() command to switch to a writable MBeans hierarchy that contains all of the configuration MBeans of the domain. WLST also provides the ability to browse a server's JNDI tree in the same manner as the MBeans hierarchies through its jndi() command.

Because navigating the WebLogic Server MBeans hierarchies can be tricky, a good way of finding the path of the MBeans for a specific setting that needs to be managed through a WLST script is through the admin console's "record WLST scripts feature." This feature allows you to make a set of modifications through the admin console and ensure that a WLST script snippet is created that represents the steps that were performed through the console during your recording session.

It should be apparent by the description of WLST provided in this section that the capabilities it provides present a powerful mechanism for the automation of domain creation and modification tasks for the management of multiple environments. WLST is, however, best used in concert with the domain configuration template and deployment plan capabilities of WebLogic Server's configuration framework. It often makes sense to create a domain template for a specific environment that is then used as the basis of a WLST script to create the actual domain and modify it for its specific context—for example, setting the appropriate JDBC connection strings based on the target database instance being provisioned. The deployed archive's configurations can then further be modified at deployment time through the use of environment-specific deployment plans.

Although a more detailed description of WLST and its commands is out of the scope of this section, we will be using WLST throughout the use cases sections of this book and will therefore have a chance to describe some of its different capabilities in more detail. As a general note, a simple way of familiarizing oneself with WLST and its commands is through the use of its "help" command. The parameterless help() command provides a list of all available WLST commands, and the help command can subsequently be used with the name of a specific command as a parameter to obtain detailed information for it.

Authentication and Authorization Services

In this section, we will examine WebLogic Server's security services and their architecture from the perspective of application authentication and authorization. Although important, a discussion of network security (that is, SSL and connection filtering) and credential and certificate management will be deferred to Chapter 9 of this book. The following diagram illustrates the main components of the WebLogic Server authentication and authorization security services that we will be discussing in detail in the following sections.

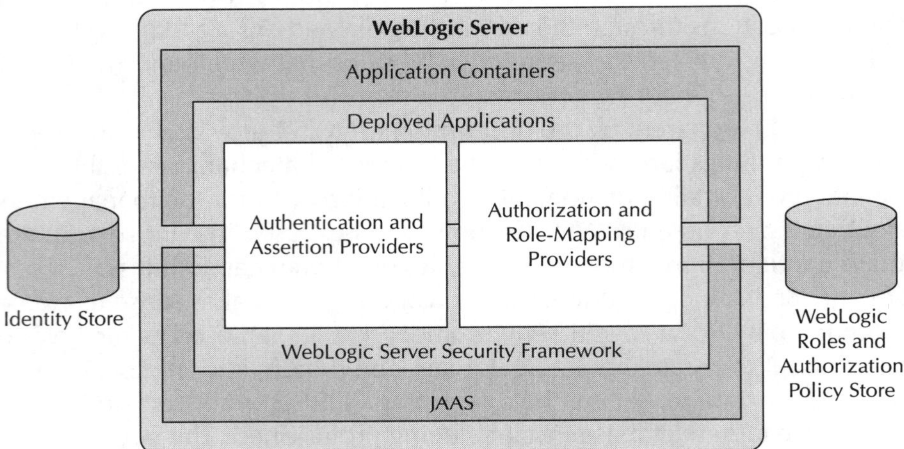

Embedded LDAP

WebLogic Server contains an embedded LDAP server that is used by its default authentication, authorization, and role-mapping providers as an identity as well as role-mapping and authorization policy store. In general, the embedded LDAP server is not recommended as an identity store in production for environments with a large user population. This is due to the fact that the content of the embedded LDAP is replicated between managed servers by the administration server, and this model does not scale very well when the LDAP's content becomes very large. The recommended production practice is therefore to use a dedicated LDAP server such as the Oracle Internet Directory or the Oracle Directory Server Standard Edition. The use of the embedded LDAP within all environments (including production) as a role-mapping and authorization policy store is, however, harmless and common; therefore, an understanding of its architecture is important. The configurations of the embedded LDAP server discussed in the remainder of this section can be modified through the admin console's "domain/Security/Embedded LDAP" tab.

An instance of the embedded server exists on each server instance and stores its data on disk within the DOMAIN_HOME/servers/<server-name>/data/ldap directory. The admin server is the only server allowed to edit LDAP content, and it ensures that the data is replicated to the managed servers on a periodic basis. Each server instance is by default configured to perform an automatic backup of its data once a day into a subdirectory called /backup. WebLogic Server uses a default administrative user called "Admin" and a randomly generated password as the LDAP server's administrator credentials. Therefore, to access the LDAP server directly through a generic LDAP client, the Admin user's random password needs to be changed, after which you can point to any server's listen address/port and use a Base DN (dc) value of the same name as your domain and a username (cn) value of "Admin".

Security Providers

WebLogic Server application security services are implemented through security providers. A security provider is a WebLogic Server construct that exposes its configuration through a JMX MBean and provides a specific type of security service. The scope of a security provider is at the level of a WebLogic Server security realm. Although multiple realms can be defined within a domain, only the single realm configured as the default can be active. WebLogic Server comes prepackaged with a number of existing security providers, some of which are configured by default for all new domains. Although possible, the creation of custom providers from scratch is rarely necessary because the prepackaged providers cover a wide range of functionality and are generally very customizable through the configurations they expose. The sections that follow describe the most important types of WebLogic Server security providers and their default configuration within a domain's security realm.

Authentication and Identity Assertion Providers

Authentication providers are used to integrate a domain with an identity store containing information about the users and groups, and to authenticate the credentials provided as part of the login of deployed applications with these stores. WebLogic Server comes packaged with a set of authentication providers designed for integration with the most widely used LDAP servers as an identity store. Additionally, an authentication provider for RDBMS-based identity stores is also provided. The default authentication provider configured with WebLogic Server uses the domain's embedded LDAP server as an identity store. The architecture of WebLogic Server authentication providers is based on the Java Authentication and Authorization Services (JAAS) specification, and as such it is possible to define multiple authentication providers (each using their own JAAS LoginModule), each with a different control flag that describes the provider's authentication success needs.

Identity assertion providers are a special type of authentication provider used for the implementation of a perimeter authentication scheme. In this type of authentication, another entity (usually a Single Sign-On server) sitting in front of the WebLogic Server domain has already performed the required authentication of the user. In such cases, an identity assertion provider is used to map the authenticated user's information—which is usually obtained from the incoming request's headers—to a valid authenticated JAAS subject that can then be used as part of the application's role-mapping and authorization policies. The application's role-mapping and authorization policies are, in turn, managed by their own set of security providers. These providers are described in more detail in the next section.

Role-Mapping and Authorization Providers

A role-mapping provider is responsible for the management of application and container scoped roles as well as the mapping of authenticated principals to their proper roles based on an application's role-mapping policies.

An authorization provider is responsible for the management of application and container scoped authorization policies. After a user has been authenticated, WebLogic Server uses the configured authorization providers to determine whether the authenticated user has access to any protected function or resource based on the authorization policies in context.

By default, WebLogic Server domains are configured with an eXtensible Access Control Markup Language (XACML) based role-mapping and authorization provider. By default, these providers store the domain's role-mapping and authorization policies in XACML form within its embedded LDAP server, although they can also be configured to use an external, RDBMS-based store.

Users, Groups, Roles, and Authorization Policies

When a domain is configured with an authentication provider pointing to an identity store, deployed applications can use the users and groups defined within that store for the purpose of their security by defining authorization policies on the usage of their resources. To do this, Java EE applications depend on the concept of a role that maps to a set of users and groups. In WebLogic Server, the application's roles and their mappings to users and groups can be defined in two ways. The first is within the application, either through annotations or within deployment descriptors. The second is at the container level, after application deployment, through the admin console's security realm page or through WLST online.

From an administrative point of view, it is important to inventory the exact set of roles expected by an application in order to ensure their proper mapping for each environment. Therefore, it is important to know whether the development team has built-in the roles within their application through its deployment descriptors or expects the provisioning of the applications roles to be performed completely at the container level. If the former is the case, and if deployment descriptors are used, the required roles can be deduced from them. However, if annotations are used or no roles are defined within the application in expectation of container-defined roles, then it is important to work with the development team to explicitly inventory the application's expected set of roles in order to identify the appropriate mappings to the users and groups within the application's different environments. We will see a good example of this process within this chapter's use case. Container-defined roles can be defined at the global scope (visible by all) or at the scope of a domain, a specific set of servers, the application itself, or JDBC data sources or JMS modules.

The benefits brought by roles, as opposed to applications directly referencing users and groups for the definition of their authorization policies, are two-fold. First, roles can be scoped to a specific deployment archive and mapped to users and groups within the target domain's specific identity store at configuration time. This flexibility allows for the development of the application's security to be decoupled from the specific content of the domain's configured identity store, which can vary from one environment to another. Second, WebLogic Server allows for the mapping of users and groups to container roles based on date/time interval and request context (HTTP request and session parameters as well as EJB method parameter values). This capability allows for the authorization aspects of an application to be based on business rules—for example, to ensure that a certain type of administrative task that could be more disruptive is not allowed during business hours.

To be useful, role mappings need to be complemented with a set of authorization policies that protect an application's functionality or resources based on the user's Subject, which is the object containing the user, groups, and roles to which the identity of the authenticated user belongs. Just like roles, authorization policies can also be defined either within the application or at the container level. When specified within the application, authorization policies can be specified either programmatically or declaratively through annotations or through deployment descriptors. Again, from an administrative point of view, it is important to understand if the application being deployed already contains its required authorization policies or expects them to be defined at the container level. Just like container-level role mappings, container-level authorization policies can be defined through the admin console's security realm page or through WLST online.

The way in which the application's role definitions, role mappings, and authorizations policies, as defined by the application itself and at the container-level interact, is controlled through the chosen deployment-time security model. WebLogic Server provides four different types of security models: Deployment Descriptor Only, Custom Roles Only, Custom Roles and Policies, and Advanced. The first three models should suffice for most applications' security needs. Their effect on the container's treatment of the different types of role definitions, role mappings, and authorization policies is described in Table 2-7.

The advanced security model is used at deployment time to customize the manner in which the application-defined role definitions, role mappings, and authorization policies need to be used in conjunction with their container-defined counterparts. As mentioned before, this behavior is rarely needed and should be used with caution.

	Role Definitions	Role Mappings	Authorization Policies
Deployment Descriptor Only	DD roles scoped at the level of the application at which they were defined for all of the application's URL patterns. Application scoped container roles cannot be defined.	Principals mapped to roles as defined in DD. DD can delegate the mapping to the container by using the <externally-linked> element, in which case global or domain-based roles matching the DD defined role names are required to specify the mapping.	All EJB and URL scoped authorization policies must be defined at the DD level and cannot be defined externally at the container level.
Custom Roles	DD role definitions are ignored by the container.	DD principal-to-role mappings are ignored by the container. Principals are mapped to roles through container-level role policies.	All EJB and URL scoped authorization policies must be defined at the DD level and cannot be defined externally at the container level. DD authorization policies must use role names that match container-level roles.

TABLE 2-7. *Security Model Role Definition, Role Mapping, and Authorization Policies Treatment*

	Role Definitions	Role Mappings	Authorization Policies
Custom Roles and Policy	DD role definitions are ignored by the container.	DD principal-to-role mappings are ignored by the container. Principals are mapped to roles through container-level role policies.	DD authorization policies are ignored by the container and only container-level authorization policies are used.

TABLE 2-7. *Security Model Role Definition, Role Mapping, and Authorization Policies Treatment* (continued)

JDBC Services

Java EE applications access the database through JDBC data sources that abstract the database integration and connection management for them. A WebLogic Server JDBC data source encapsulates a JDBC driver, a set of connection information—pointing to a specific schema within an RDBMS of the type matching the data source's driver—and a pool of active connections to the schema that is referred to by the connection information. Figure 2-2 illustrates the main elements of a WebLogic JDBC data source.

Upon startup, each WebLogic Server instance initiates its configured data sources with a certain number of active connections. Data sources are accessed by clients through a JNDI lookup, and the availability of the data source to a client's scope is determined by its server targeting. In other words, a data source's JNDI name is only available to the WebLogic server instances to which the data source is assigned at creation time. As clients access a data source, it provides them with an active connection from its pool for their use. If the pool runs out of connections, the data source can expand its connection pool size until it reaches a maximum count. The initial, maximum, and incremental size increases of a data source are all configurable parameters of its connection pool. As a general rule, it is often best to ensure that the initial and maximum size of the data source's

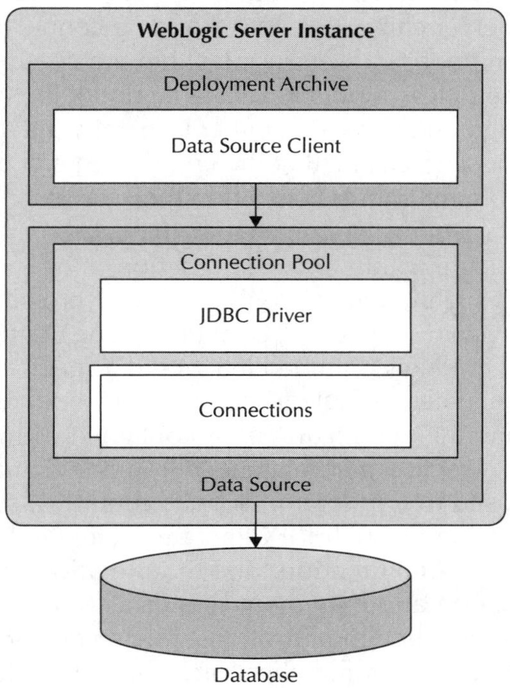

FIGURE 2-2. *WebLogic Server JDBC data sources architecture*

connection pool is set to the same value. This is meant to ensure that the backend database is not overloaded with expensive new connection requests at peak times and that all necessary connections are obtained in advance at server initialization. Each data source also performs a periodic test on all of its connections to ensure that they are still available, although this testing can be turned off. Connection pools can also be configured, through their "Test Connections on Reserve" property, to test connections just prior to handing them off to requesting clients.

The transactional behavior of data sources is another important configuration consideration. In a nutshell, if a data source is meant to be used by resources that are participating in JTA transactions and the JDBC driver used is non-XA (that is, it does not have the ability to participate in a distributed transaction as resource manager, according to the X/Open XA standard), then the data source's "Supports Global Transactions" must be set so that WebLogic Server can ensure that the same connection (from the data source's connection pool) is always used within the context of a particular JTA transaction. The different options available under the "Supports Global Transactions" configuration are used either to specify the algorithm that the data source should use to ensure that the connection can participate in XA-based two-phase commit transactions or, in the case of the "one-phase commit" option, to specifically indicate that the data source's connections should never participate within an XA transaction.

It is important to highlight that WebLogic Server provides application scoped as well as system scoped JDBC modules. The configuration of application scoped modules is embedded within a specific application deployment archive, whereas system scoped JDBC modules are defined at the domain level and their configuration is contained within the DOMAIN_HOME/config/jdbc directory and referenced from the domain's config.xml directory. As opposed to application scoped modules, system scoped modules are accessible through JMX and can be extended with new resources after their initial creation. The modification of each type of module's configuration at deployment time is also different in that for system scoped modules such modifications need to be addressed at the JMX and/or WLST level, whereas for application scoped modules deployment plans would need to be used. Due to the more flexible options available in managing system scoped JDBC modules, application scoped JDBC data sources are in general not frequently used.

Real Application Clusters Integration

Real Application Clusters (RAC) is a feature of the Oracle RDBMS that allows for multiple database server instances to provide access to the same database. Such server instances are known as nodes of a RAC cluster. Users of a specific schema can use any of the RAC nodes to submit their data access requests, and the RAC infrastructure manages the submission of parallel requests across a cluster. A RAC cluster thus allows for increased fault tolerance (if a RAC node is shut down, the others continue to serve requests), load balancing (across the hosts of the RAC nodes), and scalability (new nodes can be added to accommodate increases in request traffic). WebLogic Server JDBC provides two different features for integrating Java EE applications with RAC: multi data sources and GridLink data sources. The following diagram illustrates the way in which these features allow for the integration of WebLogic Server–deployed Java EE applications to integrate with a RAC database.

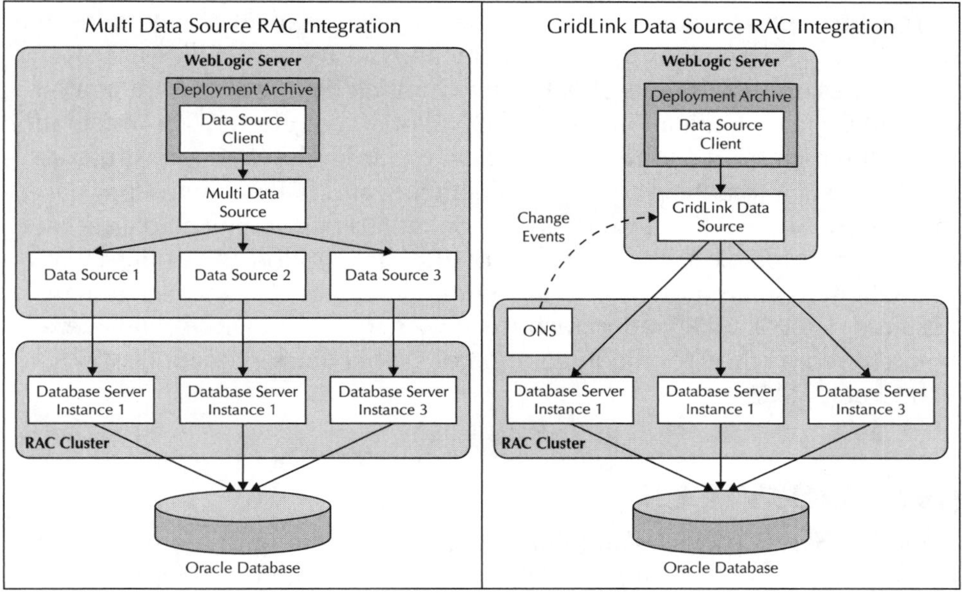

A multi data source abstracts access to a set of JDBC data sources and allows for load balancing and failover across them. Multi data sources have their own JNDI name and are configured within a domain with references to one or more actual JDBC data sources. Each of the data sources under a multi data source is a generic JDBC data source and, as such, multi data sources can be used for integration with other databases than Oracle. The only thing special about a multi data source when used for integration with RAC is that its individual JDBC data sources must be configured with the Oracle JDBC thin driver and each data source must be configured to point to a different RAC node within the RAC cluster. Otherwise, a multi data source is a generic mechanism that can be used for any clustered database technology similar to Oracle RAC. Client applications refer to the multi data source instead of the individual JDBC data sources it aggregates. As clients use the multi data source to execute SQL statements, it ensures that requests are load-balanced across the different data sources. As a result, when a multi data source is used with the nodes of a RAC cluster, it can ensure load-balancing of requests across the different nodes of a RAC cluster.

GridLink data sources are a special type of data source designed exclusively for integration with RAC. A GridLink data source is composed of a single JDBC connection pool, as is the case with a normal JDBC data source, but it can be configured with the connection of all of the nodes of a RAC cluster and provides load-balancing and failover capabilities across these nodes on behalf of its clients. The GridLink data source is integrated with the Oracle Notification Service (ONS) of a RAC cluster. This integration allows the data source to receive notifications from the RAC infrastructure, which allows it to adhere to its load-balancing and failover algorithm based on the state of the RAC cluster and its configured performance goals at the RAC layer. GridLink data sources offer tighter integration capabilities with RAC when compared to multi data sources, which are meant as a generic clustered database integration technology. As such, GridLink is considered the preferred method for the integration of WebLogic Server applications with Oracle RAC.

JMS Services

WebLogic Server provides an infrastructure that allows it to serve as a Java Messaging Services (JMS) provider in order to facilitate asynchronous messaging between clients using the JMS API. In this chapter we will explore the architecture of the WebLogic Server JMS Services and discuss its most important administrative considerations. Figure 2-3 illustrates the main elements of the WebLogic Server JMS architecture and the relationship between them.

JMS Servers

At the core of the WebLogic Server JMS architecture is the concept of a JMS server. JMS servers are responsible for managing their destinations by receiving messages sent to them by JMS client senders, honoring the properties of the messages (such as their persistence and retry requirements) and their destination, and, finally, ensuring delivery of the messages to the destination's consumers and/or subscribers. A JMS server must be targeted to a single managed server and cannot be targeted to a cluster. As such, a JMS server is considered a singleton service and relies on WebLogic Server's server migration capabilities—the details of which are beyond the scope of this book—for automatic migration of its destinations and associated

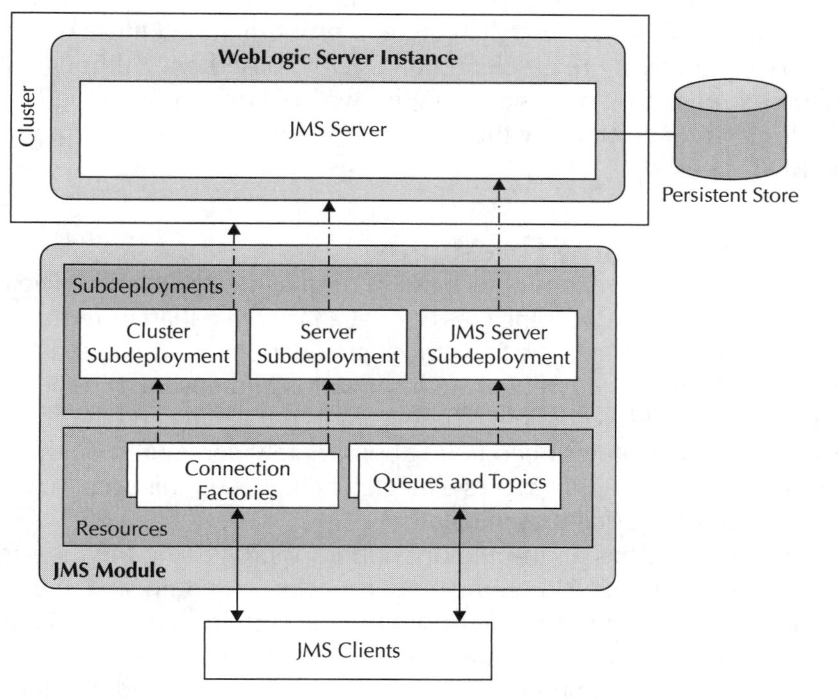

FIGURE 2-3. *WebLogic Server JMS architecture*

messages from one managed server to another in cases of failure. In the sections that follow, we will examine the most important configuration aspects of a JMS server.

Persistence Store

A JMS provider must guarantee the *persistent* delivery mode of JMS messages it is sent by ensuring that the messages are not lost before they are delivered to the recipient(s). WebLogic Server's implementation of this guarantee is through the association of a JMS server with a persistence store that is used to persevere the content of in-flight JMS messages with a persistent delivery mode. By default, each JMS server is associated with a file-based persistent store within its managed server's DOMAIN_NAME\servers\<server-name>\data\store\default directory. This store can, however, be changed to an explicitly defined file-based or JDBC-based persistence store. As a general statement, a properly tuned file-based repository is usually more efficient than a JDBC-based one, although a JDBC-based repository presents a simpler way of configuring a highly available persistence store by the virtue of the high availability capabilities of the RDBMS used.

Paging, Quotas, and Thresholds

Messaging-based integrations have a risk of running into a situation where the producer of messages is sending messages at a faster rate than its receivers can consume them. The WebLogic Server JMS provider offers a number of features designed to mitigate the effect of such scenarios and ensure that they are handled as gracefully as possible. These features are paging and thresholds. To be effective, these features need to be appropriately configured on the JMS servers to fit the client application's expected behavior. In this section, we will describe each of these features in detail.

Each JMS server has an in-memory buffer for processing the messages of its targeted destinations. When this buffer reaches a certain size, the server automatically overflows the buffer onto the file system to ensure that the message buffer does not consume all of the WebLogic Server instance's available memory. This process is referred to as "paging" and, by default, a JMS server "pages" the content of its buffer to its managed server's DOMAIN_NAME\servers\<server-name>\tmp directory when the buffer reaches less than a third of the JVM's heap size, or 512MB. Both the location of the paging directory and the maximum buffer size are configurable attributes of a JMS server.

Paging protects against memory overflow but does nothing to ensure that the paging and/or persistent stores themselves are not filled up when messages are produced on a destination at a faster rate than they can be consumed for a long period of time. To ensure that this does not happen, a JMS server can impose quotas on the maximum number of messages, maximum memory used, and maximum size of a single message on all of the destinations targeted to it. When the maximum number of messages or memory quota is reached on a server, the producers of new messages will be asked to wait for the period of time indicated by the timeout setting of their connection factory. If the required space for the new message becomes available during this time, the producer can complete its send operation. Otherwise, the producer will receive an exception that it will have to handle. Quotas can also be defined at the level of a JMS module and be associated with specific destinations within the module. When defined on the JMS server, the quota's restrictions apply to all of the server's destinations that do not have a module-level quota associated with them.

Whereas quotas are the last resort for dealing with degenerate destinations, thresholds are the mechanism that allows for WebLogic Server JMS to try and prevent quotas from being reached by throttling the rate of message production on the producers when all of the messages within the server reach a certain size or when the total number of messages on all of the server's destinations reaches a certain count total. A JMS server defines a high threshold and a low threshold value for both total message size and count. When one of the high thresholds is reached, the server initiates the flow control algorithm on all message producers by starting with an enforcement of a maximum production rate and bringing this rate down to a minimum production rate over a specific period of time, until the low threshold is once again reached. The specific elements of the flow control algorithm used are dictated by the configuration of the JMS connection factory used by the message producers. Thresholds can also be defined on specific JMS destinations, and in such cases the settings on the destination take precedence on the JMS server's settings.

JMS Modules

A JMS module contains the JMS resources needed by a set of JMS message producer and consumer's clients to integrate. The resources of a JMS module not only define the destinations used by such clients, it also contains the configurations that drive the behavior of the messaging integration between such clients. In this section we will analyze the key resource types that can be deployed as part of a JMS module and the concepts behind them.

Connection Factories

Connection factories are a type of JMS module resource used by JMS clients to make a connection to the JMS server in order to produce and consume messages. JMS clients look up a connection factory through JNDI. A connection factory's attributes determine the behavior of the connections it produces and, in turn, the behavior of the messages created from these connections by clients. Some of the main attributes that can be modified at the connection factory level are the default delivery quality of service settings (such as a persistent delivery mode) of JMS messages, default client acknowledgement policy, whether the operations performed through the connection factory can participate in distributed transactions, and the flow control algorithm settings of message producers using the connection factory. By default, each managed server is configured with two default connection factories that can be accessed using the weblogic.jms.ConnectionFactory and weblogic.jms.XAConnectionFactory JNDI names, respectively. The only difference between these two connection factories is that the XAConnectionFactory is configured to create connections that participate in distributed JTA transactions with other XA-aware resources. It should be noted that the settings of the default connection factories cannot be modified and that their server target is also fixed.

Queues, Topics, and Templates

JMS queues and topics, known generically as "destinations," are the collections that store messages sent by producers and are awaiting delivery to consumers. Both destination types can be defined as a resource within a JMS module. Queues follow a point-to-point delivery model, whereas an incoming message is always delivered to a single consumer. Topics, on the other hand, follow a publish/subscribe model, where an incoming message is delivered to all clients that have subscribed to it. Just like connection factories, JMS destinations are looked up by clients through JNDI. The key configuration parameters of a destination are its thresholds, quotas, and delivery failure setting. We discussed the first two of these parameters in the "Paging, Quotas, and Thresholds" section of this chapter. The delivery failure setting of a destination determines how many times the server tries to redeliver a rolled-back message, how many attempts it makes at such a redelivery and, finally, the name of an alternate destination (referred to as the error destination) where messages are placed that could not be redelivered after their number of redelivery attempts expired.

JMS templates are another JMS module resource type that allows for the definition of a configuration on which newly created destinations can be based. Templates are often used by JMS clients that dynamically create temporary destinations in order to minimize the level of configuration that needs to be specified by such clients.

JMS Module Types and Targeting

As was the case with JDBC modules, WebLogic Server provides application scoped and system scoped JMS modules. The configuration of application scoped modules is embedded within a specific application deployment archive. System scoped JMS modules, on the other hand, are defined at the domain level and their configuration is contained within the DOMAIN_HOME/config/jms directory and referenced from the domain's config.xml directory. As opposed to application scoped modules, system scoped modules are accessible through JMX and can be extended with new resources after their initial creation. The modification of each type of module's configuration at deployment time is also different in that for system scoped modules, such modifications need to be addressed at the JMX and/or WLST level, whereas for application scoped modules deployment plans would need to be used.

The resources of a JMS module must be targeted to a set of WebLogic Server instances, or a specific JMS server and JMS destination resources can only be targeted to a JMS server. Each resource within a module can be targeted differently. The way this is accomplished is through the concept of a subdeployment. A subdeployment is defined at the level of a JMS module and identifies a set of potential targets for the resources of the JMS module. Module resources are then associated with a specific subdeployment that targets them accordingly. This targeting mechanism is illustrated by the dashed arrows in Figure 2-3.

Foreign JMS Servers

A foreign JMS server resource can be used to point to an external third-party JMS provider and to allow its JMS resources (connection factories and destinations) to be accessible within the server's local JNDI tree, thus allowing for integration with third-party JMS providers. Foreign servers have their own associated connection factories and destinations that each have a local JNDI name (the JNDI name to be used by clients running on the local server) and a remote JNDI name (the JNDI name that the local JNDI name should map to within the external server's JNDI tree).

WebLogic Server Request Management

The ability to efficiently process incoming application requests in parallel is an important element of the WebLogic Server architecture. WebLogic Server's request management infrastructure ensures that incoming requests are associated with a server thread and properly dispatched to their destination—be it a servlet, EJB, or any other container. In this section we will analyze this infrastructure in more detail.

Connection and Port Management

Incoming requests must be sent to a server's listen port. Although, by default, a server has a single listen port, there are three ways in which this can be changed:

- *Enable the server's SSL port.* As its name suggests, this port is used for all SSL-based connections. We will cover SSL connections in more detail within Chapter 9 of this book.
- *Enable the domain-wide administrative port.* This is an SSL port enabled on all servers within the domain for the exclusive use of administrative traffic. The administrative port allows for the separation of administrative traffic—such as all JMX MBeans requests and configuration synchronization between managed and admin servers—from incoming application traffic. The administrative port of servers must be accessed using administrator credentials.
- *Create network channels.* A network channel is WebLogic Server's mechanism for creating new listen ports and/or listen addresses on a given server.

Each listen port is associated with a single listen thread, the sole job of which is to create socket connections for all connection requests and store them in an active connection collection. WebLogic Server maintains a special pool of threads—known as the muxer thread pool—that are responsible for monitoring each active socket connection for incoming request events, reading such requests from the connection, and associating them with a valid protocol (HTTP, IIOP, and so on) as well as a target application. After a request has been processed by a muxer thread, it is handed off to a Work Manager that is responsible for the prioritization and dispatching of the request to an execute thread, which, as the name suggests, will execute the request within its application context. We will discuss Work Managers in more detail in the next section. The following diagram illustrates the logical WebLogic Server request flow on its way from a listen port to an execute thread.

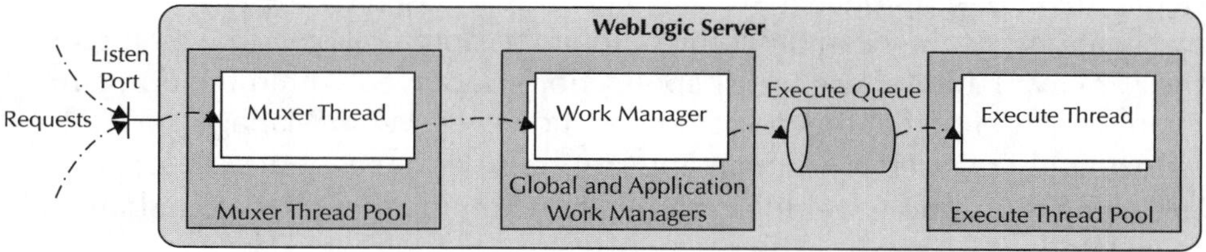

Work Managers

As we saw in the previous section, each incoming request to a WebLogic Server instance is ultimately executed within the context of an execute thread. Each server has a single pool of execute threads from which all requests are assigned their threads. Because the maximum number of threads with which an active process can run in an optimal manner is bounded, incoming requests compete for their share of available execute threads and are placed on an execute queue when no thread is available to serve them. WebLogic automatically tunes the size of the execute thread pool every two seconds, and this number cannot be changed manually. The entity that is instead used to control the way in which requests are dispatched to threads is called a Work Manager.

Work Managers can be thought of as the agent in charge of representing an application's execute thread interests within the context of a server instance process. Put another way, Work Managers are responsible for ensuring that the application's incoming requests are assigned an appropriate share of the server's available execute threads. By default, each deployed application is associated with its own Work Manager, which is responsible for all requests targeted to the application. The default Work Manager of all applications ensures that each application has an equal chance of obtaining an execute thread for its requests. Applications can continue using their default Work Manager and configure it as needed, or they can be configured to use new Work Managers for specific types of requests. In the remainder of this section we will review how such specialized Work Managers can be configured, and we discuss the type of thread-dispatching configuration parameters that they expose.

Custom Work Managers can be configured using a deployment archive's deployment descriptors, where they can only be used by the archive's applications, or they can be configured at the domain level, in which case they are available for use by all applications deployed within the domain. Even when defined at the domain level, however, Work Managers need to be explicitly referred to from an application's deployment descriptor. The following is a sample weblogic-application.xml file that refers to a domain-level Work Manager:

```
<work-manager>
  <name>pricing-service</name>
</work-manager>
```

A custom Work Manager's policies apply to all applications at the level of the deployment descriptor in which they are defined and to all applications below the descriptor's hierarchy within the archive. A Work Manager has three main types of policies: request classes, thread constraints, and capacity constraints. Instances of any of these three entities can be configured on any given Work Manager to specify their policy details. We will now discuss each of these policy types in turn.

A custom Work Manager can refer to three different types of request classes: response-time, fair-share, and context. Response-time request classes define a response time goal for the requests they manage. When such a request class is defined, the server constantly examines the response times achieved for the given request type, and if the request class's goal is not being met as a result of a lack of available request threads, it ensures that the request type's thread-dispatching priority is increased. Fair-share request classes define a numeric value (between 1 and 1000) that determines the relative priority of the Work Manager's associated requests compared to other Work Managers with a fair-share request class. As an example, if applications FOO and BAR are associated with fair share values of 60 and 40, respectively, when the server is running at full thread capacity, FOO-bound requests will, over time, end up with 60 percent of the server's requests threads, whereas BAR-bound requests will end up with approximately 40 percent. Finally, context request classes allow you to associate either response-time or fair-share request classes with a type of request based on its authenticated principals (user name or groups).

Minimum and maximum thread constraints allow you to, as can be deduced by their name, specify the least and most number of execute threads that the Work Manager's associated request types can be allocated by the server. In general, the use of these constraints is not necessary because request classes provide a more flexible way to specify the application's thread-scheduling requirements.

The last type of Work Manager policy that can be defined is a capacity constraint. This policy determines the maximum number of requests that can be queued within the server's execute queue after which the server will start responding with an error to clients sending the particular type of request.

Before we leave our discussion of Work Managers, it should also be mentioned that Work Managers and their policy configurations can be shared among multiple applications. As an example, the following listings show the weblogic-application.xml snippet of two different applications that refer to the same request class. The following is the listing for the first application:

```
<work-manager>
  <name>pricing-service</name>
  <fair-share-request-class>
    <name>priority-application-share</name>
  </fair-share-request-class>
</work-manager>
```

And here is the listing for the second application:

```
<work-manager>
  <name>pricing-web</name>
  <fair-share-request-class>
    <name>priority-application-share</name>
  </fair-share-request-class>
</work-manager>
```

The priority-application-share request class is a global request class with the following definition within the domain's config.xml file:

```
<self-tuning>
  <fair-share-request-class>
    <name>priority-application-share</name>
    <target>cluster1</target>
    <fair-share>80</fair-share>
  </fair-share-request-class>
</self-tuning>
```

In cases where multiple Work Managers refer to the same request class, min/max thread, or capacity constraint, the policies defined by these entities are shared by the request types of the referring Work Managers. For the example described by the preceding listings, this means that if a single other Work Manager with a fair-share request class value of 20 was defined within the domain, the request types associated with the priority-application-share request class would altogether consume about 80 percent of the server's execute threads at peak time.

The discussion of the WebLogic Server request management infrastructure brings us to the end of our overview of WebLogic Server's main subsystems and their architecture. We can now turn our attention to a use case in order to demonstrate the applicability of some of the concepts we have covered in this chapter in a real-life scenario.

Chapter Use Case

We will now go through a use case with the goal of putting to work some of the concepts covered in this chapter within the context of a realistic scenario. Our use case in this chapter goes through the required steps in rolling out a simple development-ready custom Java EE application built for WebLogic Server to an environment for evaluation purposes by a subset of its intended users.

Use Case Description

You have just been hired within the IT department of a mid-sized household goods manufacturing company as an Oracle Fusion Middleware expert. As your first assignment, you are asked to meet with the manager of the specialty products business development team, Jane, in order to understand the hosting needs for a new application that she has in mind. Upon meeting with Jane, you have found out that she has contracted the work to a freelance developer who has managed to complete the development of the application during the summer. Jane would like the IT department to ensure that the application is appropriately tested and that it is hosted for availability to a few members of Jane's team (about three people) for experimental use. Jane also explains that knowing that the IT department had standardized on Oracle WebLogic Server, she had instructed the contractor to build the application as a Java EE application running on WebLogic.

After discussing the situation with your manager, you are both in agreement that given the new application's departmental and experimental usage, the best way to manage it is as a special case that does not require full rollout to the IT department's hosting infrastructure. Instead, you decide to treat the application as an isolated service to be accessed and used only by Jane's group. With this strategy in mind, you set up a meeting with the application's sole developer in order to better understand the application's nature so that you can plan its rollout.

Understanding the Application and Its Environment

After meeting with the application developer, you have discovered a great deal more about the nature of the application and its architecture. The application in question is a pricing engine that is used by the specialty business development team to obtain a suggested price for specific products based on market condition variables. The application is deployed as a single EAR file and provides the following two external interfaces:

- **Pricing Model Web Service** A web service interface providing a single operation (called modifyModel) that can be used by external systems to add new products to the pricing engine's model or to update the model parameters for existing products. To update the model, the web service converts its operation's input into a JMS message, which is then placed on a JMS queue. The consumer of the JMS queue is an MDB that de-queues the message and updates the database (through a JPA entity) accordingly.

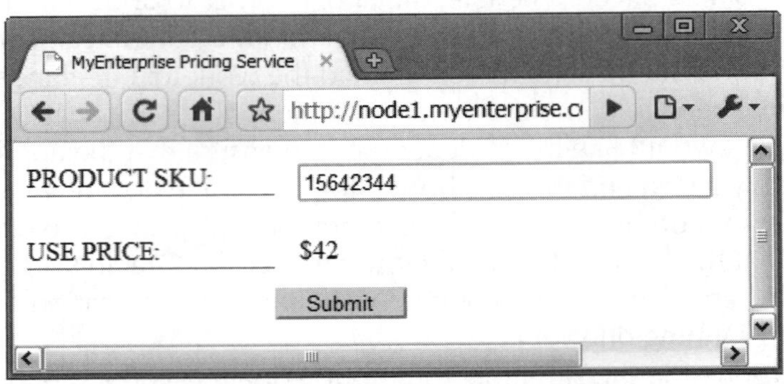

FIGURE 2-4. *Pricing Engine web application query page*

- **Pricing Engine Web Application** A simple web application to be used by the business development team to query the suggested price of a product by entering its SKU. Figure 2-4 shows the application's query page (actually the only other page the application has is a login page). The application is implemented through JSPs and servlets that call an EJB (SLSB) interface that in turn queries the database to retrieve the queried product's attributes and calculate the suggested price.

Given that the application's exposed interfaces are only through a web service and a web application, you are glad to know that you don't have to worry about any external JNDI referencing configurations for external client access. To make matters simpler, the application's web service interface is not expected to be used at this point and was developed only as a forward-looking feature (which we will be taking advantage of in the use cases in upcoming chapters). The security of the web application is enabled through a form-based login page, and the only secured page is the query page, which is protected so that only users within the "sales" role can access it through the following policy at the web.xml level:

```
<security-constraint>
    <web-resource-collection>
        <web-resource-name>query page</web-resource-name>
        <url-pattern>*.jsp</url-pattern>
```

```
        <http-method>GET</http-method>
        <http-method>POST</http-method>
        </web-resource-collection>
    <auth-constraint>
        <role-name>sales</role-name>
    </auth-constraint>
</security-constraint>
```

Because the developer has been the only user of the application up to now, he has simply mapped the "sales" role to the administrative user "weblogic" within the weblogic.xml deployment descriptor of the application, as follows:

```
<wls:security-role-assignment>
<wls:role-name>sales</wls:role-name>
<wls:principal-name>weblogic</wls:principal-name>
</wls:security-role-assignment>
```

The developer currently uses a domain on his own laptop for the development of the application. The domain has a single server: the admin server, which is also used as the deployment target for the application. After closer examination of the domain directory with the developer, you note the following:

- The application is deployed using a "staged" staging mode and a "DD only" security model.
- The domain contains two data sources, both pointing to the same MySQL RDBMS schema. One of the data sources uses and XA JDBC driver, and the other uses a non-XA driver with the supporting global (JTA) transactions flag set to false. The developer explains that both data sources are required as a result of the JPA entities used by the application.
- The developer has made the MySQL JDBC data source JAR file available to the server by placing its path on the admin server's system class path through modification of the startWebLogic.cmd script.
- A JMS server targeted to the admin server is configured without any customized configurations.
- A single global JMS module containing two resources—a ConnectionFactory and a Queue—has been configured. Both

are targeted to the JMS server through a subdeployment configuration, and neither has any nondefault configuration.

With this understanding of the application in mind and the application EAR file and development domain directory in hand, you set about to plan the evaluation environment where the application is to be hosted for use by Jane's team.

Designing the Evaluation Environment

It is clear to you that for the creation of the evaluation environment, the configuration of the application and its environment must undergo some changes. The following sections describe the changes you are considering to introduce for the configuration and the creation of the evaluation environment.

Application Topology

You know that the application needs to be deployed within a managed server instead of the admin server, but given that there are only a few users who will be using the application on an occasional basis, and because the application is not business critical, you decide to use a single managed server and have the entire domain run on the same host. However, to ensure that the scale-out of the topology is simplified in the future, you create the managed server within a cluster that will have a single member for the time being, but which can easily be extended with new cloned managed servers as required in the future.

NOTE
When creating a topology with a single managed server, consider assigning it to a cluster in order to allow for simpler scale-out if the addition of new servers is required in the future.

Furthermore, you decide to enable node manager on the evaluation host and configure it for server startup and automatic server restart in cases of failure. Finally, given the extremely low number of users for the web application, you decide to skip the need for a fronting web server for now

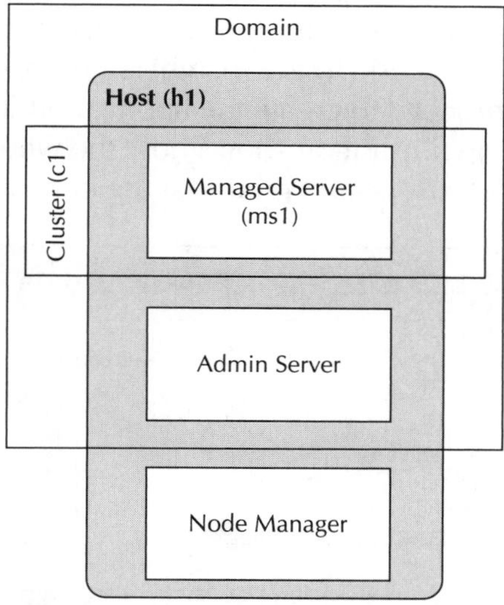

FIGURE 2-5. *Pricing application's evaluation topology*

and have browser requests be directly targeted to the one managed server. Figure 2-5 shows the evaluation topology you have designed.

Application Security

With the application's domain topology sorted out, it is time to plan its security configuration. Given that the application's user base is expected to be very small and that the application is being rolled out for experimental usage only, you decide to keep using the WebLogic Server embedded LDAP for the storage of both the users and groups as well as the application's roles and authorization policies. This means that you don't have to worry about configuring any new authentication or authorization providers within the domain and that you can use the domain's admin console to provision the required roles, groups, and users.

Because you are not planning on introducing new authorization policies but do want to modify the mapping of the role "sales" from the default "weblogic" user chosen by the developer within the application's deployment descriptor, you decide to deploy the application with a "Custom Roles" security model. This will allow you to create a container-level role with the name "sales," the membership policies of which will control the set of authorized users for the application. You also create a group called "SpecialtySales," which you add to the membership policies of the container-level "sales" role and proceed to create the application users you assign to this group. The following illustration shows how the web.xml authorization policies map to the roles, users, and groups at the container level.

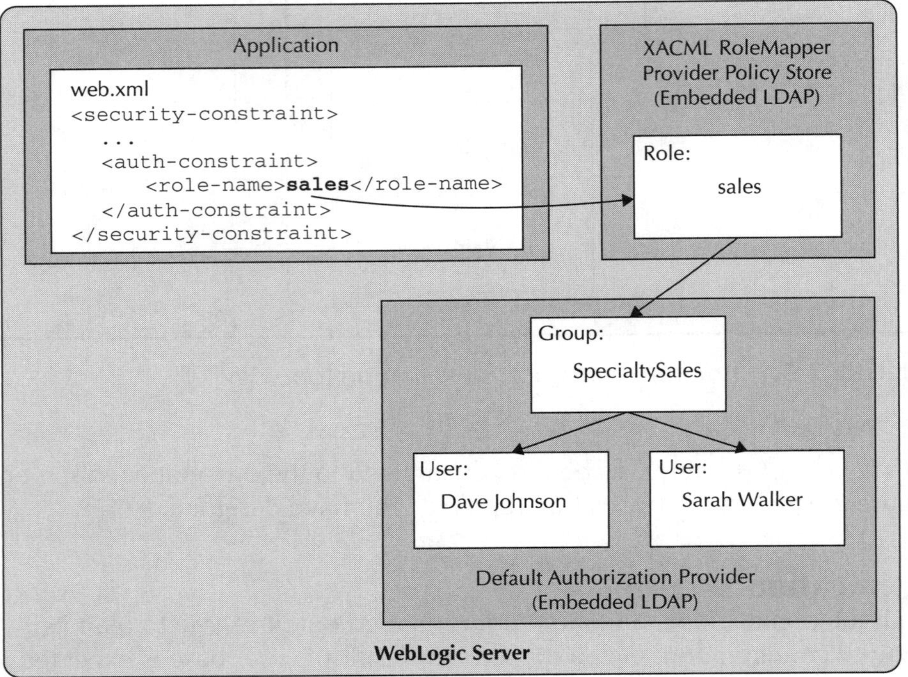

JMS and JDBC Configurations

The next step in ensuring a quality deployment is to understand the required JMS and JDBC configurations of the pricing application. One of the first things you would like to change from the developer's setup is the configuration of the application's system class path (which was set in the development environment through direct modification of the startWebLogic.cmd startup script) for accessing the MySQL JDBC driver. There are two problems with the method used by the developer. First, because you are planning to use node manager, the managed servers will not be started through the startManagedWebLogic.cmd script and therefore you cannot simply add the drivers to the system class path on this script. Second, you know from experience that the direct modification of the system class path can lead to longer-term issues that can be difficult to troubleshoot. You therefore choose to make the JDBC drivers available to the evaluation environment by adding its JAR file to the domain's /lib directory to ensure that it is made available as a direct child of the server's system class loader and therefore available to the domain's data sources no matter which servers they are targeted to. Other than these changes, you decide that no other modifications are required to the JDBC configurations from the development environment other than the targeting of the JDBC module, which needs to be made to the cluster rather than the admin server. To finalize the RDBMS configuration of the container, you work with the DBA department by providing them with the application's expected database space and usage needs (which are both expected to be minimal) as well as the application's DDLs, which were provided to you by the developer and which contain the scripts for creating and seeding the required pricing engine tables. The DBA department, in turn, creates a schema for you with appropriate credentials that you use for the configuration of the domain's data sources.

From a JMS configuration point of view, you are not worried with much customization and tuning because the web service that produces the application's JMS messages is not planned for usage at this point. You do, however, want to adjust the targeting of the JMS resources accordingly. You do this by first making sure that the JMS server is targeted against the single managed server. You then proceed to create two subdeployments within the JMS module. The first is for the targeting of the connection factory to the cluster, and the second is for the targeting of the queue to the JMS server.

Provisioning the Evaluation Environment

Up to this point, you have been working on setting up the application's eventual evaluation configuration within a staging environment by creating a domain using the WebLogic Server configuration wizard and then customizing it using the domain's admin console. When you are satisfied with this environment and have appropriately tested the application within it, you need to work on a plan to make it ready for evaluation. To do this, you decide to use the WebLogic Server domain configuration template capabilities to create a domain template from your staging domain that you will use to create the evaluation domain. You therefore run WLST within your domain's DOMAIN_HOME directory in offline mode and execute the following commands to create the template:

```
wls:/offline>readDomain('.');
wls:/offline/pricing>writeTemplate('pricingdomaintemplate.jar');
```

These commands read the domain's configuration and capture it within the pricingdomaintemplate.jar file. This template not only captures the domain's topology, all of its resources, and their configuration, but it will also include the content of the domain directory, including the /lib directory's MySQL JDBC JAR file as well as the archives of all applications deployed to the domain in staged mode. The template will not, however, include roles, groups, and users that have been created within the domain's embedded LDAP. You can now carry over the template file to the evaluation host targeted for the pricing application and create the evaluation domain using WLST. Before you do that, however, you have to install WebLogic Server on the evaluation host machine and configure node manager accordingly.

To create the destination domain using the application's domain template that you just created from the staging environment, you have to be aware of two important details: First, the domain template created also contains the pricing engine application deployment archive, which you deployed to the staging environment domain by placing it within your home directory and deployed to the domain's cluster using a staged mode. You now need to ensure that the creation of the evaluation domain places the deployment archive within an appropriate location for the admin server to pick up and deploy. To do this, you use the WLST setOption() command to set the location where the archive should be placed as part of domain creation. Second, you also need to use the setOption() command to ensure that the evaluation domain's servers are running in "production" mode. This mode sets a number of domain parameters values that are more suitable for production environments. Some of the main values affected by this mode are:

- The admin server's auto-deployment setting is disabled. This setting comes in handy in development where frequent redeployment can be done by placing an application within the domain's DOMAIN_HOME/autodeploy directory, but this is not necessary in production environments.

- The Java Runtime chosen for the environment is set to Oracle JRockit instead of the Oracle Sun HotSpot virtual machine.
- The admin console's change control settings are enabled so that changes cannot be done without explicit locking of the configuration and subsequent activation of the changes performed.

The WLST commands you run to create the evaluation domain within a directory called /domains are therefore as follows:

```
wls:/offline/prcingEval>readTemplate('pricingdomaintemplate.jar');
wls:/offline/prcingEval>setOption('AppDir',
'/domains/prcingEval/pricingapp');
wls:/offline/prcingEval>setOption('ServerStartMode','prod');
wls:/offline/prcingEval>writeDomain('/domains/prcingEval');
```

Because the domain template does not carry over the customized content of the embedded LDAP, you now have to re-create the domain's users and groups and map them to a new "sales" role, as we discussed in the "Application Security" section. Finally, to make it easier for users to access the application, you contact the IP department's networking team to ensure that the application's access URL (http://<host-name>:7002/PricingServiceWeb) is mapped to an appropriate user-friendly address (for example, http://myenterprise/sales/pricing). With this last step, the pricing application is now available in its evaluation environment for assessment by Jane's team.

Conclusion

We now conclude our overview of the WebLogic Server architecture. In the next chapters of this book we will discuss, in the same fashion as we did in this chapter, the other components of the Fusion Middleware stack and their dependencies on the WebLogic Server infrastructure. The elements of the WebLogic Server architecture we have covered in this chapter will play an important role in our exploration of the remaining Fusion Middleware components. We begin this exploration in the next chapter with an overview of the infrastructure components used by all Fusion Middleware components.

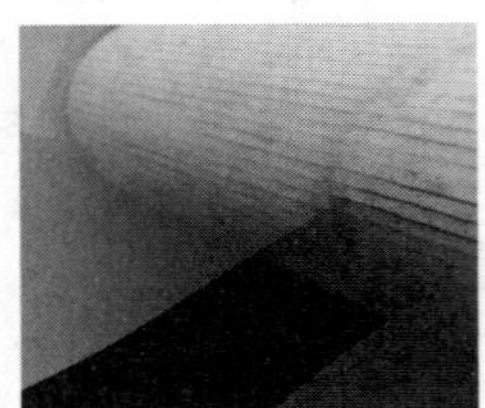

CHAPTER 3

Fusion Middleware Common Infrastructure

racle has built a set of components that together provide common services used by Fusion Middleware products. Not only do these services facilitate a consistent architecture, they also provide common management capabilities across the Fusion Middleware products. In this chapter we will examine the core elements of these common components, which we will refer to as the Fusion Middleware common infrastructure. In doing so, we will look at the services provided by this infrastructure and their relationship with the WebLogic Server services we discussed in the previous chapter. As we will see, the Fusion Middleware common infrastructure not only provides a rich set of capabilities for the layered Fusion Middleware products built on top of it, but in some cases it can also be used by custom applications built on WebLogic Server to extend their capabilities and simplify their management.

Introduction to Fusion Middleware Common Infrastructure

In this section we review the core concepts required for an understanding of the Fusion Middleware common infrastructure and review its installation and configuration artifacts.

System Components, Instances, and Farms

As we saw in the previous chapter, the concept of a domain containing servers and clusters forms the basis of the WebLogic Server administrative management and administrative scoping model. The Oracle Fusion Middleware infrastructure extends this model with the concepts of a farm, instances, and system components. The addition of these elements is designed to allow for the management of products that have components not based on Java EE and therefore do not have a natural place within the WebLogic Server domain model. A number of products within the Fusion Middleware product set have such non–Java EE components. These products include:

- Oracle Portal, Reports, Forms, and Business Intelligence Discoverer
- Oracle Internet Directory (OID) and Oracle Virtual Directory (OVD) products of the Oracle Identity Management (IDM) Suite
- Oracle WebCache and the Oracle HTTP Server (OHS) web server

In the context of this book, the non–Java EE products we will be discussing are limited to the IDM products and the OHS web server. We will discuss the IDM products in more detail in the next chapter and briefly discuss the Oracle HTTP Server in this chapter's use case.

The following diagram illustrates the relationship of the administrative elements of a farm, instances, and system components within a WebLogic Server domain. We will discuss each of these new elements in more detail in the remainder of this section.

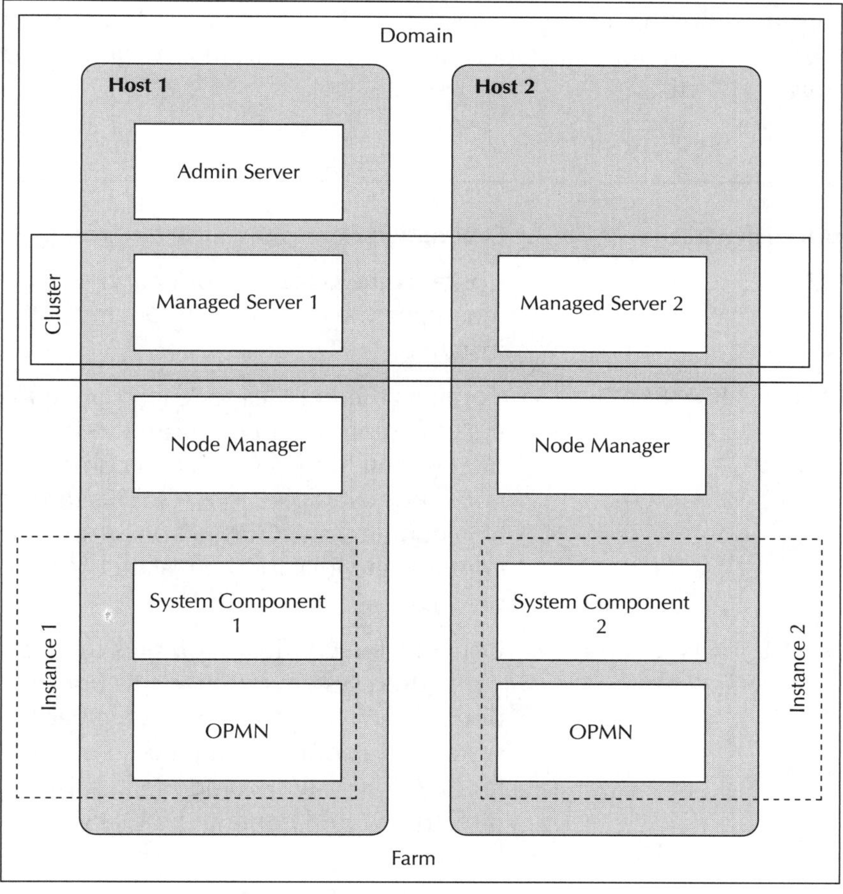

System component refers to the configuration of a non–Java-EE-based Fusion Middleware product component (the underlying technology behind the component could be anything, including C/C++ or Java Standard Edition). A system component process is therefore the actual runtime operating system process (or a set of processes) that uses a particular configuration. The life cycle of system component processes is managed by a Fusion Middleware common infrastructure component called Oracle Process Manager and Notification (OPMN). The set of system components managed by the same OPMN entity and share single parent directory for their configuration is referred to as a Fusion Middleware instance. Table 3-1 provides a description of the most important paths directly under the directory structure that encapsulates the content of a Fusion Middleware instance's configuration, the root of which we will from now on refer to as INSTANCE_HOME.

Directory/Filename	Description
INSTANCE_HOME/bin	Contains the opmnctl command for managing the system components of this instance.
INSTANCE_HOME/ diagnostics/logs	Contains the log files for each configured system component under directories with names matching each system component's name (for example, "ohs1"). This directory also contains an "OPMN" directory, which contains the logs for the instance's OPMN process.
INSTANCE_HOME/config	Contains the configuration files for each configured system components under directories with names matching each system component's name. As an example, for an OHS system component, this directory would contain the OHS httpd.conf.

TABLE 3-1. *Instance Home Directory Structure*

A Fusion Middleware instance can be registered with a single WebLogic Server domain, which allows for the system components within that instance to be managed by the Enterprise Manager Fusion Middleware Control web application. We will discuss the Enterprise Manager capabilities in detail within a dedicated section later in this chapter. Finally, we need to introduce the concept of a farm. The set of Fusion Middleware instances registered with the same domain for management by Enterprise Manager is referred to as a farm. In other words, a Fusion Middleware farm consists of a single domain and its set of registered Fusion Middleware instances, each of which is a group of system components managed by a single OPMN entity.

Oracle Process Manager and Notification

Oracle Process Manager and Notification (OPMN) consists of a set of artifacts that together allow for the management of the Fusion Middleware system components. As mentioned in the previous section, a single OPMN entity—that is, the set of artifacts that form OPMN—is associated with each instance of system components within a farm. An OPMN entity is composed as follows:

- An opmn.xml file within the INSTANCE_HOME/config/OPMN/opmn directory. This file contains the configuration of OPMN itself as well as the list of all system components that belong to the single Fusion Middleware instance managed by it.
- An OPMN process that constitutes the OPMN runtime. This process is known as "process manager" and is responsible for the life cycle of system components in terms of starting, stopping, registering with a domain, and detecting failures. An instance of OPMN is configured as a set of UNIX daemons or Windows processes as part of the system component's instance configuration. On UNIX, OPMN is actually made up of two daemon processes: a parent that only watches the child and restarts it if necessary, and a child that does all the work. On Windows, it is typically run as a Windows service, where the service process serves the purpose of the parent process on UNIX. However, it is possible to run OPMN in the same two-process setup on Windows if a service is not desired. A command-line tool called opmnctl serves as the main interface for user

interaction with OPMN. One copy of this tool resides within the ORACLE_HOME/ opmn/bin/opmnctl directory and is used for the creation and deletion of instances. Additionally, each instance has a copy of opmnctl under its INSTANCE_HOME/bin directory for the management of that particular instance, such as the starting and stopping of system components and their registration or deregistration with a particular domain.

OPMN serves three main purposes within the Fusion Middleware architecture. First, OPMN serves as an agent that allows for the starting, stopping, and automatic restarting of system components. In this regard, OPMN very much provides the same purpose as the WebLogic Server node manager process, except that it does so for non–Java EE components. Second, OPMN allows for the collection of status, metrics, and log information from system components and provides a central access point to this information. Finally, OPMN serves as the bridging point for the integration of a Fusion Middleware instance with a domain within a farm by exposing all of its information and capabilities through an MBean within the farm's admin server. We will be analyzing in more detail how OPMN provides these capabilities within the "Enterprise Manager Fusion Middleware Control" section of this chapter.

Installation and Configuration Artifacts

The Fusion Middleware common infrastructure components do not have a dedicated installation program and are therefore not installable in isolation. These components are instead installed as part of the installation of the Fusion Middleware products that rely on them. The installation tool for such products is the Oracle Universal Installer (OUI). When the OUI for a particular Fusion Middleware Product is executed, it installs the product-specific binaries within a dedicated directory referred to as the product's Oracle Home (ORACLE_HOME). In addition to the installation of a Fusion Middleware product's binaries within its ORACLE_HOME, OUI also creates a directory known as a common Oracle home (COMMON_OH) as a child of its target MW_HOME directory if one does not already exist. The COMMON_OH is populated with the binaries of the Fusion Middleware infrastructure. Table 3-2 provides a description of the most important paths directly under the COMMON_OH directory.

Directory/Filename	Description
COMMON_OH/modules	Contains the Java libraries and binaries that form the functionality of the Fusion Middleware infrastructure components.
COMMON_OH/bin	Contains the common tools for the administration of all Fusion Middleware products installed within MW_HOME.
COMMON_OH/common/templates	Contains the WebLogic Server domain configuration templates that contain the domain configuration for the Fusion Middleware infrastructure components.
COMMON_OH/doc	Contains a snapshot copy of the Fusion Middleware documentation library.
COMMON_OH/OPatch	Contains the Oracle Patch (OPatch) tool, which is used for the application of one-off patch updates to any of MW_HOME's installed Fusion Middleware products.
COMMON_OH/rda	Contains the Remote Diagnostic Agent (RDA) engine, which is a tool used to capture detailed information from a specific Fusion Middleware environment to aid Oracle support in assisting with service requests.

TABLE 3-2. *Common Oracle Home Directory Structure*

Beyond its use for the installation of the product's ORACLE_HOME and COMMON_OH within a specific MW_HOME, OUI is also used for the configuration of a farm environment for Fusion Middleware products with OPMN-managed (non–Java EE) components. For this purpose, OUI can be used for the following specific tasks:

- Creation of a domain with the component's Java EE–specific elements deployed

- Creation of an instance and system configuration for the component's OPMN-managed elements
- Registration of an instance with a domain to form the farm that can be centrally managed through Enterprise Manager

The first task listed can only be performed by OUI for products such as the Oracle Portal that have both Java EE and OPMN-managed components. For products with only OPMN-managed components, such as the Oracle HTTP Server (OHS), the creation of a farm, including its domain, as part of the configuration of a specific environment is not required, and the instance can be optionally registered with an existing domain. Also, note that the creation of an instance configuration and its registration with a domain can also be performed through opmnctl instead of OUI. For the creation of configuration environments for products that are purely Java EE based (for example, Oracle SOA Suite and Oracle WebCenter), no creation of instance configuration and registration with a domain is necessary and therefore the creation of the domain is performed through the use of the WebLogic Server domain template configuration tools, which we covered in the "Domain Creation and Templates" section of Chapter 2. We will discuss the domain creation process for these products in more detail in later chapters dedicated to these topics. Table 3-3 summarizes the installation and configuration process we just discussed for each of the Oracle Fusion Middleware products that are part of the scope of this book.

As described in Table 3-3, each Fusion Middleware product that requires a WebLogic Server domain for the hosting of its Java EE component's deployment archives has a top-level WebLogic Server domain configuration template. This template ensures that the product's required deployment archives are deployed to all domains that have been created through it. Furthermore, the template ensures that the archive's target servers are configured with the required WebLogic Server resources as needed by the product's deployment archives.

Each top-level product template has a dependency on three other templates that deploy the components of the Fusion Middleware common infrastructure within the domain being created. These three templates are Java Required Files (JRF), Enterprise Manager Fusion Middleware Control (from now on simply referred to as Enterprise Manager), and Oracle Web Services Manager (OWSM). We will discuss Enterprise Manager and OWSM

Product	Installation	Configuration
Oracle WebLogic Server	Performed through the WebLogic Server installation program as covered in the "Installation and Domain Artifacts" section of Chapter 2	Performed through the WebLogic Server configuration framework and via the use of the base WebLogic Server domain configuration template, as covered in the "Domain Creation and Templates" section of Chapter 2.
Oracle HTTP Server	Performed through OUI	Instance configuration and domain registration are performed through OUI, opmnctl, or Enterprise Manager.
Oracle Internet Directory (OID)	Performed through OUI	Instance configuration and domain registration are performed through OUI, opmnctl, or Enterprise Manager. Optional domain configuration for the management of OID is also performed through OUI.
Oracle SOA Suite, Oracle WebCenter, Oracle Application Development Framework (ADF), and some identity management products	Performed through OUI	Performed through the WebLogic Server configuration framework and via the use of the product's top-level domain configuration template.

TABLE 3-3. *Oracle Fusion Middleware Product Installation and Configuration*

in dedicated sections later in this chapter. The JRF template contains the common Java libraries required by each Fusion Middleware product. These libraries provide common security, logging, and diagnostics, as well as metadata repository services to their consuming Fusion Middleware applications. They are made available to a WebLogic Server instance through the provisioning of Java EE applications, shared libraries, MBeans, WebLogic Server startup classes, or JVM system class path JAR files. We will discuss the security services of the JRF template, known as the Oracle Platform Security Services (OPSS), in more detail in Chapter 4 and later in Chapter 9. The logging and diagnostics services contained in the JRF template are discussed in detail in Chapter 11, but we also touch upon them within the "Enterprise Manager Fusion Middleware Control" section of this chapter. Finally, we explore the capabilities provided by the Metadata Repository Services (MDS) component of JRF later within a dedicated section of this chapter. The following diagram illustrates the relationship between these three different components that form the WebLogic Server domain-level elements of the Fusion Middleware common infrastructure and the three domain configuration templates we just discussed.

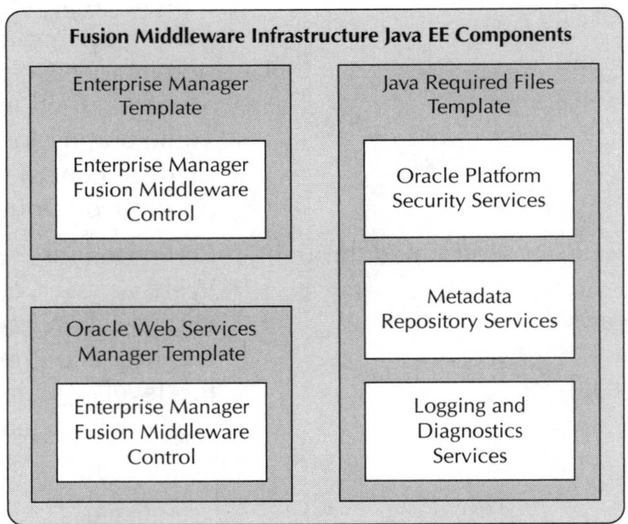

Before concluding this section, it is important to note that in most cases the Fusion Middleware common infrastructure as well as layered Fusion Middleware products provide their own WebLogic Server Scripting Tool

(WLST) commands. As reviewed in the previous chapter, WLST is a Jython-based scripting tool for the administration of WebLogic Server–based environments. Fusion Middleware products enhance the WLST set of commands with their own in order to enable a consistent scripting interface for the management of WebLogic Server domains with layered Fusion Middleware products. However, the execution of the WLST shell commands located within the WL_HOME/common/bin/wlst.sh|cmd directory or the direct execution of WLST through the Java command line does not provide access to the Fusion Middleware common infrastructure or layered product's command extensions. To be able to execute such commands, the copy of the WLST shell command within each product's ORACLE_HOME/common/bin directory must be used instead.

NOTE
To execute WLST commands provided by the Fusion Middleware common infrastructure or layered products, the WLST command located within each product's ORACLE_HOME/common/bin installation directory must be used.

Repository Creation Utility (RCU)

Some Fusion Middleware products have dependent database schemas that need to be created and seeded as part of their installation. The Repository Creation Utility (RCU)—a standalone tool downloaded separately from each Fusion Middleware Product—allows for the proper creation of such schemas. RCU allows users to specify a prefix to the product's schema names and thus allows for the existence of multiple schemas for the same product within the same RDBMS instance. RCU is also aware of the dependencies of a given product's schema on other schemas and ensures that all of them are created. Furthermore, RCU is designed to be used for use by DBAs and provides advanced schema management capabilities, such as the ability to specify a schema's table space configurations prior to its creation. The following illustration shows the RCU screen used to specify the schemas to be created and seeded.

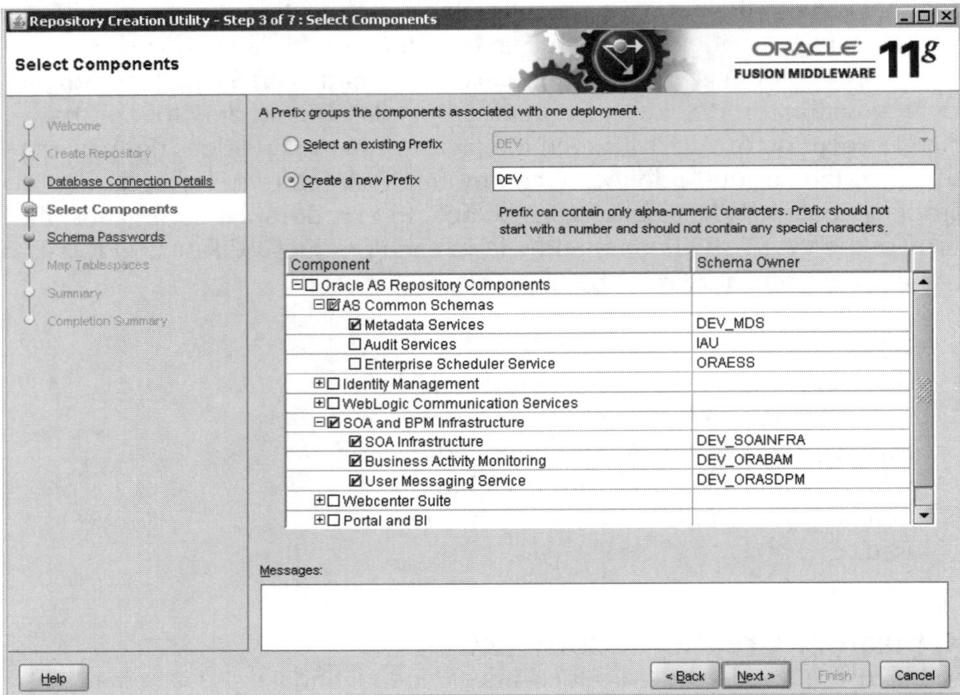

RCU maintains a schema (and creates it when it does not exist) called schema_version_registry that contains information about all Fusion Middleware schemas housed within a particular database instance. This table is used by the Fusion Middleware life-cycle tools and also provides a convenient way of querying and analyzing metadata about a given RDBMS instance's schema set. The information contained within the schema_version_registry includes the following:

- Short name (for example, SOA)
- Long name (for example, Oracle SOA Suite)
- Owner (name of schema)
- Version (for example, 11.1.1.4.0)

- Upgrade (N or Y)
- Status (Upgrading, Valid, Invalid)

The schema_version_registry is created as a system-level schema. Users with DBA roles have access to the entire content of the schema_version_registry, and RCU-created users have access to their associated schemas.

To conclude our discussion of the RCU, we should note two other important aspects of this tool. First, the tool provides an extensible framework that allows end users, through a set of XML configuration and DDL files, to configure their own application-specific schemas to be created through it. Second, RCU is packaged separately from any Fusion Middleware product and does not require installation. To run the RCU, one simply has to execute the rcu.sh|bat file from the /bin directory of the RCU package.

Enterprise Manager Fusion Middleware Control

Enterprise Manager Fusion Middleware Control (Enterprise Manager) is a web-based application that allows for the centralized management of all the components of a specific Fusion Middleware farm. The management capabilities of Enterprise Manager span the farm's domain as well as all of its registered instances of system components. Enterprise Manager provides its capabilities through integration with the WebLogic Server infrastructure, which we covered in Chapter 2, as well as the Fusion Middleware common infrastructure components. In this section we will be discussing in more detail Enterprise Manager's capabilities, architecture, and dependencies on the WebLogic Server and Fusion Middleware common infrastructure. Note that in this section we do not discuss the security, MDS, and OWSM functionality exposed through Enterprise Manager. Instead, we discuss security in Chapter 4 and MDS and OWSM functionality in dedicated sections later in this chapter.

Enterprise Manager Core Functionality and Architecture

Just like the WebLogic Server admin console, Enterprise Manager can be primarily thought of as a web-based JMX client that surfaces a key set of

JMX MBeans for simplified management through its graphical user interface. The difference is that although the admin console strictly surfaces WebLogic Server–specific MBeans, Enterprise Manager surfaces key Fusion Middleware infrastructure (as well as a small subset of WebLogic Server) MBeans in order to provide a centralized management console to a Fusion Middleware farm. The following is a screenshot of an Enterprise Manager window when a Java EE–deployed application is selected.

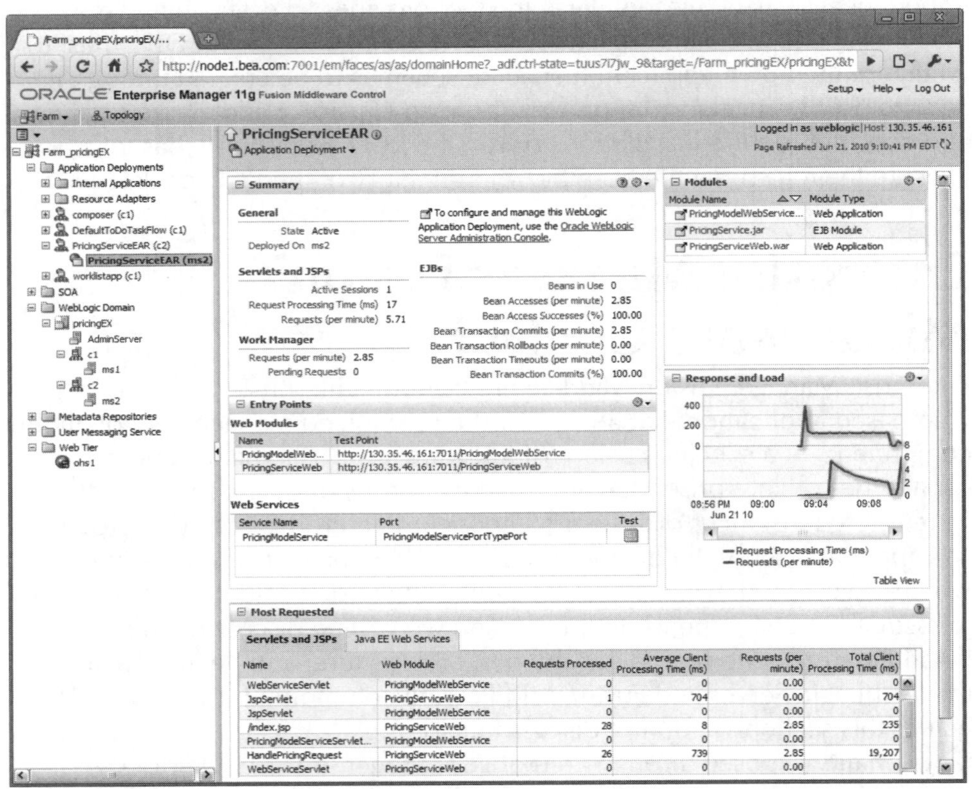

Enterprise Manager offers a wide range of functionality through a rich and context-sensitive web-based interface. Each Fusion Middleware product expands Enterprise Manager with its own product-specific functionality. Furthermore, Enterprise Manager allows for a view of a Fusion Middleware domain's deployments organized into internal Fusion Middleware product-specific archives and custom WebLogic Server application deployment archives. This view comes in handy because the Fusion Middleware infrastructure components as well as the layered Fusion Middleware products each introduce a significant set of WebLogic Server deployment archives, which to the administrator of custom applications built on top of them are for the most part irrelevant.

There's a core set of functionality provided by Enterprise Manager that concerns all Fusion Middleware components. In the next few sections we will explore the different categories of capabilities that this core Enterprise Manager functionality falls into and discuss their associated architecture and integration with the Fusion Middleware common infrastructure. The following diagram illustrates the Enterprise Manager integration with OPMN and the domain components we will be discussing in more detail in each of the following sections.

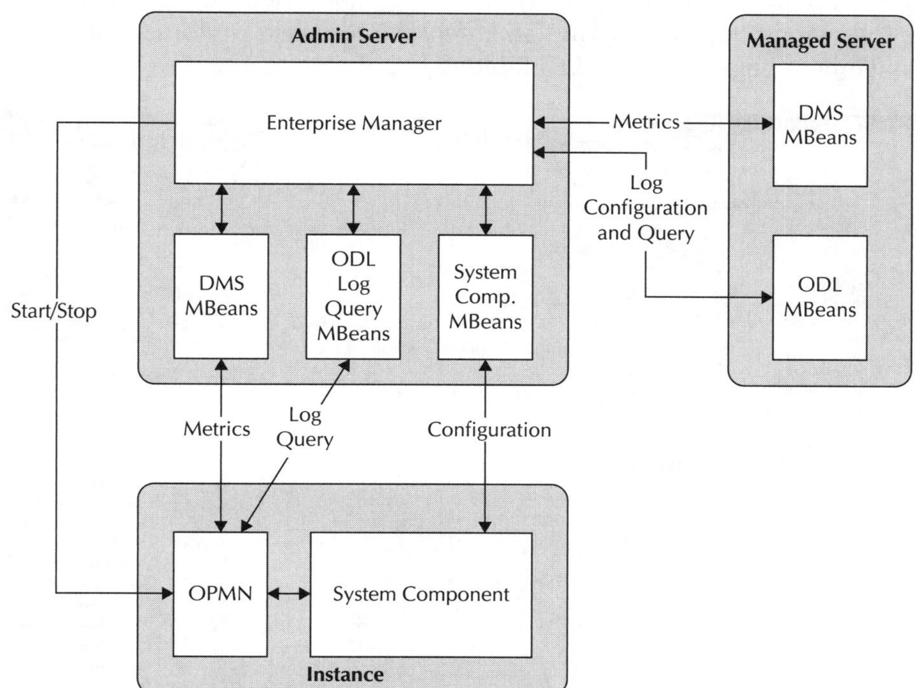

Component Startup and Shutdown

Enterprise Manager can serve as a central point of control for starting and stopping a Fusion Middleware farm's deployed Java EE applications, domain servers, and system components. To start/stop applications as well as WebLogic Server instances, Enterprise Manager uses the underlying WebLogic Server MBeans. Note that to start a WebLogic Server instance, the node manager on which the server is running must be configured, as is the case for a plain WebLogic Server domain. For the stopping and starting of system components, Enterprise Manager makes direct calls to the system component instance's OPMN process, which in turn executes the operation on the target system component.

Metrics Monitoring

Enterprise Manager provides a consolidated view of performance data captured from all of the farm's components. Although this information is distributed in a context-sensitive manner throughout a number of Enterprise Manager pages, it can also be centrally accessed through the Enterprise Manager performance management page, which provides a wide range of analysis options, including graphing, filtering, and selecting specific metrics. The following screenshot shows an Enterprise Manager performance management page for a Java EE–deployed application.

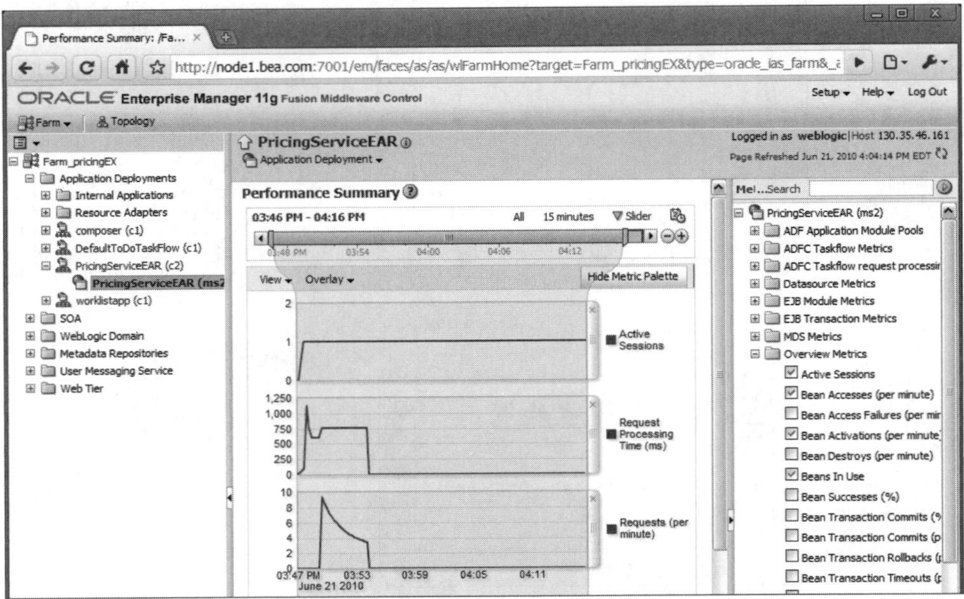

The metrics surfaced through Enterprise Manager are obtained through a JRF layer component known as the Dynamic Monitoring Service (DMS). For managing WebLogic Server instances and Java EE applications, DMS registers a runtime MBean within each managed server's Runtime MBean server. This MBean collects a set of metrics for each Fusion Middleware component running on its host server and exposes the information for collection from a special DMS collection MBean on the admin server. The DMS collection MBean periodically queries the DMS MBean on each manager server to collect a snapshot of its metrics. For the collection of performance metrics from system components within the farm, the DMS collection MBean queries each instance's OPMN process manager for performance data. OPMN, in turn, queries a specific DMS interface, which each Fusion Middleware system component makes available for the querying of its metrics. This DMS interface uses a custom RPC protocol, known as the Oracle Notification Server (ONS), for direct communication between OPMN and the system component process. Upon collection of a metrics snapshot from managed servers and system components, the DMS collection MBean on the administration server stores the information within an in-memory historical collection. Enterprise Manager, in turn, queries the DMS collection MBean to display the information available within its performance management windows.

NOTE
The metrics data displayed in Enterprise Manager is not persisted and is stored within the administration server's heap only. As such, a restart of the administration server clears all historical metrics data for a given farm.

DMS also provides WLST-based interfaces for access and management of a farm's metrics.

Log Management

Enterprise Manager provides central logging management for all farm components. The log management capabilities for a domain, its servers, and applications consists of both log querying as well as log configuration capabilities, whereas for system components only log-querying capabilities are available. The log configuration capabilities of Enterprise Manager consist of the ability to set logging parameters, such as the maximum log level for a specific Fusion Middleware layered component, and the ability to customize log file rolling parameters. The Enterprise Manager log-viewing capabilities consist of the ability to query log messages—at either the farm, domain, server, system component, or layered component specific artifact (for example, SOA composite) level—and to filter them based on date range, message type, message content, and/or originating component. The following is a screenshot of an Enterprise Manager Log Query page at the farm level.

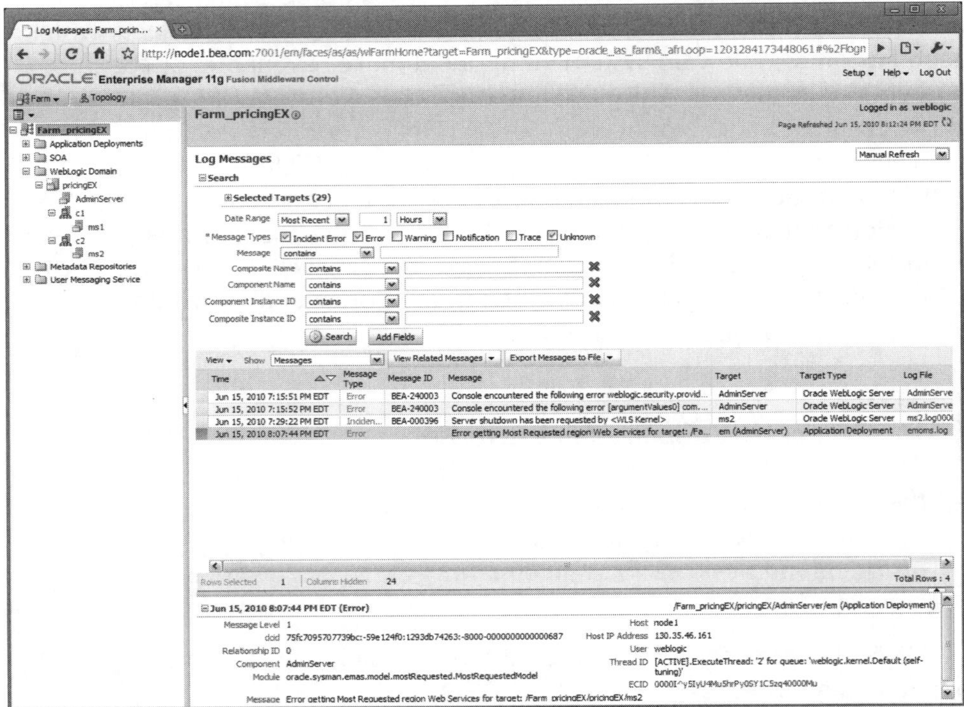

The log management capabilities of Enterprise Manager are exposed through a JRF layer component called Oracle Diagnostic Logging (ODL). ODL is a Java logging API-based framework used by Fusion Middleware components to log their messages in a standard format. Fusion Middleware layered components that run on WebLogic-managed servers log their messages to the domain's DOMAIN_HOME/servers/<server name>/logs/<server-name>-diagnostics.log file (where <server-name> is a placeholder for the actual managed server name concerned). System components log their messages to their instance's INSTANCE_HOME/diagnostics/logs/<system-component-type>/<system-component-name>/<system-component-name>.log file. In a similar fashion to the DMS component, ODL registers a runtime MBean within the server's Runtime MBean server for each managed server within a domain. This MBean provides access to the server's ODL log messages and their logging configurations. On the admin server, ODL provides an MBean that exposes the domain's aggregated ODL configuration and log messages by communicating with each managed server's ODL MBean. The admin server ODL MBean can also query a farm's OPMN process manager for the ODL logs of their associated instance; however, it does not provide the capability to configure the ODL logging configuration of system components. When OPMN receives a log query request, it looks through the log directory of the target system component within the instance directory structure and returns the requested results to the ODL MBean. Enterprise Manager uses the admin server ODL MBean to provide its centralized log management capabilities.

ODL exposes some of its management capabilities through WLST. We will be exploring ODL and the Fusion Middleware logging capabilities in more detail in Chapter 11.

Other Capabilities

Beyond the startup/shutdown, performance monitoring, and logging capabilities we discussed in the previous sections, Enterprise Manager provides three other notable cross-cutting capabilities. The first of these is a web service testing tool that can be invoked through the application page of any deployed Java EE application with web services. This tool simplifies the testing of web services interfaces and provides some advanced testing capabilities, such as the ability to specify the credential information that would need to be carried out by test invocations for web services with security policies. The second capability is a system MBeans browser that can be invoked through the context-sensitive pop-up menu from any of the Enterprise Manager's tree pane entities. This tool provides the capability to graphically browse, view, and (in the case of configuration MBeans) edit a farm's MBeans directly. The third and final capability to highlight comes into play when new managed servers need to be added to an Enterprise Manager–managed domain. As we discussed within the "Installation and Configuration Artifacts" section of this chapter, JRF components are enabled on managed servers at domain configuration time through the use of the JRF domain configuration template. However, for managed servers created after the initial creation of a domain, the JRF components required are not automatically provisioned. Enterprise Manager automatically detects such servers and within their server information page provides an Apply JRF button, which can be used to deploy the appropriate JRF components on the server and therefore enable full Enterprise Manager management capabilities. Note that this operation can also be performed through the WLST "applyJRF" command.

Metadata Repository Services

Metadata Repository Services (MDS) is a component of the Fusion Middleware common infrastructure that provides the ability for layered Fusion Middleware products to decouple their metadata from their core logic and content data by storing it within a shared repository. The services and management model provided by MDS facilitate a simple administration and customization of the metadata of the layered Fusion Middleware components. An understanding of MDS is important for the management of Fusion Middleware environments, and in this section we will review its main capabilities and architecture.

Metadata Management

Fusion Middleware applications often have a dependence on metadata in order to allow for a flexible approach for the customization and extension of their custom application logic to fit specific usage scenarios. As we will see in detail within the next section, a good example of such metadata includes the definitions of predefined web services policies that are available for the runtime used within a Fusion Middleware domain. The purpose of MDS is to provide a service that allows for centralized management of such metadata. In the subsequent chapters of this book we will discuss in detail the specific usages of MDS-managed metadata by individual Fusion Middleware products, but some examples include Oracle Application Development Framework (ADF) application customization information and Oracle SOA Suite composite's configurations.

MDS metadata content is stored in repositories that can be either file based or database schema based. Schema-based MDS repositories are created using the RCU, whereas a file-based repository can be any file system directory. To be usable by an application deployed to a Fusion Middleware domain, MDS repositories must first be registered with the domain and must have one or more partitions. A partition is a logical subdivision of the content of a particular repository, and in most cases applications that share an MDS repository each have their own dedicated partition. Both domain registration and partition management can be done either through Enterprise Manager or through WLST commands.

As part of its metadata management capabilities, MDS provides versioning, purging, and import/export capabilities to its consuming applications. Versioning allows changes to any metadata object by its consumer applications to lead to a new version of that object, thus leading to auditable and recoverable changes. For recovery, MDS's label management commands—available through WLST—must be used to create a label for an application's current MDS content. Rollback of the metadata content to a previous state across all of the application's metadata objects is then possible through label promotion. MDS's WLST purging command allows for cleanup of old versions of metadata content for maintenance purposes. It should also be mentioned that MDS provides customization capabilities that allow for changes made to an application's initially seeded metadata to be treated as separately managed customizations. This MDS capability is heavily used by the Oracle Application Development Framework and Oracle WebCenter, and we will be discussing it in more detail in the context of these products' needs within upcoming chapters dedicated to these topics. Finally, the MDS import and export capabilities can be used to export the content of an MDS repository to a file and later import it into another file-based or RDBMS-based MDS repository.

Deployment Model

Applications associated with Fusion Middleware layered products that use MDS (such as SOA Suite and ADF) have two MDS-specific deployment-time considerations that are important to note. First, they need to be explicitly associated with a specific MDS repository and partition for the storage of their metadata information. This association is contained within an MDS-specific application deployment descriptor and can be specified either at development time through JDeveloper, prior to deployment through the use of the MDS WLST "getMDSArchiveConfig" command, or through the Enterprise Manager Deployment Wizard, which provides the option of performing this association on the deployment archive prior to deployment to its WebLogic Server targets. Second, application archives that have MDS dependencies can contain seeded metadata (for example, Oracle SOA Suite composite definitions) that needs to be deployed to the layered component's MDS repository upon the deployment of the archive to a WebLogic Server domain. This seeded metadata must be packaged in a special archive file, known as the Metadata Archive (MAR) file, within the EAR deployment archive of the application. Upon deployment of a Fusion Middleware application with a MAR file, the MDS runtime imports its metadata content into the application's associated MDS repository partition.

Runtime Architecture

The MDS runtime components consist of the MDS runtime engine and a set of MBeans that are applied to a domain as part of the JRF template. The following diagram illustrates how these MDS components interact.

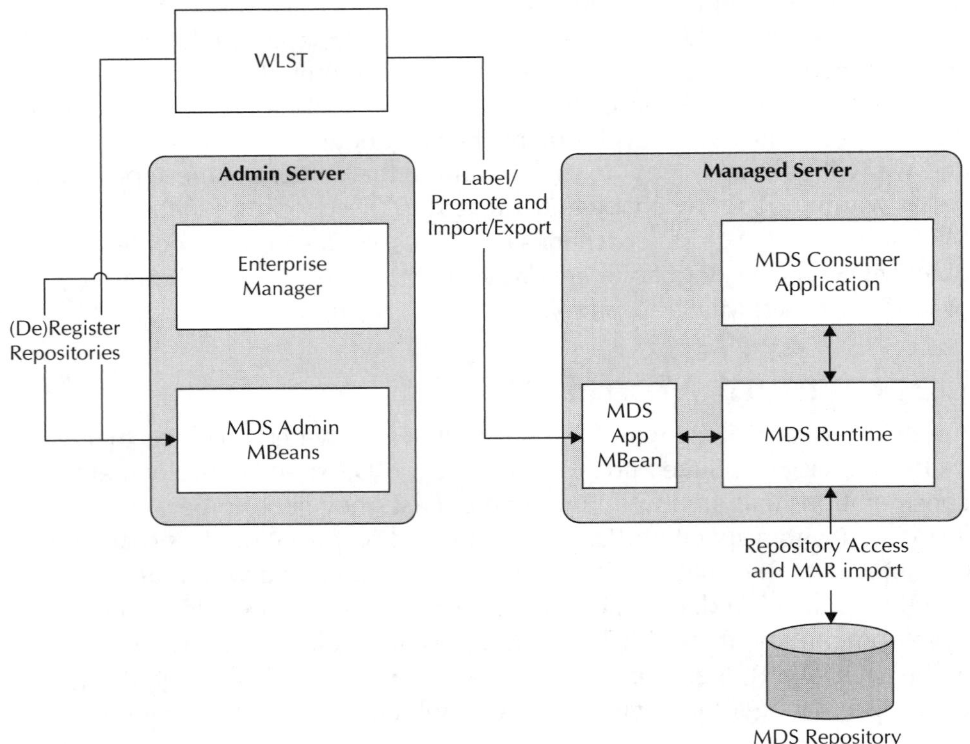

The MDS runtime engine provides the implementation for the MDS services used by consuming applications to interact with their MDS repository and is also the entity that triggers the deployment of an EAR file's MAR content into MDS upon deployment. The runtime engine also exposes a set of MBeans used by Enterprise Manager and MDS WLST commands to provide the MDS label management and import/export capabilities. Finally, the runtime engine provides a built-in cache for each application's accessed metadata objects. The parameters for the tuning of this cache—as well as other MDS engine runtime parameters—are exposed for each application as MBeans and can be modified for each WebLogic Server instance through the Enterprise Manager System MBeans browser. MDS also exposes a set of MBeans on the domain's admin server that are used by Enterprise Manager and MDS WLST scripts for the registration and deregistration of existing MDS repositories.

Oracle Web Services Manager

Oracle Web Services Manager (OWSM) is a component of the Fusion Middleware common infrastructure that provides the ability to create, manage, and enforce security and management policies that can be attached to web services deployed within a WebLogic Server domain. In this section we will review the core capabilities and architecture of OWSM.

Policy Management

Web services deployed to a Fusion Middleware environment often need to be enhanced with specific configurations that tune their behavior to match environment-specific security, quality of service, and management requirements. Such enhancements are usually better managed separately from the implementation of the web services through externally defined policies applied to web services at invocation time. This separation allows for the addition or modification of polices and their specific configuration to happen independently from the modification of the web services implementation logic and thus to be easily adjusted to suit the application's needs. OWSM enables such separation of policies from web services implementation by providing the capability to define web services policies either at development time or runtime and by attaching them to specific web services endpoints within a Fusion Middleware domain. For web services deployed to the WebLogic Server container we discussed in the "Web Services Container" section of Chapter 2, OWSM policies can only be defined and applied to JAX-WS-based web services. OWSM, however, does support a third type of web services known as Fusion Middleware infrastructure web services. This is used by the Fusion Middleware layered products—namely Oracle SOA Suite, WebCenter, and Application Development Framework—and will be explored in more detail in upcoming chapters.

Development-time web services are only available for Fusion Middleware infrastructure web services and can be defined through Oracle JDeveloper, Oracle Fusion Middleware's primary integrated development environment (IDE), and embedded within the application's deployment archives. Given this book's focus on the runtime and environment-specific architecture of the Oracle Fusion Middleware components, we will not be discussing the development-time management of OWSM web services policies, but instead will focus on OWSM's runtime capabilities.

Within a domain, OWSM stores its policies and their attachment information—in terms of the endpoints to which a policy is attached—within a dedicated MDS partition that is configured when the OWSM domain configuration template is used. MDS allows OWSM to support versioning of policies as they are modified through its built-in versioning capabilities. Also by the virtue of MDS, the migration of OWSM policies can be performed through MDS-level import and export commands, as we discussed in the "Metadata Repository Services" section.

At runtime, the domain's OWSM policies are managed through two different Enterprise Manager pages. The first page (accessed through the domain node's Web Services | Policies option) allows for the definition of new policies and or modifications of existing policies. The second page (accessed through a specific application's Web Services | Web Services Endpoint | Policies option) allows for the attachment of specific policies to the application's web services, known as service endpoint policies, or its web services clients, known as client endpoint policies. Service endpoint policies are attached to the web services implementation interface and lead to a set of tasks performed on incoming web services requests prior to the request's processing by the web service. Client endpoint policies, on the other hand, lead to a set of tasks performed on outgoing requests messages and are as such attached to web services consumer endpoints. Note that the attachment of client policies at runtime are only supported for Fusion

Middleware infrastructure web services. This means that they apply only to web services consumers that are either SOA composites or ADF applications.

Although custom policies can be created through the Enterprise Manager policy creation and modification page, OWSM comes with a set of prepackaged policies designed to be sufficient for addressing the most common web services policy requirements. The set of prepackaged OWSM policies fall into the following different categories.

- **Security** Security-based policies form the majority of the OWSM policies. Such policies are used to indicate a request's required security characteristics in terms of the type of authentication information needed, SSL requirements, and/or authorization rules for the web service's invocation.
- **Message Transmission Optimization Mechanism (MTOM)** MTOM policies are used to validate compliance to the MTOM specification for SOAP requests with binary content.
- **Web Services Addressing and Reliable Messaging** Policies falling in these categories allow for the checking of the SOAP request headers for compliance with their respective web services specification.
- **Management** Currently OWSM only provides a single prepackaged management policy that is used to specify that a request's content must be logged at the client or service endpoint to its server's log file.

Note that only security policies are supported for WebLogic Server JAX-WS-based web services and the remaining category of web services policies is only supported for Fusion Middleware infrastructure web services. Security policies that require authentication lead to the web service's request thread within the WebLogic Server to have an authenticated subject upon successful authentication through the domain's configured authentication providers. From an authorization policy point of view, web services calls cannot be protected through the WebLogic Server's default XACML authorization provider policies. To define policies that can be enforced using a subject that has been authenticated through an OWSM security policy, the attachment of a separate authorization policy that specifies the web service's authorization rules is required. The OWSM authorization policies use the Oracle Platform Security Services (OPSS) authorization policy management services, which we will be discussing in detail in the next chapter.

NOTE
WebLogic Server authorization provider policies are not enforced on web services security endpoints that are protected using OWSM security policies. For this purpose, OPSS authorization combined with OWSM authorization policies must be used instead.

In addition to the Enterprise Manager interfaces available for managing policies and their attachment to web services endpoints, OWSM also offers a set of WLST management commands for the attachment and detachment of policies to web services endpoints. For a detailed description of these commands, please refer to "Oracle Fusion Middleware Security and Administrator's Guide for Web Services."

The Anatomy of a Policy

Each OWSM policy consists of an ordered set of assertions that are themselves instances of assertion templates. Assertion templates describe a set of tasks that need to be performed on a web service's request content. On top of the set of prepackaged policies, OWSM also comes with a prepackaged set of assertion templates that can be used for the creation of custom policies. Aside from its sequenced set of assertions, other important attributes of a policy are as follows:

- **Category** Can be one of MTOM (Message Transmission Optimization Mechanism), Security, Addressing, Management, or Reliable Messaging. As we will see in the next section, a policy's category affects its order of execution at runtime.
- **Local Optimization** Can have a value of "on," "off," or "check identity." A value of "on" signifies that when a web service invocation's client and server endpoints are located on the same managed server—and thus running within the same local operating system process—then the policy does not need to be executed, whereas a value of "off" means that the policy must always be executed. A value of "on" is used for optimization purposes in order to save the performance costs of the policy's execution for nonremote and therefore potentially more trusted, invocations. A value of "check identity" signifies that the policy is not executed upon local invocation only when the request thread is associated with an authenticated subject.

With this understanding of OWSM policies in mind, we can now turn our attention to the OWSM runtime architecture and the way in which policies are enforced.

Runtime Architecture

To provide the policy management functionality we covered within the last section, Enterprise Manager interacts with an application known as the policy manager. WLST OWSM commands also lead to interactions with the policy manager applications, although they are first directed to OWSM-specific MBeans that are deployed to the domain's administration server. The policy manager application is deployed to a single server within any Fusion Middleware domain as part of its creation through the OWSM domain configuration template. As such, the OWSM policy manager is a singleton service, and the failure of its managed server signifies that the attachment, addition, or modification of policies will not be possible until the server is brought back up. However, a failure of the policy manager application does not prevent policy enforcement on web services endpoints within the domain.

The policy manager is responsible for maintaining the OWSM MDS policy repository, which contains all policy and assertion template definitions as well the mapping of attached policies to their target endpoints. The mapping of policies to web services endpoints uses information about the managed servers on which the endpoint's web services or its clients are deployed. For this reason, the content of the OWSM MDS policy store is tightly coupled with the domain's managed server and application deployment topology.

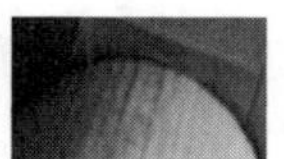

NOTE
When using the MDS import/export functionality on the OWSM partition in order to migrate it from one environment to another, one needs to ensure that the two environments have the exact same topology in terms of the number and names of managed servers that have applications with OWSM attached policies.

Each web service deployed to an OWSM-enabled domain is automatically extended with its own OWSM agent. An OWSM agent is a web services handler that is associated with its associated web services client or service endpoint and is responsible for the enforcement of all OWSM policies attached to its endpoint. OWSM agents discover their attachments by periodically polling the domain's policy manager application, through an entity known as the Policy Enforcement Point (PEP), for information about their policy attachment changes. A single PEP instance exists per managed server, and it is responsible for the polling of the domain's policy manager for the discovery of attached policies and their changes to the managed server's web services endpoints. The PEP also caches these policies in memory for use by the managed server's agents. Whenever the PEP detects policy changes for a web services endpoint, it stops the deployment archive associated with that web service, modifies its web service's WSDL to reflect the attached policy set's needs using WS-Policy statements, and restarts the archive so that it can start serving requests again. Figure 3-1 illustrates the OWSM architecture we have discussed so far in this chapter.

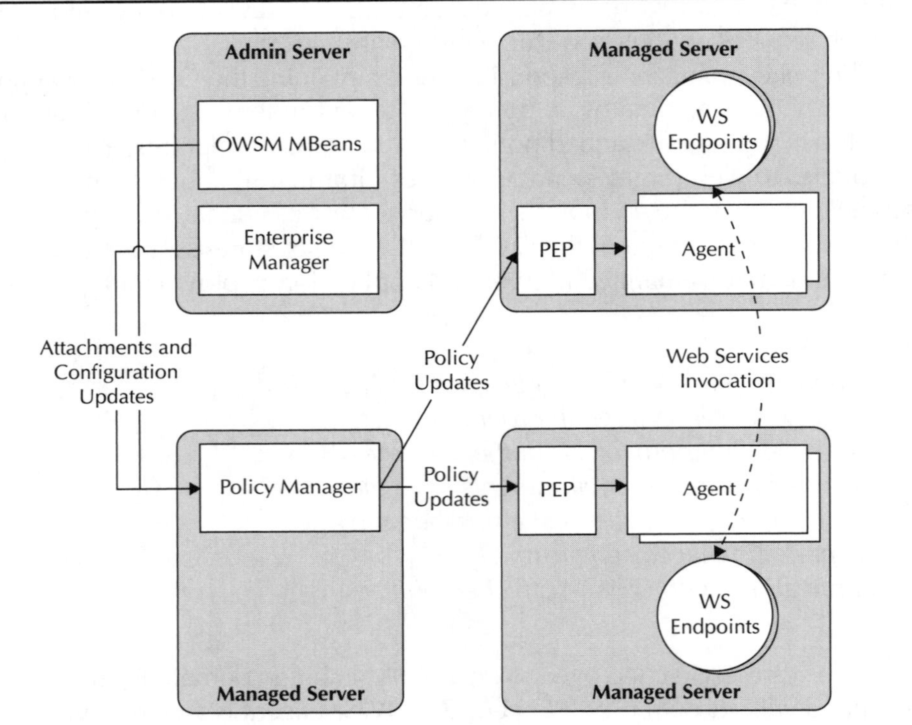

FIGURE 3-1. *Oracle Web Services Manager architecture*

Policy Execution Flow

As it should be apparent from our discussion in this section so far, each OWSM agent is essentially a policy execution engine that performs a web service's attached policies for all its invocation. The order in which a set of policies associated with a web service endpoint are executed depends on the policy's category and the endpoint type. For services endpoints, the order of precedence used by OWSM agents is as follows:

1. MTOM
2. Security
3. WS-Addressing
4. Management
5. WS-Reliable Messaging

On the other hand, the order of precedence for the execution of client endpoint policies is exactly the reverse, with Reliable Messaging policies being executed first and MTOM policies last. For security policies, where it is possible to have both authentication and authorization policies associated with the same endpoint, the authentication policies are always executed prior to the authorization policies because the authentication of the request's subject is required for the processing of authentication policies. The following diagram illustrates the OWSM policy execution flow between a client and service endpoint.

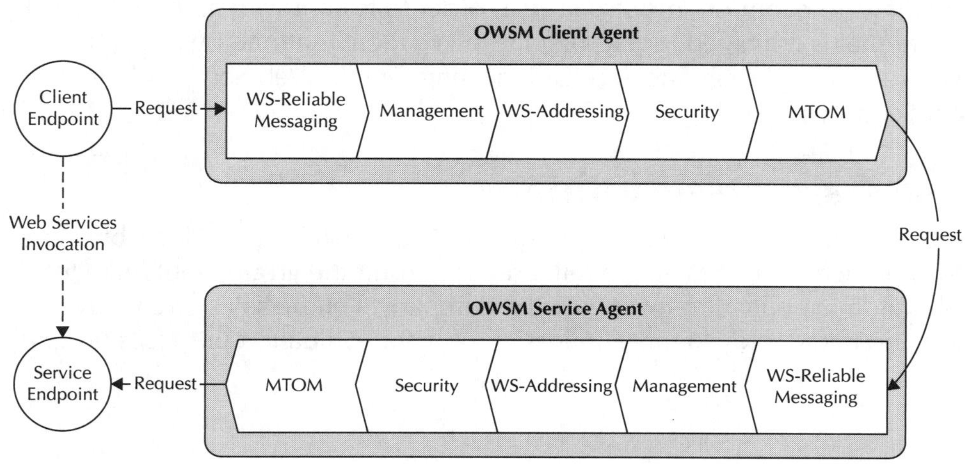

The execution of a policy by an OWSM agent translates into the execution of its individual assertions. The order in which policy assertions are executed is the order in which they are specified.

Runtime Configuration

A number of parameters that control the runtime behavior of the OWSM policy manager and the domain's PEPs and agents are configurable through the Enterprise Manager platform policy configuration page (accessed through the domain node's Web Services | Platform Policy Configuration option). A detailed discussion of the configuration options provided by this page are beyond the scope of this book. We will, however, highlight two important configuration properties related to the caching behavior of the PEP instances running on a domain's servers. The first property is called cache.tolerance and indicates the polling interval for the PEP polling the policy manager in order to refresh the server's policies. The default value for this parameter is 60000 (1 minute). The second property is called cache.size, and it indicates the maximum number of policies that can be stored within the policy cache. Both of these parameters are modified through the policy configuration page's Policy Cache tab.

Chapter Use Case

In this chapter's use case, we pick up where we left off with the Chapter 2 use case. We begin by extending the pricing application with the Fusion Middleware common infrastructure in order to front it with an Oracle HTTP Server that is managed as part of a farm. We then continue by protecting the web service of the pricing application using Oracle Web Services Manager WS-Security policies.

Use Case Description

The evaluation of the pricing application by the specialty products business development team has gone well, and as a result the group would like to roll out the application for use by the company's entire sales force. Given that you had deployed this application only for evaluation purposes up until now, you have worked out a plan for its deployment for wider use within the enterprise and have been assigned a project by your management to execute on this plan. The two main milestones of your project are as follows:

- Integrating the pricing application with the company's identity management infrastructure through the use of the company's enterprise LDAP server as the identity store and the company's Oracle Access Manager (OAM) as the Single Sign-On (SSO) provider.
- Integrating the pricing application web service interface with the company's Enterprise Resource Planning (ERP) system through the use of Oracle SOA Suite.

To lay the groundwork for these milestones, you should begin by enhancing the existing pricing application's domain—which is currently a vanilla WebLogic Server–based domain because it was not built using any Fusion Middleware product domain configuration template—with the Oracle SOA Suite template. The enhancement of the domain will allow you to front the application with a centrally managed Oracle HTTP Server (OHS) instance, which is needed for integration with OAM. The domain enhancement will also allow you to protect the application's web services endpoint with an appropriate OWSM WS-Security policy so that it can only be accessed by the company's ERP system. In this chapter's use case, we will go through the details of accomplishing these first steps in achieving the two project milestones identified for rolling out the pricing application for use by the company's sales force.

In the following sections we outline the steps required to extend the pricing application's domain with Oracle SOA Suite, front it with an OHS instance managed by the domain, and secure its web service through OWSM. After the completion of these steps, the evaluation topology we created in Chapter 2 (and as shown in Figure 2-5) will be modified to resemble the one shown in Figure 3-2.

In the next two chapter's use cases, we will outline the remaining steps required to complete the two milestones and ensure that the pricing application is ready for use by its enterprise audience.

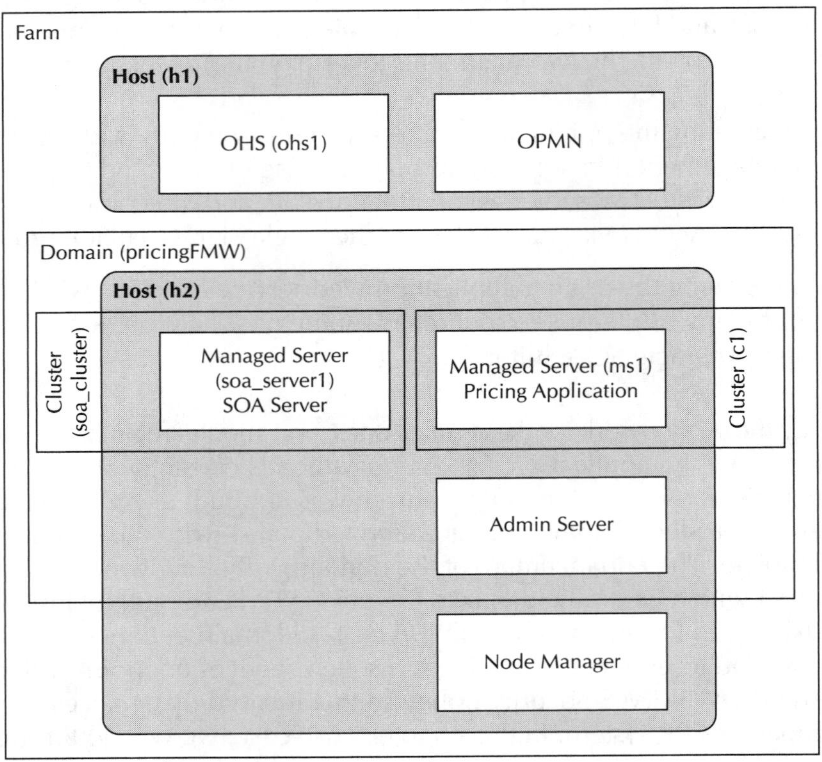

FIGURE 3-2. *Pricing application's intermediate topology for company-wide rollout*

Creating the Extended Application Domain

The extended pricing application domain will need to be an Oracle SOA Suite–based domain because it will need to host SOA Suite deployment artifacts that will be integrating the company's ERP system with the pricing application's web service. Having both SOA Suite and the pricing application as part of the same domain will simplify the administration of the pricing application because they will be manageable in the context of a single farm and therefore a single Enterprise Manager, admin console, and WLST scripts. We will work on deploying the SOA Suite artifacts in Chapter 5, but in this chapter we begin the required configuration work by building a SOA Suite domain that also has a dedicated managed server for hosting the pricing application.

To create this domain you should begin by installing Oracle SOA Suite 11*g*R1 within the same MW_HOME directory where your existing pricing application's WebLogic Server installation resides. This installation also lays down the domain configuration templates for SOA Suite and the Fusion Middleware common infrastructure templates on which they depend. Prior to using these templates to begin the domain creation process, you will need to download and use the RCU to create the schemas required by SOA Suite and the Fusion Middleware common infrastructure. Once the schemas have been created, you can use the WebLogic Server Configuration Wizard to create a SOA Suite domain (called pricingFMW) by selecting the Oracle SOA Suite (this leads to the automatic selection of the OWSM and JRF templates as dependencies), Oracle Business Activity Monitoring, and Enterprise Manager templates, as illustrated next.

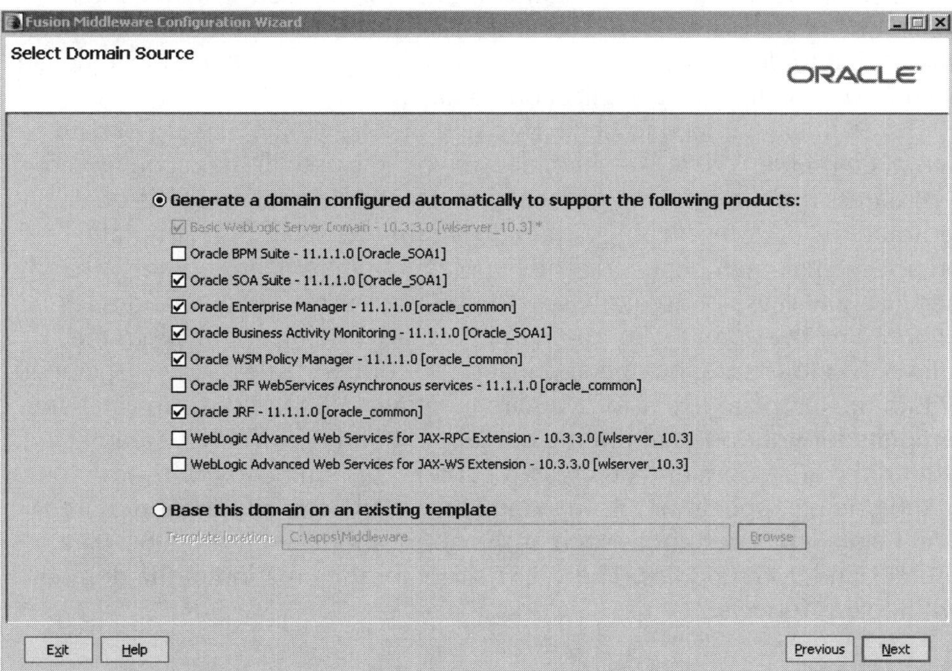

Note that the configuration wizard will prompt you for information regarding the schemas you created using the RCU in order to create the associated JDBC data sources within the domain. By default, the SOA Suite templates we have selected lead to the creation of two managed servers—named soa_server1 and bam_server1—to which are deployed the required SOA Suite deployment archives we will review in detail in Chapter 5. As per the best practice we discussed in the previous chapter's use case, you should also ensure that each of these managed servers is assigned to its own cluster so that they can more easily be scaled out in the future if the need arises. Once you have completed the execution of the configuration wizard, you will have a domain suitable for the deployment of SOA Suite applications, but is not yet configured for the deployment of the pricing application itself. Because you already have a domain with all the required resources configured for the pricing application—that is, the domain we created as part of the use case for Chapter 2—ideally you would be able to just extend the SOA Suite domain you just created with your existing pricing application so as to skip the need for the manual modification of the SOA domain with the managed server and resources needed. The WebLogic Server configuration framework allows you to do this by creating a domain configuration extension template from your existing pricing application domain.

To do this, you need to begin by using the WebLogic Server Domain Template Builder Wizard—which allows you to create domain configuration templates from an existing domain—to create a domain extension template from your existing pricing domain (let's call this template pricingextensiontemplate.jar). The template builder wizard comes in handy because it allows you to easily specify the extra users, groups, and roles required by the domain. For the purpose of the pricing application, this allows you to ensure that the application's required "sales" role is specified within the template extension you are creating. With the domain extension template for your original pricing domain in hand, you are now ready to extend the SOA domain you created earlier. This will lead to the addition of the pricing application, its managed server, cluster, and other required WebLogic Server resources such as the applications required JDBC data sources and JMS modules. The WLST script for the creation of the domain will look as follows:

```
readDomain('pricingFMW');
addTemplate('./pricing_extension_template.jar');
updateDomain();
```

Although the domain created by this script can be used for the deployment of your pricing application, there is one more task you will need to perform to ensure that you can take full advantage of the Fusion Middleware infrastructure stack—and that is to ensure that the pricing application's target cluster (c1) is extended with JRF by using the "applyJRF" WLST command, as follows:

```
applyJRF('c1','/domains/pricingFMW');
```

This command ensures that the JRF components are appropriately deployed and targeted to the "c1" cluster and its single managed server so that they can be appropriately managed through the farm's Enterprise Manager. With the preceding steps you have developed a simple and repeatable way of creating a pricing domain that not only has all of the Fusion Middleware common infrastructure components but also the Oracle SOA Suite components enabled. The following diagram illustrates the high-level steps we discussed in this section in order to create this domain.

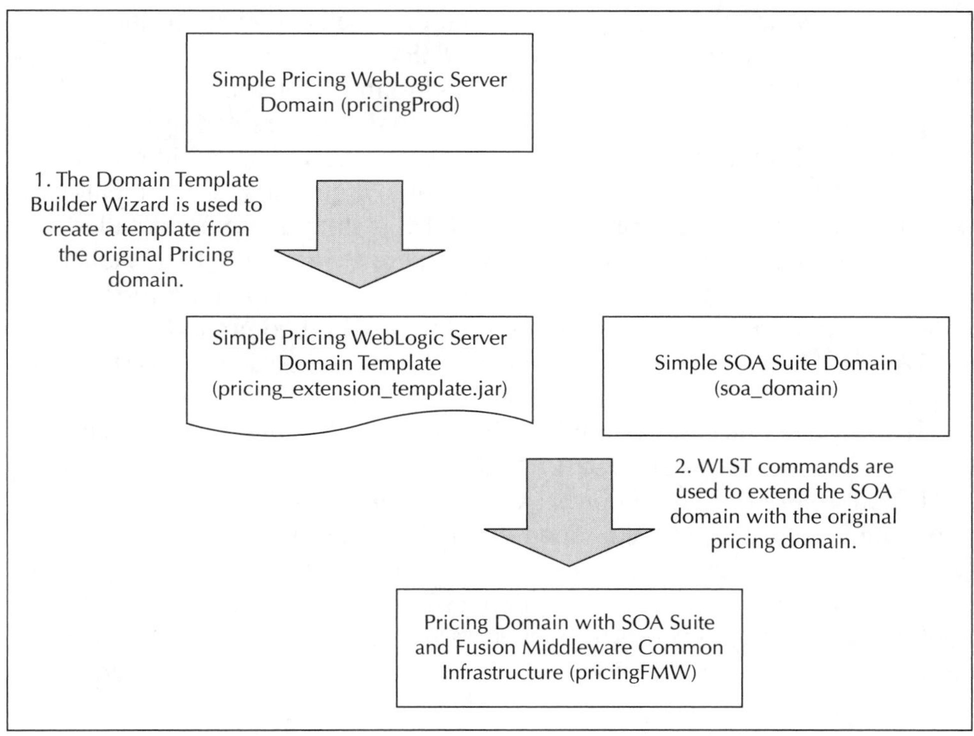

In the next section we discuss how to extend this domain with a fronting OHS instance that can be centrally managed through the domain's Enterprise Manager.

Fronting the Application with Oracle HTTP Server

In this section we complete the creation of the topology illustrated in Figure 3-2 by configuring an OHS system component that is managed as part of the same farm as the pricing application's domain and that proxies requests to the pricing application's web application. The registration of the OHS system component with our pricing application's farm will allow us to simplify the administration of the application's environment through central monitoring and configuration of the OHS instance with the farm's Enterprise Manager.

To configure an Enterprise Manager–managed OHS instance, you should begin by running the Oracle Fusion Middleware Web Tier OUI installer and selecting the Oracle HTTP Server option as well as the Associate Selected Components with WebLogic Domain option. Because you are installing OHS on its own, you need to install the OHS ORACLE_HOME within a new MW_HOME directory. To register the OHS instance that you are configuring with the "pricingFMW" WebLogic Server domain you created in the last section, you should specify the domain's administration server information as part of the Specify WebLogic Domain window and proceed to create an instance called "pricingwebtier" with an OHS system component called "ohs1." After completion of the ohs1 system component, the OHS Apache processes as well an OPMN process manager process should be running on your host, and you should be able to use the opmnctl command within the INSTANCE_HOME/bin directory of the ohs1 system component to start and stop its processes. Also, if you navigate to the Enterprise Manager page of the farm, you should notice that the ohs1 instance has been added to the bottom of the management tree.

To make sure those OHS proxies send requests to the pricing web application appropriately, you need to configure a module known as mod_wl_ohs. This is a WebLogic Server–specific module that is prepackaged and preconfigured with OHS for convenience. The mod_wl_ohs module can be configured to proxy requests to backend WebLogic Server deployed web applications. To configure mod_wl_ohs, you can right-click on the ohs1 node within Enterprise Manager and select the Administration | mod_wl_ohs Configuration option. This should bring you to the OHS configuration page, shown here.

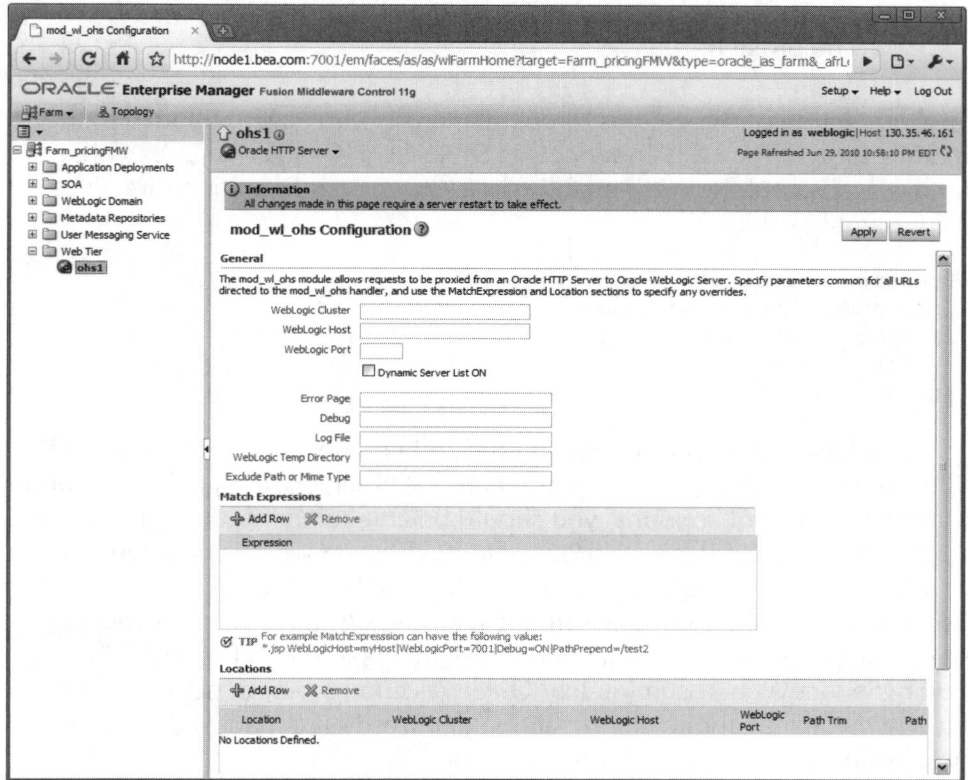

To ensure that the mod_wl_ohs is configured to proxy incoming requests targeted at the pricing web application to the domain's managed server it has deployed, you need to add a row to the "Locations" section of the Enterprise Manager's mod_wl_ohs configuration page and fill in the following values:

- **Location** This field identifies the context root portion of the request URLs that need to be proxied.

- **WebLogic Host** This field identifies the host where the WebLogic managed server containing the target application is running.
- **WebLogic Port** This field identifies the listen port of the managed server specified in the WebLogic Host field to which requests need to be proxied.

Completion of these fields through Enterprise Manager will lead to the modification of the OHS instance's INSTANCE_HOME/config/OHS/ohs1/mod_wl_ohs.conf file with the following Apache configuration directives, using sample values:

```
<Location /PricingServiceWeb>
  SetHandler weblogic-handler
  WebLogicHost node1.oracle.com
  WebLogicPort 7002
</Location>
```

For a basic proxy setup through OHS, all you need are these fields. After filling in this information and restarting the OHS server through the Enterprise Manager's "control" options, you should be able to access the pricing web application by pointing your browser to the host on which you have configured OHS and using port 7777, which is the default port the OHS listens to. Using the example from the directives listed here, to access the pricing application's URL you would specify node10.oracle.com:7777/PricingServiceWeb (assuming that OHS was configured on node10), even though the actual application might be deployed on a managed server on host node1.oracle.com and listening to port 7002.

Securing the Application Web Service with Oracle Web Services Manager

The web services interface of the pricing application exposes a single operation (modifyModel), which is used to modify the pricing model for a given product. Model modifications are driven by business parameters that have their sources within the company's ERP system. Given the knowledge that the sole client of this web service will be a SOA Suite application that will be interacting with the ERP system in order to detect changes to these business parameters (we will work through the deployment of this SOA application in Chapter 5's use case), you can protect the web service endpoint so that only the authenticated SOA composite can invoke it. This will prevent unknown users from pointing a web services client to the web service's WSDL to perform "modifyModel" operations.

To secure the application's web service endpoint, you can use the OWSM prepackaged wss_username_token_service_policy and binding_permission_authorization_policy. The first policy ensures that incoming requests have an appropriate WS-Security user name and password header and that the value of these headers is authenticated through the WebLogic Server authentication providers in order to obtain an authenticated subject. The second policy ensures that the invocations to the web service will lead to an authorization check to the domain's Oracle Platform Security Services (OPSS) policy store, where you will need to configure the authorization permission for this web service's access. We will discuss OPSS and the way to create the required permissions for this web service in the next chapter's use case. An important note to make is that even though the policies you have configured do not require SSL encryption of the message content—including the user name and password—you should be comfortable with this choice for the following reasons:

- The open text values of the modifyModel operation contain only numerical parameters that do not reveal any sensitive information that would otherwise have to be protected.
- The credential information being propagated will always be dedicated to the SOA composite and not associated with a specific individual.
- The service invocation will be occurring between company servers behind firewalls; therefore, the web service's request traffic will not be accessible to any external entities.
- The absence of SSL for the web service endpoint will simplify the architecture of the pricing application and will lead to a more efficient execution of the pricing service.

You can attach these policies through Enterprise Manager or by using the attachWebServicePolicies WLST online command. Once it's attached, you can check the WSDL of the pricing service web service (through its http://<host-name>/PricingModelWebService /PricingModelService?WSDL URL) and should notice that its definition has been prefixed with the WS-Policy WssUsernameToken10 definition shown in the following listing. This policy is then associated with the service through the WSDL's binding definition.

```
<wsp:Policy xmlns:wsp=" … ">
   <sp:SupportingTokens
xmlns:sp="http://schemas.xmlsoap.org/ws/2005/07/securitypolicy">
     <wsp:Policy>
         <sp:UsernameToken sp:IncludeToken="http://
schemas.xmlsoap.org/ws/2005/07/securitypolicy
/IncludeToken/AlwaysToRecipient">
            <wsp:Policy>
               <sp:WssUsernameToken10/>
            </wsp:Policy>
         </sp:UsernameToken>
      </wsp:Policy>
   </sp:SupportingTokens>
</wsp:Policy>
```

Although ideally you would proceed to test the web service through the Enterprise Manager web services test page, we cannot go through that step at this point because no OPSS authorization permissions have been associated with this web service despite its binding_permission_authorization_policy permission. In the next two chapter's use cases we will complete the work required to achieve the two milestones defined at the beginning of this section—namely, to roll out a version of the pricing application that is integrated with the enterprise's Oracle Fusion Middleware IDM infrastructure as well as the corporate ERP system through Oracle SOA Suite.

Conclusion

In this chapter we discussed the most important aspects of the Fusion Middleware common infrastructure through an overview of how it is installed, configured, and managed within a Fusion Middleware environment. We also discussed the Metadata Repository Services and Oracle Web Services Manager services, which are key components of this infrastructure. In the next chapters we begin our exploration of the specific layered Fusion Middleware products that are built on top of the common infrastructure we discussed in this chapter.

CHAPTER 4

Oracle Fusion Middleware Platform Security Services and Identity Management

his chapter introduces the Oracle Platform Security Services (OPSS), which is a set of services used by all Fusion Middleware layered components. OPSS is built on top of the standards-based WebLogic Server security services, which we reviewed in Chapter 2. In this chapter, we explore the various services within OPSS and discuss the ways in which they can be used to secure enterprise applications. As we will see, when the overall life cycle of an enterprise application is considered, the key objective of OPSS is to provide the right level of abstraction, the right tools for the different persons involved, and the right methodology to properly implement, deploy, and maintain the application.

This chapter also introduces the full set of products within the Oracle Identity Management suite and reviews their dependencies on OPSS and other Fusion Middleware products to complete the overall picture of Fusion Middleware security. It is important to note that middleware security and identity management are broad subjects. The intent of this chapter is to give an introductory treatment of these subjects in the context of Fusion Middleware components rather than a comprehensive coverage.

Introduction to Oracle Platform Security Services

Oracle Platform Security Services (OPSS) provides a security platform for both Java Standard Edition (Java SE) and Java Enterprise Edition (Java EE) applications. As a platform-independent and application-server-independent layer, OPSS expands beyond the application server security providers to include features such as Credential Store Framework, Audit Framework, and User & Role API, which we will review in this chapter. At development time, OPSS services can be directly invoked from the developer environment (for example, Oracle JDeveloper) to help developers create the necessary security artifacts for their applications. In the runtime environment, systems and security administrators can access OPSS services for configuration purposes through Enterprise Manager Fusion Middleware Control (Enterprise Manager) and command-line tools such as WebLogic Scripting Tool (WLST). Application and business owners can manage authorization policies through the OPSS Oracle Authorization Policy Manager (APM). All of these features are properly integrated into each stage of the application life cycle—from development to packaging of the application; from deployment to administration; and from testing to production. Please note that although OPSS is designed to be application server independent, we will discuss it in the context of WebLogic Server only.

Architecture Overview

Built on top of WebLogic Server security services, OPSS provides a rich API for application security integration. Underneath, WebLogic Server's service provider interface (SSPI) layer delivers a set of pluggable security providers for flexible and custom implementations of a particular security service. It also allows OPSS to integrate with the security repositories, including flat files, LDAP directories, and database servers. Figure 4-1 shows the high-level OPSS architecture.

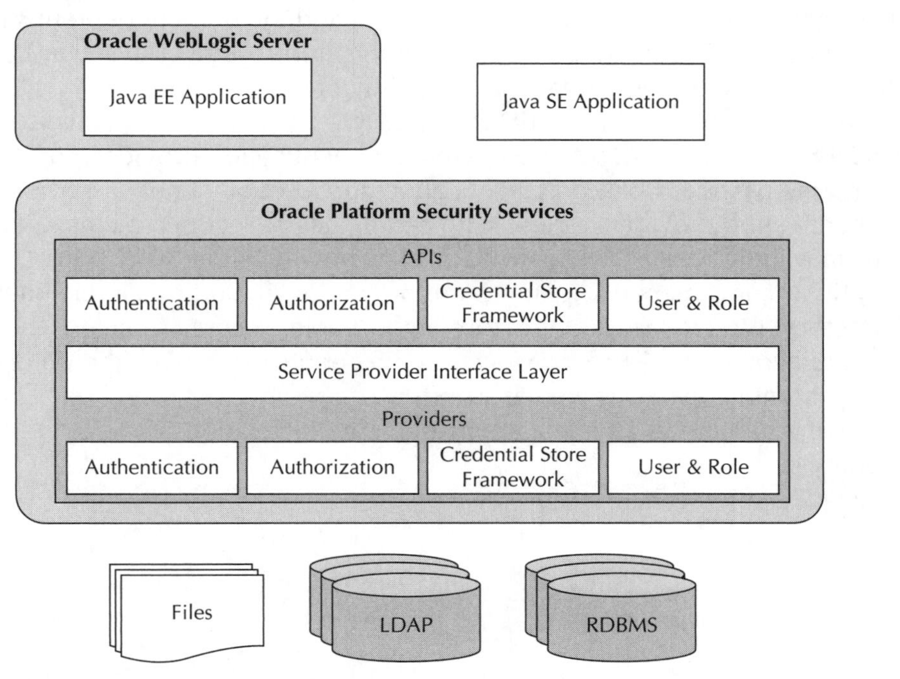

FIGURE 4-1. *Oracle Platform Security Services architecture*

Identities, Identity Store, and Authentication Providers

A domain identity store must be configured in order for OPSS to recognize any end users. OPSS leverages WebLogic Server authentication providers to define where the identity store is. When not integrated with an external Single Sign-On system, these authenticators validate user credentials through mechanisms such as username/password and digital certificates. They also allow user attributes and group information for the user to be retrieved from the identity store. Applications running in the domain can query user profile and group information from the identity store via the User & Role API, which we will be discussing later on in this chapter.

Out of the box, the DefaultAuthenticator, also known as WebLogic Authentication Provider, is configured to leverage the embedded LDAP server as described in Chapter 2. Just like with a standard LDAP server, users and groups can be created within the embedded LDAP server. However, this server is only recommended for use in development environments where the number of users is below 10,000 entries and the number of groups is below 25,000. The reason for this is that the embedded LDAP server lacks the robustness, performance, and scalability of a production-quality LDAP server such as Oracle Internet Directory.

OPSS comes with a set of predefined authentication providers for username/password-based authentication and a set of identity assertion authentication providers for use with certificates or security tokens. Oracle Fusion Middleware also ships with turnkey providers that work with Oracle Identity Management components out of the box, including Oracle Internet Directory, Oracle Virtual Directory, and Oracle Access Manager. The configuration of the OPSS providers can be performed through the WebLogic Server admin console as well as WLST.

Figure 4-2 shows a typical application and its relationship with the identity store.

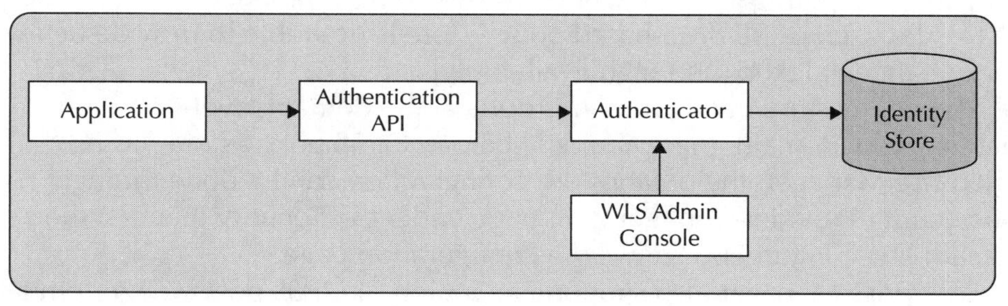

FIGURE 4-2. *Authentication flow with the identity store*

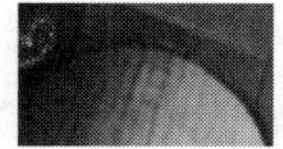

NOTE
The administration of identity data in any LDAP-based identity store is done outside of OPSS and not through Oracle Fusion Middleware. An enterprise LDAP server is typically a part of the overall enterprise identity management infrastructure where identity administration is being handled. We will discuss some of these identity management components in the context of Oracle Identity Management later in this chapter.

Policies and the Policy Store

The key to the OPSS lies in its policy model consisting of permissions, entitlements, application roles, application policies, and the various mappings and relationships among these objects. We will discuss the details of these objects and the overall application policy model later on in the chapter. The OPSS policy store serves as the repository for all these security artifacts. OPSS supports file-based, LDAP-based, and RDBMS-based policy stores. During the development phase, all the application policies are stored in an XML-based policy store named jazn-data.xml. When an application is deployed using Enterprise Manager or WLST, these application policies are deployed in the domain policy store automatically. The out-of-the-box domain OPSS policy store is file based. However, in a production environment, an LDAP-based or RDBMS-based policy store is desirable to provide better performance, backup, and high availability.

The policy store configuration is done at the domain level—implying that for every domain, there can only be one OPSS policy store. Using Enterprise Manager, the policy store configuration can be done through the Security Provider Configuration page under the Security menu at the domain level. Figure 4-3 shows the configuration page.

Enterprise Manager also supports migration of OPSS policy data from a file-based or LDAP-based policy store to another LDAP-based policy store. This process is also known as reassociation, which can be done through

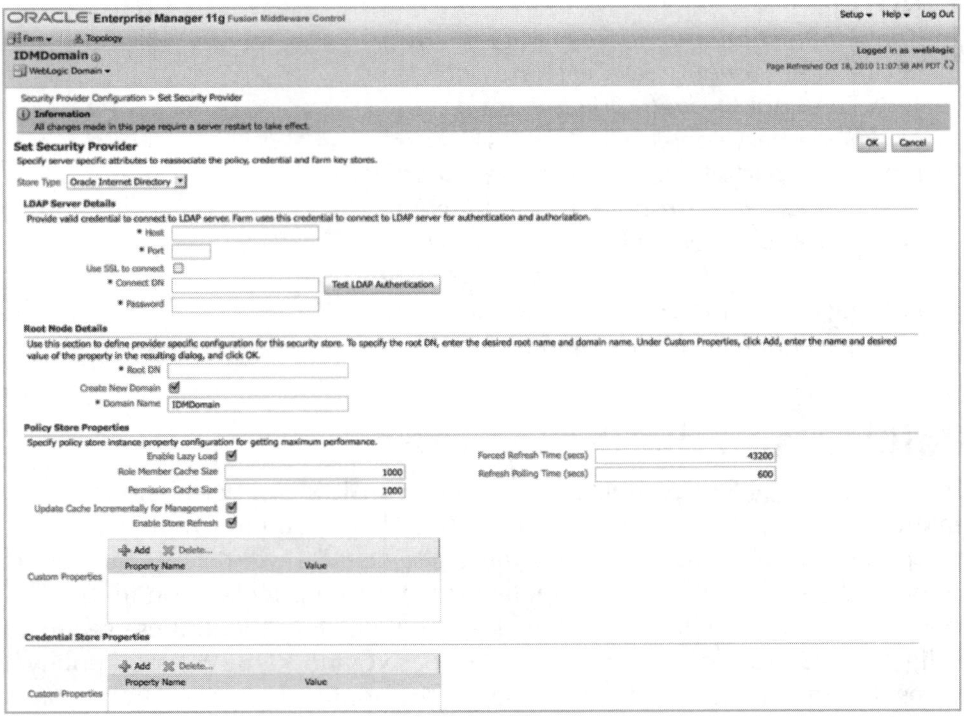

FIGURE 4-3. *The OPSS Security Provider Configuration page in Enterprise Manager*

Enterprise Manager or WLST. Migration of policies is needed in scenarios where an entire domain or a single application is migrated from one domain to another, thus requiring policies to be migrated from one policy store to another. For example, a domain might be promoted from a staging to a production environment, or a new version of an application may be pushed from staging to production where an older version of the application already exists. To ensure the integrity of the policies, the reassociation logic searches the target LDAP and looks for a match for each policy within the source policy store. If a match is found, the matching policy is updated. If no match is found, the policy is copied and migrated as is. The migration can be done at the global level, where all the policies in the domain are migrated, or at the application level, where only policies for a specific application are migrated. The OPSS policy store reassociation capabilities provide a convenient method for migrating policies in development-to-production or test-to-production scenarios.

Credentials and the Credential Store

Application developers often have to deal with the storage of credentials such as username and password combinations, tickets, tokens, and public key certificates. To address these needs, OPSS provides a comprehensive Credential Store Framework, including a set of APIs and support for a file-based or LDAP-based credential store.

OPSS supports two types of credentials: a password credential consists of a username and password combination, and a generic credential encapsulates any customized data or arbitrary token, such as a symmetric key. The APIs allow applications to create, read, update, and manage these credentials, which are typically used to access an external application or an external repository such as databases or LDAP directories.

Figure 4-4 shows a typical application and its relationship with the credential store.

Similar to the policy store, OPSS supports a default file-based credential store in the form of an Oracle Wallet. The recommended production setup is to leverage an LDAP-based or RDBMS-based credential store. In fact, when an LDAP-based or RDBMS-based repository is set up, OPSS treats the policy and credential store together using a single repository configuration, as shown in Figure 4-4.

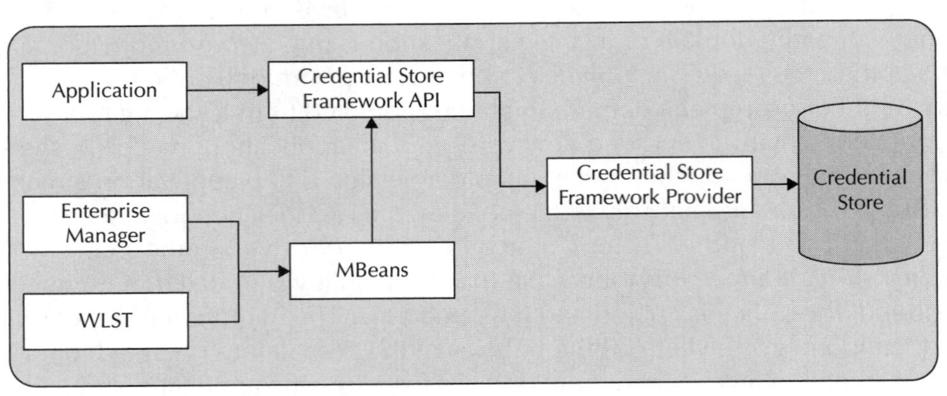

FIGURE 4-4. *Credential Store Framework*

User & Role API

A key objective of OPSS is to provide an abstraction layer for application developers dealing with users and roles that doesn't require them to worry about the intricacies of the underlying repositories where users and roles are stored. Developers can therefore rely on the User & Role API to access this information, which enables applications to work seamlessly against different repositories without any code changes to the application itself. The User & Role API acknowledges the runtime configuration of the OPSS identity store. By default, it uses the first configured WebLogic Server authentication provider within the domain's security realm. If more than one authentication provider exists, the precedence is determined by the control flag priority, and the higher-priority one is selected. At any time, the User & Role API can only work with a single WebLogic Server authentication provider.

Figure 4-5 shows a typical application and its relationship with the identity store through the User & Role API.

Audit Framework

The Fusion Middleware Audit Framework is an OPSS service designed to provide a centralized audit framework for the Fusion Middleware family of products. The framework provides audit services for Fusion Middleware Common Infrastructure and Oracle SOA Suite components, including

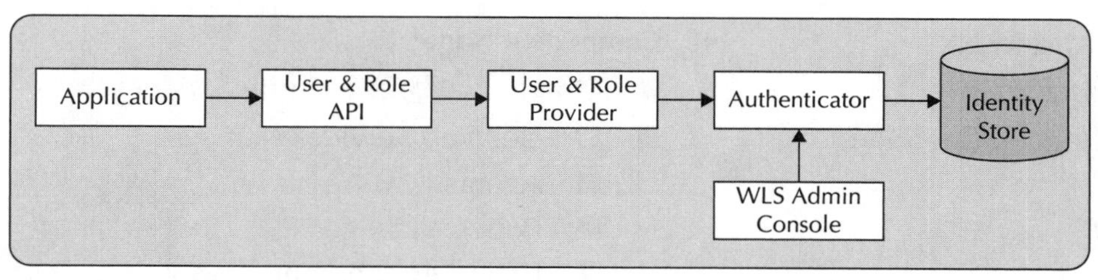

FIGURE 4-5. *Application accessing the identity store with the User & Role API*

OPSS and web services. Some of the system components, such as Oracle Internet Directory and Oracle HTTP Server, are also integrated with the Audit Framework. However, the main objective of the Audit Framework is to provide a set of services for all Java EE components within Fusion Middleware and eventually to allow custom Java EE development to leverage this framework. In Fusion Middleware 11*g*, the Audit Framework is integrated with many Fusion Middleware Java EE components, including Oracle Access Manager and Oracle Identity Federation. Table 4-1 shows a partial list of components that are integrated with the OPSS Audit Framework.

Integration with the Audit Framework starts with the audit APIs, which allow applications to specify audit event details where appropriate. The audit event data is then pushed to the centralized audit repository, an RDBMS instance containing the audit schema created by the Repository Creation Utility (RCU). It is generally recommended that a dedicated RDBMS instance be used for audit purposes because the audit store is expected to be cumulative and will grow over time.

NOTE
It is recommended that the Audit Framework schema be placed within its own dedicated RDBMS instance because it is expected to grow over time and will require special maintenance.

The Audit Framework allows each audit-aware component to define a set of events. Each event definition identifies the set of attributes with names

Category	Component Name
Platform	■ Oracle Platform Security Services

Oracle SOA Suite	■ Oracle Web Services Manager
	  ■ Agents
	  ■ Policy Manager
	  ■ Policy Attachment
	■ SOA Suite Web Services

System components	■ Oracle HTTP Server ■ Oracle WebCache ■ Oracle Internet Directory ■ Oracle Virtual Directory
Java EE components	■ Oracle Identity Federation ■ Oracle Access Manager ■ Oracle Adaptive Access Manager ■ Directory Integration Platform ■ Oracle Reports

TABLE 4-1. *List of Products Supporting Fusion Middleware Audit Framework*

and data types to be recorded as part of the audit event itself. A component audit policy is a declaration of which audit events and how the audit data will be captured. Audit policies of all the audit-aware components are centrally managed through Enterprise Manager or through WLST. Although the current audit framework is restricted for use by Oracle Fusion Middleware components only, Oracle may expose its functionality for enterprise applications deployed to a Fusion Middleware environment.

Once the audit data is collected in the audit repository, Oracle Business Intelligence Publisher (BI Publisher) can be used to view the audit data through predefined or custom reports. The audit data collected contains information about the time, component, operation, and user information for each audit event, thus allowing the data to be filtered and analyzed across different dimensions. In addition, Fusion Middleware Audit Framework supports the notion of an Execution Context Identifier (ECID), which is used to track the flow of a particular request through the various layers of the product stack, thus providing efficient tracking of end-to-end flow of a particular request spanning across multiple components.

Oracle Security Developer Tools

Oracle Security Developer Tools (OSDT) provides application developers with advanced security features in the area of cryptography, Public Key Infrastructure, web services security, and federated identity management. Many of these features are used internally by Fusion Middleware components such as the Oracle SOA Suite BPEL service engine and Oracle Web Services Manager. Table 4-2 provides an overview of all the OSDT features as described in the Fusion Middleware Documentation library.

TIP
Oracle Crypto and Oracle Security Engine, although still shipped with Oracle Security Developer, are no longer recommended for use. Instead, the Standard Java Cryptography Extension (JCE) interface should be used whenever possible.

OPSS Policy Model and Authorization Policy Manager

Developers and administrators should be familiarized with the OPSS policy model. Many components in Fusion Middleware and Fusion Applications rely heavily on OPSS. Fortunately, Oracle Authorization Policy Manager (APM) delivers a user-friendly interface for administration of OPSS policies across applications,

OPSS Policy Model

To avoid any confusion, it is important to understand the precise definitions of the security terms within OPSS because many of these terms are used in a wide variety of contexts and are often interpreted differently. The definitions shown in Table 4-3 are based on the Oracle Fusion Middleware Documentation library.

Tool Name	Description
Oracle CMS	■ Supports Cryptographic Message Syntax (CMS), an IETF standard ■ Provides a pure Java API for reading and writing CMS objects, including sample programs and supporting tools for developing secure message envelopes
Oracle S/MIME	■ Supports Secure/Multipurpose Internet Mail Extension(S/MIME), an IETF standard ■ Provides authentication, digital signature, and encryption support for message integrity, data security, and encryption
Oracle PKI SDK	■ Supports Public Key Infrastructure (PKI) ■ Provides support for Certificate Management Protocol (CMP), Online Certificate Status Protocol (OCSP), time-stamping, and digital certificate publishing/retrieval to and from a directory server
Oracle XML Security	■ Provides support for standard security requirements, including confidentiality, integrity, message authentication, and nonrepudiation for XML documents
Oracle SAML	■ Security Assertions Markup Language (SAML) ■ Provides support for cross-domain Single Sign-On and federated access control solutions conforming to SAML 1.0/1.1 and SAML 2.0 specifications
Oracle Web Service Security	■ Provides a complete implementation of the OASIS WS Security 1.1 standard
Oracle XKMS	■ XML Key Management Specification (XKMS), W3C specification for public key management ■ Provides a pure Java toolkit for PKI functionality, complete key/certificate life cycle, and XML signature

TABLE 4-2. *Oracle Security Developer Tools*

Term	Description
User	A *user,* or an *enterprise user,* is an end user accessing a service. Such an end user must be present in the domain identity store in order to be recognized by OPSS. The identity store is instantiated via WebLogic Server DefaultAuthenticator as part of OPSS identity store configuration. An *authenticated user* is a user whose credentials have been validated, which is typically required when one is accessing protected resources where authorization is needed. An *anonymous user,* or *unauthenticated user,* is one whose credentials have not been validated and is typically permitted to access unprotected or public resources.
Role	The OPSS authorization model has two main types of OPSS roles: enterprise and application. An *enterprise role,* also known as *enterprise group* or *external role,* is a collection of users and other enterprise roles. These roles are typically implemented as LDAP groups in an LDAP identity store and they can be hierarchically structured. An *application role* is a collection of users, groups, and other application roles by means of an application role hierarchy. These roles are defined by application policies and are not necessarily known to a Java EE container. Application roles can have a many-to-many relationship with enterprise roles.
Resource Type	A *resource type* is a template for creating a particular type of secured resource or a secured artifact such as a flow, a job, or a web server. It is associated with a permission class governing the actions that can be invoked on instances of the resource type.

TABLE 4-3. *OPSS Policy Model Terminology*

Term	Description
Resource	A *resource* or a *resource instance* represents an actual instance of an application resource. The implemented resource type determines the permissions allowed on this resource. At runtime, the permissions are evaluated to determine the right level of access by the principal.
Permission and Entitlement	A *permission* aggregates a permission class and resources and defines the actions allowed on these resources. An *entitlement* or *a permission set* is a collection of permissions typically grouped together to represent a particular set of resources and their associated privileges needed to perform a particular business function.
Principal	A *principal* is the identity to which the authorization in the policy is granted. A principal can be a user, an external role, or an application role. Most frequently, it is an application role.
Application Stripe	An *application stripe* is a logical subset of the domain policy store where the application policies are kept. This subset may be shared by more than one application.
Resource Catalogue	A *resource catalogue* is a detailed catalogue of all the resource types, resources, permissions, and entitlements and how they are related to each other.
Application Policy	An *application policy* is a functional policy that maps either to one or more permissions or to an entitlement to specify the exact set of permissions allowed for a principal to access application resources. When combined with enterprise roles and application roles, the runtime evaluation of the relationship between enterprise roles, application roles, and these application functional policies drives the application authorization decisions.

TABLE 4-3. *OPSS Policy Model Terminology* (continued)

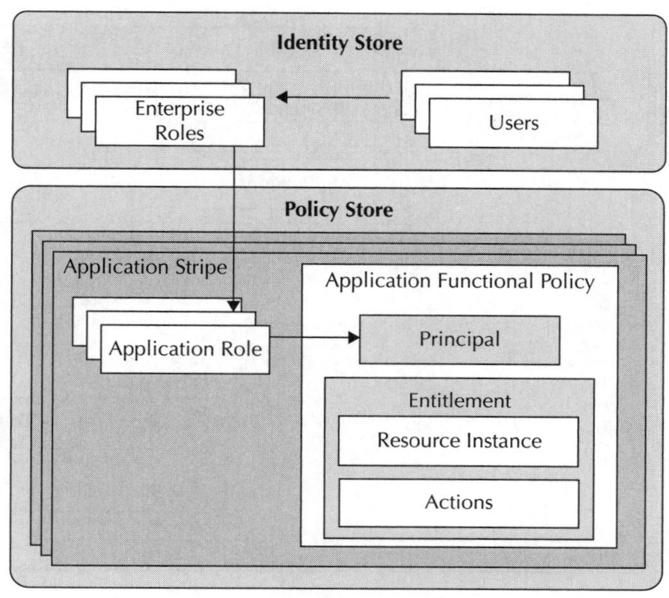

FIGURE 4-6. *OPSS application policy model*

Figure 4-6 shows this logical OPSS application policy model.

At runtime, when an end user attempts to access a resource, the appropriate application policy with the corresponding permissions on that resource will be evaluated through its relationship with the application role and the mapping to the enterprise role. The applications built on top this model will result in a large volume of manageable security artifacts based on this policy model. Although Enterprise Manager and WLST provide some management capabilities, Oracle has introduced Oracle Authorization Policy Manager (APM) to provide a comprehensive management tool for OPSS policies.

Oracle Authorization Policy Manager

Figure 4-7 shows APM and its relationship with the identity and policy stores.

Oracle Authorization Policy Manager (APM) is a graphical user-interface console for managing OPSS-based authorization policies. It is designed for the management of enterprise applications that use services. APM provides

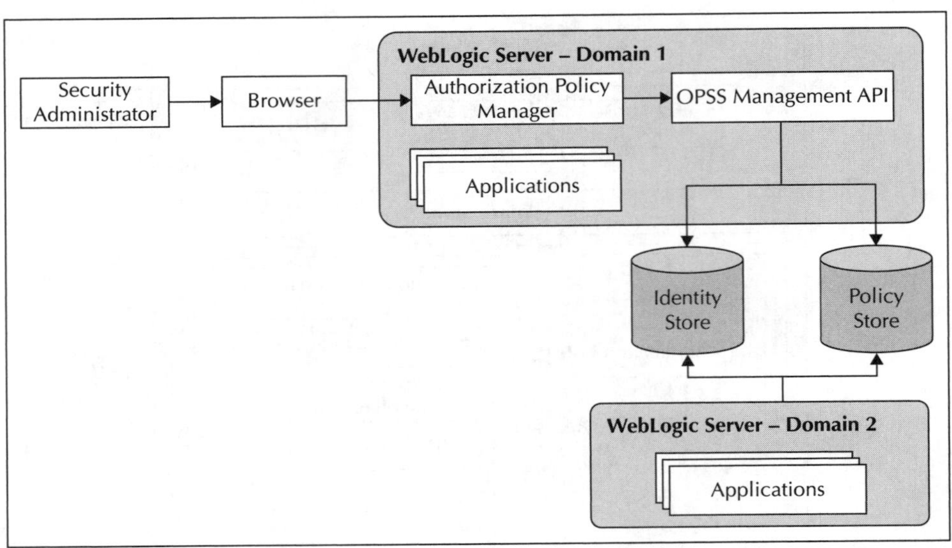

FIGURE 4-7. *Authorization Policy Manager*

the following key capabilities for application owners and business users to administer the OPSS policy store:

- **Managing application security artifacts** This capability provides easy lookup of all the security artifacts in the application policy model. For roles, resource types, resources, entitlements, policies, and role categories, APM supports full CRUD capabilities to add, view, and delete these artifacts.
- **Viewing the enterprise role hierarchy** This capability essentially picks up the groups from the LDAP where enterprise roles are stored. APM allows the expansion of enterprise roles to show the deeper levels of the application policy hierarchy in the UI.
- **Managing the application role hierarchy** This capability allows a delegated administrator to modify the application role inheritance.
- **Mapping between application roles and external roles** This capability allows for the mapping of application roles to external roles residing in an external LDAP server. This mapping ultimately ties the end user to the policy model, enabling runtime evaluation to occur.

Users and external roles (that is, LDAP groups) can be viewed within APM in the context of application policies. However, APM does not provide any management capability on this data, which is typically managed through LDAP tools or in a broader provisioning environment by an identity provisioning solution such as Oracle Identity Manager.

Introduction to Oracle Identity Management

Although OPSS provides a comprehensive set of platform security services for application development and runtime abstraction, the end-to-end management of the security needs of enterprise applications spawn many aspects that are not addressed by OPSS. This is due to the fact that from a security and identity management perspective, an identity-enabled application itself does not necessarily address all of the identity management requirements, such as the following:

- What is my corporate identity store?
- Is there a single authoritative identity store where all my users reside?
- Can the application recognize users from multiple identity stores without synchronizing all the data into a single store?
- How are end users logging in to various applications?
- Do end users need web Single Sign-On?
- Do end users require desktop Single Sign-On? (Windows Native Authentication.)
- Is additional web access authorization required?
- Is it possible to enhance application security with a risk-based access solution?
- How to efficiently authenticate users with a partnering organization?
- How are user accounts being created or provisioned across different systems?

- How is access being granted to an end user? Is approval required?
- How are passwords being managed?
- How to determine who has access to what and how a user was granted the access?
- How to review and certify user access per compliance regulations?
- How to revoke access?

OPSS shields application developers from worrying about these questions and provides the foundation for a service-oriented security architecture that allows integration with the appropriate identity services. The Oracle Identity Management suite of products enables the creation of this service-oriented security architecture. In the following sections we review the individual products that are part of the Oracle Identity Management suite of products.

Oracle Internet Directory

The Oracle Internet Directory (OID) is a robust and scalable LDAP v3–compliant directory that is built on top of the Oracle RDBMS. OID can be used in large enterprise deployments in order to handle a large volume of data while delivering the performance needed. Thanks to its use of the Oracle RDBMS, OID can be deployed in a high-availability configuration by leveraging Oracle Real Application Clusters (Oracle RAC). In addition, other high-availability options such as multimaster replication and Oracle Internet Directory Clusters are also available. From a security perspective, OID also benefits from Oracle RDBMS options such as Oracle Database Vault and Oracle Transparent Data Encryption.

OID can also be deployed in conjunction with the Directory Integration Platform (DIP) component to provide meta-directory functionality. DIP supports synchronization of LDAP data with other directories, including Oracle Directory Server Enterprise Edition, Microsoft Active Directory, Tivoli Directory Server, Novell eDirectory, and other LDAP v3–compliant directories. Directory Integration Platform can also support integration with RDBMs containing identity data such as the backend of Oracle Human Resources Management System, part of Oracle E-Business Suite.

As part of Fusion Middleware, OID benefits from some of the common infrastructure. For system management, Enterprise Manager and WLST provide the UI and command-line interfaces for the day-to-day administration of the product. It is also integrated with Oracle Fusion Middleware Audit Framework. OID is also tightly integrated with many Fusion Middleware components. WebLogic Server security services provide an out-of-the-box authenticator for Oracle Internet Directory, which can be easily configured as the enterprise identity store for OPSS and WebLogic Server domains. Similarly, Oracle Internet Directory is certified as the preferred OPSS LDAP-based policy and credential store.

Oracle Directory Server Enterprise Edition

Oracle Directory Server Enterprise Edition (ODSEE—formerly Sun Directory Server Enterprise Edition) is a market-leading directory server and one of the most supported directory servers by independent software vendors (ISVs). The core directory service architecture is built on top of an embedded database. The product ships with an integrated Directory Proxy Server to provide load-balancing, high-availability, and distribution capabilities. The product can also be configured in a replication environment to ensure data availability. Out of the box, it also supports synchronization with Microsoft Windows identity data, password, and group information residing in Microsoft Active Directory.

Depending on the deployment preferences of an enterprise, both Oracle Internet Directory and Oracle Directory Server Enterprise Edition can be used to deliver an enterprise-grade LDAP directory to the server.

Oracle Virtual Directory

Although having a single LDAP server as a corporate identity store is ideal, many enterprises are forced to deal with more than one identity store. They might need to deal with multiple LDAP servers from customers, partners, or another organization. Authoritative identity information might also be found in other identity repositories, such as a human resources management system or an identity-enabled application carrying specific user information. Using synchronization to consolidate this data is one solution, but this is usually not practical due to technical and oftentimes, nontechnical reasons, such as political, regulatory, or corporate boundaries when dealing with customers and partners. Oracle Virtual Directory (OVD) delivers a solution that provides an elegant solution and quick ROI through virtualization.

OVD provides a virtualization layer on top of the existing identity stores and presents a single, unified view of the data through an LDAP interface. It also possesses transformation capability to achieve the following:

- Unify identity data across multiple sources in a virtual manner and return a single search result
- Transform data from non-LDAP data, such as databases and web services, and expose them to LDAP clients
- Transform data to create application-specific views or dynamic views of the data—with a different schema, structure, attribute name, and values.
- Improve security and compliance through additional access control and denial-of-service protection.

Figure 4-8 shows a typical usage of Oracle Virtual Directory.

OVD is integrated with Enterprise Manager and WLST for system management. It is also integrated with Fusion Middleware Audit Framework. Like Oracle Internet Directory, WebLogic Server security services provide an out-of-the-box authenticator for Oracle Virtual Directory to configure the

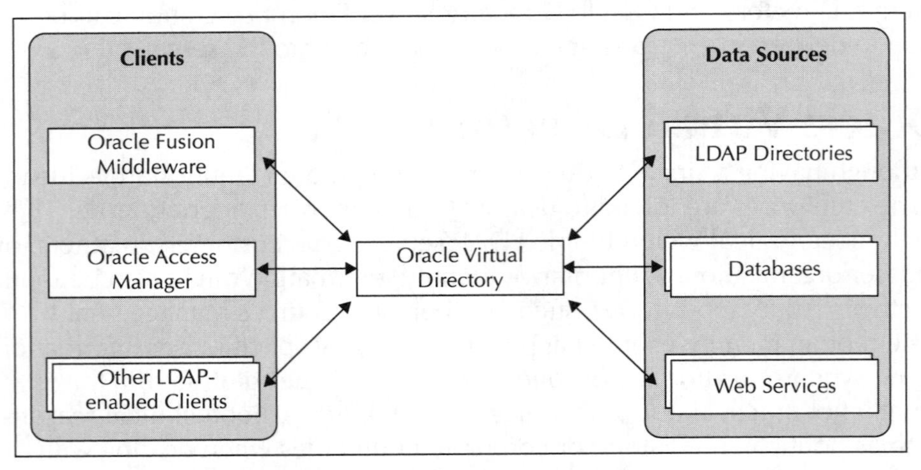

FIGURE 4-8. *Oracle Virtual Directory typical usage*

virtual directory as the enterprise identity store for OPSS and the domain. The Oracle Virtual Directory Local-Store Adapter (LSA) option is certified with OPSS as a lightweight option of an LDAP-based policy store.

Oracle Access Manager

Oracle Access Manager (OAM) centralizes web access control by delivering a solution for authentication, authorization, and Single Sign-On, accompanied by comprehensive policy administration, session management, and agent management capabilities. OAM integrates with an LDAP user identity store where user data resides, including credentials. A database backend is required to store OAM policy data and user session data.

In order for an application to achieve Single Sign-On, it needs to delegate user authentication to the Single Sign-On provider. OAM refers to such an application as its "partner application." In OAM, the configuration of a partner application is done by deploying policy enforcement agents in the form of Oracle Access Manager WebGates and AccessGates, which handle the communication with the Access Manager server. A registration process is required for the agent to establish the relationship between the OAM and the partner application.

Figure 4-9 shows a typical topology of an OAM deployment.

WebGates are agents at the HTTP layer. They intercept HTTP requests coming into the web server and redirect them to the OAM server. An AccessGate is a custom agent to be used in conjunction with the Access Software Development Kit to process requests for non-HTTP resources. The agent registration is done from the OAM web UI, which manages the agent life cycle—from registration to diagnostics and real-time monitoring.

The OAM Administration Console provides both system and policy configuration capabilities for administrators. The OAM Session Management Engine (SME) can monitor and control real-time user sessions. Policies can be defined in the administration console to enforce certain constraints against any user session—for example, limiting the number of concurrent sessions by a single user at any given time. The Session Management Engine also keeps track of all the active sessions. An administrator can easily look up the active sessions of a particular user and can terminate the sessions remotely from the OAM administration console.

In order for OAM to authenticate users, it must be configured against the centralized identity store, which is typically an LDAP repository. Out of the box, OAM is configured against the WebLogic embedded LDAP. It readily

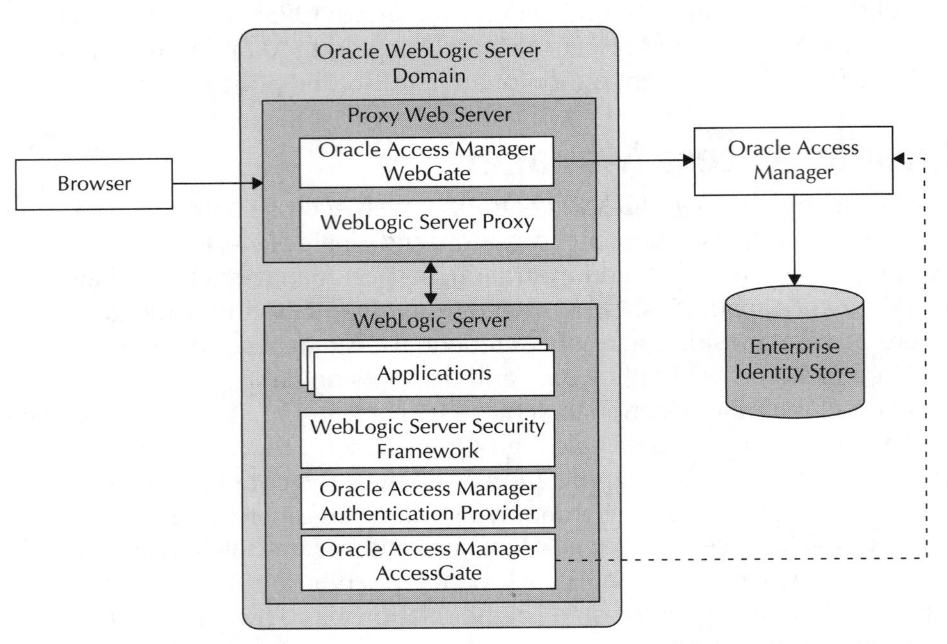

FIGURE 4-9. *Oracle Access Manager deployment topology*

integrates with Oracle Internet Directory, Oracle Directory Server Enterprise Edition, and Oracle Virtual Directory, along with other well-known LDAP servers, including Novell eDirectory and Microsoft Active Directory.

A protected application in Fusion Middleware must be configured to properly delegate authentication and be able to recognize the authenticated users and to retrieve the necessary data about these users, including additional user profile and group information from the identity store. Depending on how the resource is being protected, OAM provides, out of the box, the WebLogic Authenticator and Identity Asserter to handle different scenarios. In the typical Single Sign-On scenario where a WebGate is present with an Oracle HTTP Server, the OAM Identity Asserter is configured in conjunction with an LDAP Authenticator. The Identity Asserter takes care of the identity assertion portion of the Single Sign-On process, while the LDAP authenticator allows the application (through WebLogic Server) to fetch additional user profile and group information from the associated LDAP identity store.

For Microsoft Windows customers, OAM supports desktop sign on—commonly known as Windows Native Authentication. This allows Microsoft Internet Explorer to automatically authenticate a desktop user accessing a protected web application using her desktop credentials. The user login credentials are passed through Microsoft Internet Explorer to OAM in the form of a Kerberos ticket. This Kerberos ticket is first validated against the Key Distribution Center server on the Windows domain server. The credentials are then used to authenticate the user against Windows Active Directory, which acts as the identity store for OAM.

For further details, please refer to the Oracle Access Manager document in Fusion Middleware documentation library.

Oracle Identity Federation

Within a single security domain such as a single enterprise, a Single Sign-On solution and a centralized identity store provide the necessary infrastructure for centralized authentication and sharing of user data. Most importantly, a Single Sign-On solution reduces the need for users to provide credentials repeatedly to access resources. However, this solution breaks down in a federated environment where users and resources span across a single domain—for example, a company's boundary. There is an increasing need for customers, vendors, and business partners to integrate with each other where access to resources and user information is required. Another main driving factor for extending beyond a company's security domain is the rapid adoption of Software-as-a-Service (SaaS) providers, where seamless and secured access to these SaaS services in a cloud is needed.

Oracle Identity Federation (OIF) provides a solution to protect resources across a federated environment by enabling identity information to be shared across security domains. OIF supports many of the standard federation protocols, including SAML 1.0/1.1/2.0 and WS-Federation. By implementing cross-site access and authentication, OIF delivers Single Sign-On capability across domains and gives administrators the ability to control access to external sites. It readily integrates with various authentication providers, including LDAP directories such as Oracle Internet Directory and Oracle Virtual Directory as well as access management solutions such as Oracle Access Manager.

OIF also allows applications and access control systems in the federated environment to obtain authenticated assertions and user identity attributes directly through a set of integration modules that comes with the product.

An application may use this information for setting up user preferences or creating audit records. An access control system may define policies based on user identity attributes to determine access privileges for a particular user.

Other features of OIF include support for X.509 certificate validation and out-of-the-box Microsoft CardSpace authentication provider.

Oracle Enterprise Single Sign-On

Many enterprises still have the need to deal with passwords for non-web-based systems such as legacy mainframes, Unix logins, and application access through Java-based thick clients for client/server-based applications that a web-based Single Sign-On solution cannot handle. Oracle Enterprise Single Sign-On (ESSO) suite fills the gap by providing the end user with a Single Sign-On experience to access all these resources. A user signs in once through her Windows desktop or other mechanism, such as biometrics or smartcard. Once the user is logged in, Oracle ESSO can retrieve the user record and look up the appropriate credentials when the user attempts to access the Oracle ESSO–enabled application and then send the credentials to the downstream application to authenticate the user. Here are some of the key features of Oracle ESSO:

- Eliminates the need for users to remember multiple username and password combinations by storing, fetching, and applying these credentials during user login
- Supports web-based and non-web-based system logins, including Telnet logins for Unix systems, mainframes, Java-based applications, and other client/server-based applications.
- Supports password resets for Windows logon
- Supports secure access in shared kiosks or workstations through session monitoring and automatic user sign-off
- Supports any combination of advanced authentication mechanisms, including biometrics, smartcards, and secure tokens to control user access
- Supports integration with identity provisioning systems to programmatically add and remove credentials for applications, which enables provisioning and deprovisioning of users to all applications governed by Oracle ESSO

Oracle ESSO can readily integrate with all the Oracle LDAP offerings, including Oracle Internet Directory and Oracle Directory Service Enterprise Edition as its user profile and credential repository, along with other LDAP vendors such as Microsoft Active Directory or a SQL-based RDBMS. Oracle ESSO can also integrate with OAM for user authentication against web-based applications protected by OAM. What's more, Oracle ESSO integrates with Oracle Identity Manager (OIM), allowing automatic user and credentials provisioning to be driven by the enterprise provisioning solution.

Oracle Adaptive Access Manager

Oracle Adaptive Access Manager (OAAM) provides a next-generation access management solution that goes beyond user authentication. Although authentication is still an important part of today's enterprise access management solution, authentication alone cannot prevent fraudulent activities such as phishing, malware, transaction fraud, and insider fraud. OAAM can strengthen an identity management deployment through many of its features, including the following:

- **Device fingerprinting** For each user session, OAAM generates a unique single-use fingerprint based on the device used during access requests and transactions by monitoring the device attributes in a clientless fashion. Any changes to these attributes during a user session may indicate session hijacking. Any reuse of the single-use fingerprint may indicate a fraudulent attack.
- **Virtual authentication devices** OAAM provides a set of advanced authentication devices to harden the authentication process. OAAM TextPad provides a device for entering a password or a pin with a personal image and a phrase displayed to ensure the prompt is generated from a valid site. OAAM QuestionPad presents a Knowledge-Based Authentication (KBA) challenge question to the end user to serve as an additional challenge during authentication. The QuestionPad question text is also embedded into the image to protect from screen scrapers.
- **One-time Password Anywhere (OTP Anywhere)** OAAM can generate a one-time password challenge that can complement a KBA challenge or be used as the KBA. The one-time password can be delivered via the Short Message Service (SMS), e-mail, instant messaging, or voice message.

OAAM provides an out-of-the-box integration with Oracle Access Manager, enhancing the login security with these advanced login devices. It can also be integrated with a third-party Single Sign-On solution through custom integrators.

At the application level, OAAM can be embedded natively in the application itself to provide highly customizable security inside the protected application through the Java API. A SOAP interface is also available for an application to integrate with OAAM through web services.

Oracle Entitlements Server

Oracle Entitlements Server (OES) provides a centralized authorization service to support externalization of authorization policies and entitlements from within the application. It provides a set of security modules that act as policy decision points (PDPs). These security modules evaluate entitlement policies on behalf of an application or a service. Applications and services can then act as policy enforcement points (PEPs) to ask the security modules for decisions as to whether a user can perform an action on a particular resource. This externalization allows application code to be simplified by avoiding security policies and logic being mingled into the application logic. It also allows entitlement policies to be reused across applications and provides a centralized and consistent mechanism to manage application access.

Oracle Entitlements Server provides the ability to easily leverage existing enterprise data (RDBMS, LDAP, web services, customer sources, and so on) in the policies for highly data-driven policy definitions for applications. Entitlement policies can leverage attributes from these data sources to implement an Attribute-Based Access Control (ABAC) system if so desired. In addition, extensions such as custom attribute retrievers and evaluation functions can be implemented to cater to customer-specific requirements.

In terms of standards, Oracle Entitlements Server supports eXtensible Access Control Markup Language (XACML). Applications may use the XACML request/response protocol to obtain authorization decisions from the security modules. For interoperability, Oracle Entitlements Server policies can be imported and exported in a standard XACML format.

OES also provides a set of prebuilt PEPs for certain structured runtimes such as Oracle Database, WebLogic Server, and Microsoft SharePoint Server. Integration with Oracle Data Service Integrator and Oracle Virtual

Private Database gives way in defining and enforcing data-level security by providing an intermediate layer between the database client and the database that can enforce data security based on policies defined in OES.

While OES can serve as an authorization engine for any custom applications, it is also the underlying authorization engine for many of the Oracle Fusion Middleware components, including Oracle Platform Security Services, Oracle Access Manager, and Oracle Identity Manager.

Oracle Identity Manager

The components discussed so far have laid down a strong foundation to secure an application at the runtime level. However, to properly enforce security, a comprehensive identity administration solution must be in place to manage the life cycle of a user and control how access is provisioned to a user. Oracle Identity Manager (OIM) brings together a broad set of features that complements the security infrastructure in Oracle Fusion Middleware to support the various stages of the identity life cycle, including on-boarding, account provisioning, transfer, access request, delegated administration, and off-boarding scenarios. It also provides integration with other Oracle applications, Oracle Database, common security infrastructure components, including those in Oracle Identity Management, and other third-party or custom applications.

Here are some of the key features of OIM:

- Self-service user profile management
- Delegated administration
- Role-based and policy-based automated provisioning of user accounts and fine-grained entitlements
- Self-service request support for account and entitlement requests, along with real-time request-tracking capability for end users and business owners
- Comprehensive approval workflow support based on Oracle Business Rules, part of Oracle Fusion Middleware SOA Suite
- Advanced password policy management, including syntax, password age, and historical passwords

- Self-service password management to support password reset, password expiration, and forget-password scenarios
- Password synchronization, supporting bidirectional password synchronization across targets where necessary
- Identity reconciliation, to ensure integrity of accounts and entitlements granted to users across all the managed targets
- Rogue account (an account created out of process for a known user) and orphan account (an operational account without a mapping to a valid user) management
- Automated user identity, account, and access provisioning, which can be role based, policy based, request-approval driven, or achieved through direct provisioning by a delegated administrator

When developing an identity-enabled application, you should consider many of the identity administration features listed here. Rather than building an application-specific implementation, by externalizing these features and integrating with Oracle Identity Manager, you can allow your applications to benefit from this rich set of features. End users and administrators will also benefit from a common user interface. But most importantly, the identity life cycle across all the resources and applications are managed centrally. From an identity compliance perspective, this is crucial in providing an audit and historical trail of key events.

Oracle Access Manager readily integrates with OIM to leverage its password policy management capabilities, including its self-service feature. This combination can be further enhanced by a supported integration with Oracle Adaptive Access Manager, thus delivering a power solution with the following features supported by the trio of products:

- Password entry protection through personalized virtual authenticators
- Knowledge-Based Authentication (KBA) challenge questions for secondary login authentication based on risk
- One-Time Password (OTP) challenge for secondary login authentication based on risk

- Registration flows to support password protection and KBA and OTP challenge functionality
- User preference flows to support password protection and KBA and OTP challenge functionality
- Password management flows

In the context of Oracle Platform Security Services and its application policy model, OIM would facilitate the creation of users in the identity store, along with user profile management that ties to the user attributes stored in the identity store. These attributes may be used by Oracle Entitlements Server policies for authorization. The application policy model also depends on the notion of enterprise roles in the form of LDAP groups residing in the identity store. Oracle Identity Manager can manage these enterprise roles. Reconciliation from the identity store will bring in changes of these enterprise roles into OIM if the changes are made directly in LDAP. Conversely, if the enterprise role is being requested, or is assigned to a user based on a policy in OIM, the change will be pushed out to LDAP to allow Oracle Platform Security Services to properly enforce security at runtime.

Oracle Identity Analytics

Oracle Identity Analytics (OIA) provides a business-user-centric component to look at the overall identity and access information across the enterprise. The intended users are business owners, application owners, and line managers who are required to perform duties such as audit violation monitoring and remediation and periodic access certifications. Reports and dashboards are also important tools for these types of business users and auditors to review certain aspects of the identity data.

The key to effectively performing identity audits, access certification, and analytics on identity data is a centralized repository of identity and access data. This is the core of OIM in the form of the Identity Warehouse. OIM can directly integrate with applications and resources to pull in identity and access data. It is also readily integrated with several provisioning solutions, including Oracle Identity Manager.

Key features of access certification include the following:

- Consolidation and correlation of identity and access data from various enterprise applications and resources
- Dynamic generation of access certifications with full life-cycle support, including notification, delegation, expiration settings, escalation options, and reminders
- Comprehensive risk analysis and assessment of a user based on previous audit violations, provisioned methods, certification history, and so on
- Variations of certification types available for different audiences—user entitlement certification for managers, data owner certification for application owners, and role certification for role owners
- Closed-loop remediation in case of revocation of access to automatically remove access through provisioning integration (with Oracle Identity Manager, for example) along with remediation tracking

OIM also includes a comprehensive identity audit module to detect any toxic combinations of user access. Policies can be defined at the role and entitlement level—and can be defined across applications and resources to catch any violated conditions. A remediation workflow is available along with closed-loop remediation. When scheduled, the identity audit scans act as a detective mechanism to catch any violations. When integrated with a provisioning solution such as Oracle Identity Manager, the identity audit scans can also be triggered during an access request to perform preventive simulation and warn of any possible violations before the actual provisioning is carried out.

Chapter Use Case

In Chapter 3, we laid down the foundation for integration with some of the key security infrastructure components in the enterprise. The ultimate goal is to deploy and provide the pricing application to the rest of the employees in a secured manner. A corporate LDAP directory, an Oracle Internet Directory, has been identified as the corporate directory containing all the users. This corporate LDAP will serve as the identity store for this domain. In addition, per company policy, all web applications must be protected and accessible via the corporate Single Sign-On solution—Oracle Access Manager. Although there is no OPSS policy defined at this moment, to plan for the eventual uptake of Application Developer Framework (ADF), we will also configure the domain policy store to be LDAP based. As a result, the credential store will now be LDAP based, and this can be used immediately by the pricing application to store the database credentials to access the backend pricing data.

In this section, we will first go through the steps to configure the domain identity store to point to the corporate Oracle Internet Directory. To test this, we will write a small piece of code using the User & Role API to fetch some user information from the configured identity store. We will then register the pricing application as a partner application and go through the high-level steps to enable Single Sign-On with Oracle Access Manager. Finally, we will enable auditing for some of the key components deployed so far in our topology, including Oracle HTTP Server and Oracle Internet Directory.

Configuring the Identity Store

The goal here is to configure an LDAP Authenticator to point to the instance of Oracle Internet Directory. To configure the identity store, log on to the WebLogic Server Administration Console. From the left pane, under Domain Structure, click on Security Realms and select the active security realm you are using on the main pane. The main pane should now show the realm settings. Select the Providers tab to see the current list of providers configured. A DefaultAuthenticator and a DefaultIdentityAsserter are typically available out of the box. Click on Lock & Edit in the Change Center region to unlock the main pane, which should now be unlocked. To create a new LDAP Authenticator, select New and choose OracleInternetDirectoryAuthenticator from the drop-down list. Once created, your new OracleInternetDirectoryAuthenticator should be available on the provider list. Select it to open the configuration tabs for the provider. The key configuration is under the Configuration | Provider Specific tab.

You will notice that most of the values have been prepopulated according to the out-of-the-box settings in Oracle Internet Directory. Here are a few of the key values that will need to be configured:

Parameter	**Description**
Host	The host name or the IP address of the LDAP server.
Port	The port number of the LDAP server. 389 is the default non-SSL LDAP port.
Principal	An LDAP Distinguished Name (DN) is needed to connect to the LDAP server.
Credential	The credential corresponding to the principal just specified.
User Base DN	The base Distinguished Name identifying the root of the tree in the directory containing users.
Group Base DN	The base Distinguished Name identifying the root of the tree in the directory containing groups.

The rest of the parameters should work with the out-of-the-box settings of Oracle Internet Directory. When you are finished, save the configuration and click on Activate Change in the Change Center region. To activate the setting, WLS server needs to be rebooted. But before doing so, make sure you consider the following points.

You may not want to rely solely on a single LDAP Authenticator because it becomes a single point of failure if the LDAP server becomes unavailable. In this case, WebLogic Server will not come up upon rebooting. Keeping the DefaultAuthenticator with at least a user with Administrator privilege is a good option to avoid this situation. By default, the "weblogic" user will be there. Speaking of the "weblogic" user, if you wish to create an end user in LDAP that has similar Administrator privilege within the domain, make the user a member of an LDAP group. This LDAP group must then be added to the Admin role under Global Roles using the WebLogic Server Administration Console on the Realm Roles page.

Using the User & Role API

Oracle Platform Security Services leverages the underlying LDAP Authenticator to access users and groups from Oracle Internet Directory. The User & Role API provides an application with a way to retrieve user and group information without dealing with the identity sources directly. At this point, we have configured only one LDAP Authenticator pointing to Oracle Internet Directory.

We will write a simple Java class to create a user:

```
import java.util.*;
import oracle.security.idm.*;
import oracle.security.jps.ContextFactory;
import oracle.security.jps.JpsContextFactory;
import oracle.security.jps.JpsContext;
import oracle.security.jps.service.idstore.IdentityStoreService;
public class CreateUser
{
  public static void main(String args[]) throws Exception
  {
    String username = args[0];
    String passwd = args[1];
    IdentityStore idStore = null;

    ContextFactory ctxFactory = JpsContextFactory.getContextFactory();
    JpsContext ctx = ctxFactory.getContext();
    IdentityStoreService iss =
ctx.getServiceInstance(IdentityStoreService.class);
    System.out.println(iss);
    // obtaining the ID store instance
    idStore = iss.getIdmStore();
    System.out.println(idStore);
    // UserManager is the object used for most of the operations
    UserManager usrMgr = idStore.getUserManager();
    try{
      // Do search of the username to be created.  The sample
      // program will drop the user if exists
      User user = store.searchUser(username);
      usrmgr.dropUser(user);
      System.out.println(username + " is found and has been deleted.");
    }catch(IMException e){}
    // Create the user setting the password value
    User user = usrmgr.createUser(username, passwd.toCharArray());
    System.out.println("user created : " + user.getUniqueName());
    // Now modify the display name of the user
    System.out.println("Modifying property UserProfile.DISPLAY_NAME");
    UserProfile usrprofile = usr.getUserProfile();
    ModProperty mprop = new ModProperty(UserProfile.DISPLAY_NAME,
                        "Sample Display Name",
                        ModProperty.REPLACE);

      usrprofile.setProperty(mprop);
      System.out.println("Now fetch UserProfile.DISPLAY_NAME");
      Property prop = usrprofile.getProperty(UserProfile.DISPLAY_NAME);
```

```
        List values = prop.getValues();
        Iterator itr = values.iterator();
        // Depend on the attribute, there may be multiple values.  The
        // while loop iterates through the result set.
        while(itr.hasNext()) {
          System.out.println(UserProfile.DISPLAY_NAME+": "+ itr.next());
        }
        System.out.println();
      }
    }
```

Note that in this entire program, there is no specifying of connection information (such as login user and credentials) or any specifying of the type of identity store in the code. The developer is completely abstracted from the details underneath because OPSS is aware of the identity store configuration. More importantly, without any code change, this code will work against all the different types of identity stores—whether they are file based, LDAP based, or through other custom providers—as long as they are supported by OPSS.

Configure Single Sign-On with Oracle Access Manager

We have configured the identity store and tested it with our sample program. The pricing application, per company policy, needs to be protected by the corporate Single Sign-On solution, which in this case is Oracle Access Manager. One assumption here is that Oracle Access Manager shares the same identity store, the corporate Oracle Internet Directory, to authenticate the users.

In Chapter 3, we configured Oracle HTTP Server to front our pricing application. We will first install Oracle Access Manager 11g WebGates where Oracle HTTP Server resides. However, a couple prerequisites should be noted before proceeding:

- If you are installing WebGates on a Linux or Solaris system, some GCC libraries need to be downloaded and compiled beforehand. Please refer to the Oracle Access Manager documentation for details.
- If you are installing WebGates on a Microsoft Windows 2003 64-bit or 2008 64-bit platform, you need to install Microsoft Visual C++ libraries. Please refer to the Oracle Access Manager documentation for details.

From your Oracle Fusion Middleware installation download, locate webgate.zip, which contains the installer for the WebGate installation. Unzip the file, launch the installer, and follow the installation wizard. For Linux and Solaris, you will be prompted for the directory containing the GCC libraries. Once the installer finishes, perform the post-installation steps as documented to properly deploy the WebGate on the Web Tier host.

Now that the WebGate is properly set up on the Web Tier, we need to register the WebGate with Oracle Access Manager. As mentioned before, only registered WebGate agents can communicate with the Oracle Access Manager server in order to protect our partner application. This registration can be done from the Oracle Access Manager Administration Console under the Agent Configuration panel by following the steps as documented. The base URL would be pointing to http://node10.oracle.com:7777, which is the HTTP setting based on the use case in the previous chapter. Under the Protected Resource List, "/PricingServiceWeb" should be added. The agent configuration contains many other parameters. For further details, please refer to Fusion Middleware documentation library.

Once the registration has completed on the console, one additional step is required to copy the updated Oracle Access Manager Agent ObAccessClient.xml configuration file (and any certificate artifacts, if created) from the Oracle Access Manager domain home to the WebGate installation directory on the Web Tier host to complete the registration.

Oracle Fusion Middleware ships with a predefined OAMAuthenticator and OAMIdentityAsserter—both of which should now be configured, in that order, in the pricing application WebLogic Server domain.

The final step is to ensure centralized logout is configured. Without this, a user session may not be properly terminated. The general guideline is that the application should not have its own logout page when being protected by Oracle Access Manager. It should allow for configurable logout links to be set accordingly, based on the Oracle Access Manager setup. To configure logout options for a WebGate, access the Agent Registration page in Oracle Access Manager Administration Console where certain key logout parameters need to be populated.

This section has provided a high-level set of tasks to be performed and considered when registering a partner application. For detailed steps, please refer to Fusion Middleware documentation library.

Managing Credential Store

Our pricing application needs access to its backend RDBMS for the pricing data. To better manage the credentials for database access, we will create the credentials in the domain credential store. Log in to Enterprise Manager and navigate to the Domain | Security | Credentials menu.

First, we will create a new map for our application. Click on Create Map and enter **PricingApp** as the map name. The Pricing App folder should now appear on the UI. Now, to create the key and configure the actual values of the credentials, click on Create Key. Select PricingApp as the map and provide a unique key within this map for your credentials. This key will be used by your code to access this information at runtime. For type, select "password" because this will be a database credential. Enter the appropriate user name and password values needed to access the pricing application backend, as shown here in Figure 4-10.

In Part II of this book, we will see how the credential store can be used by the pricing application at runtime.

Configuring Component Audit

We now have a setup where our pricing application is running in a domain where Oracle Internet Directory is the identity store. The application is

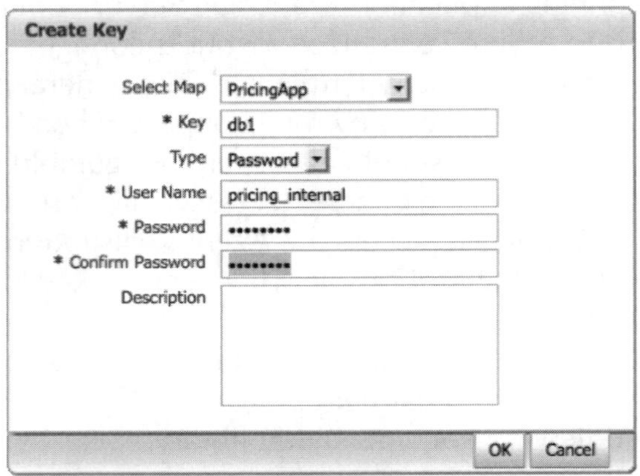

FIGURE 4-10. *Credential store configuration in Enterprise Manager*

fronted by an Oracle HTTP Server that is configured with an Oracle Access Manager WebGate registered in Oracle Access Manager to provide Single Sign-On. Out-of-the-box audit support is available for many of these components. We will focus on the application deployment rather than the identity management deployment. Because we have just created a new key in the credential store, we enable a simple audit policy for the credential store under Oracle Platform Security Services.

To access the audit configuration, log in to Enterprise Manager. Select the domain from WebLogic Domain on the left pane. From the menu, go to WebLogic Domain | Security and you will see two audit related menus: Audit Store and Audit Policy.

Out of the box, the audit store is file based. If an RDBMS-based audit store is available with the appropriate audit schema created, the audit store can be changed accordingly. For now, we will stay with the file-based audit.

The Audit Policy section presents all the components that are audit-enabled in the domain (see Figure 4-11). There are two predefined levels (Low and Medium) along with a Custom option. With the predefined levels, each audit-enabled product has associated a set of audit events for these levels to provide a quick way of enabling the common audit events for the entire domain. For a more fine-grained approach, an administrator can choose the Custom option to enable individual events. A filtering option is also available for a subset of the events to filter out unwanted events and focus on the necessary ones. In general, many of these audit events occur at a very high volume (for example, permission checks or user authentication). The filtering option allows you to optimize the audit results.

In our use case, we want to make sure any existing credentials are closely monitored. We will audit all deleting events and modification events. By selecting Custom from the Audit Level drop-down, all the check boxes will now be enabled on the UI. Next, expand Oracle Platform Security Services to see the list of audit categories. Click on CredentialManagement to view the list of audit events available. Under the Enable Audit column, check DeleteCredential and ModifyCredential to enable these two audit events. Click Apply to activate the events.

In Part II, we will touch on the RDBMS-based audit repository as well as the reporting aspect of audit through Oracle Business Intelligence Publisher.

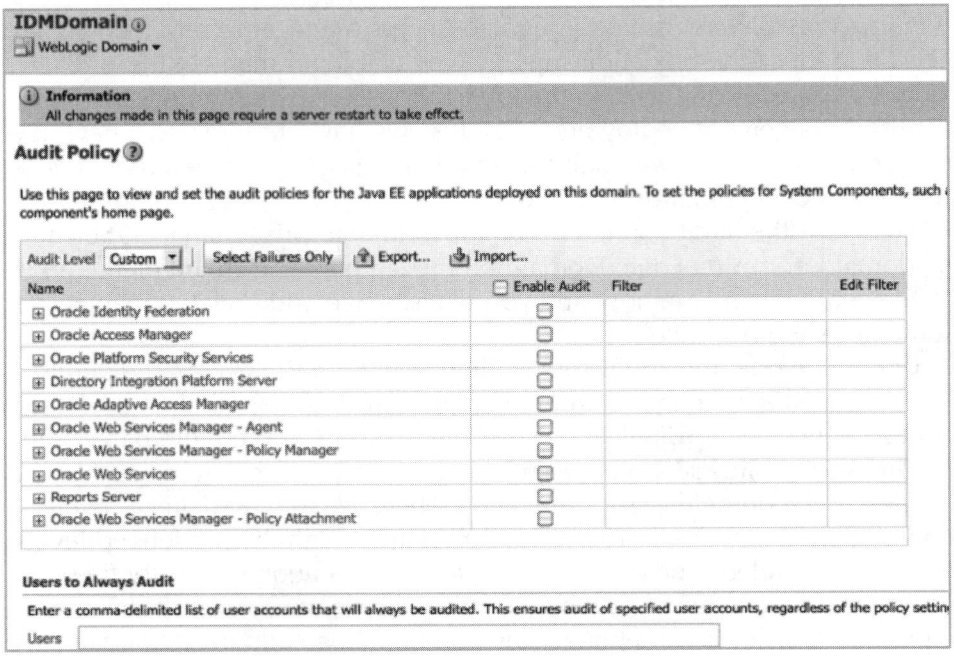

FIGURE 4-11. *Fusion Middleware Audit Framework configuration in Enterprise Manager*

Conclusion

In this chapter we have touched on a broad set of topics around Oracle Platform Security Services and Oracle Identity Management. A portable and comprehensive set of services is provided through Oracle Platform Security Services to enable every stage of the application life cycle—including development, packaging, deployment, and runtime. Developers are abstracted from having to deal with the underlying security and identity management infrastructure in the enterprise. Oracle Identity Management provides many of the key identity infrastructure components to support directory services, web access management, identity federation, risk-based access management, user provisioning, role management, and audit and access certification. Now that we have reviewed Oracle Platform Security Services and Oracle Identity Management, we will move on to further enhance our pricing application in the next few chapters, and some of these enhancements will involve the security foundation laid down in this chapter.

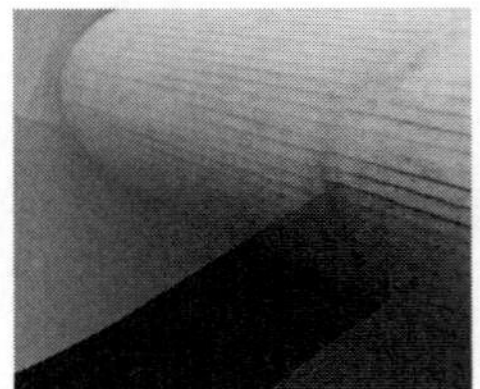

CHAPTER 5

Oracle Service-Oriented Architecture Suite

he Oracle Service-Oriented Architecture (SOA) Suite of products provides a platform that enables an enterprise to adopt a unified service-oriented IT infrastructure. Such an infrastructure allows for more effective and flexible management of enterprise IT services as well as more efficient creation of new value-added services. In addition to providing a SOA platform upon which services can be built and managed, Oracle SOA Suite also forms the basis of a number of other Oracle Fusion Middleware products that use it for the implementation of their own service-oriented design. Given these key roles within the Fusion Middleware stack, a solid understanding of Oracle SOA Suite is essential. In this chapter we introduce the core components of Oracle SOA Suite and review their architecture and management capabilities.

Introducing Oracle SOA Suite

We begin our discussion of the Oracle SOA Suite of products (from here on referred to simply as SOA Suite) by introducing the SOA principles it is designed to facilitate. We then describe the components of SOA Suite in terms of these principles.

The Case for a SOA Platform

So far in this book the Fusion Middleware pieces we have covered—namely, WebLogic Server, the Fusion Middleware shared infrastructure, and the Identity Management components—provide a solid infrastructure on which secure Java EE applications can be built and managed. It is therefore fair to ask why another abstraction layer, such as the SOA Suite components we are about to discuss, is at all needed for the enablement of an enterprise IT infrastructure. The short answer to this question is that the SOA products provide a standard platform that facilitates the creation and management of applications that adhere to SOA principles. Therefore, to understand the benefits of SOA Suite—and, of course, to properly implement a SOA infrastructure using them—one has to be familiar with these principles. Although a thorough discussion of SOA principles is beyond the scope of this book, the following points describe some of the fundamental SOA principles facilitated by the core SOA Suite capabilities:

- **Decoupling of service interfaces from their implementation** The implementation of enterprise applications changes over time. These changes can be holistic in nature, such as implementation rewrites using a new language, or they can be evolutionary, such as the application of defect patches or upgrades of a service over time. To ensure that implementation changes do not affect the consumers of an application's publicly exposed services, it is important to make sure these services are described through an interface that can remain independent from their implementation. Although this type of decoupling of interface from implementation is usually possible through sheer discipline, regardless of the underlying technology, the capabilities of the underlying technology can play a big part in making this separation simpler to sustain.
- **Component-based development** The implementation of business services can span various functions and implementation types that together realize the capabilities of their services. Component-based development allows for the elements of a service's implementation that are responsible for a common function to be separated into abstracted components with clearly defined interfaces. These components are then integrated and packaged together to compose the overall implementation of a service. Component-based development lessens the impact—in terms of cost and downtime—of changes to a component's implementation.
- **Integration of applications through orchestration of business processes** Enterprise business processes typically consist of activities that consist of interaction with departmental staff, integration with automated enterprise services, and application of business rules. In a non-service-oriented architecture, the integration of these endpoints is typically achieved through Enterprise Application Integration (EAI) techniques, which involve point-to-point integrations of systems. It is then left to "paper" procedures and the organization's employees to properly orchestrate an end-to-end business process (such as the approval of a business trip). The EAI method lends itself to a number of issues, including a high level of complexity in the

management of end-to-end integration points (which tend to propagate and lead to what is commonly referred to as a "spaghetti integration") as well as the inability to provide a holistic view (in terms of change management and monitoring) of individual business process. A SOA platform facilitates the implementation of business processes as end-to-end orchestrations of heterogeneous endpoints that can be managed and monitored as a unit.

- **Decoupling of business rules from application logic** Service implementations often encapsulate business rules that are key to the core capabilities of the enterprise. These rules often need to be adjusted, either by expert end users or external systems, to account for organizational or environmental changes. The implementation of a service should therefore externalize such business rules parameters in a way that facilitates their frequent changes and does not require the redeployment or, worse, the reimplementation of the service itself. A SOA platform should allow for a consistent way for services implementations to expose business rules and a centralized mechanism for their modification at runtime.
- **Business activity monitoring** The runtime business metrics from the various applications of an enterprise provide important insight into the health of its operations and business activity. A central way of capturing, browsing, and visualizing such metrics can therefore be of significant strategic benefit. A SOA platform should provide a unified mechanism for the capture and centralized monitoring of such metrics.
- **Service mediation** No matter how diligent an enterprise is with standards, in order to keep its service-oriented environment consistent, major deviations are bound to occur over time as a result of various internal factors (such as diverging views on the "right" standards to follow) as well as external factors (such as mergers and acquisitions activities). To enable a more seamless integration of heterogeneous business services—and hence to act as a shock absorber for nonstandard services and service changes—a mediation layer that allows for the mapping of diverging interfaces, data types, or communication protocols as well as for the implementation of routing logic for incoming service requests is essential. A SOA platform should provide flexible and rich service mediation capabilities to facilitate heterogeneous service integration.

These principles and their rationale form the basis for the need for a SOA platform that acts as their enabler. The different components of SOA Suite are designed to facilitate the implementation of business services that adhere to these principles. In the next section we introduce the core components of this suite.

SOA Suite Components

The core components of SOA Suite that are discussed in this chapter are the SOA infrastructure, Business Activity Monitoring (BAM), and the User Messaging Service (UMS). Beyond the components falling into these categories, SOA Suite also contains three other important elements that should be mentioned: Business-to-Business (B2B), which provides a platform for formal interorganizational communications using protocols (such as ebXML or EDI) specially designed for this purpose, Complex Event Processing (CEP), which allows for the real-time processing of high-throughput message streams for the detection of specific patterns, and the Oracle Service Bus (OSB), which provides a platform for the centralization of complex service mediation and routing logic. A discussion of these three components (beyond the brief overview of OSB within the next box) is, however, beyond the scope of this book. Therefore, the remaining content of this chapter focuses on the other areas of SOA Suite illustrated in the following diagram.

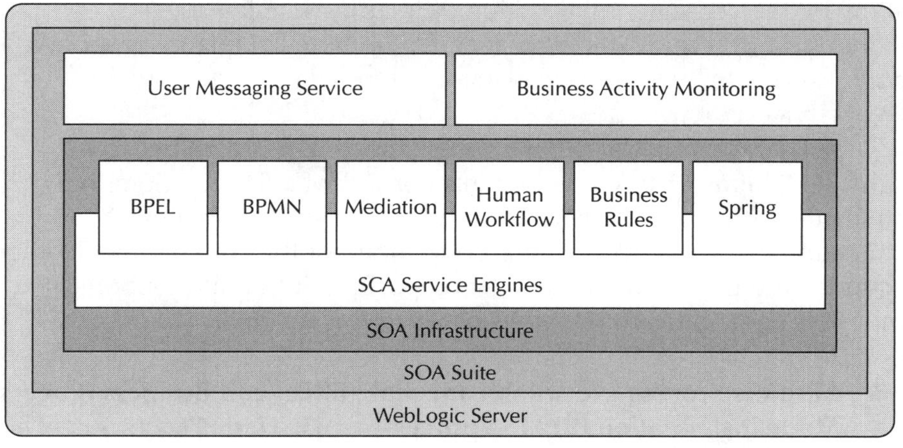

Oracle Service Bus Overview

The Oracle Service Bus (OSB) is a component of the Oracle SOA Suite that provides message routing and mediation logic capabilities. OSB routing and mediation logic are modeled within an entity known as a message flow. A message flow defines a set of routing and transformation nodes between proxy services and a business service. A proxy service is an outbound interface meant to be used by external components, whereas a business service is a reference to an existing interface that may be invoked as part of an OSB message flow. OSB executes as a WebLogic Server application and is designed for high-throughput message processing. Beyond the capture of complex routing logic and message transformations (specified using the XQuery language), OSB supports a wide range of transport protocols (web services, EJB, JMS, MQ, FTP, and so on) and allows for a message flow's proxy service interface and protocol to be different from those of its business services, thus allowing for mediations at these levels.

OSB message flows can be configured directly on an OSB server instance through a web-based console or they can be developed within a development environment (through the Oracle Enterprise Pack for Eclipse) and deployed to an OSB server separately. The OSB web console provides a central management tool for the monitoring and management of message flows. The management capabilities of OSB allow for the central administration of security policies, logging, monitoring, and service-level agreement (in terms of quality of service policies such as average processing time) for all message flows and their services.

The SOA infrastructure components consists of a Service Component Architecture (SCA) based environment (see "Service Component Architecture [SCA] Primer" in the next section) for the creation, deployment, execution, and management of SCA composites. SOA Suite supports SCA composites containing components of the following types:

- **Business Process Execution Language (BPEL) and Business Process Modeling Notation (BPMN) processes** Two distinct component types used to define end-to-end business processes that involve orchestration of human user tasks, business rules, and service invocations

- **Mediations** Used to define mappings between system interfaces that need to be contained and managed within the scope of a composite application
- **Human Tasks** Used to define the detailed parameters (for example, a task escalation algorithm) of specific human interactions
- **Business Rules** Used to expose composite application parameters that need to be adjusted over time based on business needs
- **Spring Service Component** Used to create components that use the Spring framework to implement their logic using Java

Business Activity Monitoring (BAM) is the second key component of SOA Suite we will be discussing in this chapter. This component provides an infrastructure that allows for the central monitoring of key business metrics captured from SOA Suite composites as well as other applications within the enterprise. Finally, we will examine the User Messaging Service (UMS) component of SOA Suite. UMS provides a common infrastructure used by the SOA infrastructure and Oracle BAM to send different types of notifications (SMS, e-mail, and so on) to end users.

SOA Infrastructure

The SOA infrastructure (also referred to as the "SOA fabric") is the SCA runtime engine of SOA Suite. The development of SOA SCA composites that are deployed to the SOA infrastructure is done through Oracle JDeveloper. In this section, we discuss the SOA infrastructure and its deployment artifacts, SOA SCA composites, in terms of their runtime behavior and management capabilities.

Composite Container

All application business logic developed for the SOA infrastructure is in the form of SCA composites. SOA Suite developers design and implement an application's functional logic within the model of a composite using the

Oracle JDeveloper integrated development environment. The following screenshot shows the SCA composite design pane within JDeveloper.

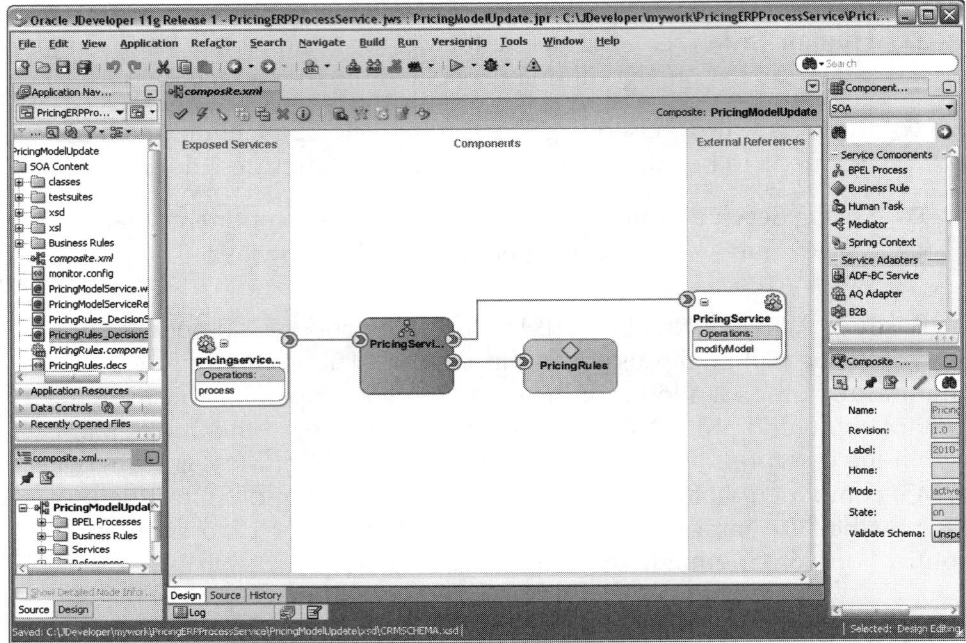

After the development of an SCA composite is completed, it is executed within a SOA infrastructure–enabled WebLogic Server runtime (from here on referred to as the SOA infrastructure container). The SOA infrastructure container can consist of a single managed server or a cluster of managed servers that have been created with the SOA Suite domain configuration template. This runtime executes the components of a composite within the context of a service engine that is effectively a container in its own right executing within the scope of the SOA infrastructure container. Each component implementation type is associated with its own service engine. Table 5-1 provides a description of each of the available SOA Suite component types.

Component Type	Description
BPEL and BPMN	BPEL and BPMN are specifications that allow for the modeling of business processes. Both specifications are supported as a component type in SOA Suite and both are executed within their own service engine. The choice of which specification should be used for the modeling of an application's business processes is a design decision that depends on a number of factors such as the expected level of post-deployment process customizations by business users (if more such customization are required, then BPMN is usually preferred) and whether the process is more geared toward the orchestration of system-to-system integrations as opposed to human workflow modeling (if so, then BPEL processes are usually preferred). BPMN processes can be created and modified at runtime through a web application called the BPM Composer, which is accessible by default on any SOA server at the /bpm/composer context root. The BPM Composer is meant for use by business users (instead of JDeveloper) for the design of business processes. The end result of BPM Composer is a composite—with a single component of type BPMN—that follows the same deployment life cycle as a composite developed through JDeveloper.
Mediator	The Mediator component type is used to implement interface mapping and message routing logic. Mediator components are generally used to implement adaptation logic between heterogeneous interfaces (through message transformations and/or protocol mediation) or to expose a façade interface that abstracts a set of internal interfaces.

TABLE 5-1. *SOA Suite Component Types*

Component Type	Description
Business Rules	BPEL, BPMN, and Mediator component types can use a Business Rule component to expose key decision parameters for runtime modifications by business users. A composite's Business Rules components can be modified at runtime through a web application known as the SOA Composer, which is accessible by default on any SOA server at the /soa/composer context root. The SOA Composer is meant for use by business users for the direct design and modification of business rules at runtime.
Human Task	The Human Task component type is used by other components to interact with end users through task assignments. The component implementation details the content of the task (for example, title, payload information, and so on) as well as its flow (escalation path, expiry rules, and so on). End users interact with human tasks through a task list application. SOA Suite servers have a default task list web application that can be accessed at the /integration/worklistapp context root. Additionally, custom task list clients can be created through a web service API provided by SOA Suite. Finally, Oracle WebCenter provides a worklist application within its Spaces component, which is described in more detail in Chapter 7. It is important to note that this component type's implementation leads to the assignment of tasks to a specific set of users, groups, or Oracle Platform Security Services (OPSS) application roles. Therefore, an important aspect of the deployment of composites with Human Task components is the provisioning of the appropriate users, groups, and OPSS application roles within the domain's identity and policy stores.

TABLE 5-1. *SOA Suite Component Types* (continued)

Component Type	Description
Spring Context	The Spring Context component type allows any Plain Old Java Object (POJO) that extends an interface available through a Spring Framework application context to form the implementation of a component within a SOA Suite composite. This component type is used to expose functionality developed directly in Java as a component to a composite.

TABLE 5-1. *SOA Suite Component Types* (continued)

In the next sections we discuss the life-cycle management and deployment model of the SOA infrastructure container. In line with the post-development scope of this book, we will not be discussing the implementation aspects of SOA Suite composites and instead focus on the aspects of the SOA infrastructure container's architecture that are most important for the post-composite implementation aspects of the management of a SOA Suite environment. For more information regarding the development of SOA composites, please refer to "Developer's Guide for Oracle SOA Suite" within the Oracle Fusion Middleware documentation library.

Service Component Architecture (SCA) Primer

A software application can be defined in terms its components and their interactions. In fact, that is one of the premises of object-oriented programming, which allows software programs to be defined in terms of objects abstracted through well-defined public interfaces that are used by other objects. As the size of a software program increases, however, the definition of interfaces at the object level alone become too granular, and different modules of the program—groups of objects, each with its own area of functionality—must be defined. Software engineering teaches us that in a well-designed application, these modules are highly cohesive and loosely coupled. Component-based development seeks to increase these attributes of the subsystems of a large software program by organizing its internals into components: a module that encapsulates all semantically related logic of the software programs and exposes a clearly defined interface with all information required for external entities to access its functionality. Enter Service Component Architecture (SCA), a specification that seeks to define a metadata-driven (XML) model for the description of software applications composed of loosely coupled components that can be implemented through different technologies.

Software applications defined through SCA consist of a set of components that are integrated to provide the application's functionality and together are referred to as an SCA composite. Within the application's composite, each component must define its type. The set of component types that can be used depends of the SCA platform being used. For SOA Suite, the available types are BPEL and BPMN processes, Business Rules, Java (through the Spring component type), and Human Workflow.

In addition to its type, each component can identify a set of services and references. A *service* is a description of the operations that the component exposes through a set of interfaces (for example, WSDL operations or Java interfaces) as well as the protocols and endpoints that can be used to access the component's interfaces through a set of bindings (for example, SOAP over HTTP or RMI-IIOP). A *reference,* on the other hand, is a pointer to other services (either internal to the composite or external) that are needed by the component. A reference contains a pointer to a description of the interface of its target service (for example, the service's WSDL in case of a web service) as well as the binding (for example, Oracle Advanced Queuing [AQ] or JMS) that the component intends to use when accessing the reference. In SCA terminology, the "wiring" of a one component to another indicates the creation of a reference from a source component to a destination component's service. It should also be noted that not all services and references require a binding: The protocol used for component interactions within a composite can be determined (and optimized) by the SCA runtime. Services and references, however, can be externalized at the composite level (meaning that a service becomes available for use by external entities, including other composites, and a reference points to an entity outside of the composite, such as an external JMS Queue) and only require a binding that explicitly identifies their protocols.

We can use an example to clarify some of the SCA concepts we covered in the previous paragraph. Imagine the creation of an SCA composite to encapsulate an application that implements an end-to-end business process for the handling of events that affect the pricing model for an enterprise pricing service. From the composite point of view, its external entities are the agents that produce price modeling change events (for example, ERP systems) and the pricing service that would need to be invoked with appropriate model modification messages based on the content of modeling change events. The external view of the composite and its services as well as references could therefore be represented by the following SCA diagram.

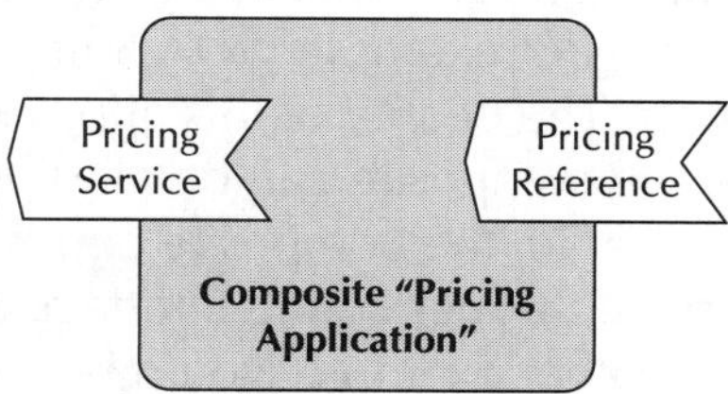

The internals of the composite consist of the individual components and their dependencies. In this case, the pricing composite contains two components: a Pricing Update Process component with a BPEL component type (that is, the implementation of the component is in BPEL) and a Pricing Rules component with a Business Rule (a proprietary SOA Suite technology) implementation type. The internal view of the composite and its components can be represented by the SCA diagram shown in Figure 5-1.

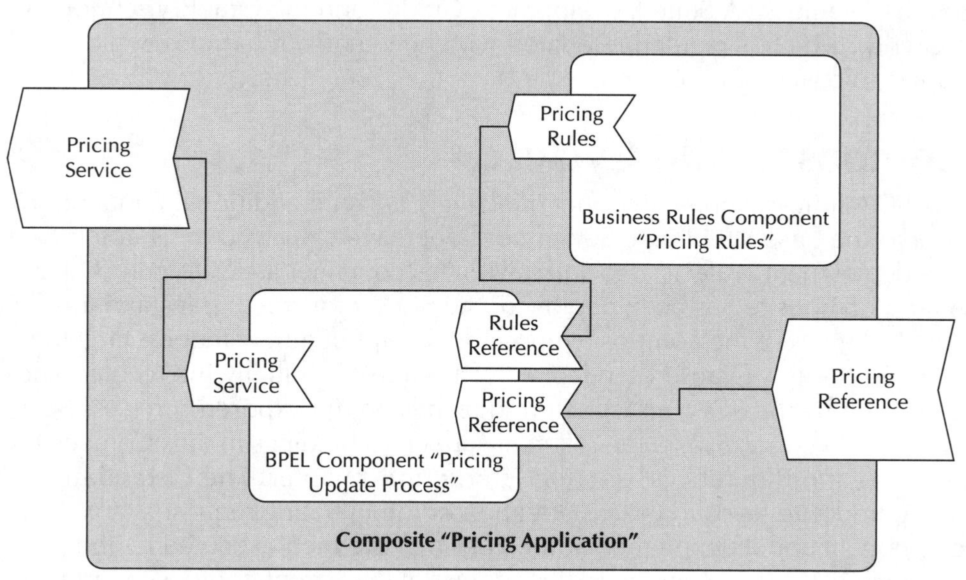

FIGURE 5-1. *Internal view of Pricing SCA composite*

Using an SCA modeling technology (such as the SOA Suite development capabilities exposed through JDeveloper), the content of the pricing composite would be captured in SCA metadata, which could in turn be deployed to an SCA runtime (for example, SOA Suite's SOA infrastructure SCA runtime) for execution. The beauty of this approach is that key internal and external elements of the composite can be modified in isolation with minimal impact. As an example, the composite could expose a new service that would expose its service through a JMS interface as well as its existing Web Services interface. Another example would be a scenario where the implementation of the Pricing Rules component would need to be changed from the Oracle Business Rules implementation to Java. In such a case, the implementation change can be made without any impact to the Pricing Update Process component or the composite's external interfaces so long as the Pricing Rules service's metadata is kept intact—something that should be easily doable given the clear separation of the interface information from the component's implementation logic, thanks to SCA.

This discussion was meant as a quick introduction to SCA and its merits. SCA is, however, a rich specification, the proper description of which would be worth a book on its own. For more resources regarding SCA, please refer to the "Oracle SOA Suite Development Guide" and the Oracle Technology Network, which is regularly updated with new material (articles, white papers, blogs) on the subject.

Composite Life Cycle

The SOA infrastructure container effectively adds an additional container type to the base WebLogic Server containers we reviewed in Chapter 2. The deployment artifacts associated with this container are SOA composites. After a composite has been deployed, the SOA infrastructure instantiates new instances of the composite upon the receipt of a new request targeted to a composite's exposed service. How a request is initially intercepted and processed by the SOA infrastructure depends on the exposed service's SCA bindings. We will discuss the different supported bindings in the "Composite Services and References" section later in this chapter. The instantiation of a composite leads to the instantiation of the initiating request's target component and its implementation types that are then executed by the component's service engine in the context of the parent composite instance and the initiating request. As an example, when a request is targeted to the "Pricing Service" (a service with a Web Service binding) of the composite illustrated in Figure 5-1, the following chain of events is triggered:

1. The SOA infrastructure creates an instance of the "Pricing Application" composite and executes the composite's "Pricing Service" interface with the incoming request's SOAP message.
2. The execution of the composite's "Pricing Service" interface leads to the instantiation of the "BPEL Component Pricing Update Process" component and its underlying implementation, which in this case is a BPEL process.
3. The BPEL process is executed within the SOA infrastructure's BPEL service engine with the incoming request's SOAP message.

To manage a composite's runtime behavior, each composite's component can be associated with an OWSM policy in the same fashion as web services endpoints can have such policies attached and detached, as we reviewed in Chapter 3. Components can have either security authorization (to allow for checking against the domain's OPSS policies) or management category policies. The attachment of these policies can be made either at the composite's development time through JDeveloper or after the composite has been deployed through Enterprise Manager. The assertions of the policies associated with a component are executed at component instantiation time (for example, step 2 in the preceding list). Each component implementation's transaction participation behavior is derived from the transactional properties of the services that it exposes and its implementation type's implicit transaction participation model (for example, BPEL processes are always executed within the context of at least a single JTA transaction).

In some cases (depending on the component's implementation type and nature) the SOA infrastructure persists the state of the composite instance to a database and passivates it until a particular event requiring the reactivation of the composite occurs. This process is known as "hydration," and the RDBMS tables to which the SOA infrastructure persists the state of the process is known as the "hydration store." As an example, any BPEL process that contains a receive node in the middle of its execution (requiring the process instance to wait until a new request message targeted to it is received) is automatically hydrated. When a SOA server is shut down, all existing active composite instances are lost except for those that had been hydrated.

Deploying Composites

SOA composites are packaged into a JAR file—known as a SOA Archive (SAR)—for deployment to a SOA server. Packaging of a SOA project's artifacts into a SAR file can be performed either through JDeveloper or by using the WLST sca_package command. To deploy SAR files to a SOA server, either JDeveloper, Enterprise Manager, or the WLST sca_deployComposite command can be used. When deployed to a SOA server, the SOA infrastructure stores the content within an MDS repository and activates the composites within it. After a SAR file's composites have been deployed, all management of its content is done at the composite level through SOA infrastructure WLST scripts and through Enterprise Manager. This is an important difference when compared to Java EE archives, which are deployed directly to WebLogic Server, and it is an implication of the fact that SAR files are not managed by the WebLogic Server deployment runtime and administration tools.

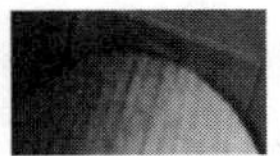

NOTE
SOA Suite composites are deployed (through SAR files) directly to the SOA infrastructure container and managed strictly by this layer. As such, they are not exposed for management through WebLogic Server–specific administration tools.

The SOA infrastructure persists its deployed composites through MDS. The MDS repository that the SOA infrastructure uses for this purpose is named mds-soa. By default, the SOA Suite domain configuration template configures this repository to use the same physical schema as the OWSM MDS repository, although this can be changed at domain configuration time. The mds-soa repository has a single MDS partition named soa-infra, with the following three subpaths. The first is named "deployed-components" and, as the name suggests, is the location under which all deployed composites are stored. Each subdirectory of the deployed-components path within the MDS repository is known as a SOA Suite deployment "partition," which should not be confused with an MDS partitions. When a composite is deployed, a deployment partition can be specified; if it is not, the default partition (named "default") is used. Partitions can be created and deleted through Enterprise Manager's SOA folder. The purpose of SOA Suite deployment partitions is to group related SOA composites that are deployed through separate SARs.
The second soa-infra subpath is named "soa," and it is used by the SOA

infrastructure for the storage of some of its internal configuration artifacts. The final soa-infra subpath is named "apps," and it is used for metadata artifacts that need to be shared among multiple composites. This shared content can be XSD, WSDL, or any other file that needs to be shared among a number of composites that are deployed as part of different SARs to avoid duplication. The content of this subpath is populated by bundling an MDS MAR file containing the shared metadata within a ZIP file along with any number of other SAR files. Such a SAR/MAR ZIP bundle (referred to as a SOA bundle) can be deployed directly to the SOA infrastructure. Composites that refer to elements within the shared subpath of the SOA MDS repository use the "oramds" suffix. As an example, the following reference from a component's BPEL process implementation refers to a WSDL file stored within the shared soa-infra MDS subpath:

```
oramds:/apps/PricingModelUpdate/PricingModelService.wsdl
```

The following diagram summarizes the organization of the SOA infrastructure mds-soa repository, as we have discussed so far in this section.

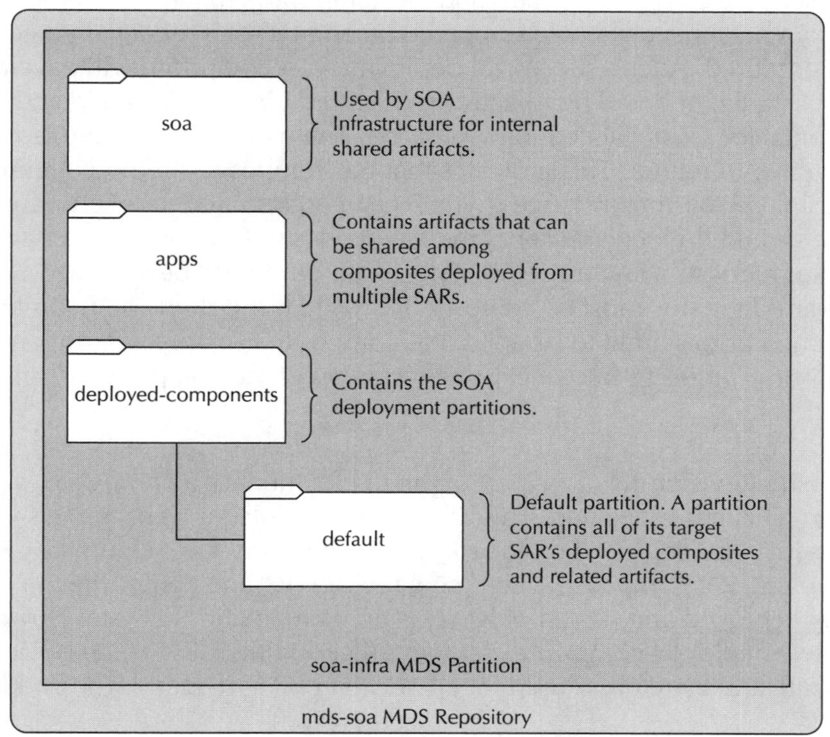

Prior to a composite being deployed, the security realm of the target SOA domain needs to be configured with an appropriate authentication provider as well as appropriate application roles within its policy store. Specifically, Human Task components can have explicit dependencies on the content of the domain's authentication provider's identity store as well as OPSS policy store application roles. The reason for this is that Human Tasks may contain task assignment algorithms that might expect a certain set of users, groups, or OPSS application roles to be present.

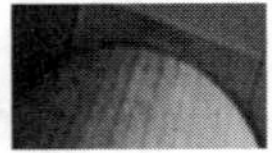

NOTE
Prior to the deployment of a composite, the target SOA domain's authentication provider and OPSS policy store need to be seeded with the appropriate users, groups, and application roles.

Once deployed, the state of a composite is determined by two different parameters: the composite's status and the composite's mode. The composite's status can be either started or stopped. The composite's mode can be either active or retired. After a successful deployment, a composite will have a status of started and will be in active mode. Only in such a started/active state can a composite accept new requests. The mode of a composite can be switched to retired. This indicates that the composite should continue processing all existing instances (which resulted from requests processed so far) but should no longer accept any new requests. To allow the composite to accept requests again from this state, its mode should be switched back to active and its status must be set to started. When the status of a composite is switched from started to stopped, the composite not only will no longer process new requests, but all existing instances of the composite are also aborted.

Composite Revision ID As part of the deployment of a composite, a revision ID can be specified. This allows for multiple versions of the same composite to be deployed on the same SOA infrastructure. Upon the deployment of a composite with a new revision ID, the composite that is already deployed and has an older revision ID maintains its state. However, the newly deployed composite assumes all endpoints URIs of the older composite and therefore is used for all new incoming requests. The endpoint

URIs of the older composites is changed to include their old revision ID. This SOA Suite capability allows for multiple versions of the same composite to be actively deployed on the same SOA Suite domain, with only the latest one processing new requests from existing clients, but with older versions allowed to coexist and be explicitly accessible by clients through their versioned URI endpoints.

Configuration Plans Oftentimes SOA Suite composites must reference external resources that can have different endpoint coordinates, depending on their environments. As an example, an external web service that is invoked by a BPEL process would have a development and QA environment service endpoint URI that differs from the one in the production environment to ensure that testing activity does not impact the production system's state. Obviously the implementation of such changes through direct modifications of the SAR's content or through modification of the composite's JDeveloper project would be highly inefficient. To accommodate for the effective management of such environment-specific changes at deployment time, SOA Suite provides a mechanism known as configuration plans. Configuration plans are similar in concept to WebLogic Server deployment plans, except that instead of acting on a deployment archive's deployment descriptors, they are used for accommodating the configuration changes required by the XML files (for example, WSDLs, XSDs, or composite.xml) contained within a SAR. Configuration plans can be attached to a single SAR or a SOA bundle file using either JDeveloper or SOA Suite's WLST deployment commands. The following listing is an example of a SOA configuration plan that, when used, replaces all instances of the local host URI string within the SAR file's WSDL and XSD files with a URI string pointing to the production URI http://myenterprise.com:8080:

```
<?xml version="1.0" encoding="UTF-8"?>

<SOAConfigPlan xmlns:jca="http://platform.integration.oracle/blocks/
adapter/fw/metadata"
               xmlns:wsp="http://schemas.xmlsoap.org/ws/2004/09/policy"
               xmlns:orawsp="http://schemas.oracle.com/ws/2006/01/policy"
               xmlns:edl="http://schemas.oracle.com/events/edl"
               xmlns="http://schemas.oracle.com/soa/configplan">
  <wsdlAndSchema name="*">
    <searchReplace>
      <search>http://localhost:7002</search>
      <replace>http://myenterprise.com:8080</replace>
    </searchReplace>
  </wsdlAndSchema>
</SOAConfigPlan>
```

Configuration plans provide a flexible way of tailoring a SOA composite application's content for different environments throughout its life cycle without the need for direct modifications.

Composite Services and References

A deployed composite can expose services that allow external entities to consume its functionality. A service exposed by the composite is described by the SCA services element within the composite.xml file. The services element is key in enabling the decoupling of a composite application's implementation from its interfaces, which (as we discussed in this chapter's introduction) is one of the key Service-Oriented Architecture principles. As we will see in this section, SOA Suite offers a large number of service types, ranging from standard SOAP/HTTP web services to a pure TCP-based socket service. However, thanks to SCA and SOA Suite's implementation of it, the actual business logic encapsulated within a composite's component implementation is completely independent from the interface types that it can be associated with through a service. This is in great contrast to the application deployment artifacts deployed to WebLogic Server application containers we reviewed in Chapter 2, where the application's implementation type (for example, servlet) is tightly coupled with the type of interface it can offer (for example, HTTP only for a servlet). The following is a snippet for the description of a service exposed as a web service:

```
<service name="pricingserviceprocess_client_ep"
           ui:wsdlLocation="PricingServiceProcess.wsdl">
    <interface.wsdl
interface="http://xmlns.oracle.com/PricingERPProcessService_jws/
PricingModelUpdate/
PricingServiceProcess#wsdl.interface(PricingServiceProcess)"/>
    <binding.ws port="http://xmlns.oracle.com/PricingERPProcessService_jws/
PricingModelUpdate/PricingServiceProcess#wsdl.
endpoint(pricingserviceprocess_client_ep/PricingServiceProcess_pt)"/>
</service>
```

A composite can also have dependencies on services exposed by external entities that may need to be invoked as part of its components' implementation logic. Such dependencies are described through SCA reference elements within the composite.xml file. The following is a composite.xml's reference snippet for a reference of type HTTP binding:

```
<reference name="pricingServiceHTTP"
            ui:wsdlLocation="pricingServiceHTTP.wsdl">
    <interface.wsdl interface="http://xmlns.oracle.com/pcbpel/adapter/http/
PricingERPProcessService/PricingModelUpdate/
pricingServiceHTTP#wsdl.interface(Request_Response_ptt)"/>
    <binding.ws port="http://xmlns.oracle.com/pcbpel/adapter/http/
PricingERPProcessService/PricingModelUpdate/pricingServiceHTTP#wsdl
.endpoint(pricingServiceHTTP/Request_Response_pt)"
                location="pricingServiceHTTP.wsdl" supports="http">
      <property name="http.verb" type="xs:string" many="false">POST
      </property>
      <property name="endpointURI" type="xs:string"
any="false">http://myenterpriseapphost/products</property>
      <property name="http.payload" type="xs:string" many="false">xml
      </property>
    </binding.ws>
</reference>
```

Composite services and references are described through two elements. The first is an interface element. For a service, the interface describes the operations that are made available by the endpoint, whereas for a reference, the interface points to the description of the dependent interface's operations. In SOA Suite, interface descriptions are always provided either through the SCA interface.wsdl element, which references the portType element of a WSDL file, or through the SCA interface.java element, which references a Java interface. For a service, the interface's abstract WSDL is generated at development time by the SOA Suite JDeveloper service creation wizards. The second element that describes a composite's service or reference is the binding element. The binding describes the transport protocol and endpoint coordinates of the service or reference. The way bindings describe this information is different for each type of service or reference. The following sections describe the available SOA Suite service and reference types as well as the attributes of the binding associated with each.

Web Services

Web service SCA services are used to accept SOAP messages over an HTTP protocol and by default use the WebLogic Server listen address and port (although this can be changed through the SOA Administration common properties described later in this chapter) for receiving such messages.

The details of the service's binding are specified through a reference to a concrete WSDL that is generated by the SOA Suite infrastructure at composite deployment time based on the service interface's abstract WSDL (generated at development time). The service type can be associated with predefined OWSM policies at development time or at runtime through Enterprise Manager. Additionally, the transaction participation model of a web service binding can be controlled using WS-Atomic Transaction property elements that specify the service's transaction participation level, as follows:

- **Never** No transaction participation occurs.
- **Supports** If the request is associated with an existing transaction, the composite's execution will participate in that transaction.
- **Mandatory** Same as Supports, except that a fault is returned if the request is not associated with a transaction.

The web service binding effectively allows SOA Suite composites to act as a third type of implementation to the two existing WebLogic Server web services implementation types (that is, POJO and EJB) we covered in Chapter 2. It is, however, worth noting that strictly speaking, the web service is not managed by the WebLogic Server web services container (either JAX-WS or JAX-RPC) but that it is managed by a web services container provided by the Fusion Middleware infrastructure layer.

Composite web service references have the same characteristics as the service type, except that instead of exposing a web service interface, the reference is used for invoking such an interface and therefore only client-side OWSM policies are applicable. Web service references also provide the extra WS-Atomic Transaction property element of WSDL Driven, which indicates that the transaction participation model is dictated by the target web service's WS-Atomic Transaction directives contained within its WSDL.

HTTP

The HTTP services and references are typically used for enabling a Representational State Transfer (REST) style service interface. Services with an HTTP binding accept HTTP messages either through URL encoding for POST and GET messages or optionally through an XML payload for POST messages.

Messages are received through the WebLogic Server listen address and port, and the service can be associated with predefined OWSM policy types. No transaction propagation is possible for this type of service. Just like a service of type web service, an HTTP service's binding details are also described through a concrete WSDL generated at deployment time.

Composite HTTP references have the same characteristics as the service type, except that instead of exposing an HTTP interface, the reference is used for producing such messages and directing them at a service of the same type.

Application Development Framework Business Components

The Application Development Framework (ADF) Business Component (BC) service binding is used to provide an interface that accepts XML messages over an RMI protocol. The attributes of the message and the RMI endpoint are described through a web services WSDL. No transaction propagation is possible and no OWSM policies can be associated with this type of service. Security propagation happens automatically when the caller of the service is deployed within the same domain or within a different domain with domain trust established. To access this type of service, clients use the SOA Suite Fusion Middleware Infrastructure Management Java API. The ADF BC service binding does not have any specific relationship with ADF as the name might suggest.

When used on a reference, the ADF BC binding can be used by BPEL process component types to interact with ADF BC application module web services. The ADF BC features allow for applications to interact with an RDBMS database through an abstract object model—exposed by the web service using a specification known as Service Data Object (SDO). BPEL processes can use ADF BC references to interact with ADF BC objects through a special type of process variable known as entity variables. We will be discussing ADF and its Business Components capabilities in more detail in Chapter 6.

Java Connector Architecture

Java Connector Architecture (JCA) based service and reference bindings are characterized by the fact that the integration point they expose (either for inbound messages through a service or outbound messages through a reference) is managed by an underlying JCA adapter deployed to the SOA WebLogic Server instance. The SOA domain configuration template configures a number of JCA adapters for the purpose of enabling this type of binding. Table 5-2 describes the different types of JCA-based bindings (as well as their associated JCA adapter deployment archive name) that a SOA Suite composite can expose. Note that the Oracle Applications JCA adapter used to integrate with Oracle Applications such as E-Business Suite is not listed within this table because its description is beyond the scope of this book.

In a number of cases—as called out in Table 5-2—the JCA adapter associated with the binding type needs to be configured at the WebLogic Server level in order for a composite that contains a service or reference using the binding type to be deployable. In such cases, the JCA adapter needs to be configured with an outbound connection pool instance through

Type/Adapter Name	Description	Transport Protocol
Database/ DbAdapter	■ Service type used to initiate a request whenever a specific table undergoes any changes. ■ Reference type used to call a stored procedure or function in Oracle or MS SQL RDBMS databases, perform an SQL operation, or execute a SQL script. ■ An adapter connection pool instance needs to be configured for each data source being used by deployed composites.	Determined by the JDBC driver of the data source used

TABLE 5-2. *JCA Service and Reference Binding Types*

Type/Adapter Name	Description	Transport Protocol
File/ FileAdapter	■ Service type used to read the content of a file or list the set of files (and related typical file system information such as size, path, and last modification date) from a specific location on the server's file system. ■ Reference type used to write content to a file.	Not applicable because no remote invocation is involved
FTP/ FtpAdapter	■ Service type used to perform FTP GET operations from a specific location on an FTP server. ■ Reference type used to perform FTP PUT operations to a specific location on an FTP server. ■ An adapter connection pool instance needs to be configured for each FTP server being used by deployed composites.	FTP
AQ/ AqAdapter	■ Service type used to perform a dequeue operation on an AQ queue. ■ Reference type used to perform an enqueue operation on an AQ queue or to perform an enqueue operation (to put in a request message) followed by immediate dequeue operation (to receive the corresponding response message). ■ An adapter connection pool instance needs to be configured for each AQ server being used by deployed composites.	AQ proprietary

TABLE 5-2. *JCA Service and Reference Binding Types* (continued)

Type/Adapter Name	Description	Transport Protocol
MQ/ MqAdapter	■ Service type used to perform GET message operations on an MQ queue. ■ Reference type used to perform PUT message operations on an MQ queue. ■ An adapter connection pool instance needs to be configured with the server connection information of each MQ server being used by deployed composites.	MQ proprietary
JMS/ JmsAdaper	■ Service type used to perform receive or subscribe operations on JMS destinations (queue or topic, respectively). ■ Reference type used to perform send or publish operations on JMS destinations. ■ The JMS binding can be used to provide integration points with WebLogic Server JMS server destinations or third-party JMS servers through the creation of a foreign JMS provider at the WebLogic Server level. ■ An adapter connection pool instance needs to be configured for each JMS connection factory being used by deployed composites.	Protocol dictated by target JMS provider (for WebLogic Server that is T3)

TABLE 5-2. *JCA Service and Reference Binding Types* (continued)

Type/Adapter Name	Description	Transport Protocol
Socket/ SocketAdapter	■ Service type used to perform receive operations on a specific TCP socket endpoint. ■ Reference type used to perform request or synchronous request/ reply (where the send operation on the socket is followed by an immediate receive to obtain a response message) operations on a TCP socket endpoint. ■ An adapter connection pool instance needs to be configured for each socket TCP endpoint being used by deployed composites.	TCP
Oracle BAM	■ The Oracle BAM binding type is used on reference endpoints only and allows for the modification of Oracle BAM objects on a specific Oracle BAM server instance. ■ An adapter connection pool instance needs to be configured for each Oracle BAM server being used by deployed composites.	HTTP or RMI

TABLE 5-2. *JCA Service and Reference Binding Types* (continued)

WebLogic Server using the admin console or WLST. The connection pool instance needs to be appropriately configured with properties for the adapter to be able to connect to the target integration point of the composite's associated binding as well as a JNDI name that corresponds to the binding's configured JNDI name (for all composites that use the adapter) to allow the deployed composite to appropriately reference the correct connection pool for its desired integration point. The following diagram illustrates this configuration for the database adapter that needs to be configured with the JNDI name of its target JDBC data sources.

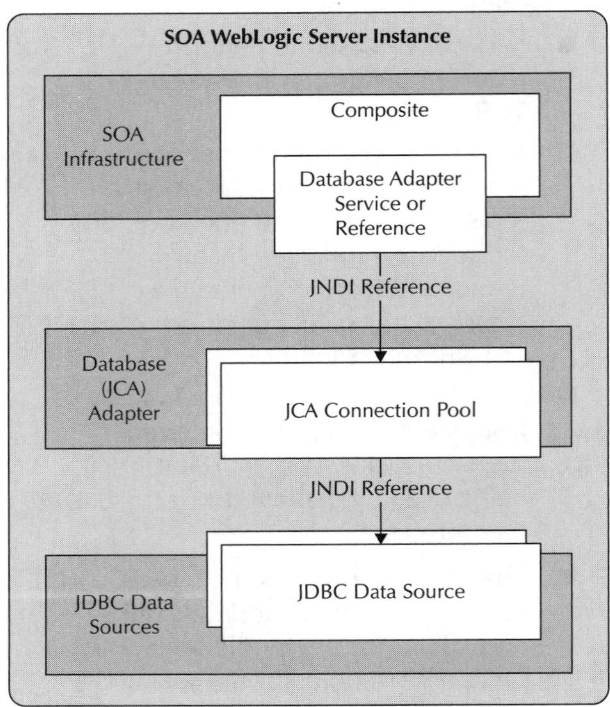

The configuration required for each type of JCA adapter is complex and can vary depending on the scenarios involved (for example, using secure FTP, setting up authentication, and so on). A thorough discussion of each adapter's required configuration prior to the deployment of composites is beyond the scope of this book. The reader is instead referred to "Oracle Fusion Middleware User's Guide for Technology Adapters," which offers a detailed discussion of each adapter type and its configuration requirements.

Enterprise Java Beans

The Enterprise Java Beans (EJB) service binding is used to expose operations that can be invoked by external entities as a stateless session bean EJB. The EJB reference binding allows components to invoke an existing external EJB. In both cases, the interface can be described in two ways. The first is through WSDL (using a interface.wsdl element), in which case invocations (both inbound and outbound) are performed via a web service (SOAP over HTTP) call and the parameters of the operations in question are marshaled into XML format (using the SDO specification). The second is through a Java-based interface (using an interface.java element), in which case invocations are performed via the standard EJB RMI-IIOP protocol.

Direct

The direct service binding is used to provide a proprietary Oracle interface. This binding can be used by other SOA Suite composites or by Oracle Service Bus (OSB) message flows. It allows for both security context (Subject) and transaction propagation and is more efficient than other remote protocols. When used as a reference binding, it allows a composite to invoke services of other composites with direct binding interfaces as well as OSB message flows.

In concluding the discussion of SOA Suite services and references, it is worth noting that no matter which service type is used to instantiate a SOA composite, the SOA infrastructure uses the standard WebLogic Server request management infrastructure for all requests received through any of the composite's service endpoints. In fact, each SOA Suite server has a dedicated WebLogic Server Work Manager (named wm/SOAWorkManager).

NOTE
The SOA infrastructure is configured with a dedicated WebLogic Server Work Manager (called wm/SOAWorkManager) for the processing of composite requests.

This Work Manager is responsible for the prioritization of all requests targeted to deployed SOA composites on a specific WebLogic Server instance.

Composite Management

As with the rest of the Oracle Fusion Middleware products, the main tools available for the management of a SOA Suite environment are Enterprise Manager and WLST. SOA Suite exposes functionality specific to its administration in both of these tools. In this section we will be reviewing the core elements of this functionality.

Enterprise Manager

When the SOA Suite domain creation templates are used to create or extend a domain, the Enterprise Manager capabilities of that domain are extended by these templates to include SOA Suite management tasks. This capability is then exposed within Enterprise Manager through the SOA folder as illustrated next.

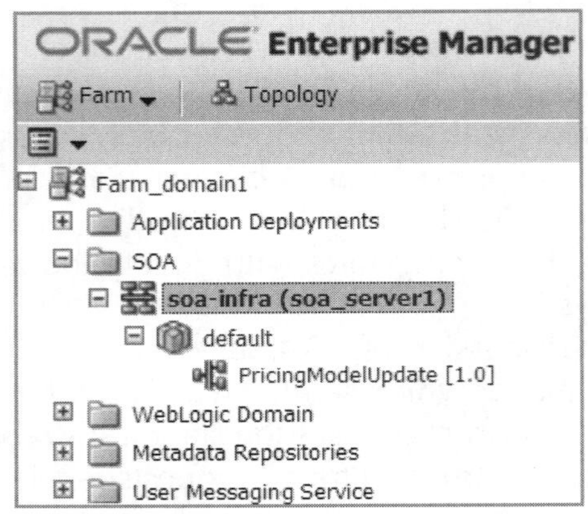

It should be noted that the SOA management folder is only available through Enterprise Manager when one or more managed servers that have been configured within the SOA infrastructure in the domain are up and running. The folder tree structure, as illustrated here, is divided into three nodes. Each root node of the SOA folder, known as a "soa-infra" node, represents either a WebLogic Server managed server (when not clustered) or cluster that was created with the SOA domain configuration template and therefore enabled with the SOA infrastructure components. Under each such node is a list of the SOA deployment partitions, which as we discussed in the "SOA Composite Container" section is a grouping mechanism for the management of deployed composites. Finally, under each partition is a list of composites deployed to it. In addition to the general composite life-cycle management capabilities provided by the SOA Suite Enterprise Manager features—such as composite deployment and composite state management—each node level under the SOA folder provides a subset of management functionality at its respective scope, as described in the following sections.

Metrics Monitoring Two types of metric information are available through the SOA Enterprise Manager pages. The first set of metrics is displayed through the dashboard graphs (or optionally table) showing historical trends such as the number of active composite instances and runtime faults that might have been raised by them. The second set of metrics is per composite and component instance statistics, such as the number of running instances, number of faults, and total execution time. These metrics are captured by the SOA infrastructure, persisted in its database, and exposed as Dynamic Monitoring Services (DMS) metrics, as we reviewed in Chapter 3. The following screenshot shows an example of SOA runtime metrics exposed through Enterprise Manager.

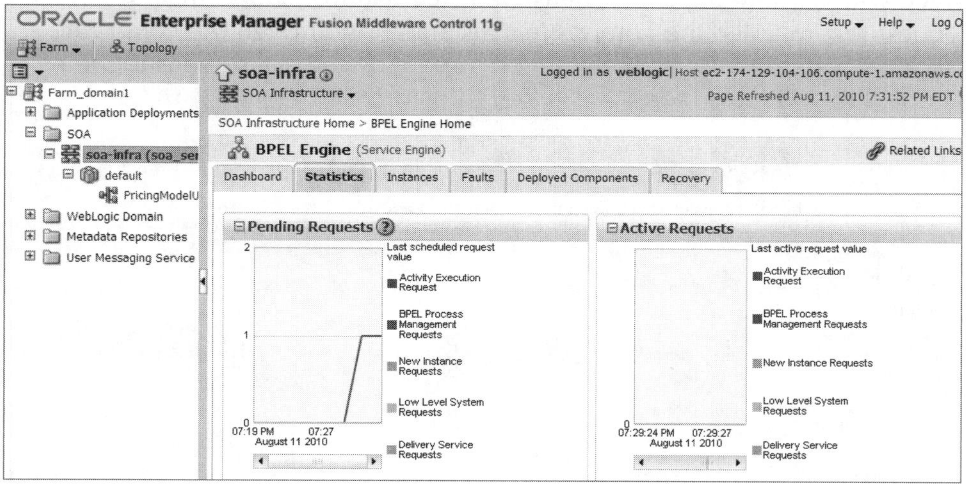

The level of audit metrics captured by the SOA infrastructure can be controlled through the SOA administration properties pages, as discussed in the "SOA Infrastructure and Service Engine Properties" section.

Service and Reference Properties An important management feature of SOA Suite exposed through Enterprise Manager is the ability to dynamically modify the properties associated with a composite's services and references. As we reviewed within the "Composite Services and References" section, each different component binding type exposes properties that control the behavior of the interfaces it exposes. SOA Suite allows for the properties associated with any service or reference bindings to be modified through the composite's Enterprise Manager "Services and References" window. This capability allows for the modification of binding attributes in staging or production environments without the need for the composite's redeployment.

A sample scenario where this capability can be useful is the modification of the PhysicalDirectory property of the JCA File adapter binding, which allows the customization of the PhysicalDirectory used by this binding for the reading or writing of file content.

Instance Flow Trace SOA Suite exposes Enterprise Manager composite instance management capabilities for both active (that is currently under execution) as well as completed instances. Instance information can be browsed by clicking the instance ID of a composite and using the Flow Trace window that pops up. The Flow Trace window shows the path of the request that initiated the composite's instantiation through the composite's services, components, and references. The following is a screenshot of a sample Flow Trace window.

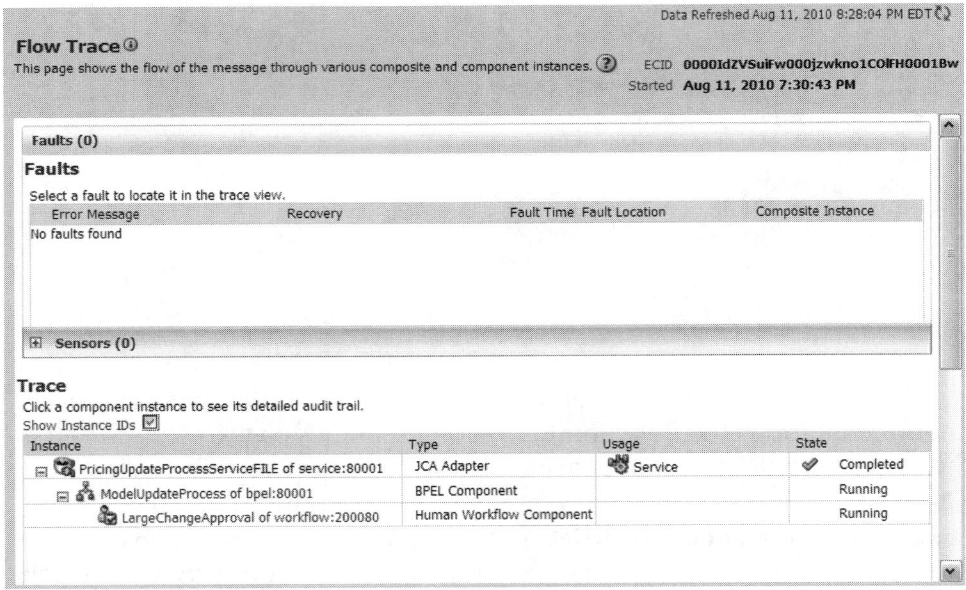

The Flow Trace window allows for a drill down into each component of the request's path by clicking the component name within the composite instance Flow Trace page. The drill-down information provided for each component is dependent on its type but is generally concerned with the details audit trail of the elements of the component that have executed, the faults that might have been raised, step-by-step performance statistics, and the component's latest state.

The Enterprise Manager SOA pages also provide an audit trail of all of the composite instance's execution history, which can be viewed in the dashboard tab and further analyzed within the instances tab, with detailed query capabilities that allow for the narrowing down of the audit search to a specific point in time or for composites with specific instance ID, name, or conversation ID attributes. The instance search capabilities exposed through the lower-level nodes of the SOA management folder provide more detailed query capabilities as their scope is narrowed to a specific composite or component type. The instance history information is managed by the SOA infrastructure runtime components and is stored within the SOA RDBMS schema configured at domain-creation time.

The level of flow trace information captured by the SOA infrastructure can be controlled through the SOA administration properties pages as discussed in the "SOA Infrastructure and Service Engine Properties" section.

SOA Infrastructure and Service Engine Properties Through the SOA Infrastructure node of the Enterprise Manager SOA folder, it is possible to access a SOA Administration menu that provides access to a set of pages for setting common and service engine–specific runtime properties. These enterprise manager pages are used to view and modify properties that are specific to the SOA infrastructure. These properties control the behavior of the SOA infrastructure container and are exposed as a set of common infrastructure MBeans. A set of these MBeans can be modified through the pages accessed through the SOA Administration option's "properties" items. However, the complete list of properties is available through the Enterprise Manager system MBeans browser. Some notable SOA properties include the settings to control the composite life-cycle audit behavior and the URI endpoint parameters that should be used for the compilation of a composite's web services endpoints as part of its concrete WSDL generation. The BPEL, BPMN, Mediator, and Human Task service engines also expose properties that allow for the tuning of their specific runtime parameters, such as their transaction and thread management setting. We will be reviewing some of the specific MBean properties of the SOA Administration properties pages in more detail in Part II of this book.

Composite Fault Management The execution of a composite can lead to errors that result in runtime faults that are managed by the SOA infrastructure. The Enterprise Manager capabilities of SOA Suite allow for a detailed examination of such faults and in some cases fault recovery options.

Sensors and Sensor Actions

Sensors are entities that are added to SOA Suite composites at design time in order to expose specific instance data for detailed monitoring. A good analogy to describe sensors is as debugger "watches" that allow developers to identify specific variables to be monitored as part of a debugging session. In the same way, sensors allow for the runtime monitoring of specific composite variables. At the time of this writing, SOA Suite only makes available sensors at the BPEL process level and, with some limitations, at the composite service and reference level. Within a BPEL process, the following three types of sensors can be enabled:

- **Variable sensors** Variable sensors identify a specific BPEL process variable for runtime monitoring.
- **Activity sensors** Activity sensors are similar to variable sensors, except that they are associated with a specific BPEL activity (or group of activities) and are only triggered—that is, the variable information they are associated with is exposed—when the activity has reached a specific life-cycle event (activation, completion, and so on).
- **Fault sensors** Fault sensors identify a specific BPEL process fault for runtime monitoring.

The information targeted by a sensor is, by default, exposed at runtime for detailed monitoring within a BPEL process instance's Flow Trace page. BPEL process developers can, however, choose to expose sensor information to other channels. The mechanism by which this is achieved is known as a sensor action. Sensors are associated with sensor actions at design time. A sensor action allows for sensor information to be sent to the following targets:

- **JMS destination** Both local server JMS destinations as well as JMS destinations accessed through the SOA Suite JMS adapter can be configured as targets.
- **Database** This target ensures that the sensor information is persisted within the SOA Suite RDBMS schema.
- **Java class** Targets the sensors information to a POJO that implements a specific SOA Suite interface. This target allows for a customized sensors information handling mechanism.

- **Oracle Business Activity Monitoring (BAM)** Targets a data object within an Oracle BAM server instance. We will be reviewing the capabilities of this type of sensor action in more detail in the "Oracle Business Activity Monitoring" section of this chapter.

SOA Suite also allows for the definition of sensors that are associated with composite services and references. In such cases, the sensor exposes the payload of the binding associated with the service or reference. Only database sensor actions can be associated with composite sensors. The following diagram illustrates the function of sensors and sensor actions within SOA Suite.

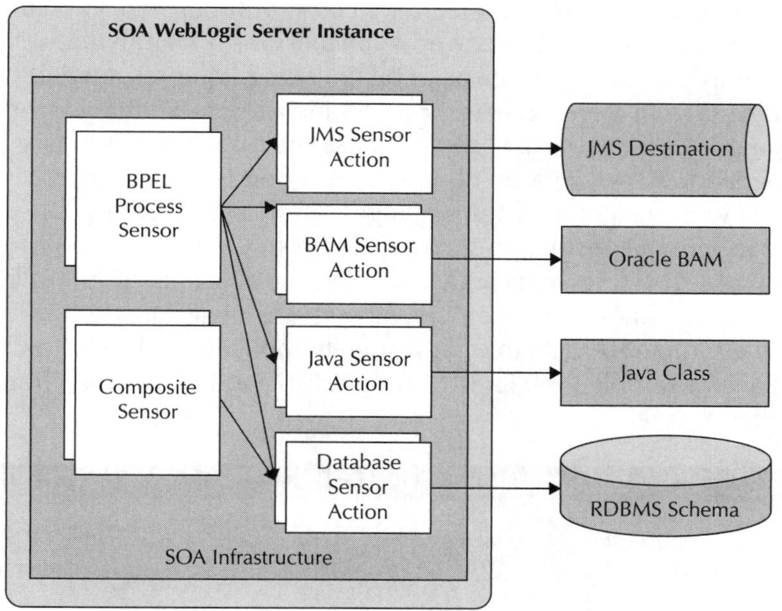

WebLogic Scripting Tool

As with other Fusion Middleware products, the SOA infrastructure can be managed through WLST scripts and commands. The WLST shell within the SOA Suite Oracle home directory's /common/bin path is used to execute such commands. For a detailed description of these commands, please refer to the "WebLogic Scripting Tool Command Reference" document within the Oracle Fusion Middleware documentation library.

Oracle Business Activity Monitoring

Oracle Business Activity Monitoring (BAM) is a component of SOA Suite that enables the capture of runtime application data and its processing, aggregation, and exposure in the form of real-time business reports. Using Oracle BAM, business users can have access to targeted notifications and dashboards that expose real-time application data in a business-user-friendly format using elements such as Key Performance Indicators (KPI), graphs, and tables.

Oracle BAM data objects and reports form the core elements of Oracle BAM from an end user point of view. Oracle BAM data objects are data structures typically defined by a technical user with business knowledge—using the Oracle BAM Architect web application—to identify the application information that needs to be collected and presented to business users. Once Oracle BAM objects for a specific application have been defined, a power business user can then use the Oracle BAM Active Studio web application to define a set of reports. A report is a web page that lays out a set of widgets (graphs, tables, gauges, and so on) that displays updated information from a specific set of data objects. In Oracle BAM terminology, each such object is known as an active view set. Once a report has been defined, other business users can view the results of an Oracle BAM report through the Oracle BAM Active Viewer web application. The following is a screenshot of a sample Oracle BAM report displayed within the Oracle BAM Active Viewer.

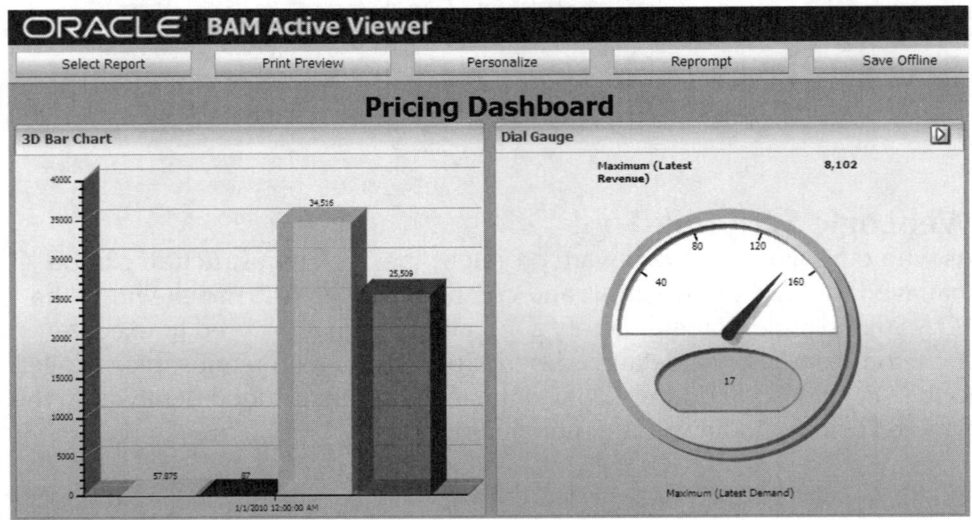

The following sections provide an overview of the Oracle BAM architecture and management capabilities.

Oracle BAM Components and Architecture

Figure 5-2 shows the different Oracle BAM components and their dependencies.

At the highest level, the Oracle BAM functionality is separated into two layers: the Oracle BAM Server layer the Oracle BAM Web layer. When a domain is created using the Oracle BAM domain configuration template, the components of both of these layers are targeted to the same WebLogic Server instances (named by default "bam_server1").

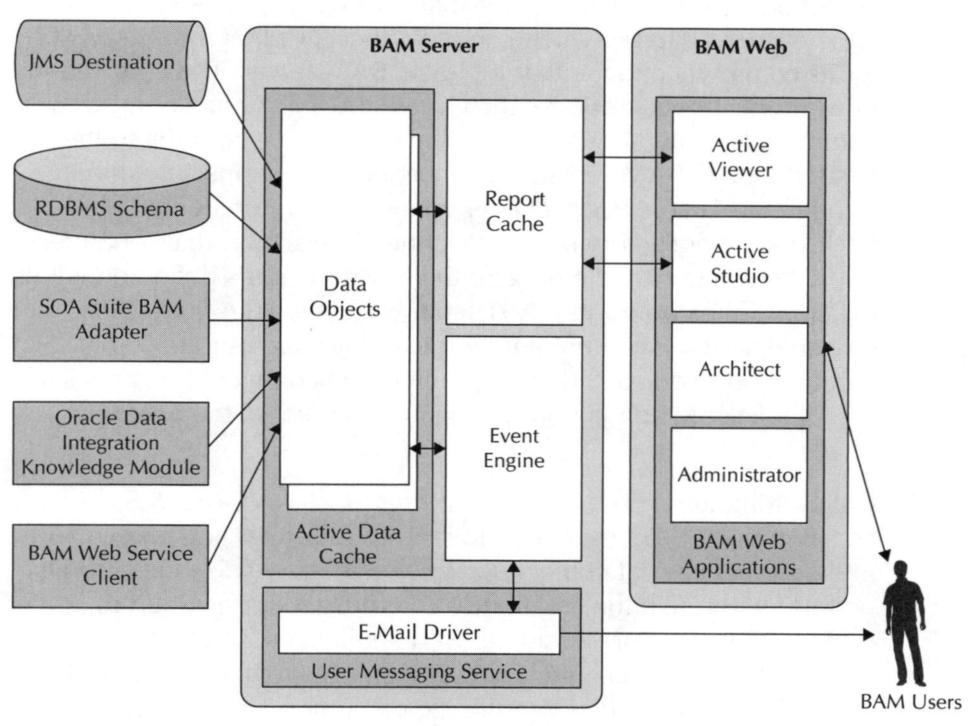

FIGURE 5-2. *Oracle BAM Architecture*

Oracle BAM Server

The Oracle BAM Server layer contains all of the components responsible for collecting information from various sources and mapping this information to specific data objects. Data object information update requests are targeted to the Oracle BAM server by external sources as Oracle BAM commands. An Oracle BAM command can be of type insert, upsert (insert and/or update), update (applied only if object already exists), or delete. The Oracle BAM server can be integrated with the following integration points for receiving data object update commands:

- **SOA Suite composites** SOA Suite composites can send data to an Oracle BAM server instance by using the Oracle BAM reference type or, in the case of BPEL components, through the use of Oracle BAM sensor actions. Both of these mechanisms use the SOA Suite JCA Oracle BAM adapter, which can use either RMI/IIOP or SOAP/HTTP for its communication with the Oracle BAM server. The connection pool connection factories of the Oracle BAM JCA adapter need to be configured—using the WebLogic Server console—to point to the desired Oracle BAM server. The choice of protocol is determined through the Oracle BAM adapter connection factory (either RMIConnectionFactory or SOAPConnectionFactory) that is pointed to by the composite reference or the sensor action's definition within the SOA Suite composite. By default, when the SOA Suite and Oracle BAM domain configuration templates are used in conjunction to create a domain, both of the connection factories of the Oracle BAM adapter are configured to point to the domain's Oracle BAM server.
- **JMS destinations** The Oracle BAM server can act as a JMS consumer to a JMS destination to receive messages and subsequently interpret them as data object update commands. This integration is performed through the creation of Enterprise Message Sources (EMS) using the Oracle BAM Architect web application. Integration with external JMS providers (including third-party providers such as IBM MQ Series) is performed through the configuration of a WebLogic foreign JMS provider, as described in Chapter 2.

- **RDBMS schemas** The Oracle BAM server can use the content of an existing RDBMS schema as its data object model. This integration is enabled through the creation of External Data Sources (EDS) using the Oracle BAM Architect web application. Each EDS points to a single RDBMS schema. Oracle BAM uses its own JDBC connection management mechanism (as opposed to using WebLogic Server JDBC data sources). To create an EDS, the JDBC driver classes needed must be made available to the Oracle BAM server instance's class loader (best performed by dropping the JDBC driver JAR file within the domain's /lib directory, as discussed in Chapter 2). Once an EDS is created, data objects can be defined that map their fields to the content of specific tables within the schema referenced by the EDS. Updates to such database tables will automatically lead to updates to the associated Oracle BAM data objects.
- **Oracle Data Integrator (ODI)** Oracle Data Integrator (ODI) is an Extract, Transform, Load (ETL) tool that can handle a wide variety of different types of data sources. Oracle BAM is packaged with a set of ODI 10.1.3 knowledge modules (note that ODI 11*g*R1 is currently not supported for this integration type) that can be used to allow an ODI installation to send update commands to an Oracle BAM server. A discussion of the configuration of the ODI integration with Oracle BAM is beyond the scope of this book; for detailed instructions on enabling such integration, please refer to the "Using Oracle Data Integrator with Oracle BAM" chapter of the "Developer's Guide for Oracle SOA Suite" document within the Oracle Fusion Middleware document library.
- **Oracle BAM web services** The Oracle BAM Server layer exposes a web service interface (WSDL exposed on BAM server instances at /OracleBAMWS/WebServices/ICommand?WSDL) to allow for the creation of web services clients that can update Oracle BAM data objects.

Once update commands are received through any of these channels, the Oracle BAM server updates an instance of the targeted Oracle BAM data object (or, if the object does not exist and the command is upsert or insert, it creates a new instance) based on the incoming command's content. The server component responsible for maintaining the state of the data objects is known as the Active Data Cache (ADC). As illustrated in Figure 5-2, two separate Oracle BAM server components actively monitor the content of the ADC. The first is the event engine, which is responsible for enforcing all configured alerts within an Oracle BAM server instance. Oracle BAM alerts are rules that are configured based on the content of the ADC data objects and lead to the server performing a specific action. These can be the dispatching of e-mail messages (through the User Messaging System, which is discussed in more detail later in this chapter), the triggering of other alert rules, the deletion of data object instances, and, finally, the invocation of a specific external web service (which can be performed securely using WS-Security user name token headers). The second component monitoring the content of the ADC is the report cache. The report cache is the server-side component that manages the state of the reports being viewed by active reports (that is, reports currently open within Oracle BAM web sessions either through the Active Viewer or Active Studio web applications). It is responsible for maintaining the current set of data objects needed by all active reports as changes are made to the underlying data within the ADC.

Oracle BAM Web

The Oracle BAM web layer contains a set of web applications that deliver the BAM functionality to end users (this functionality is, in fact, deployed as a single Web Application deployment archive). All BAM web applications can be accessed on the BAM web WebLogic Server at the /OracleBAM context root. The web applications available are as follows:

- **Oracle BAM Active Studio** Used by business users (usually expert, or otherwise referred to as "power" users) to create Oracle BAM reports based on the existing set of data objects within the Oracle BAM server ADC. Once completed, reports can be published for use by all BAM users (through the BAM Active Viewer). Beyond the management of reports, Active Studio is also used for the creation of Oracle BAM alerts that allow for the creation of rules that lead to specific actions (dispatching of an e-mail, invocation of a web service, deletion of a specific data object instance, or triggering of another alert). Active Studio uses the Oracle BAM server reports cache to ensure that all open reports are updated as the underlying data objects change.

- **Oracle BAM Active Viewer** Used by business users to view specific reports that were created through Active Studio. Open reports are updated through integration of the web application with the Oracle BAM server reports cache component.
- **Oracle BAM Architect** Used by technical users familiar with the business requirements of the BAM reports that need to be created. This application is the tool used for the definition of data object structures, enterprise messaging sources, and external data sources. Just like the Oracle BAM Active Studio, this application can also be used for the creation of Oracle BAM alerts. As part of its data object management capabilities, Oracle BAM Architect also allows for the addition of security filters with each data object that allows for the access control of Read, Update, and Delete permissions for specific users or groups. By default, all new data objects created have full access permission by all users and have no associated security filters.
- **Oracle BAM Administrator** Used by administrators for two primary purposes. The first is the management of the users and roles required for the security permissions of BAM data objects and report folders. The second is the creation of distribution lists that can be used as targets for Oracle BAM alerts that require the dispatch of an e-mail. The next section contains a more detailed discussion of BAM users and roles.

With an understanding of the Oracle BAM architecture and components in mind, we can now turn our attention to the product's management concepts and tools.

Oracle BAM Management

Oracle BAM administration is performed through three different interfaces: the BAM Administrator web application, which was introduced in the previous section, the BAM ICommand command-line interface, and Enterprise Manager. Oracle BAM is one of the few Oracle Fusion Middleware components that, as of the time of this writing, does not offer a set of WLST administration commands.

Oracle BAM Administrator Web Application and User Management

The Oracle BAM administrator web application is used for the management of BAM users, application roles, and e-mail distribution lists. Note that this tool does not provide capabilities for the provisioning of users and roles: Oracle BAM users must exist within the server's authentication providers, and the BAM application roles are managed as generic OPSS roles through Enterprise Manager, as reviewed in Chapter 4. Instead, the BAM Administrator web application is only used to associate additional properties (such as e-mail address) with specific users and groups and to browse the BAM roles and privileges that are associated with them. The Oracle BAM e-mail distribution lists, which are also created through the Oracle BAM administrator web application, are used for the creation of e-mail alerts as well as for the e-mail dispatching of reports to a group of users.

It is important to note that for users to be available to an Oracle BAM server—and therefore viewable within the Oracle BAM Administrator web application—they need to be explicitly registered. This is due to the fact that Oracle BAM uses its own security store (within the Oracle BAM schema) for the storage of data object security policies, which includes an internal representation of the users they relate to. These policies are defined through the security filter functionality of the Oracle BAM Architect web application. The registration of users with an Oracle BAM server allows for the provisioning of such policies within the BAM security store. This registration is performed implicitly when a user logs in to any of the Oracle BAM web applications. Additionally, Oracle BAM provides a command-line interface (named registerusers and located within the SOA Suite ORACLE_HOME/bam/bin directory) that allows for the explicit registration of users with a BAM server.

Oracle BAM ICommand

ICommand is a command-line tool that allows for the management of a BAM server's data objects, alerts rules, reports, and folder hierarchies. ICommand is located within the SOA Suite ORACLE_HOME/bam/bin directory. The tool can accept explicit operation input directly from the command line or instead use an XML command file. The following is a sample ICommand command file for deleting two separate data objects:

```
<OracleBAMCommands>
  <Delete name="/Pricing/PricingUpdateProcessEvent" />
  <Delete name="/Pricing/PricingDemandAttributes" />
</OracleBAMCommands>
```

The server upon which ICommand executes is determined through the content of the ORACLE_HOME/bam/config/ BAMICommandConfig.xml, which must be modified to have its <ADCServerName> and <ADCServerPort> element values point to the desired Oracle BAM server target. The operations available through ICommand are export, import, rename, clear, and delete. The export and import commands can be used to move the content of an Oracle BAM schema (data objects, reports, alerts, and so on) from one environment to another. As an example, the following command generates an XML file that contains all of the information of a BAM server's repository within a file named PricingBAMExport.xml:

```
icommand -cmd export -ALL 1 -FILE ./PricingBAMExport.xml
```

The following is a sample snippet of the resulting file generated by this command showing the content of a data object named PricingUpdateProcessEvent:

```
  <DataObject Version="14" Name="PricingUpdateProcessEvent"
ID="_PricingUpdateProcessEvent" Path="/Pricing" External="0">
    <Layout>
      <Column Name="Product SKU" ID="_Product_SKU" Type="integer" Nullable=
"0" Public="1"/>
      <Column Name="Latest Demand" ID="_Latest_Demand" Type="integer"
Nullable="0" Public="1"/>
      <Column Name="Latest Revenue" ID="_Latest_Revenue" Type="integer"
Nullable="0" Public="1"/>
      <Column Name="Current Price" ID="_Current_Price" Type="integer"
Nullable="0" Public="1"/>
      <Column Name="Update Time" ID="_Update_Time" Type="timestamp"
Nullable="0" Public="1"/>
      <Indexes>
        <Index>
          _SKU</ID>
          <Name>SKU</Name>
          <FieldName>_Product_SKU</FieldName>
        </Index>
      </Indexes>
    </Layout>
    <Contents>
      <Row ID="1">
        <Column ID="_Product_SKU" Value="1212"/>
        <Column ID="_Latest_Demand" Value="10"/>
        <Column ID="_Latest_Revenue" Value="4623"/>
        <Column ID="_Current_Price" Value="42"/>
        <Column ID="_Update_Time" Value="2010-08-22T15:41:41.0000560EDT"/>
      </Row>
```

```
<Row ID="2">
  <Column ID="_Product_SKU" Value="1212"/>
  <Column ID="_Latest_Demand" Value="12"/>
  ...
```

In a similar fashion, via the use of the import command, the content of the PricingBAMExport.xml file can be imported into a BAM schema within another environment. It should be noted that beyond the import and export commands, which are not exposed through any other Oracle BAM interface, the remaining ICommand operations can be performed through the Oracle BAM Architect web application. ICommand, however, allows for the scripting of the provisioning of an Oracle BAM environment.

Enterprise Manager

Oracle BAM exposes its performance monitoring, logging, and configuration capabilities through Enterprise Manager. In terms of performance management, both the BAM Server and BAM Web layers expose component-specific monitoring metrics as Dynamic Monitoring Services (DMS) metrics. The log management capabilities of Oracle BAM are implemented through the Oracle Diagnostic Logging (ODL) framework and are therefore used in the same manner as discussed in Chapter 2. Oracle BAM also contributes a set of common infrastructure MBeans for the management of its Server and Web layers. The most commonly changed set of these properties is exposed for direct modification through the Enterprise Manager BAM Server and BAM Web properties options available through the respective context menu of these nodes within the Enterprise Manager tree. However, as was the case for the SOA infrastructure properties, Oracle BAM has a more substantial set of MBeans that can only be modified through the Enterprise Manager system MBeans browser. The MBeans properties available for modification on the BAM server properties page include the persistence mechanism of the server report cache, ODI integration configuration settings, and the e-mail address to be used for dispatch of alert action error notifications. The MBeans properties that are available for modification on the BAM web properties page are the base URL that should be used by Oracle BAM to generate the access URL for newly created reports (this should always be set to the base URL of the BAM web server) and the host name of the BAM server layer used for cases where the BAM Web and BAM Server layers are deployed to different manager servers.

We review some of the specific MBean properties of the BAM Server and Web layers in more detail in Part II of this book.

User Messaging Service

SOA Suite composites allow applications to integrate with a wide variety of system endpoints. However, in many cases, applications must interact not only with other systems but also directly with end users. The Human Task component type provides one way of implementing such a communication path, but its capabilities are mainly designed for task-flow-based interactions and require users to use a specific client (the task list UI) to interact with the application. In many cases, however, what is required is the ability to interact with users through richer messaging mechanisms such as e-mail, SMS messages, voice mail, or instant messaging. This capability is provided by the SOA Suite User Messaging Service (UMS) component. Using UMS, applications can interact directly with end users through different types of messaging protocols. End users can, in turn, configure the system with a set of preferences (such as their phone numbers or e-mail addresses) that should be used by UMS for its interactions.

UMS consists of two primary types of components: the UMS server and UMS drivers. The UMS server is a Java EE application that provides the core of the UMS functionality. It is responsible for the interaction with its consumer applications (that need to send or receive end-user notifications) and interactions with UMS drivers, which are the entities responsible for providing the actual integration with the different types of end-user messaging endpoints. The Fusion Middleware Components that integrate with UMS are as follows:

- **SOA Suite BPEL processes** BPEL processes can use UMS activities to send instant message, e-mail, text message, or voice mail notifications to end users. The type of notification can be explicitly set as part of the BPEL process definition or could be left unspecified, in which case the user's preferred notification mechanism is used.
- **SOA Suite Human Tasks and Worklist** Human Tasks can be configured to use UMS in order to send e-mail notifications upon a change to a task's state. The SOA Suite Worklist application can also be configured to initiate tasks at the receipt of messages from UMS channels.

- **Oracle Business Activity Monitoring (BAM)** Oracle BAM uses UMS to execute alert rules that require the dispatching of e-mail messages as well as to allow for the e-mailing of reports through the Active Studio web application. As such, BAM servers only require the configuration of a UMS e-mail driver.

The UMS server is deployed to the same WebLogic managed servers (or clusters) that are configured as part of a SOA Suite domain by the virtue of the SOA Suite domain configuration template. This includes both SOA infrastructure managed servers and Oracle BAM managed servers. The UMS drivers are JCA deployment archives and in order to be used must be deployed to the same deployment targets as the UMS servers after the domain's creation (the e-mail driver is the only one that is deployed by default through the domain configuration template). The deployment and registration of these drivers is performed through the WLST deployUserMessagingDriver command. It should be noted that within a SOA Suite domain, the configuration of the UMS server and its drivers is managed on a per-managed-server basis, even when the servers are part of a cluster. As a result, configuration changes applied to these components must be performed on every managed server independently.

NOTE
UMS configuration changes must be made independently for each managed server within a SOA Suite domain.

UMS provides drivers for the following types of endpoints: Instant Messaging, E-mail, VoiceMail (using VoiceXML), SMS Text (using SMPP), and the SOA Suite Human Task worklist. UMS driver configuration is performed through a UMS-specific abstraction layer—as opposed to direct modification of the JCA deployment archive properties—that is exposed through configuration MBeans, Enterprise Manager, and WLST. Because the UMS server effectively acts as a messaging provider, it has a message store, in the form of a dedicated RDBMS schema, for persisting undelivered messages. Finally, it is important to note that to be operational, all UMS drivers must be configured with their associated gateway. As an example, for the e-mail driver to be able to send outbound messages, it must be configured with the coordinates of an SMTP server. The SOA Suite Human Task driver is special in this regard because its gateway is effectively a SOA Suite server. For this reason, this driver is not registered through the deployUserMessagingDriver WLST command but is instead deployed through the oracle.ums.driver.worklist_template_11.1.1.jar domain configuration extension template located within the SOA Suite ORACLE_HOME/common/templates/applications directory. This template deploys a composite (named sca_sdpmessagingsca-worklist-composite_rev1.0.jar) to the SOA infrastructure, and the human task UMS driver interacts with this composite in order to create human tasks as a result of UMS notifications. Table 5-3 shows the underlying protocol and the type of interaction (sending messages out to end users, receiving messages from end users, or both) supported by each of the available UMS drivers.

Driver	Gateway Communication Protocol	Supported Interaction Type
Instant Messaging	Extensible Messaging and Presence Protocol (XMPP)	Send/receive
E-mail	SMTP for sending. POP or IMAP for receiving.	Send/receive
VoiceMail	VoiceXML	Send
SMS Text	Short Message Peer-to-Peer (SMPP)	Send/receive
SOA Suite Human Task	Web service (SOAP/HTTP)	Send

TABLE 5-3. *User Messaging Service Drivers*

The following diagram illustrates the UMS architecture using the E-mail and SMS Text drivers as an example.

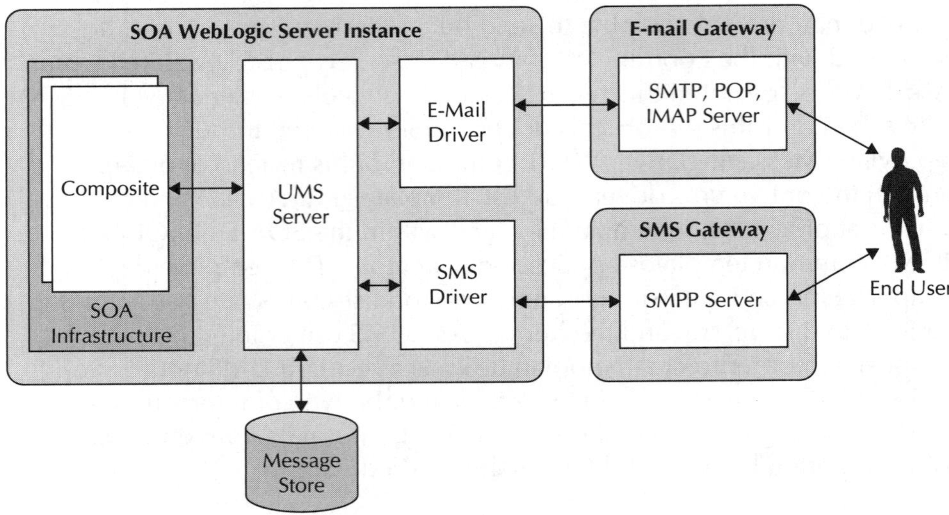

For a detailed discussion of the configuration required for enabling the different types of UMS drivers, please refer to the "Administrator's Guide for Oracle SOA Suite and Oracle Business Process Management Suite" document within the Oracle Fusion Middleware document library.

Chapter Use Case

In this chapter, we pick up where we left off in the use cases of Chapters 3 and 4. In Chapter 3, we went through the steps required for the creation of the topology shown in Figure 3-2, with the pricing application deployed to its own cluster, its web interface accessible through a fronting OHS instance, and its web service interface secured using OWSM. In Chapter 4, we proceeded to configure this domain with a central LDAP server and configure it for Single Sign-On (SSO) perimeter authentication with Oracle Access Manager. In this section we will proceed with deploying to this domain a SOA Suite composite that orchestrates the integration of the pricing application's model update web services with the corporate ERP system and exposes update data through Oracle BAM.

Use Case Description

The project team has completed its work on the SOA Suite artifacts required for the integration of the corporate ERP system with the pricing application's model update web service, and you have been asked to work with the team on deploying these artifacts to the pricing application's WebLogic Server domain, which you have set up in a staging environment. In a meeting with the development team, you are given an overview of the SOA Suite artifacts, which consist of a SOA Suite composite (named Pricing Model Update) as well as an Oracle BAM data object and associated report. The JDeveloper SCA view of the SOA Suite composite is shown here.

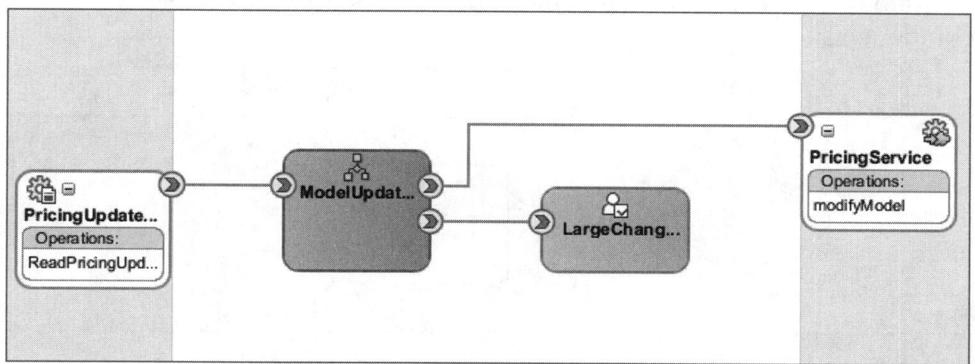

The development team explains that the SOA composite exposes a service with a File Adapter binding configured to poll a specific directory (/myerp/erp-in) for files containing pricing update messages from the ERP system. Once the service is invoked, it initiates a BPEL process that defines the orchestration flow for performing a model update on the pricing application's web service. The process logic of the BPEL process is outlined as follows:

- If the request is for the update of a product that has a current price higher than $100, then the model update requires human approval from the marketing product management group.

- If the product does not require update approval or update approval is granted, then the update to the pricing application's model is made by first mapping the data from the ERP system message to the input expected by the pricing application's web service and then invoking the service.
- Finally, the BPEL process is configured with a BAM sensor action that updates an Oracle BAM data object with the parameters of the pricing model update that is received by each request. The data object is, in turn, used within a BAM report that allows the specialty product group to have a live view of the latest updates being applied to the pricing model.

Based on this information, you jot down the following logical architecture diagram of the existing pricing application's interaction with the SOA Suite components.

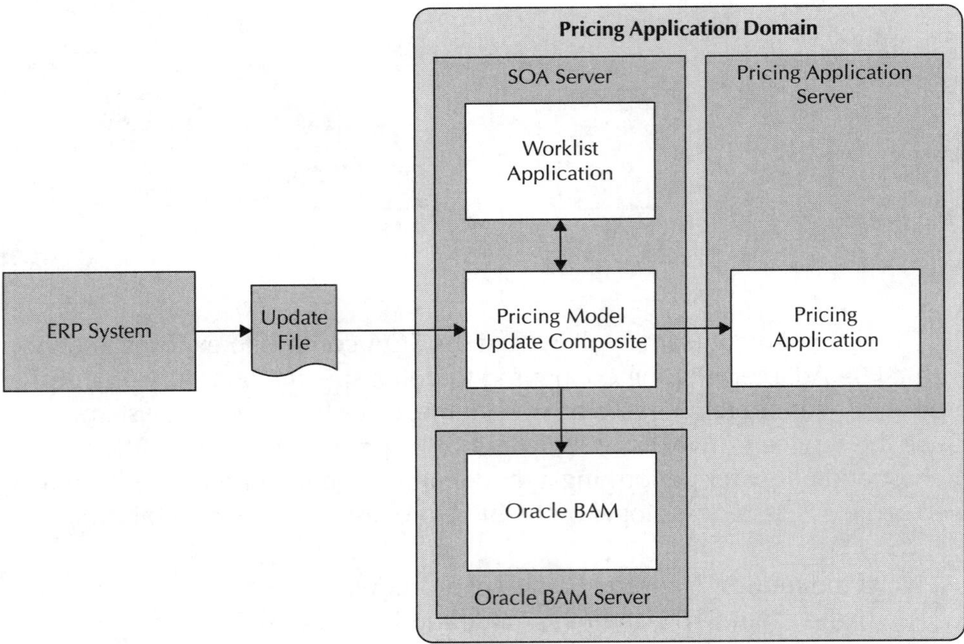

You proceed to query the business development team on the usage of the SOA Suite worklist and Oracle BAM web applications and find out that the users of these two applications are the members of the specialty products business development team. Furthermore, the only Oracle BAM web application that is needed for use is the Active Viewer, because end users will not be required to create their own reports or data objects and will be using Oracle BAM for monitoring purposes only. The development team also confirms that the SOA composite's Human Task component's task owner parameter (the entity that determines the user to which tasks are assigned) is set to the PricingAnalysts OPSS application role. Before concluding the meeting, you ask the development team to produce the following so that you can proceed with the deployment of their artifacts in the staging environment:

- A SOA Archive (SAR) JAR file for the Pricing Model Update composite
- An Oracle BAM ICommand export file containing the definition of the pricing data object and report

With the information you needed in hand, you proceed to plan the deployment of the new SOA Suite artifacts for the pricing application.

Provisioning the Appropriate Users, Groups, and Roles

Your first order of business in preparing the existing application environment for its new SOA Suite deployments is to ensure that the right users, groups, and roles are provisioned. The domain's security realm is now (as per the configuration steps discussed in Chapter 4's use case) configured with an authentication provider that points to the company's central LDAP server. Because the domain is also configured with the default authentication provider, which points to the WebLogic Server embedded LDAP, you do not need to explicitly create the SOA infrastructure system principals (that is, the OracleSystemUser belonging to the OracleSystemGroup group) because they are created by default within the embedded LDAP of the domain by the SOA Suite domain configuration templates. With the existence of the new central LDAP authentication provider, you can also be sure that the domain has access to all of the employees of the specialty product team (in fact, it has access to all of the users within the company). With this knowledge, you proceed to create the PricingAnalysts role for the SOA Suite worklist application and associate it with the specialty product team members' user IDs through a WLST script. The following is the beginning snippet of that script, showing the createAppRole command followed by repeated calls to the grantAppRole command to associate the appropriate users with the role:

```
createAppRole(appStripe="worklistapp", appRoleName="PricingAnalysts ")
grantAppRole(appStripe="worklistapp",appRoleName="PricingAnalysts",
principalClass="weblogic.security.principal.WLSUserImpl ",
principalName="djones")
grantAppRole(appStripe="worklistapp",appRoleName="PricingAnalysts",
principalClass="weblogic.security.principal.WLSUserImpl ",
principalName="mparker")
grantAppRole(appStripe="worklistapp",appRoleName="PricingAnalysts",
principalClass="weblogic.security.principal.WLSUserImpl ",
principalName=tsmith")
```

Next, you need to make sure that these users can have the appropriate access to Oracle BAM. To do this, you first register the users with the Oracle BAM server through the registerusers command, as follows:

```
./registerusers -file ./pricing_bam_users.txt
```

You use the content of the input file pricing_bam_users.txt shown here:

```
-adminuser weblogic
-host myenterprisehost1
-port 9001

djones
mparker
tsmith
```

These steps make these users available to the BAM server for the setting of data object permissions, but do not allow the users to access any of the BAM web applications. To do this, you need to ensure that the users are associated with one of the following Oracle BAM OPSS application roles:

- **BAMAdministrators** Have access to all Oracle BAM functionality, including all BAM Web interfaces.
- **BAMReportArchitects** Have access to the BAM Architect, Report Studio, and Report Viewer interfaces

- **BAMReportCreators** Have access to the BAM Report Studio and Report Viewer interfaces
- **BAMReportViewers** Have access only to the BAM Report Viewer interface

Because the specialty product's business development team only needs to access Oracle BAM for viewing the single, predefined, pricing report, you associate all of the users with the Report Viewer role through the WLST grantAppRole command. You use this command on the Oracle BAM application stripe for each user, as follows:

```
grantAppRole(appStripe="oracle-bam#11.1.1",
appRoleName="BamReportViewers",
principalClass="weblogic.security.principal.WLSUserImpl",
principalName="djones")
```

Note that for the pricing application, the creation of the Oracle BAM data objects and reports is never performed directly on the staging or production environment and is always controlled through Oracle BAM import/export commands. However, if the application required direct modification and creation of data objects and reports by end users on the production system, you would have had to assign the appropriate Oracle BAM roles other than BAMReportViewers to these users.

Provisioning the SOA Composite

With the provisioning of the users, groups, and application roles complete, you are now ready to deploy the composite you have now received from the development team as a SAR file (sca_PricingModelUpdate_rev1.0.jar) and placed within the staging host's /tmp directory. Because the URI of the pricing application web service is different on the staging environment compared to the URI of the test web service that the development team has been using on its development hosts (and is therefore contained within the SAR file's composite content), you create a SOA configuration plan XML file that uses the <wsdlAndSchema> element to map all of the references to the test URI within the composite to the pricing application's staging URI, as follows:

```
<?xml version="1.0" encoding="UTF-8"?>

<SOAConfigPlan xmlns:jca="http://platform.integration.oracle/blocks/
adapter/fw/metadata"
```

```
                xmlns:wsp="http://schemas.xmlsoap.org/ws/2004/09/policy"
                xmlns:orawsp="http://schemas.oracle.com/ws/2006/01/policy"
                xmlns:edl="http://schemas.oracle.com/events/edl"
                xmlns="http://schemas.oracle.com/soa/configplan">
  <wsdlAndSchema name="*">
    <searchReplace>
      <search>http://localhost:7002</search>
      <replace>http:// myenterprisehost1:8080</replace>
    </searchReplace>
  </wsdlAndSchema>
</SOAConfigPlan>
```

You then attach the deployment plan to the SAR file using the following WLST command:

```
sca_attachPlan("/tmp/sca_PricingModelUpdate_rev1.0.jar",
"/tmp/configplan.xml")
```

You are now ready to deploy the SAR, and you choose to perform the deployment using WLST through the following command, which uses the URI of the SOA infrastructure managed server (soa_server1):

```
sca_deployComposite("http://myenterprisehost1:8001",
    "/tmp/sca_PricingModelUpdate_rev1.0.jar")
```

At this point the pricing update composite has been deployed, but its reference still needs further configuration. The reference to the pricing web service will not work as is because that service is protected with an OWSM wss_username_token_service_policy, which was not the case for the test service used within the development environment. To allow the composite's reference to invoke the pricing web service, you need to attach to it an OWSM wss_username_token_client_policy. You can do this through the following WLST command:

```
serverConfig>attachWebServiceClientPolicy(None, 'default/
PricingModuleUpdate[1.0]','soa','PricingService',
'PricingModelServicePortTypePort','wss_username_token_client_policy')
```

Note that the user name and password that will be used by the reference's service invocations are, by default, obtained from the OPSS credential store key configured with the client policy through the OWSM policy configuration page in Enterprise Manager. However, at policy attachment time, the credential store key that needs to be used for the specific client can be overwritten through the Enterprise Manager's SOA Reference attributes page, as shown here.

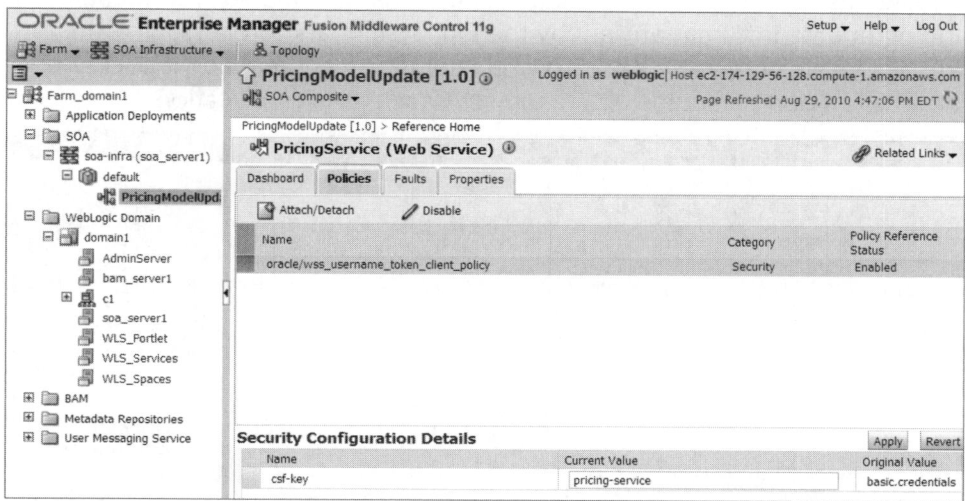

Because you have already configured the default credential store key for this policy (as part of Chapter 4's use case), you do not need to create a specific configuration for the policy attachment. With the attachment of this client policy, the composite is now operational in that it will be able to receive messages from the ERP system, execute the business logic contained within its two components, and invoke the pricing service when appropriate. However, the BAM sensor action of the BPEL process within the composite will not function at this point because you have not ensured that the Oracle BAM server contains the appropriate data object and report.

Configuring Oracle BAM

To populate the Oracle BAM repository with the pricing application's data object and report, you simply execute the following ICommand import operation using the export file provided to you by the development team:

```
icommand -cmd import -FILE ./PricingBAMExport.xml
```

Note that the content of the PricingBAMExport.xml file was generated by the development team by running the ICommand export operation on the Oracle BAM server that is used by the specialty product team to create a single Oracle BAM business object (with the path /Data Objects/Pricing/PricingUpdateEvent) and a single Oracle BAM report (named Pricing Update History). The report contains a table that is updated with the latest pricing update information sent by the ERP system and processed by the Pricing Update composite's BPEL process component. The following screenshot shows this report within the Active Viewer Oracle BAM application.

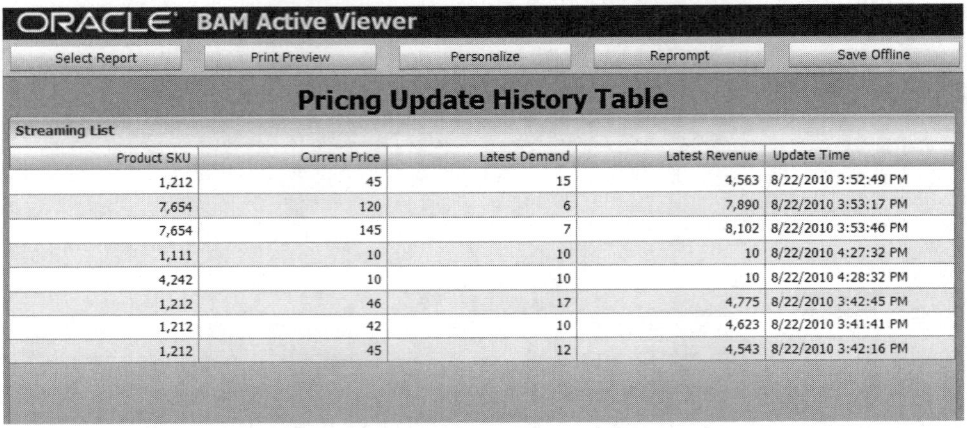

ORACLE BAM Active Viewer

Select Report | Print Preview | Personalize | Reprompt | Save Offline

Pricng Update History Table

Streaming List

Product SKU	Current Price	Latest Demand	Latest Revenue	Update Time
1,212	45	15	4,563	8/22/2010 3:52:49 PM
7,654	120	6	7,890	8/22/2010 3:53:17 PM
7,654	145	7	8,102	8/22/2010 3:53:46 PM
1,111	10	10	10	8/22/2010 4:27:32 PM
4,242	10	10	10	8/22/2010 4:28:32 PM
1,212	46	17	4,775	8/22/2010 3:42:45 PM
1,212	42	10	4,623	8/22/2010 3:41:41 PM
1,212	45	12	4,543	8/22/2010 3:42:16 PM

With the population of the Oracle BAM repository, the provisioning of the pricing application's SOA Suite elements within the staging environment is now complete.

Conclusion

In this chapter we reviewed the architecture and management capabilities of the core SOA Suite components. These components consist of the SOA infrastructure, Oracle Business Activity Monitoring (BAM), and the User Messaging Service (UMS). In our review of the SOA infrastructure, we saw how its SCA-based container complements the core WebLogic Server application containers by allowing for the deployment of composite applications that can be made up of heterogeneous interfaces and implementation technologies. We then moved on to a discussion of Oracle BAM, which allows for the capture of business data from a variety of sources, including SOA composites, and their display in reports using a variety of widgets relevant to the business users. Finally, we discussed UMS, an infrastructure that allows Fusion Middleware components to interact with end users through different messaging mechanisms such as e-mail, instant messaging, and text.

CHAPTER 6

Oracle Application Development Framework

his chapter introduces the Oracle Application Development Framework (ADF). The chapter begins with a description of the architecture of enterprise applications built using ADF technology and continues by exploring the operational aspects of administering such applications. The chapter concludes with a brief discussion of the upgrade and environment-to-environment migration of ADF applications.

Introducing ADF

Oracle ADF builds on Java Enterprise Edition (Java EE) standards to provide a complete framework for implementing service-oriented applications and highly interactive user interfaces. Applications built with this framework provide enterprise solutions across different platforms and can also integrate with various other open-source technologies. The framework supports applications to search, display, create, modify, and validate data for the web using web services, desktop user interfaces, or user interfaces for mobile devices. Oracle ADF simplifies Java EE development, through a metadata-driven framework, by minimizing the need to write code that implements the application's infrastructure and thus allowing users to focus on the features and the business logic of the application. An application built using the ADF User Interface (UI) components, which are part of the ADF framework, can seamlessly take advantage of future changes to these underlying components as the framework upgrades to newer view technologies that come up, and thus protect the investment in application development.

Several enterprise applications that are part of the Oracle Fusion Middleware are built using the Application Development Framework. The Oracle WebCenter Spaces application, which is described in detail in Chapter 7, is one such example. The Oracle Identity Management console is another such example. It uses ADF to leverage its powerful capabilities of customizability, security, and declarative development model, and it uses the rich collection of supplied ADF UI components. The Application Development Framework supports component architecture. For example, several components are provided as part of ADF Faces UI technology. Also, these components can be extended to provide more complex components. A classic example of this is the components added by other layers in Oracle Fusion Middleware—for example, the components from Oracle WebCenter and the components from Oracle Business Intelligence visualizations. The next generation of enterprise business applications, known as Oracle Fusion Applications, are all built using the ADF technology at their core. Oracle Fusion Middleware Extensions for Applications provides standardized, complex components that implement the common design patterns used in Fusion Applications, which exemplifies the component architecture and the key aspect for reuse in enterprise applications. Oracle ADF application development is supported and enabled by Oracle JDeveloper, the integrated development environment (IDE) from Oracle, and is also supported in the Oracle Enterprise Pack for Eclipse.

Architecture

This section describes the architecture of ADF. Oracle application development model via ADF is based on the industry-standard Model-View-Controller (MVC) architecture to achieve separation of business logic, navigation, and user interface. The MVC pattern isolates the application logic from the user interface, permitting independent development, testing, and maintenance of each layer. Applications built with the MVC architecture pattern typically provide:

- A model layer that manages the behavior and data of the application
- A view layer that contains the User Interface components to render the model data in a user viewable and actionable form
- A controller layer that handles input and navigation via integration with the model layer and the view layer

The ADF technology stack components support this pattern as shown next:

- Model layer via the ADF Business Components, for building business services and business logic. The model layer, also known as the business services layer, can also be implemented via Enterprise Java Beans (EJBs), Plain Old Java Objects (POJOs), or web services.

- View layer via the ADF Faces rich client UI components for web applications built with Java Server Faces (JSF). The ADF Binding layer supports declarative data binding with the model layer, thus providing an abstraction on top of the business layer for the view and controller to work with different implementations of the business layer.
- Controller layer via the ADF Controller, for input processing, navigation, and control flow.

The basic architecture of ADF is shown in Figure 6-1.

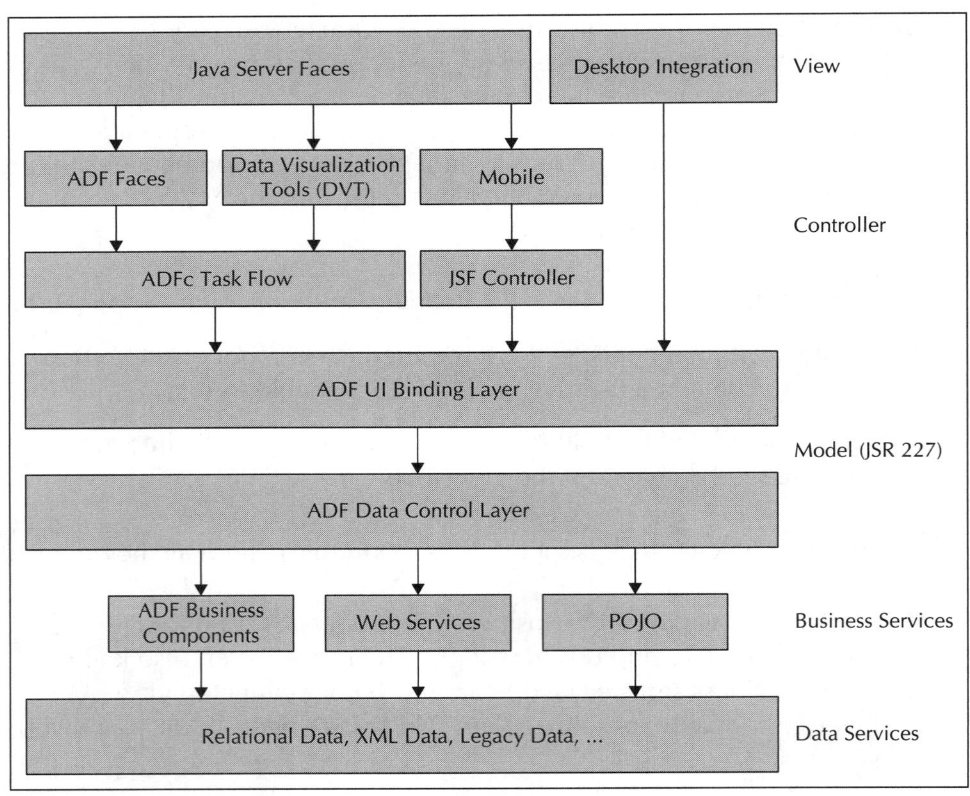

FIGURE 6-1. *ADF architecture*

Applications built using the Application Development Framework are metadata driven in all these aspects. This metadata is managed by the Metadata Services (MDS) layer, the core metadata management layer in Oracle Fusion Middleware, which is described in detail in Chapter 3. Such metadata-driven architecture provides various advantages, both in terms of functionality and in terms of application administration and management, such as centralized metadata administration, customization, and personalization capabilities. We will examine these in more detail in the next sections.

View Layer

The view layer is where the user interface of the application is implemented and is the most end-user-visible aspect of an application. In terms of implementation technologies, the view layer in an ADF application can be based on HTML, JSP, Java Server Faces (JSF), rich Java components, or XML and its variations to render the user interface. In terms of the mode of user interface, it can be a web client, a client/server Swing desktop-based application, a Microsoft Excel spreadsheet, or a UI accessed from mobile devices such as a mobile phone. In the examples in this chapter, the UI is implemented using the ADF Faces technology.

ADF Faces technology provides a large set of UI components that are built on top of the standard JSF technology and can leverage the latest browser technologies—including partial page rendering and AJAX—to provide a rich, interactive user interface. Some of the rich components in ADF Faces include tables, trees, dialogs, accordions, and a variety of layout components. There are also Data Visualization components for displaying graphs and charts that can be used in web applications. JSF provides server-side control to reduce the dependency on JavaScript and improve security. All the ADF Faces components support skinning, internationalization, and accessibility options as needed. One of the advantages provided by ADF is the support for multiple view technologies in the view layer. The ADF Faces components can be implemented with HTML5, AJAX, or Flash, and these implementations are wrapped inside the ADF Faces components. An application user interface built using the ADF Faces technology has the added benefit of being customizable with Oracle MDS, which we will discuss in more detail in later sections.

Controller Layer

The controller layer manages the application flow. For example, when the application user clicks a "save" button on a page, the controller determines what action to take (that is, to perform a save) and where to navigate to (that is, to navigate to the save confirmation page). ADF Controller provides a navigation and state management model that works with JSF. The ADF Controller extends the standard JSF controller by providing additional functionality, such as reusable task flows. The application in this book is built using the ADF Controller. An application's flow can be composed of smaller, reusable task flows, including both visual components and nonvisual components, such as method calls, using ADF Controller. These task flows encapsulate a specific task sequence and provide reusability. Task flows run inside a region of the containing page. This approach encourages maximum reusability for user interface fragments and business logic, and even provides simplified integration into portals and mash-up applications, where the reusable task flows can be embedded. For example, a reusable task flow can be built to update the details of an employee, and such a task flow can be reused in various pages of an application or even across multiple applications where this functionality needs to be integrated. The controller definition in ADF Controller, including the definition of a task flow, is metadata driven, and this metadata is managed by MDS. As a result, the controller functionality is customizable using the MDS customization methodology.

ADF Binding Layer

The ADF Binding layer is the abstraction that connects the model layer and its business services to the objects that use them in the view and controller layers. The ADF binding layer implements abstractions called data controls and data binding. Data controls abstract the business service implementation details. Data bindings expose data control methods and attributes to the UI components. Together, they provide a clean separation of the view and controller from the model. These abstractions use metadata to describe data collections, properties, methods, and types. The Oracle ADF Binding layer also serves as the basis for JSR-227: A Standard Data Binding & Data Access Facility for Java EE. The goal of this JSR is to standardize the data binding for Java EE applications. Data controls in the Application Development Framework expose data sources such as relational databases via ADF business components, data controls that expose web services, and data controls that expose EJB that can readily be used in any application. There are also data controls to expose other sources of data, such as POJOs, content management systems, JMX beans, REST/URL services, and plain files.

ADF Business Components

ADF business components are objects that operate on the business data, providing typical create, read, update, and delete (CRUD) operations as well as query capabilities. Business rules can be applied to the business components to enforce proper usage. The key components of ADF business components are the entity object, the view object, and the application module. An entity object represents a row in a database table, and also handles validation, storage, and persistence aspects of this data. It uses data manipulation language (DML) operations to modify data. A view object provides the data, typically, based on a SQL query. It can also be based on programmatic Java objects, stored procedures, or static lists. SQL query-based view objects reference one or many entity objects and also make the query result updateable. An application module (AM) exposes the data model based on the defined view objects and their relationships. An application module is the transactional component that allows UI components to access data and encapsulates business logic as a set of related business functions. It presents a data model and methods to perform certain tasks. There are other aspects of ADF business components, such as view links, which link together different view objects like in master-detail relationships.

ADF business components can also be exposed as web services where an ADF application module is mapped to a web service. During the development of an application module, the web service interface on it can be enabled to publish rows of view object data as Service Data Object (SDO) components. The SDO framework abstracts the data of the view object and standardizes the way it is passed between Java and XML. Thus, the same ADF business components can be used to support highly interactive web user interfaces and also web service clients. The JDeveloper IDE supports exposing application modules as web services so that the service-enabled application module exposes the view objects, custom methods, and the data manipulation operations as part of the web service.

ADF Metadata and Customizations

Oracle Metadata Services is a core infrastructure component in Fusion Middleware that provides a single, unified metadata repository through which all the metadata assets for all components and applications within the Fusion Middleware family are deployed and managed. In addition to the metadata management capabilities, this layer provides functionality for customizing and personalizing this metadata. This section describes how ADF integrates with MDS and provides the customization functionality to all ADF applications.

Behavior of any application, including the UI, needs to be tailored to the specific requirements of a deployment. Such requirements in each deployment are unique and thus cannot all be delivered in the enterprise application itself, and need to be performed as customizations in the deployment. It is crucial to maintain these customizations across upgrades of the enterprise application and also across migrations between environments—for example, from test instance to a product instance. MDS supports these capabilities by providing a generic framework for metadata customization. Customization changes are stored as a separate delta document in the MDS repository and are merged with the seeded artifacts (also known as "base" artifacts) at runtime. There can be multiple layers of customizations. These customizations can be done for all users (for example, as site layer customizations), for a group of users (for example, as department layer customizations), or for a single user (also known as personalization layer). Figure 6-2 shows how these multiple layers of customizations are merged with the base metadata to provide the customized metadata to the runtime engine. Caching mechanisms are established in MDS to provide better performance and scalability, even with multiple layers of customization. Customizations can be created and updated via multiple mechanisms—either in JDeveloper IDE, in a special role called customization role, or in Oracle WebCenter Composer UI, which is discussed in Chapter 7. ADF UI provides native capabilities for end users to personalize the UI. Simple user gestures such as reordering columns in a table can be configured to be saved and persisted as personalizations. Several other ADF Faces components also support such personalization capabilities, including components such as *showDetailItem, panelSplitter,* and *panelBox.*

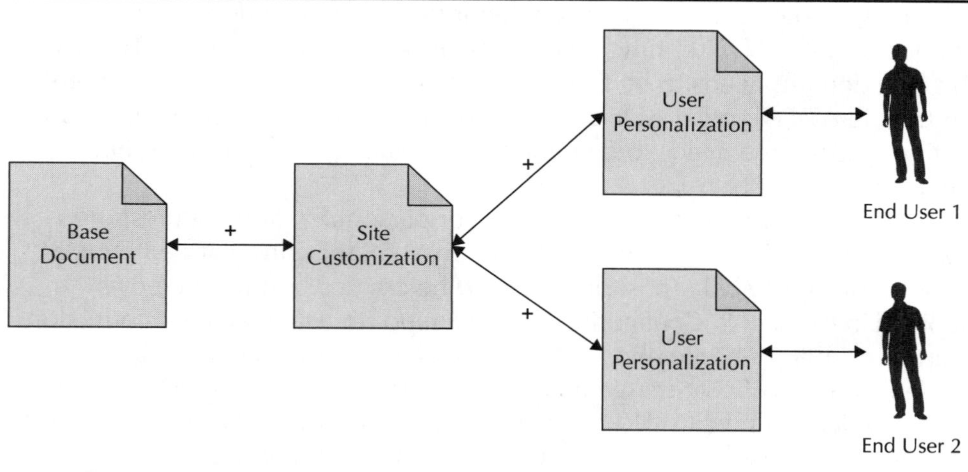

FIGURE 6-2. *MDS Layered Customizations*

Administering ADF Applications

A variety of administration tasks can be performed on ADF applications after they are deployed. These tasks can be performed using Oracle Enterprise Manager Fusion Middleware Control, WLST commands, or the WebLogic Administration Console. After the ADF application is deployed, administrators can configure the application properties. Using the Enterprise Manager MBeans browser, some configuration properties can be updated. For example, connection endpoints can be modified. Performance data on the application modules and task flows can be monitored from Enterprise Manager. These aspects are discussed in more detail in the sections that follow.

Deploying ADF Applications

An enterprise application built using the Application Development Framework is packaged into an EAR file, per the Java EE standards, for deployment. This EAR file can be deployed to the WebLogic Server in the same manner as standard Java EE application archives are deployed, as outlined in Chapter 2. This EAR file can be deployed from Oracle Enterprise Manager Fusion Middleware Control, from JDeveloper IDE, or via WLST commands.

For WebLogic Server to be prepared for the deployment of an ADF application, the ADF runtime needs to be installed on that server. To ensure this, the domain needs to be extended with the WebLogic Server template for Oracle ADF. Typical ADF applications use a database as the data source, so that data source needs to be configured in the server, as outlined in Chapter 2.

If the application uses customization or personalization features, the application needs to be configured with an MDS repository at deployment. Prior to this, the MDS repository needs to be created and registered as outlined in Chapter 2. Configuring the MDS repository connection information is a critical part of deploying an ADF application. Any contents that need to be deployed to MDS are targeted to this repository, and these are packaged in a metadata archive (MAR) inside the EAR. Any customizations, including changes to application configuration and application connections, as well as end-user personalizations, are created and persisted in this repository. An MDS repository, from the registered repositories, and an MDS partition need to be selected as the target for an ADF application from the Enterprise Manager UI in the Deployment Plan section, as shown in Figure 6-3. The best-practice recommendation is to select a separate MDS partition for each ADF application. Also, it is recommended to choose a partition name that's similar to the application name. A partition with the chosen partition

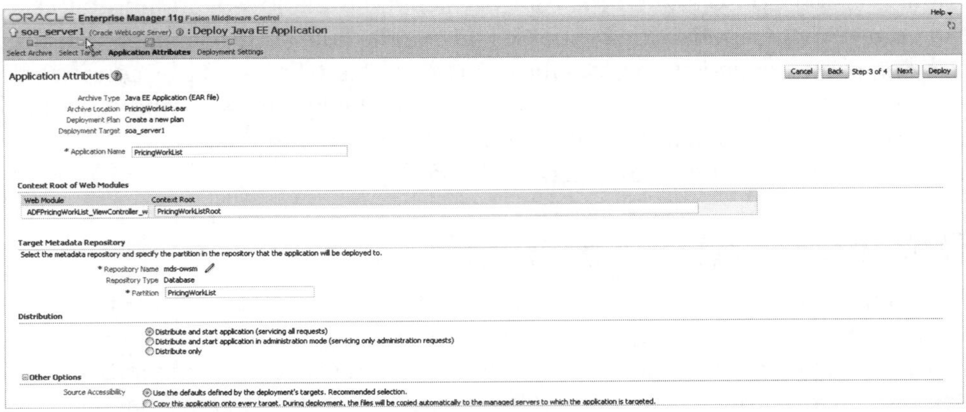

FIGURE 6-3. *Selecting MDS repository while deploying an application*

name will be created in MDS if it does not already exist at the time of deployment. In some advanced scenarios, some metadata is shared between multiple applications via shared metadata repositories. In these cases, the shared metadata repository details also need to be selected in the deployment plan UI as well. This MDS repository selection is updated into the adf-config.xml file.

If the application is deployed via WLST commands, then prior to the deploy command being executed, the MDS repository selection needs to be updated into the application archive via the following commands:

```
ArchiveToBeDeployed = getMDSArchiveConfig( fromLocation =
'<location of the ear file>')

ArchiveToBeDeployed.setAppMetadataRepository( repository='myMDSRepos',
partition='<Partition Name>', type='DB', jndi='<jndi name>')

ArchiveToBeDeployed.save()
```

The information required for the preceding commands about the MDS repository, such as the type and the JNDI name, can be obtained from the MDS repository home page in Enterprise Manager, as shown in Figure 6-4.

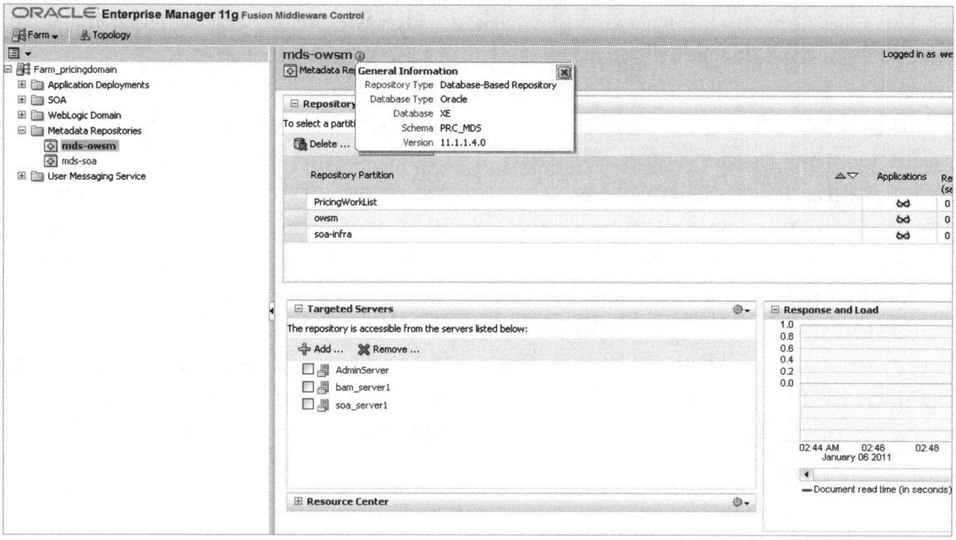

FIGURE 6-4. *MDS Repository home page*

Clicking the info icon next to the repository name in this page will result in a pop-up dialog that shows the details of this repository, as illustrated in Figure 6-4. Now the adf-config.xml file in the archive is updated with the MDS repository information, and the archive is ready for deployment via the deploy command, which can be done via the following WLST command:

```
deploy('<Application Name>', '<location of the ear file>',
 targets='<Target Server>')
```

Configuring ADF Applications

An ADF application deployed to Oracle Fusion Middleware can be monitored and configured via the Enterprise Manager Fusion Middleware Control, via the exposed MBeans, or via the WLST commands. ADF applications have a master configuration file named adf-config.xml. During application development, the adf-config.xml file is updated with the configuration based on the features used in an application. This file is further updated during deployment to capture the deployment-specific information, such as the MDS repository being used by the application. In order to differentiate the changes done after deployment from the configuration prior to deployment that the application is seeded with, the post-deployment changes are captured as MDS customizations of adf-config.xml, a delta file that contains just the changes and is merged at runtime with the deployed adf-config.xml. This will enable this configuration to be applied after any application upgrade via redeployment. If an application is deployed to several nodes within a cluster, any ADF application configuration changes will be propagated to all the other nodes. MDS will store a single set of ADF application configuration information for all versions of an application. In case of any migration from a test instance to a production instance, this customization needs to be migrated so that these configurations can be transferred to the production instance.

To update the configuration via Enterprise Manager, the first step is to launch the MBean browser by navigating to the target domain and application and then launching the ADF | Configure ADF menu. In the MBean browser, the ADFConfig folder exposes the child MBeans as shown in Figure 6-5.

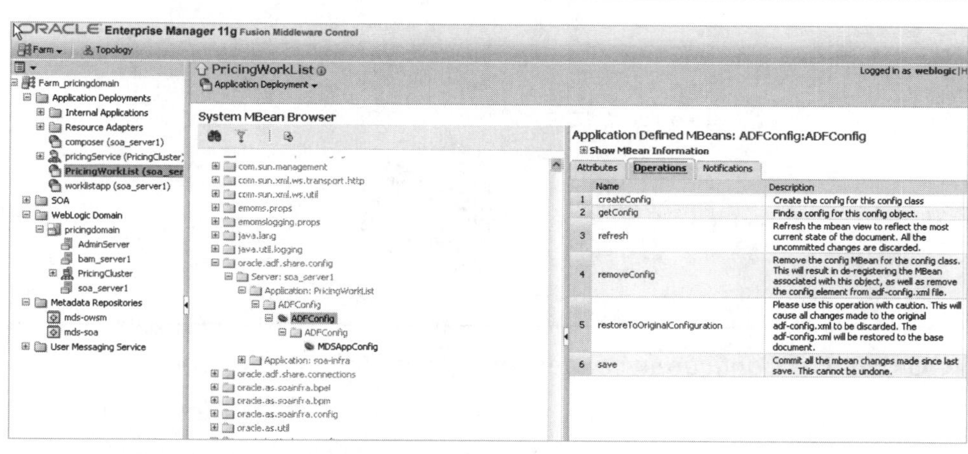

FIGURE 6-5. *ADF MBeans in the MBean browser*

Configuring Connections

The external connections used by an application are managed in the connections configuration, and these are maintained in the connections.xml file that is specific to each application. This file is part of the EAR during deployment. Typically, the connection details are some test connection details during the development phase of an application and are replaced with the real production connection configuration at deployment time. Some aspects of these connections may also be changed after the application is deployed. An example of a connection is a web service connection or a portlet producer connection that is used by an application to interact with an external application. Similar to adf-config.xml, for any post-deployment changes to connections, the connections.xml file is customized and the customization is stored in MDS.

Connections can be configured either via Enterprise Manager, via MBeans using the generic MBean browser, or via WLST commands. As part of configuring a connection, one can specify the physical connection information as well as additional details, such as cache sizes and timeout information. To update this configuration via Enterprise Manager, the first step is to launch the MBean browser by navigating to the target domain and application and launching the ADF | Configure ADF menu. In the left pane

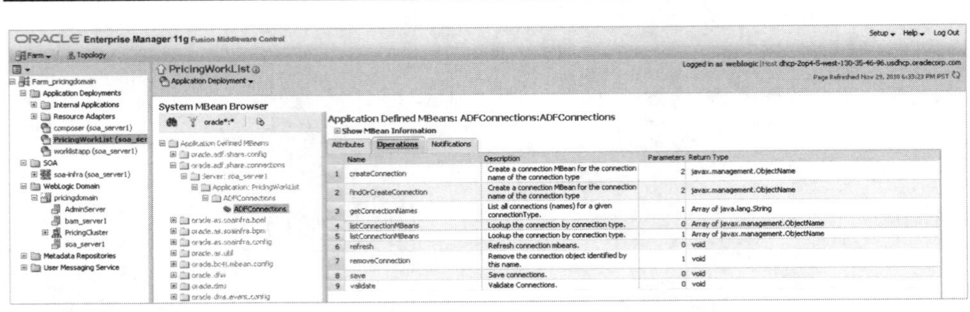

FIGURE 6-6. *Configuring connections via the MBean browser*

of the System MBean browser, navigate to the ADFConnections MBean. The MBean is in the oracle.adf.share.connections | *server name* | *application name* path, as illustrated in Figure 6-6. Several connection types are supported, including File System Connection, Mail Server Connection, Web Service Connection, and URL Connection. The properties to be configured for different connections are specific to those types of connections. For example, for a data-source-based connection, it is the data source name that is needed. For a URL connection, one can specify whether to use a proxy or not on a per-connection basis. An example where a connection needs to be created or updated is when an ADF application uses a web service in the model layer. In such an application, the web service connection needs to be set up to access the service at runtime, as previously illustrated. Several other examples in a WebCenter application will be illustrated further in Chapter 7, including examples to set up a portlet producer connection and mail server connections.

Configuring ADF Business Components

ADF Business Components configuration can be modified via the supported MBeans. Unlike ADF connections and ADF application configuration information, which can be configured once for all versions of the same application, ADF Business Components need to be configured for each version of the application.

To update this configuration via Enterprise Manager, the first step is to launch the MBean browser by navigating to the target domain and application and then launching the ADF | Configure ADF menu. In the left pane of the

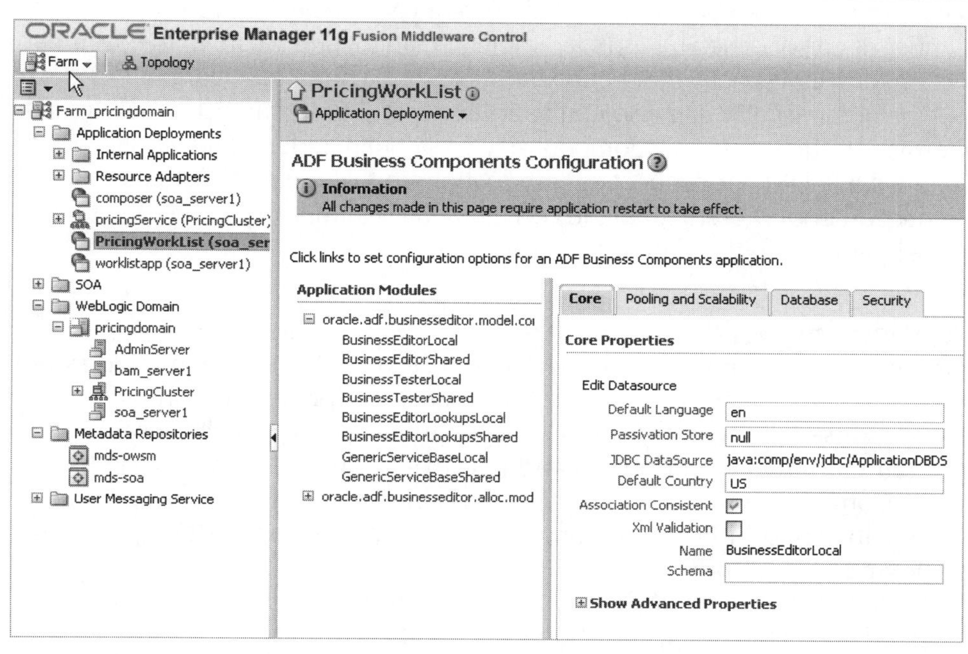

FIGURE 6-7. *Configuring ADFBC configuration via the MBean browser*

System MBean Browser, navigate to ADFBC MBeans. These MBeans are in oracle.bc4j.mbean.share | *server name* | *application name,* as shown in Figure 6-7. There are multiple sections—such as Application Modules, Pooling and Scalability (for application pool properties or connection pool properties), Core, Database Properties, and Security Properties—where the administrator can update the configuration parameters. If the application module uses data sources, they can be configured also. All of these operations can be performed via WLST commands as well.

For example, in the Application Pool section, the administrator can specify whether Application Module pooling should be used (*AmpoolDoAMPooling* property), the maximum size of the AM pool (with the default being 25), the minimum size of the pool (with the default being 5), and several other such properties. Similarly in the Connection Pool section, one can specify the initial pool size (with the default being 0), the maximum pool size (with the default being 25), and the minimum available size. In the Core section, the administrator can specify the default language, the database configuration, and so on. In the

Database Properties section, the administrator can specify the maximum number of cursors, the SQL Builder implementation, and so on. In the Security section, one can specify the security context, the security configuration, and so on. The administrator can also configure Application Module data-pooling information such as connection pool size and configuration. If the application is using a JDBC URL for connection information (so that the ADF database connection pool is used), then the configuration parameters can be used to tune the behavior of the database connection pool.

Configuring MDS

After deployment, one can tune specific aspects of MDS via Fusion Middleware Control or via WLST commands and MBeans. To update this configuration via Enterprise Manager, the first step is to launch the MBean browser by navigating to the target domain and application and then launching the ADF | Configure ADF menu. In the MBean browser, the ADFConfig folder exposes the child MBeans, and one of these child MBeans is MDSAppConfig, as shown in Figure 6-8.

Table 6-1 lists some of the MDS configuration properties that can be accessed and set at the application level via these MBeans.

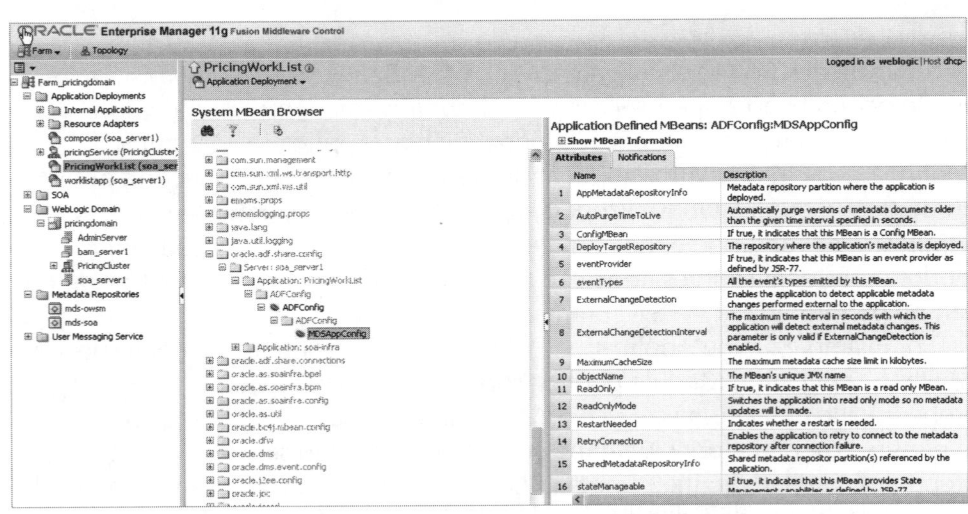

FIGURE 6-8. *MDS configuration via the MBean browser*

Attribute	Description
DeployTargetRepos	The metadata repository where the application's metadata (in the MAR) is deployed to. This same repository typically also contains any user personalizations created via the application runtime. This field is read-only.
AppMetadataRepositoryInfo	The MDS partition in the deploy target repository where the application's metadata is deployed. This field is read-only.
AutoPurgeTimeToLive	Useful to purge the unwanted versions of metadata in the repository. If the auto-purge functionality is configured in the adf-config.xml, MDS automatically purges versions of metadata documents older than the given time interval specified in seconds, if those versions do not correspond to a saved label.
ExternalChangeDetection	The value of this attribute is either true or false. If true, this enables the application to detect applicable metadata changes (for example, a personalization or customization done via a different application node).
ExternalChangeDetectionInterval	The maximum time interval, in seconds, with which the application will detect external metadata changes. The default is 30 seconds.

TABLE 6-1. *ADF-Related MDS Configuration Properties*

Attribute	Description
MaximumCacheSize	The maximum size of the metadata cache in kilobytes. If the value is 0, caching is disabled. The Metadata Services layer caches the metadata in this cache. The default is 10 megabytes.
ReadOnlyMode	The value of this attribute is either true or false. If true, this makes the application read-only with respect to the target repository. Therefore, no metadata updates can be made to this repository from this application.
RetryConnection	Enables the application to retry to connect to the metadata repository after connection failure to the same. This is typically used for high-availability configurations.
SharedMetadataRepositoryInfo	This property refers to the shared metadata partitions referenced by the application. This field is read-only.

TABLE 6-1. *ADF-Related MDS Configuration Properties* (continued)

All of these property changes affect all instances of the application running in the cluster. Some of these properties will take effect immediately—such as the external change detection interval—and some others will apply after the application is restarted. In the Operations tab of the same UI, the operation *RestoreToOriginalConfiguration* is exposed. Invoking this operation resets the ADF configuration to the values at deployment time. Other runtime operations on metadata are exposed as runtime MBeans within the MBeans browser. They can be edited as shown in Figure 6-9. Some operations that can be performed here are described in Table 6-2.

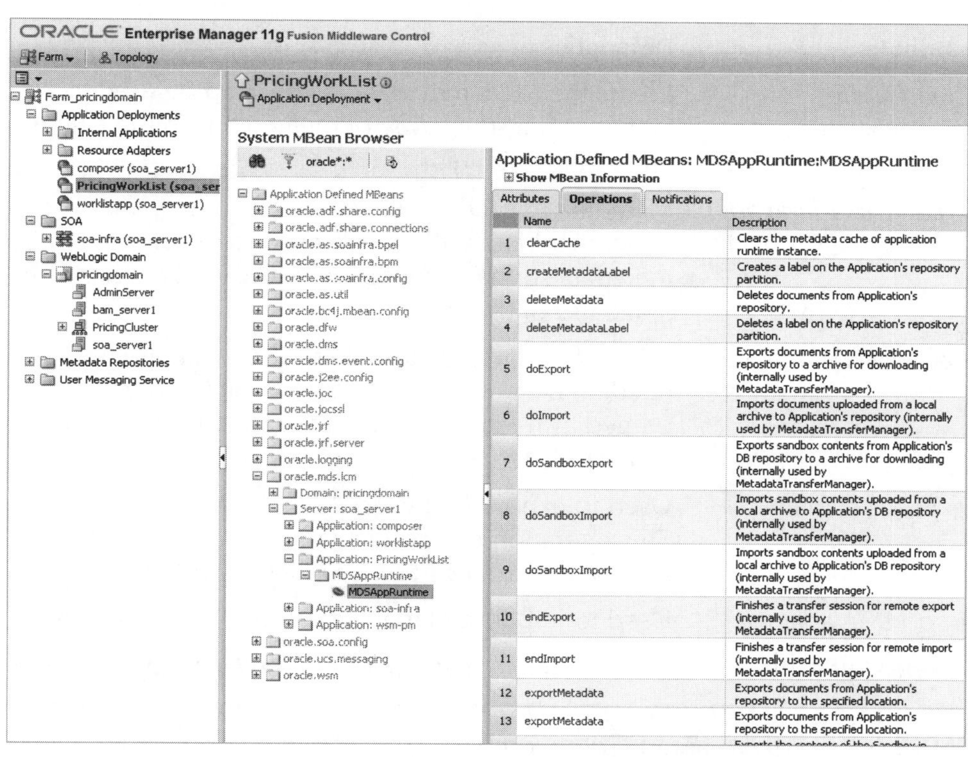

FIGURE 6-9. *MDS runtime MBeans within the System MBeans browser*

Configuring MDS Customizations

The configuration of an application to use customizations is defined in the application's adf-config.xml file. It is a development activity, not an administration activity, to configure an application for customizations. Hence, there are no MBeans to change this configuration in a running application. This includes defining the customization layers and configuring an application to use them via the adf-config.xml file. Similarly, configuring an application to persist implicit user personalization is also a development-time activity.

If an application is configured for customizations and implicit personalizations, then an administrator can turn on or off the personalizations on specific components in a page. This is stored as a customization of the page. This change needs to be done from WebCenter Page Composer. We will discuss

Attribute	Description
clearCache	Clears the MDS metadata cache. Can be used to diagnose if a stale copy of metadata is in the cache and not invalidated.
createMetadataLabel	Metadata in MDS repository is versioned, and creating a label will mark a consistent set of metadata so that a subsequent recovery or reset can make use of this label.
deleteMetadataLabel	It is a good practice to delete labels that are not needed, because unlabeled metadata will be purged as needed via the auto-purge tool described in Table 6-1.
exportMetadata	Used to export the metadata in the MDS repository. This operation can be used to migrate metadata from a test instance to a production instance.
importMetadata	Used to import metadata into the MDS repository.
deleteMetadata	Used to delete metadata from the MDS repository.

TABLE 6-2. *MDS MBean Operations*

this aspect further in the next chapter. Implicit personalizations do have some performance impact due to the additional, although optimized, cost of loading and applying personalizations. Therefore, it is a good practice to configure them only on pages where this functionality is needed, rather than turning them on for the entire application UI.

Upgrading Applications and Best Practices

After the environment is set up for executing an ADF application and the application is deployed and running, either the environment or the application may need to be upgraded to apply new functionality or patches. A typical upgrade or patch to an application comes in the form of an updated, full EAR or a patch. In a particular deployment, one can choose to apply patches to all the instances of the application or only to some. Also in a particular deployment, one can either choose to upgrade the existing instances to the new full EAR or choose to deploy the old application and the new application side-by-side. When the application is upgraded and the same MDS repository is used after the upgrade, the changes done to the configuration of the application and the changes done to the connection definitions used by the application automatically carry over and apply to the upgraded application. This is a key aspect that simplifies the upgrade process and is facilitated by the fact that these changes are maintained as customizations in MDS.

Migrating MDS Customizations

In the preceding case, where the plan for upgrading the application is to have the old and the new versions of the application side-by-side where they both use different MDS repositories, then it is important that any metadata changes done on the older version are applied to the new version. This includes any customizations and personalizations of the application metadata and also any changes to the configuration or connections of the application. These metadata customizations can be migrated from one MDS repository to another by exporting them from the source repository and importing them to the target repository. One way to do this is via the WLST commands exportMetadata and importMetadata. Another way to do this migration is to use the Enterprise Manager UI. In the Application Deployments section, the MDS Configuration option can be chosen, which shows the export and import operations. Here is a sample WLST command to export metadata:

```
exportMetadata( application='PricingWorkList', server='soa_
server1", toLocation='/tmp/MDSExport', restrictCustTo='user',
excludeBaseDocs='true')
```

This command exports all user personalizations from the MDS repository used by the specific application.

To import the same metadata, the sample exportMetadata WLST command is as follows:

```
importMetadata(application 'PricingWorkList', server='soa_server1',
fromLocation='/tmp/ MDSExport',docs="/**")
```

The preceding methodology is also used in the case where changes need to be propagated from a test system to a production system. The UI in Enterprise Manager where the operations to import and export metadata are available is shown in Figure 6-10.

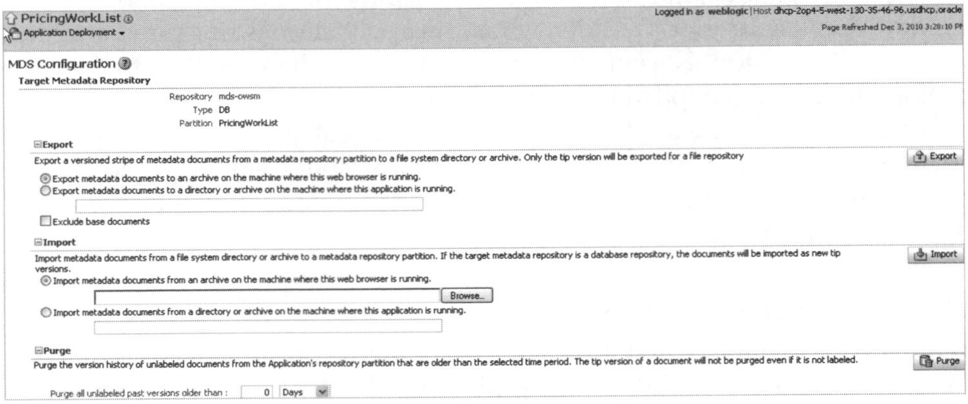

FIGURE 6-10. *MDS export/import operations from EM*

Chapter Use Case

In this chapter, we pick up where we left off in the use case of Chapter 5. In Chapter 3, we went through the steps required to create the topology with the pricing application deployed to its own cluster, its web interface accessible through a fronting OHS instance, and its web service interface secured using OWSM. In Chapter 4, we proceeded to configure this domain with a central LDAP server and to configure it for Single Sign-On (SSO). In Chapter 5, we deployed to this domain a SOA Suite composite that orchestrates the integration of the pricing application's model update web services with the corporate ERP system and exposes updated data through Oracle BAM.

In this section, we will deploy the PricingWorkList ADF application. As described in the use case section of Chapter 3, the web services interface of the pricing application exposes a single operation named *modifyModel,* which is used to modify the pricing model for a given product. A business process is executed every time changes occur to the company's ERP system that can affect the pricing application's business parameters. The process reads the change event and translates it to the parameters required by the Pricing Update web service and then invokes the web service in order to ensure that the changes are reflected within the pricing application's business model. Depending on the nature of the changes involved, the process in some

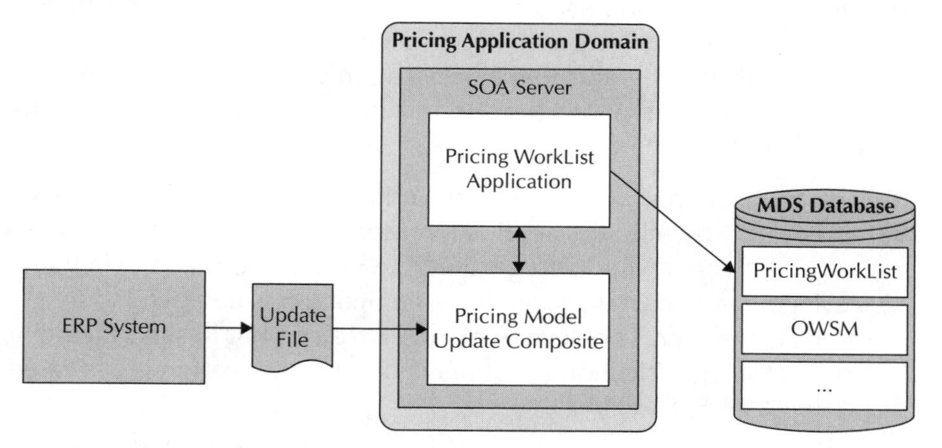

FIGURE 6-11. *Pricing WorkList application topology*

cases involves an approval from the specialty product's product management team before proceeding with the update of the pricing model. The Pricing WorkList application has the user interface where the specialty product's product management team approves these changes to the business parameters. The topology of the application is illustrated in Figure 6-11.

Use Case Description

The Pricing WorkList application provides the user interface for various users of the specialty product management group to access the worklist for these approval items. After further discussions with the application's product development and business analyst teams, you have gathered the following key aspects about this application:

- This application is contained in its EAR file named PricingWorkList.ear.
- This application is built to support personalizations for the application users to change the columns they would like to see and the order in which they would like to see them in the worklist table. Because users don't want to have to make the same changes every time they log in to this application, the application is configured to store these personalizations across sessions in an MDS repository.

- The only users who need access to the application's user interface are the pricing analysts within the specialty product management team. The access grants to the application user interface; therefore, the embedded task flows need to be granted to the "PricingAnalysts" OPSS application role.
- The application is built to get the worklist items from the SOA server and display them in the application user interface. The development team built the flexibility to get the SOA server information via the ADF connections framework if the application is deployed to a non–SOA server. The development team also built in simplification so that this specification is not needed if the application is deployed to the same SOA server.

Based on this information and the existing topology of the applications already deployed, you come up with the following plan for deploying this new application:

- You will deploy the application's EAR file to the existing soa_server1 managed server.
- Two existing MDS database repositories are created and registered with the soa_server1 managed server for use by the SOA infrastructure and OWSM, respectively. MDS supports logical partitions in a repository so that different applications can be deployed to different partitions. You therefore choose one of these MDS repositories as the target repository for the PricingWorkList.ear application and create a special partition, PricingWorklist, to use as the target partition for this application.

To deploy the application based on this plan, you use the following WLST commands (note that these are the same commands used in the "Deploying ADF Applications" section of this chapter):

```
PricingWorklistArchive = getMDSArchiveConfig( fromLocation='/home/
oracle/deployments/PricingWorkList.ear')
PricingWorklistArchive.setAppMetadataRepository( repository=
'myMDSRepos', partition='PricingWorklist', type='DB', jndi='jdbc/
mds/owsm')
```

```
PricingWorklistArchive.save()
deploy('PricingWorkList', '/home/oracle/deployments/
PricingWorkList.ear', targets='soa_server1')
```

You are deploying this application to the SOA server, so there is no specific connection information that needs to be set up for the application to connect to the SOA server. Finally, you need to ensure that the specialty product management team users have access to the Pricing WorkList application user interface. The application uses the role PricingAnalysts internally to control access to its functionality. Therefore, after deployment you need to associate this application role with the appropriate group (SpecialtyProductManagement) from the enterprise LDAP server. You do this through the following WLST command:

```
grantAppRole(appStripe="PricingWorkList", appRoleName=
"PricingAnalysts",
principalClass="weblogic.security.principal.WLSGroupImpl",
principalName="SpecialtyProductManagement")
```

Conclusion

This chapter introduced the Application Development Framework (ADF) and its architecture and described the administration and configuration aspects of an application built on this framework. The chapter also illustrated how the Metadata Services are used by customizable ADF applications and then proceeded to discuss how an administrator can migrate these customizations in the application's target MDS repository from one instance of an application to another. Finally, we extended our use case discussion to the deployment of the Pricing WorkList ADF application. In the next chapter we will explore Oracle WebCenter, a product that uses the Application Development Framework as a foundation for enabling advanced user interaction capabilities.

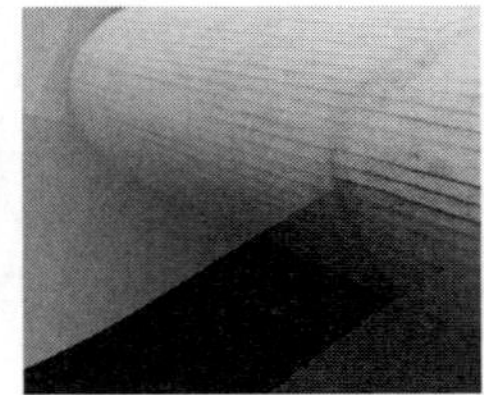

CHAPTER 7

Oracle WebCenter

This chapter introduces Oracle WebCenter, the Fusion Middleware framework that provides portal and collaboration capabilities. This chapter provides a description of Oracle WebCenter technologies and explores the architecture of enterprise applications built using the rich feature set provided by these technologies. This chapter also describes the operational aspects of administering, managing, and configuring such applications.

Introducing Oracle WebCenter

WebCenter is Oracle's portal, user interaction, and Enterprise 2.0 product suite. Enterprise 2.0 refers to integrating the new generation of web technologies (referred to as "Web 2.0"), which enable social communication, with enterprise applications to bring these productivity benefits to enterprise users. Portal technologies provide the ability to present relevant information and services from multiple applications to the target users in an effective and customizable manner. The framework that provides the infrastructure to build and integrate both the portal technologies and the Enterprise 2.0 technologies into enterprise applications also provides the benefit of accelerating the development of such applications. WebCenter technology provides complete support to build such manageable enterprise portals with embedded Enterprise 2.0 technologies. Its unified, standards-based portal platform not only allows business applications to be designed by developers but also supports the customization of applications that can be evolved by business users as business requirements change. WebCenter technology provides support for administrators to maintain and administer these applications via integration with the Enterprise Manager (EM) and with the WebLogic Server Scripting Tool (WLST) commands.

Figure 7-1 depicts the architecture of the WebCenter technology and its four key aspects (which are further described in this chapter):

- Oracle WebCenter Composer, and its integration with ADF applications, provides browser-based customizability of application UI metadata.

- Oracle WebCenter Enterprise 2.0 technology (also referred to as WebCenter Services) provides the user interaction components and the underlying support to integrate Enterprise 2.0 technology into any ADF application.
- Oracle WebCenter Portal technology builds portal applications that consume portlets and also expose portlets for consumption in other applications.
- Oracle WebCenter Spaces application is an Enterprise 2.0 application that includes social networking, communities, and enterprise application integration.

The first three technology components (WebCenter Composer, WebCenter Enterprise 2.0 services, and WebCenter Portal technology) are collectively referred to as the WebCenter framework. Applications built using the WebCenter framework are referred to as custom portal applications or custom WebCenter applications. The WebCenter Spaces application is an application built using the WebCenter framework.

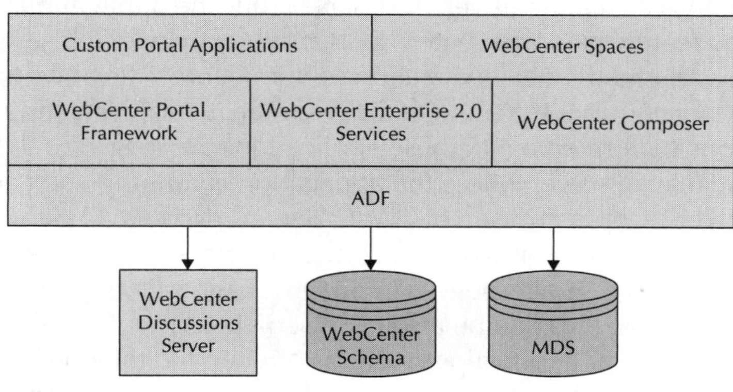

FIGURE 7-1. *WebCenter architecture*

WebCenter Installation

This section briefly introduces the steps in installing Oracle WebCenter. The first step is the installation of the database and the Fusion Middleware WebLogic Server, as described in previous chapters. As shown in Figure 7-1, WebCenter framework requires the WebCenter database schema to be installed, and this needs to be done using the Repository Creation Utility (RCU) scripts provided by WebCenter.

The next step is to create the managed servers and the applications required. WebCenter installation results in the creation of five managed servers to host various WebCenter components. The installation creates a WebCenter domain that contains the admin server and the required managed servers. A managed server called WC_Collaboration is created to host the Discussions server. Several WebCenter services, such as Discussions and Announcements (described further in the "WebCenter Services" section), use this server. A managed server called WC_Spaces is created to host the WebCenter Spaces application. A managed server called WC_CustomPortal is created to host the portal applications built using the WebCenter portal and collaboration technologies. Any custom WebCenter portal application can be deployed to this server. A managed server called WC_Portlet is created to host the OmniPortlet server, which is described further in the section on portal technologies. The fifth managed server created is the WC_Utilities server. This server runs the applications needed for advanced features in WebCenter, such as the activity graph server, analytics server, and the personalization server. Figure 7-2 shows the Enterprise Manager (EM) screen with the five managed servers installed.

Operations performed by all these applications are logged to the WebLogic managed server where the application is running and can be accessed at <base_domain>/servers/<WC_Server>/logs/<WC_Server>.log. For example, WebCenter Spaces diagnostics are logged to the file /<base_domain>/servers/WC_Spaces/logs/WC_Spaces-diagnostic.log. As explained in Chapter 3, the log files can be also accessed via EM.

Oracle WebCenter applications store data related to the configuration and content for the various features. To facilitate disaster recovery and the full production life cycle—from development through test instance and production instance—WebCenter provides a set of utilities to back up this data, moving the data between test and production environments. Each of the following sections discusses the test-to-production migration aspects of applications using the WebCenter technology.

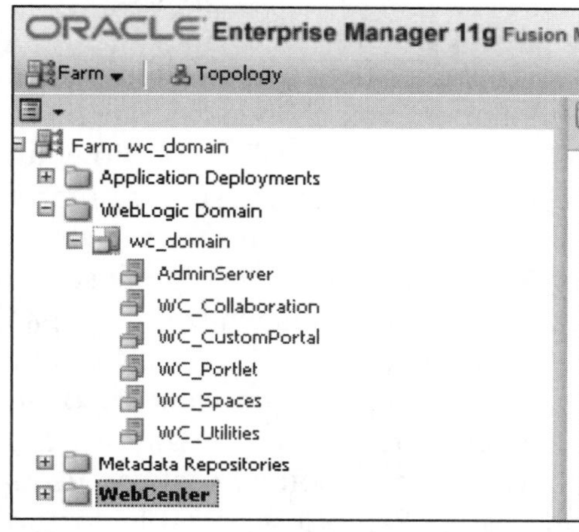

FIGURE 7-2. *Managed servers installed in the WebCenter domain*

WebCenter Composer

Businesses often have requirements to tailor enterprise applications to their needs. Very often these are simple functionality changes such as a slightly different page layout, additional text, a change of the order in which components appear on a page, or some change in the business logic. Such requirements are typically unique to each deployment and therefore cannot be delivered in the enterprise application itself; hence, the need to do be performed as customizations in each deployment. Ideally, business users should be able to use a browser-based user interface to change the behavior of the running application without going through a development and testing process. Oracle Metadata Services (MDS) infrastructure and customization capabilities were introduced in Chapter 6. Oracle WebCenter Composer provides an easy-to-use, browser-based user interface for business users so they can create and update such MDS-based customizations to tailor the user interface and business logic of ADF applications.

Any page integrated with WebCenter Composer has two modes: view mode and edit mode. The view mode is the regular runtime view of the page. The Faces components in the Composer technology provide the mechanism to edit a page by changing the mode of the page from view mode to edit mode. Composer technology provides two key mechanisms to provide customization capabilities. One is via the Composer components in view mode to support user gestures that result in personalizations. The second is support for more complex changes in the edit mode.

The capabilities provided by the ADF technology for implicit personalizations—for simple user gestures such as reordering the columns of a table to be persisted as personalizations in the MDS repository—were introduced in Chapter 6. Oracle WebCenter Composer provides additional components that offer such implicit personalization capabilities, and these are called "customizable components." The PanelCustomizable component provides capabilities for end users to rearrange components via drag-and-drop gestures. The ShowDetailFrame component provides an Actions menu that has Move Up and Move Down options that can be used to move these components within any parent PanelCustomizable component. The ShowDetailFrame component also provides a collapse option that can collapse the component and only display its header. Similarly, the expand icon on a collapsed ShowDetailFrame component enables users to display the component. The LayoutCustomizable component allows users to switch between a set of predefined layouts. All these components together provide a high degree of dynamic customization capabilities in the view mode of a page for end users. As described in Chapter 6, the application configuration and the page metadata can control whether all or some of these actions get persisted in MDS as personalizations.

The customizable components just described enable simple personalizations that end users can perform on a page. However, these are not sufficient for the customizations that business users and administrators need to perform on pages to meet the requirements at any specific deployment, and WebCenter Composer supports such more complex customizations in edit mode. Once an ADF page is running in edit mode, WebCenter Composer functionality provides capabilities to add content, to edit page properties and user interface component properties, to delete user interface components, to rearrange components, and to change the page layout. ADF pages need to include the Page Customizable component to integrate with Composer. The Change Mode Link and Change Mode Button components provide the support to switch a page from running in view mode to running in edit mode. When a page is running in edit mode, one can add additional content to the page via the "add content" action shown

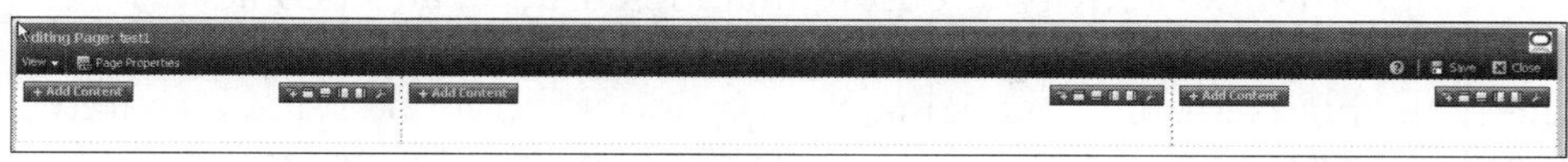

FIGURE 7-3. *A page rendered in Edit mode*

by Composer. The user interface components that can be added to the page are displayed in a catalog called the resource catalog. The resource catalog configuration determines which components are shown. The catalog can include basic ADF Faces components (such as outputText and button), reusable ADF taskflows, or portlets from registered portlet producers (this aspect is described further in the section on portal technologies). Figure 7-3 shows a page rendered in edit mode in Composer and the "add content" capabilities.

Some applications have pages that need to provide a higher degree of personalization capabilities than those provided by the customizable components in the view mode of the page. For example, end users may want to personalize the home page or the landing page of their portal application to add widgets that they use frequently. In such cases, the Composer edit mode can be exposed to end users so that they can perform such personalizations. During the development of an application, the ability to edit a page can be restricted to certain roles or privileges, thus ensuring that such end-user personalization capability is restricted to only those pages where it is needed. This can be achieved by controlling the rendering of the Faces component that exposes the mode-change capability, such as ChangeModeLink or ChangeModeButton, to check for specific security privileges and to be rendered only when those privileges are granted to the logged-in user. Advanced functionality in Composer supports the application logic to configure the resource catalog to show different contents based on the user (end user, business user, or administrator) or based on the page being edited.

Note that it is the same Composer technology that is used both by end users to personalize a page and by business users to customize a page. The MDS customization layers configured in the application (as discussed in Chapter 6) determine the scope at which such changes are saved in the MDS repository (this is referred to as the "customization context"). It is a development-time activity to ensure that the customization context is appropriately set up. It should be set up to be the user customization layer when the end user is personalizing a page, and it should be set to a shared layer (such as the "site" layer) when changes done by a business user or an administrator are intended to impact a broader set of users of the application.

WebCenter Composer Management

The customizations created from Oracle WebCenter Composer are saved in the MDS repository. These customizations are stored as separate "delta" documents in the Metadata Services Repository, as explained in Chapter 6. These customizations are upgrade safe and will continue to apply even after the application EAR is patched or upgraded. These customizations can be exported from the MDS repository via the exportMetadata WLST command or in the EM UI.

The Composer toolbar provides capabilities to manage the customizations performed in edit mode, as shown in Figure 7-4. The Save button enables all the changes done in the current edit session to be saved to the MDS repository in a single transaction. The Cancel button shown in the Composer toolbar cancels the current edit session and does not save any changes made in the current session to the MDS repository. Composer provides the ability to reset the customizations on a page or to reset the customizations on an ADF taskflow, which results in deleting all the customizations performed at the current customization layer.

Oracle Composer provides advanced functionality via the Save and Label button in the Composer toolbar to save the customizations performed in the current edit session to the MDS repository and also to create a metadata label at the same time. As explained in Chapter 6, a label in the MDS repository will mark a consistent set of metadata. Metadata as of

FIGURE 7-4. *Composer toolbar*

a given label can be exported using the MDS commands, or the application can be configured to access metadata as of that label instead of the latest metadata. The labels created in the MDS repository can be maintained via the label management WLST commands. For example, the deleteMetadataLabel WLST command can be used to delete a label in the MDS repository. Any customization created from Oracle Composer will result in a new version of the customization document in the MDS repository. These additional versions created in MDS can be purged when they are not needed via the purgeMetadata command and also via the auto-purge configuration, as described in Chapter 6.

Test-to-Production Migration of Customizations

In typical systems where the application behavior can be customized, one best practice is to maintain two systems—a test system and a production system. Any customizations are performed in the test system using WebCenter Composer. Then, after proper validation, testing, and approval, they are migrated to the production system. There is support in EM and WLST commands to migrate such customizations from the test system to the production system. Figure 7-5 shows the EM user interface for performing such operations.

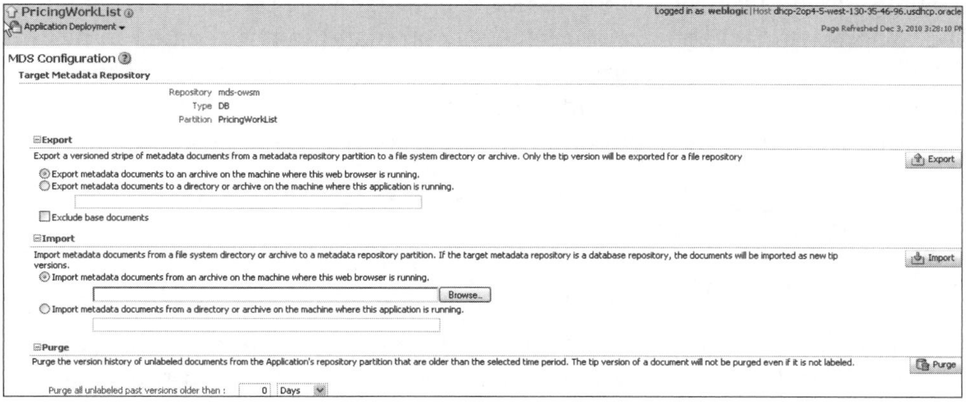

FIGURE 7-5. *Exporting and importing metadata via the EM user interface*

The exportMetadata WLST command supports exporting customizations of an application from the test system. The WLST command shown next exports all the customizations from the application to a target file location:

```
exportMetadata(application=<appName>, server=<serverName>,
toLocation='/tmp/myrepos', docs='/**', excludeBaseDocs='true')
```

The importMetadata WLST command supports importing customizations into the target production system. The following command can be used to import the documents in the *fromLocation* to the target application from a file location:

```
importMetadata(application=<appName>, server=<serverName>,
fromLocation='/tmp/myrepos', docs='/**')
```

As explained in Chapter 6, an application can use multiple layers of customization. For example, there may be "site" customizations that apply to the users of the whole site, and also "business unit" customizations that provide specific customizations to the users of individual business units. Finally, there can be user layer customizations to support personalizations. The WLST commands to export and import customizations can be used to selectively migrate customizations that correspond to a specific customization layer. For example, one may choose to only export the site customizations. Typically one may want to exclude any user personalizations from the test system during such a migration process because the test system may be configured with test users who are not real users in the production system. The exportMetadata and importMetadata commands are described in more detail in Chapter 6. The *restrictCustTo* option of these commands is what can be used to restrict the exported customizations to specific layers. For example, the following command will export only the site customizations:

```
exportMetadata(application=<appName>, server=<serverName>,
toLocation='/tmp/myrepos', docs=<doc pattern>, restrictCustTo=
'site',
excludeBaseDocs='true')
```

The ability to migrate customizations from a stage system to a production system is also provided via a user interface by the WebCenter propagation tool, described later in this chapter.

Troubleshooting Customizations

WebCenter Composer is a powerful tool that enables business users and administrators to make customizations to ADF pages and any embedded ADF taskflows. Because customizations evolve over a period of time, it is important to analyze which customizations exist on the page and on all the taskflows on a page. Customization Manager is such a tool for identifying and diagnosing customizations on a page; it is accessible from the Composer toolbar. Customization Manager is an Oracle Composer panel that enables business users and administrators to manage these customizations. The Customization Manager dialog box displays a list of all the taskflows and page fragments on the page, and provides details about the customization layers in which they are customized. Typically, at development time, the application is configured to restrict access so that only administrators can access the Customization Manager. Administrators can download customizations for a selected page, page fragment, or taskflow onto their desktop from the running application. Customizations can also be uploaded via the user interface from the user's desktop to the MDS repository. Additionally, Customization Manager provides options to delete customizations and promote customizations from a previously saved label. For example, an MDS label can be created to identify a good state of customizations, and the customizations associated with that state via the label can be retrieved via this promote functionality. Thus, Customization Manager is an invaluable tool for administrators to maintain and troubleshoot customizations. Figure 7-6 shows how the Customization Manager user interface is used to perform such activities.

Controlling Implicit Personalizations with Composer

As explained in the previous section, several ADF Faces and WebCenter customizable components support saving user gestures to modify the UI as MDS personalizations. The capabilities provided by the ADF technology for simple user gestures such as reordering columns of a table to be persisted as personalizations in the MDS repository were introduced in Chapter 6. The previous section discusses how various WebCenter "customizable components" provide similar personalization support. Depending on the design of any application UI, this feature may need to be turned on either for the entire application, for specific pages in an application, or for specific instances of those components in the application pages. The application can

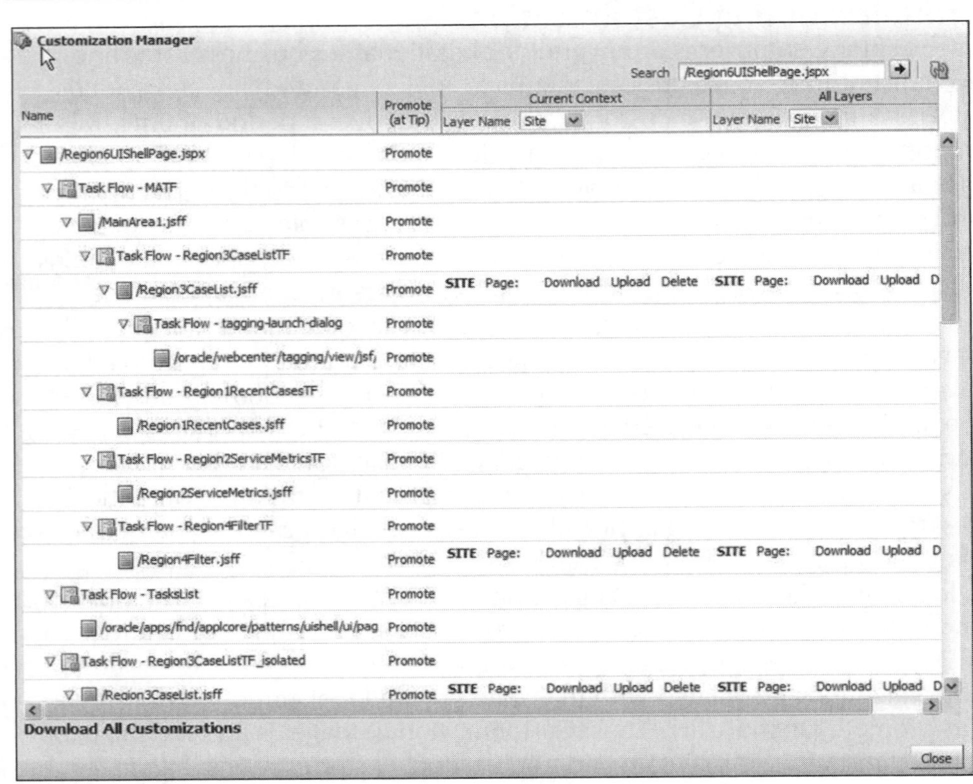

FIGURE 7-6. *Customization Manager UI*

control whether these user gestures are persisted as personalizations at various levels of granularity. This can be controlled at the component level (all instances of a component in an application) or at the instance level (only on specific instances of a component in an application), thus providing complete control for various scenarios. Therefore, an application can be configured to not save any personalizations for any occurrence of a specific component such as column in table in the application. Similarly, an application can be configured to persist personalizations for all the occurrences of such a component and then provide overridden configuration on the column component instance on specific pages to not persist the personalizations. The component-level configuration is specified in an ADF application's adf-config.xml descriptor. The instance-level control is specified on the component instance in a page via the properties *persist* and *dontPersist,* which are typically set up at application development time in the JDeveloper IDE. Because these properties are specified on the components in the page metadata, one can modify these properties via Oracle Composer like modifying any other property on the page via the property inspector exposed in Composer. These properties are not exposed by default in the property inspector in Composer, and it is a development activity to configure the application to include them in the property inspector. Thus, an administrator can customize a page via Composer to control whether or not those components on a page should result in persisting MDS personalizations.

WebCenter Enterprise 2.0 Services

Enterprise 2.0 is the term for bringing the Web 2.0 techniques that enable the social nature of the World Wide Web to enterprise applications, thus providing collaboration among enterprise application users. WebCenter technology supports various Enterprise 2.0 services that can be integrated into the business logic and user interface of enterprise applications in order to bring these productivity-enhancing and user-friendly services into these applications. These Enterprise 2.0 services include social computing services, personal productivity services, online awareness and communications, and content integration. A service is a grouping of components that may include JSF tags, ADF taskflows, data controls, application programming interfaces (APIs), and Expression Language (EL) expressions. WebCenter infrastructure has horizontal frameworks that all these services integrate with, including the Security Framework and the Configuration Framework. These WebCenter Enterprise 2.0 services can be classified into the following major categories:

- **Content Integration Services** These services provide content management and storage capabilities, including content upload, editing capabilities, file and folder creation and management, file checkout, and versioning. The following are the services in this category:
  - Document Library
  - Wikis and Blogs
  - Content Presenter

- **Collaboration Services** These services enable enterprise users to effectively collaborate with each other. The following are the services in this category:
  - Discussion Forums
  - Announcements
  - Instant Messaging and Presence
  - Mail
  - Polls
- **People Connection Services** These services enable users to connect with each other and keep track of each others' updates. The following are the services in this category:
  - Connections
  - Feedback
  - Message Board
  - Profile
  - Publisher
  - Activity Streams
- **Linking and Search Services** These services provide alternative ways to bookmark, retrieve, and find content. The following are the services in this category:
  - Tagging
  - Linking
  - Search
  - WorkList
  - RSS Viewer
  - Activity Graph
  - Analytics

Table 7-1 lists the available WebCenter Enterprise 2.0 services.

Service	Description
Activity Stream	This service provides the ability to track recent updates from other users, communities, business objects, documents, and so on, via the news feed.
Activity Graph	This service provides the ability to analyze activities to provide recommendations, similarities, and so on.
Analytics	This service provides the ability to analyze various activities in the system.
Announcements	This service provides the ability to post announcements about important activities and events.
Discussion Forums	This service provides the ability to create threaded discussions, to pose and respond to questions, and to search.
Document Library	This service provides features for accessing, adding, and managing folders and files and for configuring file and folder properties.
Wikis and blogs	This service provides features to browse, update, and manage wiki content and blog content.
Mail	This service provides easy integration with mail servers.
Instant Messaging and Presence	This service provides the ability to observe the status of other authenticated users (for example, whether they are online, offline, busy, or idle) and to contact them instantly.
Links	This service provides a way to view, access, and associate related information.
People Connection Services	This service provides the social networking tools for enhancing connection and communication throughout an enterprise.

TABLE 7-1. *WebCenter Services*

Service	Description
Polls	This service provides ways to create, edit, and take online polls on application pages.
RSS Viewer	This service provides ways for application users to add and view RSS 2.0–formatted feeds.
Tagging	Tags enable users to apply their own meaningful terms to items, making those items more easily discoverable in search results.
WorkList	This service provides a way to show Business Process Execution Language (BPEL) WorkList items assigned to the currently authenticated user.

TABLE 7-1. *WebCenter Services* (continued)

Administering Enterprise 2.0 Services

This section discusses various aspects related to the administration of the WebCenter Enterprise 2.0 services used in an application.

Connections

Several of the Enterprise 2.0 services require a backend server and a connection to that server. The connection information of the backend server is stored using the ADF connection framework, which was described in Chapter 6. A connection can be created and managed with JDeveloper IDE wizards at design time. The connection information in a deployed environment is supplied as a configuration during or after deployment of the application via EM or WLST commands.

Table 7-2 lists the various backend server connections and some WebCenter services that use the corresponding connections.

WLST commands are available to set up these server connections and to update their properties. To invoke any WLST command supported by WebCenter, the wlst.sh script needs to be invoked from the WebCenter Oracle Home's common/bin directory (for example, /Oracle/Middleware/Oracle_WC1/common/bin, in a default install).

Connection Name	Properties	Description
Content Repository	Connection Name Repository Type Primary Connection Flag Configuration Parameters Login Timeout Identity Propagation Flag External Application Flag External Application ID	Used by Document Library, Wikis, Blogs, and Content Presenter services to connect to the content repository
Discussion Server	Connection Name Default Connection Flag URL Admin User Connection Timeout Policy URI for Authenticated Access Policy URI for Anonymous Access Recipient Key Alias	Used by Discussion Forum and Announcements services to connect to the Discussion Forum server
Instant Messaging and Presence	Connection Name Connection Type Default Connection Flag URL Domain Connection Timeout User Domain Pool Name	Used by the Instant Messaging and Presence service to connect to an Instant Messaging server

TABLE 7-2. *Backend Server Connections and Services*

By running the following command, one can get the full list of all available WLST commands supported by WebCenter as well as detailed syntax help:

```
help("webcenter")
```

All the commands discussed next support two parameters: *server* and *applicationVersion*. They are not shown in the following syntax examples in order to focus on the other parameters relevant to these examples. In all the commands specified in this chapter, the optional parameters are indicated with square brackets, as in [*optionalParameter*].

The following WLST command creates the discussion forum connection:

```
createDiscussionForumConnection(appName, name, url, adminUser,
[timeout, default, policyURIForAuthAccess, policyURIForPublicAccess,
recipientKeyAlias])
```

The setDiscussionForumConnection WLST command can be used to edit properties on an existing discussion forum connection:

```
setDiscussionForumConnection(appName, name, [url, adminUser,
policyURIForAuthAccess, policyURIForPublicAccess, recipientKeyAlias,
timeout, default])
```

Additional connection properties can be set via the setDiscussionForumConnectionProperty WLST command. This command provides an extensible way to add any connection property using a key and a value. For the properties that can be set via the setDiscussionForumConnection command, setting them via setDiscussionForumConnectionProperty has no effect. One example of a property that can be set using this command is the *application.root.category.id* property, which specifies the root category ID under which all discussion forums are created in the WebCenter Spaces application.

```
setDiscussionForumConnectionProperty(appName, name, key, value, [secure])
```

Properties set via the preceding command can be deleted via the deleteDiscussionForumConnectionProperty command, as shown here:

```
deleteDiscussionForumConnectionProperty(appName, name, key, [server,
applicationVersion])
```

The following WLST command configures the content server connection to an Oracle Content Server:

```
createJCRContentServerConnection(appName, name, socketType, [url],
[serverHost], [serverPort], [keystoreLocation], [keystorePassword],
[privateKeyAlias], [privateKeyPassword], [webContextRoot],
[clientSecurityPolicy], [cacheInvalidationInterval],
[binaryCacheMaxEntrySize], [adminUsername],
[adminPassword], [extAppId], [timeout], [isPrimary])
```

The WLST command setJCRContentServerConnection can be used to edit an existing content server connection. Configuration changes made using these WebCenter WLST commands to the content server connection are only effective after restarting the managed server on which the custom WebCenter application is deployed.

Several other services, such as the Tagging service and the Links service, use the WebCenter database itself as the backend server to store information. For such services, no special server connection is needed, and the WebCenter database connection is set up during the deployment of the application.

All of these configurations can also be done via Enterprise Manager. Figure 7-7 shows the menu used to access the service configuration screen.

Figure 7-8 shows the service configuration screen in Enterprise Manager where properties for various services can be set.

Service Properties

In addition to the server connection and the properties on the server connection, each service itself supports a certain set of properties for configuring how the application uses the service. These properties can be set in EM or via WLST commands. For example, the Discussion Forum service properties can be set via the setDiscussionForumServiceProperty command. There are also corresponding commands to remove properties and to list the service properties: removeDiscussionForumServiceProperty and listDiscussionForumServiceProperties, respectively.

```
setDiscussionForumServiceProperty(appName, property, value)
removeDiscussionForumServiceProperty(appName, property)
listDiscussionForumServiceProperties(appName)
```

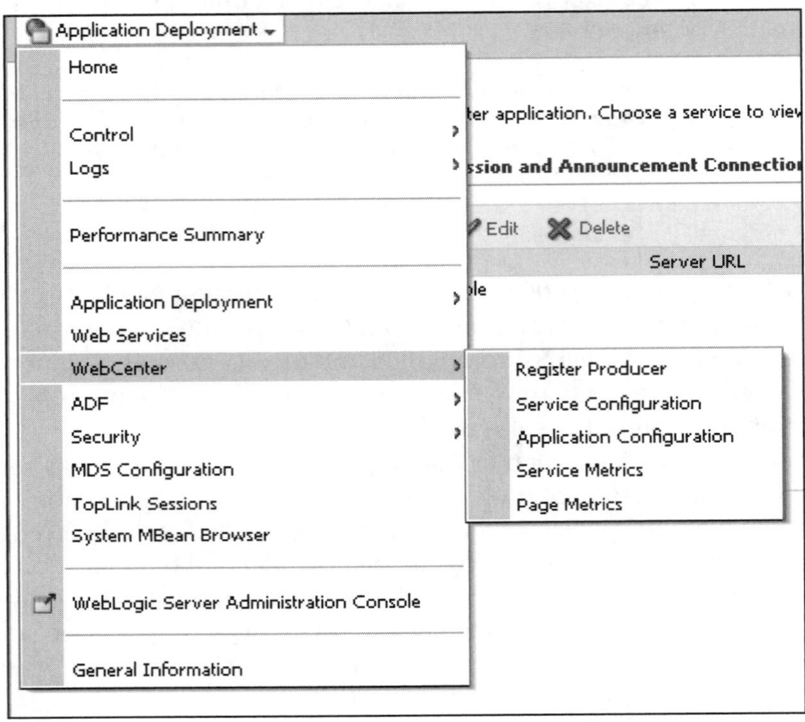

FIGURE 7-7. *WebCenter menu in Enterprise Manager*

Here are some properties that can be set via the preceding commands:

- **topics.fetch.size** Maximum number of topics fetched by the Discussions service and displayed in the Topics view
- **forums.fetch.size** Maximum number of forums fetched by the Discussions service and displayed in the Forums view
- **recentTopics.fetch.size** Maximum number of topics fetched by the Discussions service and displayed in the Recent Topics view
- **watchedTopics.fetch.size** Maximum number of topics fetched by the Discussions service and displayed in the Watched Topics view

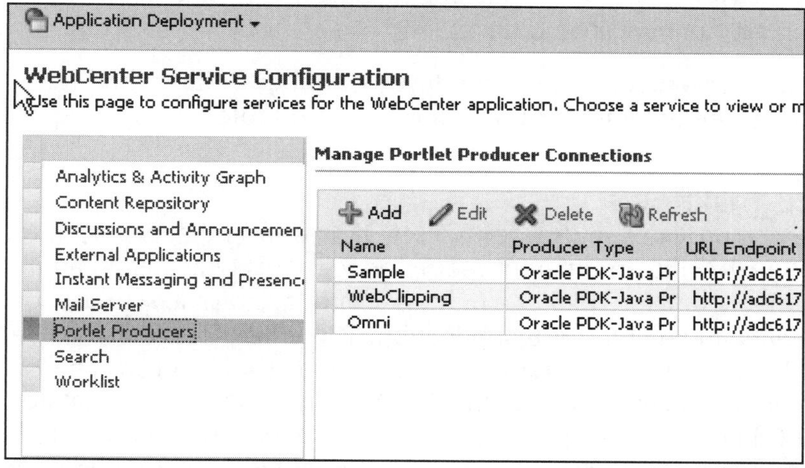

FIGURE 7-8. *Service Configuration user interface in Enterprise Manager*

- **watchedForums.fetch.size** Maximum number of forums fetched by the Discussions service and displayed in the Watched Forums view

The Announcements service also provides WLST commands as shown next. These commands provide support for setting, removing, or listing service specific properties.

```
setAnnouncementServiceProperty(appName, property, value)
removeAnnouncementServiceProperty(appName, property)
listAnnouncementServiceProperties(appName)
```

Here's a list of some properties that can be set via these commands:

- **miniview.page_size** Maximum number of announcements displayed in the Announcements quick view
- **mainview.page_size** Maximum number of announcements displayed in the Announcements main view

- **linksview.page_size** Maximum number of announcements displayed in the Announcements links view
- **announcements.expiration.days** Number of days that announcements display and remain editable

Service Taskflows

Each service provides several reusable ADF taskflows that expose the service functionality in different user interfaces. It is typically an application development choice to pick the right user interface taskflow to use for a given service in an enterprise application. These taskflows can also be included in the resource catalog so that business users and administrators can customize pages by adding the suitable taskflows from the catalog. In the WebCenter Spaces application, the resource catalog is configured this way so that individual space moderators can add the taskflows that are suitable to that community via the resource catalog to the space pages. For the Discussions service, the following taskflows are available:

- **Discussion Forums** Provides controls for creating discussion forums; creating, replying to, and managing discussion forum topics; and selecting watched forums and watched topics
- **Discussions – Quick View** Provides a means of accessing all possible views of discussions: Recent Topics, Popular Topics, Watched Topics, and Watched Forums
- **Popular Topics** Provides a look at the most frequently viewed discussion topics in all the discussion forums
- **Recent Topics** Provides a look at the most recently accessed discussion topics in all the discussion forums
- **Watched Forums** Provides a means of viewing all discussion forums the user has selected to watch
- **Watched Topics** Provides a cohesive view of all the topics the user has selected to watch

Even with the variety of taskflows exposed, the need for customizing or tailoring a taskflow continues to exist. All the methodologies described in Chapters 6 and 7 can be used to customize these WebCenter service taskflows. They can be customized in the JDeveloper customization role or via WebCenter Composer. These customizations are upgrade safe and can be migrated from test system to production system using the methodologies explained earlier.

Test-to-Production Migration of Enterprise 2.0 Services

A typical best practice is to maintain two systems—a test system and a production system—and to configure the application in the test system to test the WebCenter service taskflows, before doing the same configuration in the production system. Here are some key aspects to consider while performing such a migration:

- This requires migrating any backend server connections and server properties set up in the test system. One option is to repeat the configuration WLST commands on the application in the production system. Another option is to migrate the customizations of the connections.xml file from the MDS repository of the test system to the MDS repository of the production system, which can be done via the exportMetadata and importMetadata WLST commands, as illustrated in earlier sections. Connections that include secure properties will have the secure part of the connection definition stored in the Credential Store. These types of connections, therefore, cannot be migrated simply by migrating the connection metadata in MDS; they require the connection to be reestablished in the target production application via EM or WLST.
- The ADF taskflows provided by various WebCenter services can be customized in the test system; hence, these customizations need to be migrated from the test system to the production system. Because these customizations are stored in the MDS repository, the MDS WLST commands can be used for this purpose. The following WLST

command can be used to export only such customizations done to WebCenter service taskflows. The *docs* parameter is used to restrict the customizations exported to the customizations made on the WebCenter service taskflows. Note that the value in the *docs* parameter in the importMetadata and exportMetadata commands is case-sensitive:

```
exportMetadata(application=<appName>, server=<serverName>,
toLocation='/tmp/myrepos', docs='/oracle/webcenter/**',
excludeBaseDocs='true')
```

- Typically, the data in the backend servers need not be migrated. For example, any discussions created in the discussion server for testing purposes need not be migrated. However, there are cases where some content in the underlying content server also needs to be migrated. This can be performed via the commands exposed by the content server. For example, if the Oracle Universal Content Management (UCM) solution is used as the content server backend, the UCM commands are used for such a migration. A discussion of UCM is outside the scope of this book.

WebCenter Portal Technology

Portal applications present relevant information and services from multiple applications to the target users in an effective and customizable manner, and portal technologies enable the building of such portal applications. With the advent of Enterprise 2.0 technologies and social collaboration, modern portal applications are expected to provide a blend of the traditional portal functionality along with the Enterprise 2.0 functionality. WebCenter portal technology provides the enabling technology to build such modern portal applications. WebCenter portal technology blends Composite user interfaces, collaborative Enterprise 2.0 services, and social communities with the traditional portal functionality. This section discusses portal technology in Oracle WebCenter, starting with the introduction of the architecture and key components of the WebCenter portal infrastructure and then continuing on to discuss its administration.

The two key aspects of the portal technology are applications built as portals and applications that expose portlets so that they can be integrated into other portal applications. A portlet is a reusable web component that can display content from many different sources. The application that hosts and exposes a portlet is called a "portlet producer." A portlet consumer application, referred to as a "portal," consumes portlets from other enterprise applications that are portlet producers. For example, a producer application can host a portlet that shows a stock quote, and another portal application can include this stock quote portlet on its pages. A detailed discussion of portal technology is beyond the scope of this book, and it is assumed that the reader is familiar with this technology.

Any reusable ADF taskflow can be converted into a portlet so that the content of that taskflow can be exposed as a portlet and hence consumed in any portal application. The WebCenter technology that enables this is called the JSF portlet bridge. Thus, any WebCenter application can expose key reusable functionality in the application as portlets without additional development work to build this portlet content. This aspect of developing portlets is an intrinsic part of the development of the application. When such an application with portlets is deployed, the application behaves as a portlet producer. The consuming applications need to register this application as a portlet producer in order to consume the portlets in their pages. The WebLogic managed server on which the producer applications are deployed needs to be extended by the WebCenter Producer template (which is oracle.wc_custom_services_producer_template_11.1.1.jar) either at the time of creation of the domain or subsequently by extending the domain (the methodologies are described in Chapter 2).

The two types of portlet producers are based on the implementation technology: Web Services for Remote Portlets (WSRP) producers and Portlet Developer Kit for Java (JPDK) producers. JPDK portlets are deployed to a Java EE application server and communicate with the consumer through a proprietary protocol based on Simple Object Access Protocol (SOAP) over HTTP. WSRP producers, on the other hand, communicate with consumers through Web Services. Portlets created from ADF taskflows via the JSF portlet bridge are WSRP portlets. If the producer application enforces security policies, the Web Services end point on the producer application also needs to be secured with the matching security policy. A WSRP portlet producer has four Web Services ports exposed: Service Description, Portlet Management, Markup, and Registration. Of these four ports, only the Markup port should be configured with the appropriate WS-Security policy. The consumer application should include the appropriate security configuration on the producer registration in order to successfully propagate the user identity from the consumer to the producer.

Custom portal applications built using WebCenter technology can consume portlets from portlet producers in two ways. Applications can be developed to include portlets onto their ADF pages at design time using the support in JDeveloper IDE. For these applications, the key administration aspect is to set the portlet producer connections for all the registered portlet producer connections used in the application. Typically, the portlet producer connections used during the development of the application are not those to be used in production instances; hence, this change is needed while the application is being deployed.

Applications can combine WebCenter Composer technology with the WebCenter portal technology to enable business users and administrators to customize ADF pages by including portlets. To enable this functionality, the resource catalog in the application needs to be configured, at development time, to show portlets from the registered portlet producers. The administration aspect for this is the registration of the portlet producer connection at application runtime (which is described further in the next section) and subsequent customization of the pages to include portlets from the resource catalog in WebCenter Composer, as described in the preceding section on WebCenter Composer technology.

Administering Portlet Producer Connections

Portlet producer connections are maintained in the ADF connections configuration, which, as mentioned in Chapter 6, is maintained in the connections.xml file. Any runtime changes made to this file are stored as customizations in the MDS repository. Registration of portlet producer connections can be done either from EM or via WLST commands. Portlet producer registration is dynamic. New portlet producers and updates to existing producers are immediately available in the running WebCenter application; it is not necessary to restart the WebCenter application or the managed server. Figure 7-9 shows the EM screen for WebCenter applications to register new portlet producers. The navigation path to this screen is shown in Figure 7-7 and Figure 7-8 and is accessed via the WebCenter | ServiceConfiguration | PortletProducers | Add menu.

The WLST commands to register, de-register, and manage portlet producers are based on the technology type of the producer. Following are some WLST commands to administer WSRP portlet producers:

- **RegisterWSRPProducer** This command registers a WSRP portlet producer with a WebCenter application. This creates a connection to the WSRP portlet producer in the ADF connections framework. When you create a WSRP producer connection, a Web Services connection is also created because the communication between the WSRP portlet consumer and producer is via Web Services. This Web

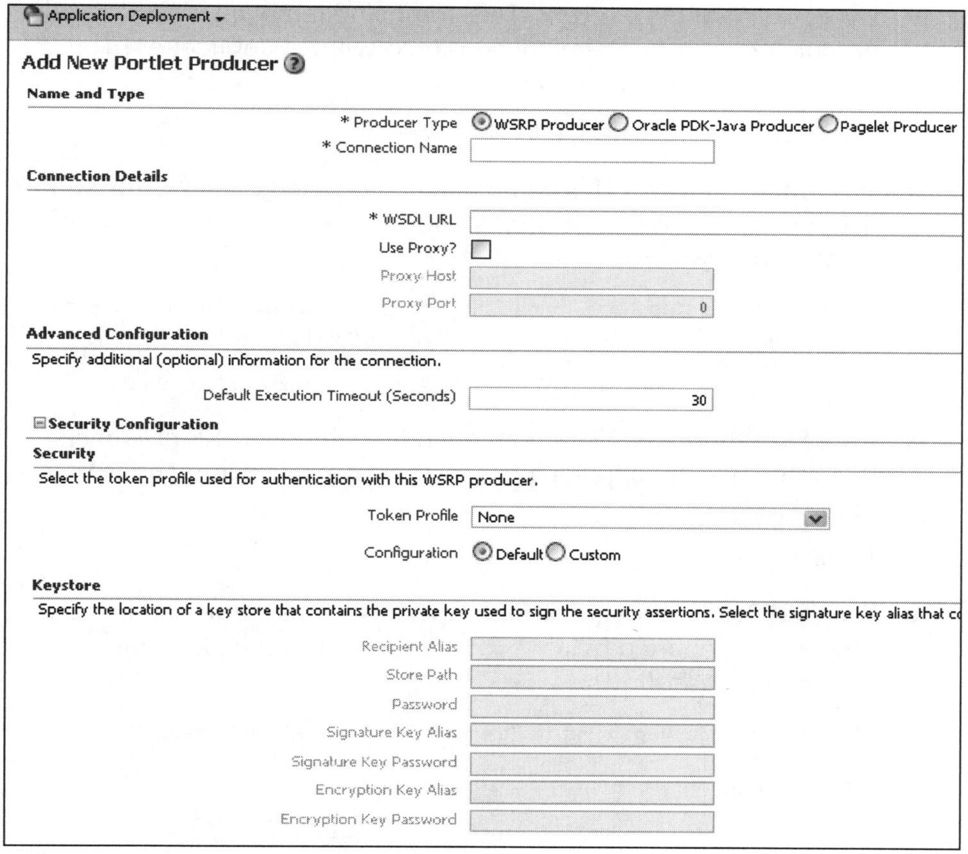
Application Deployment
Add New Portlet Producer
Name and Type
* Producer Type
WSRP Producer
Oracle PDK-Java Producer
Pagelet Producer
* Connection Name
Connection Details
* WSDL URL
Use Proxy?
Proxy Host
Proxy Port
0
Advanced Configuration
Specify additional (optional) information for the connection.
Default Execution Timeout (Seconds)
30
Security Configuration
Security
Select the token profile used for authentication with this WSRP producer.
Token Profile
None
Configuration
Default
Custom
Keystore
Specify the location of a key store that contains the private key used to sign the security assertions. Select the signature key alias that c
Recipient Alias
Store Path
Password
Signature Key Alias
Signature Key Password
Encryption Key Alias
Encryption Key Password

FIGURE 7-9. *Portlet producer registration in Enterprise Manager*

Services connection is <name>-wsconn, where <name> is the portlet producer connection. The producer application needs to be up and reachable when this command is invoked. Here is the syntax for this command:

```
registerWSRPProducer(appName, name, url, [proxyHost], [proxyPort],
[timeout], [externalApp], [registrationProperties], [tokenType],
[issuer], [defUser], [keyStorePath], [keyStorePswd], [sigKeyAlias],
[sigKeyPswd], [encKeyAlias], [encKeyPswd], [recptAlias],
[enforcePolicyURI)
```

- **DeregisterWSRPProducer** This command removes a WSRP portlet producer connection already registered with an application. The syntax of this command is as follows:

```
deregisterWSRPProducer(appName, name)
```

- **setWSRPProducer** This command can be used to edit registration details of an already registered WSRP producer. The syntax of this command is as follows:

```
setWSRPProducer(appName, name, [url], [proxyHost], [proxyPort],
[timeout], [externalApp], [tokenType],[issuer], [defUser],
[keyStorePath], [keyStorePswd], [sigKeyAlias], [sigKeyPswd],
[encKeyAlias], [encKeyPswd], [recptAlias], [enforcePolicyURI])
```

- **listWSRPProducers** This command lists all the WSRP producers registered with an application. The syntax of this command is as follows:

```
listWSRPProducers(appName,[name],[verbose])
```

- **listWSRPProducerRegistrationProperties** This command lists the properties supported by a WSRP producer. The syntax of this command is as follows:

```
listWSRPProducerRegistrationProperties(appName, url,[proxyHost],
[proxyPort])
```

Following are some WLST commands to register and set the properties for JPDK portlet producers:

- **registerPDKJavaProducer** This command is used to create and register an Oracle PDK–Java producer. For Oracle PDK–Java producers, an underlying URL connection is created that follows the naming convention *connectionname-urlconn*. The producer application needs to be up and running when this command is invoked. The syntax of this command is as follows:

```
registerPDKJavaProducer(appName, name, url, [serviceId], [proxyHost,
[proxyPort]], [subscriberId], [sharedKey], [timeout],
[establishSession],
[externalApp], [mapUser])
```

- **deregisterPDKJavaProducer** This command deregisters an Oracle PDK–Java producer that is already registered and deletes the associated connection, for a named WebCenter application. The syntax of this command is as follows:

```
deregisterPDKJavaProducer(appName, name)
```

- **setPDKJavaProducer** This command is used to edit the properties of an already registered PDK producer. The syntax of this command is as follows:

```
setPDKJavaProducer(appName, name, url, [serviceId], [proxyHost;
[proxyPort]], [subscriberId], [sharedKey], [timeout],
[establishSession], [externalApp], [mapUser])
```

- **listPDKJavaProducer** This command lists all the WSRP producers registered with an application. The syntax of this command is as follows:

```
listPDKJavaProducers(appName, [name], [verbose])
```

Two portlet producers are available in the WebCenter framework: OmniPortlet and Web Clipping portlets.

OmniPortlet technology enables developers to easily use data from various data sources in a variety of user interface layouts without writing any code. An OmniPortlet can be built on any kind of data source, such as a web service, SQL database, spreadsheet (character-separated values), XML, and even application data from an existing web page. Once the OmniPortlet producer is registered with a consuming WebCenter application, an OmniPortlet instance can be added to any ADF page in the consuming application. An OmniPortlet instance can be created in a simple wizard-driven fashion to provide a user interface on any data source.

Web Clipping is a publishing portlet that integrates part of any web application with a WebCenter Portal application. Web Clipping is designed to give quick integration by leveraging the existing user interface of a web application. With Web Clipping, one can collect web content into portlets in a single centralized web page.

The following EAR files are packaged with Oracle WebCenter: portalTools.ear (which contains OmniPortlet and Web Clipping support) and wsrp-tools.ear (WSRP Tools, which are deployed to the WC_Portlet managed server). Registering connections with these portlet producers can be done using the registerOOTBProducers WLST command. Prior to the invocation of this command, the corresponding server and the applications must be installed and accessible. The deregisterOOTBProducers command removes this already registered producer.

```
registerOOTBProducers(producerHost, producerPort, appName)

deregisterOOTBProducers(appName)
```

Portlet Customization and Personalization

Portlets can be customized and personalized for specific usages. Portlet properties can be customized so that these customizations can affect all the users of a certain portlet instance. Also, portlet properties can be personalized by authenticated users so that the logic or appearance of the portlet is personalized for that user. For example, a stock quote portlet can expose personalization choices to specify the time period for the graphical representation of a stock quote. These customizations and personalizations of portlets are stored in the portlet preference store. An application can be configured to use one of the two mechanisms of the preference store. One mechanism is to store this data on the producer application (either in the producer's local file system or, typically, in the database). This is the default mechanism used in applications built using JDeveloper IDE. The main advantage is that the producer has the option to use technology such as Java Object Cache to optimize access to the data, and this data does not need to be carried on the network for each request. This preference store data is an essential component of a consumer application, but it is not captured on the consumer side until an export is performed, typically when the ear file is packaged or in test-to-production migration. This means that until packaging, there is a vital aspect of the consumer application stored remotely on the producer side, which may not be under the control of the consumer application developer. Another mechanism is to configure the application to use a consumer-side preference store. The choice of this configuration is defined by the developer of the producer application and results in the configuration in the producer application's web.xml file via the following syntax as a child of the root element <web-app>:

```
<env-entry>
  <env-entry-name>
     oracle/portal/wsrp/server/persistentStore
  </env-entry-name>
  <env-entry-type>java.lang.String</env-entry-type>
  <env-entry-value>Consumer</env-entry-value>
</env-entry>
```

Test-to-Production Migration of Portal Applications

One best practice is for a portlet producer to be registered with an application in the test system, and to migrate the changes, after proper validation, to the production instance. The key aspects to consider in such migrations are described next.

If the same portlet producer continues to be used after migration to the production instance, no additional portlet producer metadata migration is needed. However, if the portlet producer to be used in the production instance of the application is different from the one used in the test instance, then the migration involves migrating the portlet customizations and personalizations from the test producer instance to the production producer instance. As explained in the previous section, this requires the slice of metadata from the producer that corresponds to this consumer to be migrated. The WLST command exportPortletClientMetadata can be used for this purpose. This command is run on the entire application; therefore, it exports metadata from all the producers stored in an application:

```
exportPortletClientMetadata(appName, fileName, [exportPersonalizations])
```

Similarly, to import this metadata, the WLST command importPortletClientMetadata can be used. This command imports portlet client metadata and producer customizations and personalizations from a named WebCenter export archive:

```
importPortletClientMetadata(appName, fileName)
```

Another aspect of migration is related to the security data. Security migration involves moving the identity store, credential store, and policy store from one WebCenter application to another. For more information for the migration of an environment's security configuration, refer to Chapter 4.

If some pages or taskflows are customized to include portlets via WebCenter Composer, then the corresponding customizations of those pages or taskflows need to be migrated to the target system using the MDS WLST commands exportMetadata and importMetadata, described in detail in Chapter 6.

WebCenter Portal Metadata

Creating and exposing portlets and consuming portlets are all important parts of portal applications. Another critical aspect of portal applications is the ability to build a set of pages with navigation to present business functionality to the target users. In addition, administrators need the ability to create new pages (or to customize pages) to modify or add to the navigation patterns used in the application. Oracle WebCenter Portal platform provides the infrastructure so that any WebCenter application can embed this functionality. Here are some critical features provided via the WebCenter Portal technology to support this:

- **Pages and page hierarchies** Page hierarchy organizes pages into a tree structure, with a parent-child relationship between pages. This hierarchical structure allows for the convenient propagation or inheritance of security settings from pages to subpages and thus provides an easy way of managing the security of these pages. These pages can be built using various page templates available in the application.

- **Navigation** WebCenter supports building different navigation UIs and binding them to the defined navigation model, which could be based on the page hierarchies in the portal or based on various entry-point pages in other enterprise applications.
- **Customizable and personalizable pages** This involves customizing pages for a group of users or personalizing the pages (for example, adding portlets or ADF taskflows onto a page from the resource catalog). This ability is provided via the WebCenter Composer, which is described earlier in this chapter in detail. The resource catalog definitions themselves can be edited and enhanced at runtime.
- **Content integration** Typical portal pages include content from an underlying content repository. WebCenter applications can include content via the various WebCenter services described in previous sections, such as the Document Library service and the Content Presenter service.
- **Look and feel management** Pages and page templates can be customized further to manage the application's look and feel through modifying existing skins or adding new skins.
- **Application Integration services** Although content from other applications can be included via portlet technology, it can also be incorporated via search integration and Single Sign-On capabilities.

WebCenter provides a web-based user interface, named Site Resource Manager, for administering the aspects mentioned in the preceding list. The developer of an application built using the WebCenter framework can provide ways to launch the Site Resource Manager UI to authorized administrators. Typically, a link is provided on the application to launch this UI, and this link is made available only to the administrators. Using the Site Resource Manager UI, the WebCenter Portal administrator can edit any of the aspects mentioned previously. For example, one can create new pages in a page hierarchy, create new navigation models, or edit or add skins for

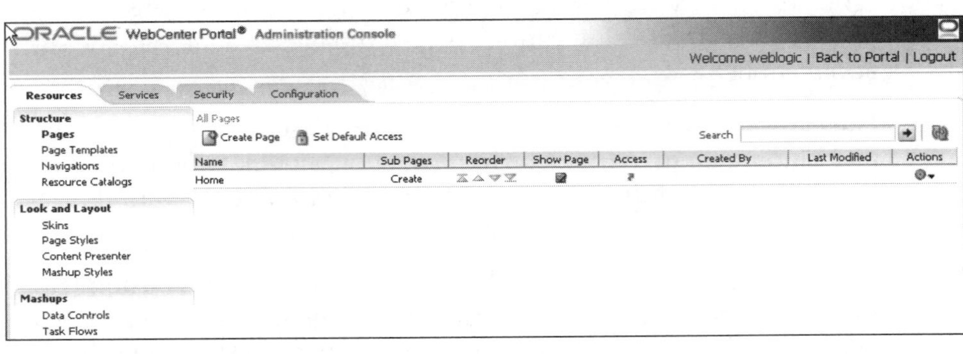

FIGURE 7-10. *Site Resource Manager user interface*

look-and-feel management. This same user interface also provides a way to export and import this metadata. Figure 7-10 shows the Site Resource Manager user interface.

The metadata created and updated via the Site Resource Manager user interface is maintained in the MDS repository. Hence, the export and import WLST commands mentioned in Chapter 6 can be used to manage this metadata. In addition, WebCenter provides the Propagation tool for fine-grained management of this metadata. This user interface can be accessed from the Site Resource Management user interface, as shown in Figure 7-11. For the Propagation tool to appear in the Site Resource Manager, a URL connection with the name *ProductionURLConnection* needs to be defined and point to the target production server as well as include the admin username and password. This tool relies on the versioning feature in the MDS repository, which is described in Chapter 6. Any update to metadata documents in the MDS repository is versioned, and consistent versions of metadata can be marked with a label. The Propagation tool allows changes between two labels in the MDS repository to be migrated. One can create labels using the MDS WLST commands mentioned in Chapter 6 to mark consistent sets of metadata. For example, if a label called "Label_At_First_Cutoff_Date" is created at the time the initial migration is done between the test and production systems on the first cutoff date and then another label called "Label_At_Second_Cutoff_Date" is created subsequently, one can

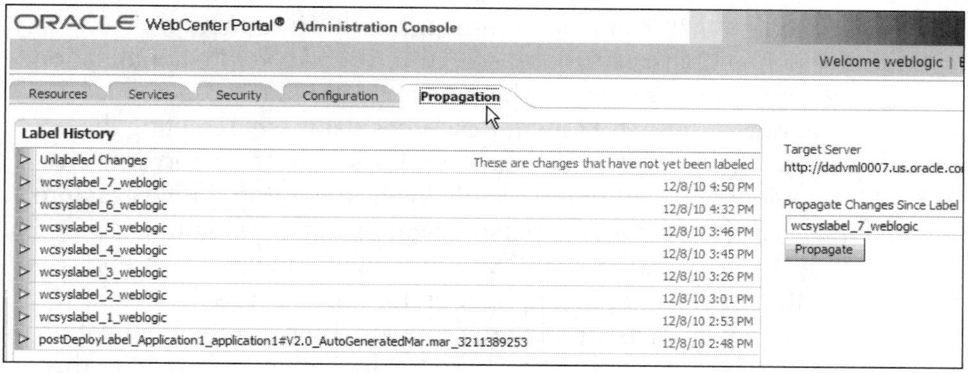

FIGURE 7-11. *Propagation tool*

use the Propagation tool to examine the metadata changes that happened between these two labels and then migrate just these metadata changes (and not any changes done after the second cutoff) to the production system. Metadata labels are automatically created by the Propagation tool each time propagation is executed. Therefore, metadata labels need to be created via the MDS WLST commands if a snapshot is needed at other times.

Advanced Features

Several advanced topics in Oracle WebCenter Portal are not discussed in detail in this chapter but a few features will be briefly mentioned in this section. First off, a *pagelet* is a reusable user interface component similar to a portlet, but whereas portlets are designed specifically for portal applications, pagelets are designed to run on any web page. The Oracle WebCenter Pagelet Producer (previously known as Ensemble) provides a collection of useful tools and features that facilitate dynamic pagelet development, and this is another application that can be deployed as part of the Oracle WebCenter Portal infrastructure.

Another feature available in the Oracle WebCenter Portal infrastructure is the Personalization service. WebCenter Personalization provides a dynamically derived user experience for any WebCenter Portal application.

WebCenter Personalization evaluates defined sources of input data, generates a decision based on that evaluation, and applies this information to a declaratively defined personalization scenario. WebCenter Personalization, for example, can return content or change application flow based on information about a user in a Human Resources database, targeting the application experience for that specific user. Personalization Server is an application deployed as part of the Oracle WebCenter Portal infrastructure. Note that this is different from the personalizations that are part of MDS customizations—the MDS personalizations provide a way for an end user to customize the metadata of an application for him- or herself. The Personalization service mentioned here provides a way for the application developer or administrator to provide business logic that is specific to the viewing user.

WebCenter Spaces

Oracle WebCenter Spaces is a J2EE application built using ADF and the WebCenter Framework. This application integrates with the WebCenter Enterprise 2.0 services, WebCenter Portal technology, and WebCenter Composer. WebCenter Spaces offers a configurable work environment that enables individuals and groups to collaborate more effectively and provides a self-service solution for managing individual and group interactions. It also provides intuitive tools that allow business users to come together and share information by adding and customizing pages and resources such as documents, charts, reports, and portlets. WebCenter Spaces provides two work environments: the home space and community spaces. The home space provides each user with a private work area for storing personal content, viewing and responding to business process assignments, and performing many other tasks relevant to his or her unique working day. Community spaces (from here on referred to as "spaces") support discrete work areas organized around an area of interest or a common goal shared by multiple users. Spaces support the formation and collaboration of project teams and communities of interest. Spaces bring people together in a virtual environment for ongoing interaction and information sharing, thus forming a social network within the enterprise. Each space is a collection of pages exposing various services and content, which can even be selectively exposed to the users collaborating in the space. The WebCenter Spaces application is also a portlet consumer application, and any page in a space can consume portlets via WebCenter Composer's resource catalog.

Administering Oracle WebCenter Spaces

The two types of administrator functions for the Spaces application are the Fusion Middleware administrator functions and the Spaces application administrator functions. The Fusion Middleware administrator performs the typical management operations on the Spaces application like on any J2EE application—via EM UI, WebLogic Console, or via WLST commands—and can also perform additional WebCenter-specific administration via the Spaces application's UI. WebCenter Spaces administrators have full administrative privileges within the WebCenter Spaces application itself and can perform various administrator functions from the Spaces application UI. Spaces administrators can assign the Spaces administration permissions to additional users via the WebCenter Spaces UI.

The Fusion Middleware administrator performs the standard administration of the WebLogic managed servers deployed as part of the WebCenter installation as well as the administration of the Spaces application. Administrators need to configure the backend server connections used by the Enterprise 2.0 services embedded in the Spaces application. This includes the connection to the discussions server and the connection to the content server. These connections need to be set up similar to the steps outlined earlier either in EM or via WLST commands. The EM home page for the Spaces application shows the different WebCenter services used in the application and their availability and performance details, as shown in Figure 7-12. Administrators can configure the application properties, including those that tune application performance. These properties are covered in more detail in Chapter 10.

Administrators can also register portlet producers with the Spaces application in EM or via WLST commands following the steps outlined earlier. The WebCenter Spaces application uses an MDS repository to manage the application metadata, and administrators can configure the MDS repository used by this application and also perform management operations such as exporting and importing metadata in EM or via WLST commands, as described in Chapter 6.

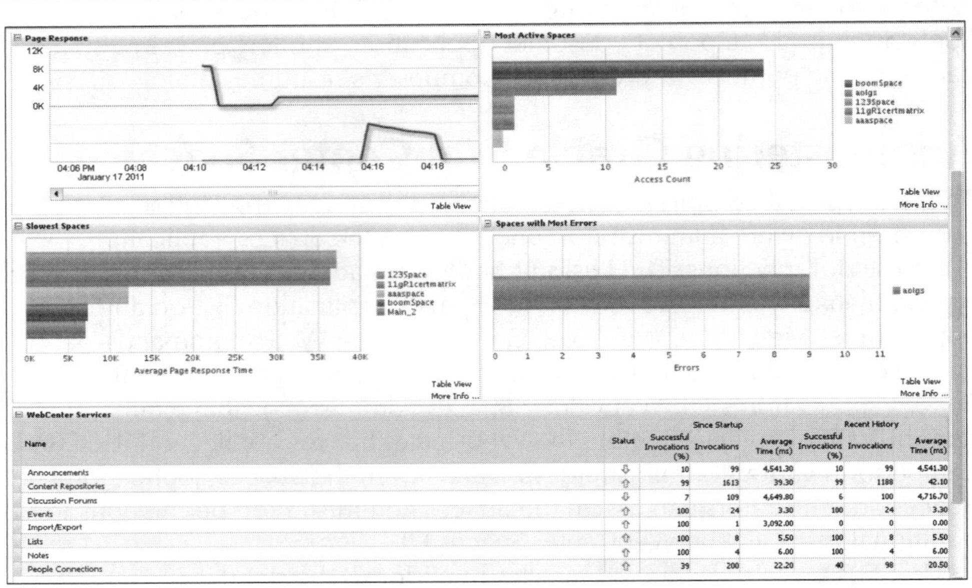

Name	Status	Since Startup: Successful Invocations (%)	Since Startup: Invocations	Since Startup: Average Time (ms)	Recent History: Successful Invocations (%)	Recent History: Invocations	Recent History: Average Time (ms)
Announcements	⇩	10	99	4,541.30	10	99	4,541.30
Content Repositories	⇧	99	1613	39.30	99	1188	42.10
Discussion Forums	⇩	7	109	4,649.80	6	100	4,716.70
Events	⇧	100	24	3.30	100	24	3.30
Import/Export	⇧	100	1	3,092.00	0	0	0.00
Lists	⇧	100	8	5.50	100	8	5.50
Notes	⇧	100	4	6.00	100	4	6.00
People Connections	⇧	39	200	22.20	40	98	20.50

FIGURE 7-12. *WebCenter service metrics in Enterprise Manager*

Spaces Application Administration

The WebCenter Spaces application administrators can perform several configuration functions on the application while it is up and running via the application user interface. Some of these configurations are discussed here. The navigation path to all these administration options is via the Administration link on the WebCenter Spaces application home page.

First of all, administrators can configure properties that affect the look and feel of the application. These include the following actions:

- Updating the name and logo for the application.
- Updating the copyright and privacy notice shown in the application user interface.
- Configuring the application's default page template. The page template selected in this user interface, as shown in Figure 7-13, will be used by all the pages in the application.

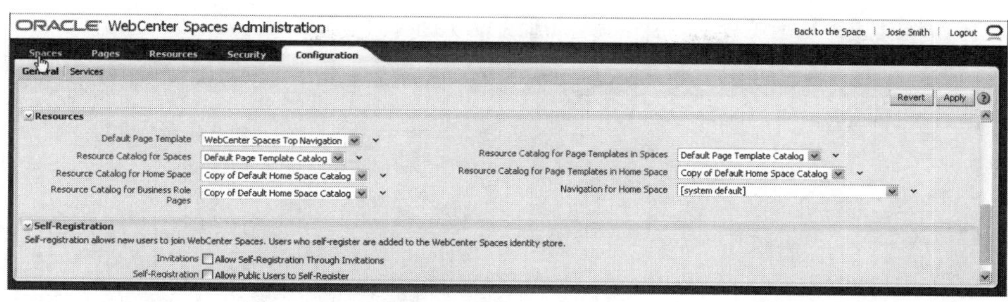

FIGURE 7-13. *Configuring the page template in the Spaces application*

- Configuring the skin to be used by the application UI. Administrators can choose between the various skin options available, as shown in Figure 7-14. Administrator can also upload new skins via the Site Resource Manager. New skins can be created in the JDeveloper IDE and uploaded via this user interface.

Second, enterprise applications typically require multilanguage support, and the Spaces application provides this support. In addition, a specific installation may require a specific supported language to be the default language for the Spaces application. Administrators can set this up via the application user interface. WebCenter Spaces supports 27 different languages, and the administrators can choose the default language from this list. Figure 7-15 shows the user interface to perform this configuration.

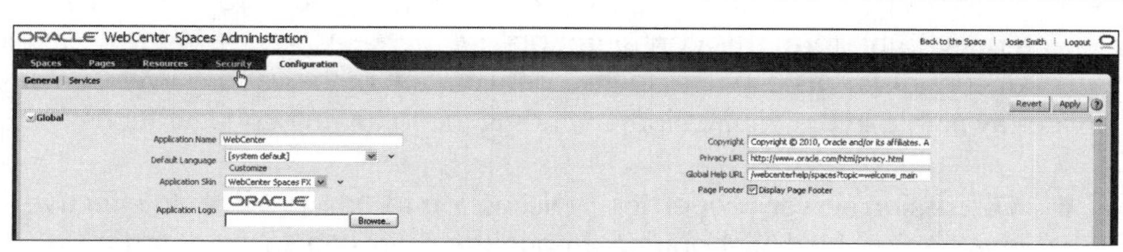

FIGURE 7-14. *Spaces Administration setting for the UI skin*

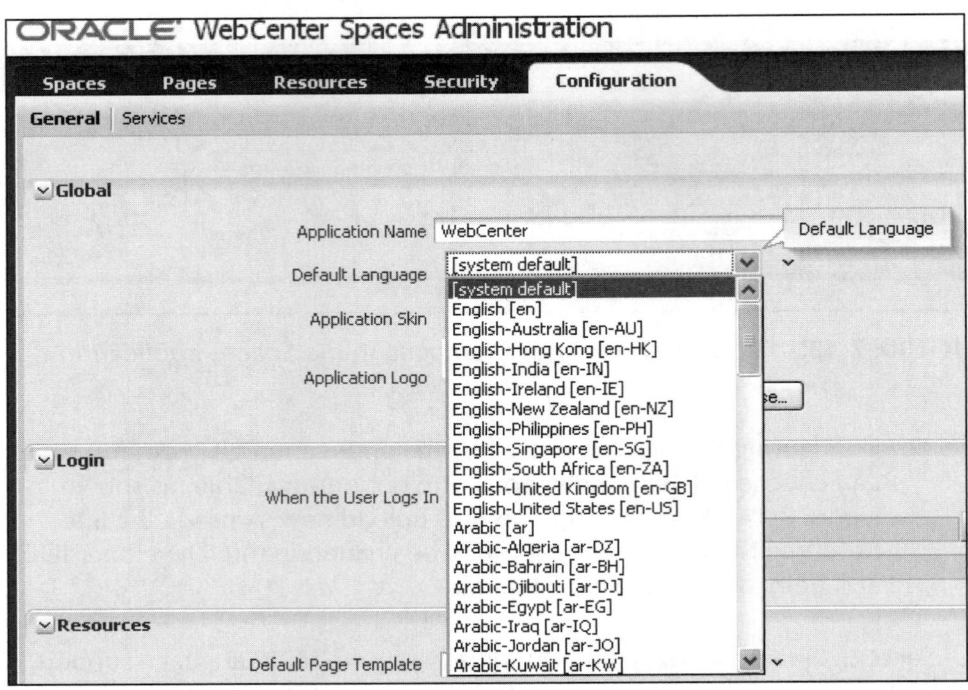

FIGURE 7-15. *Spaces Administration user interface for default language setting*

End users can personalize the language used for their view of the application via the preferences UI exposed to all the end users of the Spaces application. The language options shown to the end user can be configured by the administrator. Although WebCenter supports 27 different languages, the administrator can configure a subset of this list. Figure 7-16 shows the user interface to perform this configuration.

Third, administrators can update the configuration of the various WebCenter Services available in the application, including the following configurations:

- **Discussion server properties** Discussion forums provide an effective mechanism for collaboration among the users of a space. For the WebCenter Discussions functionality to be available, the first step is to configure the discussion server connection in the Spaces application,

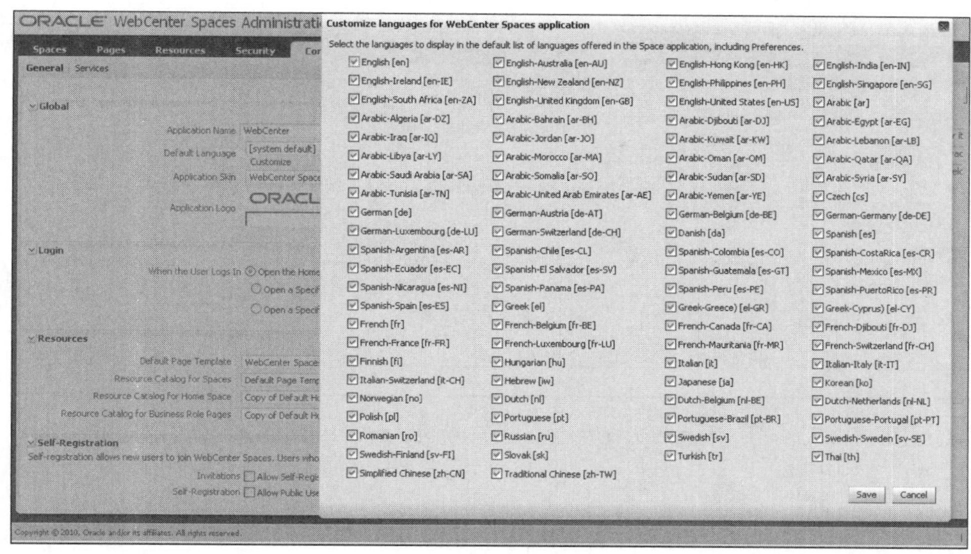

FIGURE 7-16. *Configuring the list of languages shown to end users*

which can be done in EM or via the WLST command createDiscussionForumConnection. The Spaces application administrator can set additional configuration properties on the discussion server connection in the user interface shown in Figure 7-17. Properties such as the root category and the category name can be updated here. Administrators can also select the number of most recent discussion topics and replies to be copied to a template when a group space template is created from a group space. As the help text shown in this figure says, specifying a large number impacts performance and the maximum value that can be selected is 25.

- **Portlet producers** Typically enterprises have multiple enterprise applications deployed, so it is important to include some related content from one or more enterprise applications into a space to provide additional context to the collaboration in that space. One mechanism to achieve this is to enhance the space pages to include relevant portlets exposed by enterprise applications. The first step for

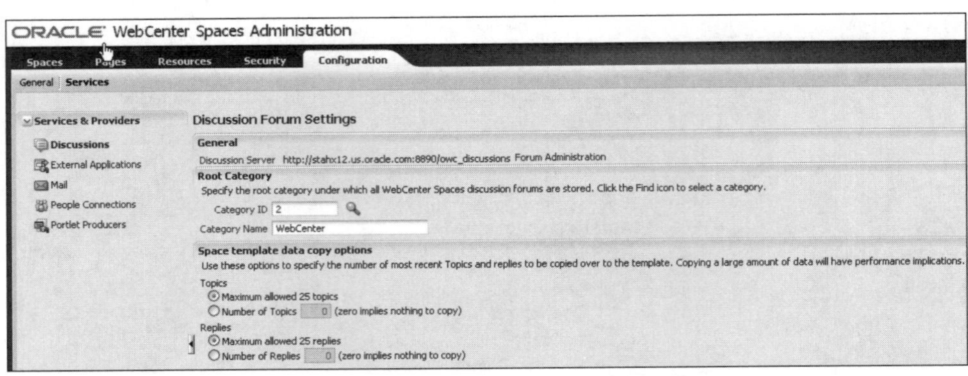

FIGURE 7-17. *Configuring discussion server properties*

this is to register the corresponding portlet producers with the Spaces application. Subsequently, the portlet can be added to any page in the space by editing the page in the page composer, via the resource catalog. Administrators can register new portlet producers (and remove any existing registrations) as well as edit the properties on existing registrations via the user interface shown in Figure 7-18. Note that this configuration can be done in EM by the Fusion Middleware administrator, but the Spaces application provides a convenient embedded user interface for the Spaces administrators to do the same.

Fourth, administrators can perform user management and role management operations in the Spaces application user interface, as shown in Figure 7-19.

It may be necessary for multiple users to have administrative access to the Spaces application. An administrator can provide administrative access to other users via this user interface. The operations in this user interface will result in permissions and grants to be specified in the Identity Management framework, which is described in Chapter 4.

Several roles are available in the application when it is installed the first time, including Administrator, Public-User, and Authenticated-User. Each of these roles has some functionality accessible. The Administrator role has all the administrative functionality accessible. The Public-User role represents the privileges of a guest user who has not logged in to the Spaces application.

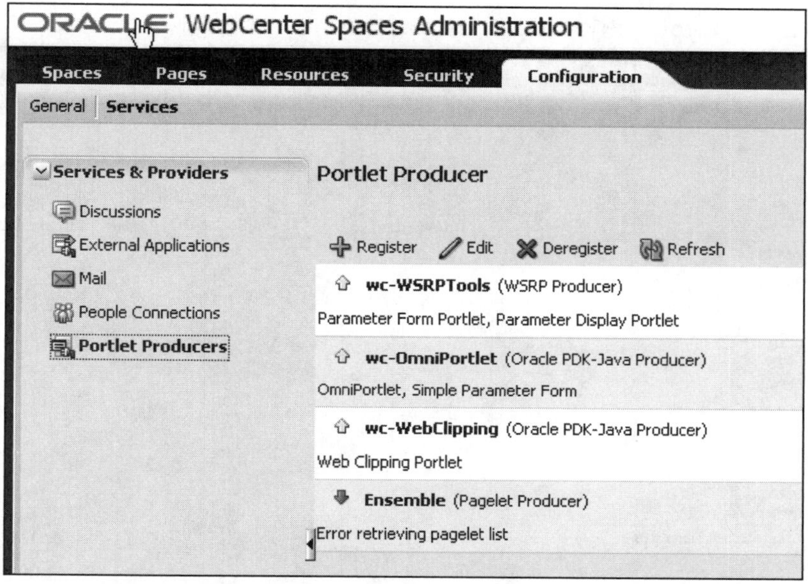

FIGURE 7-18. *Configuring portlet producers*

The functionality accessible to the Public-User role is limited. By default, this user only has access to view some application pages. The Authenticated-User role is for the users who have logged in to the application. Here's a description of some of the administrator functions:

- Administrators can create custom roles and define the functionality accessible to those roles via this user interface. For example, in a specific deployment, if there is a need for two types of authenticated users—managers and non-managers—then the administrator can create a Manager-User role in this user interface and then manage the functionality accessible to either of the roles.
- Administrators can manage the functionality accessible to any of the standard roles, just like specifying the level of access for the custom roles as described earlier.

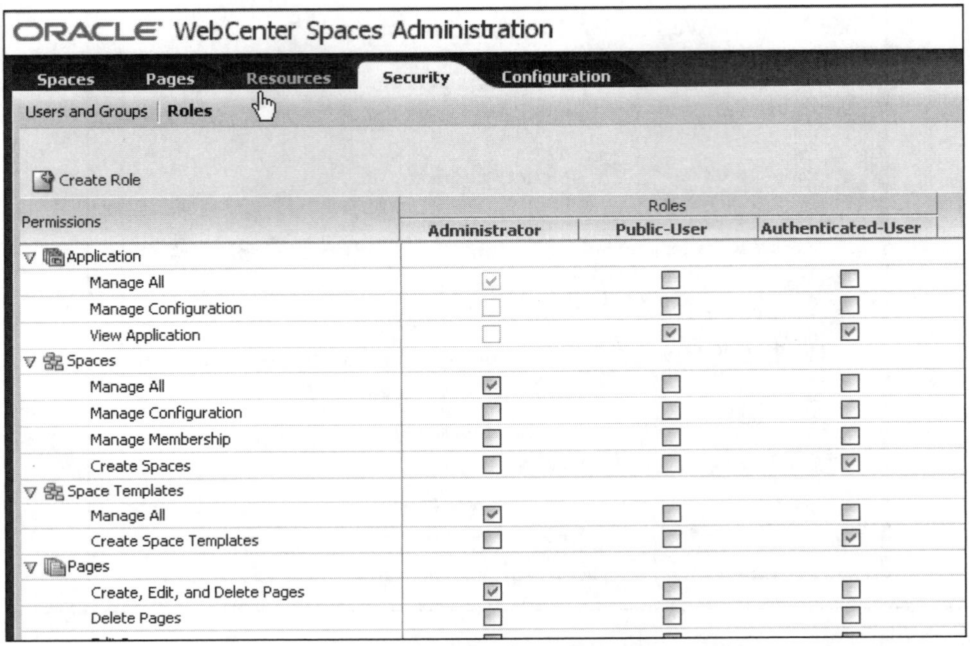

FIGURE 7-19. *Configuring security*

The final configuration discussed involves site resources, which are those resources that can be used across the Spaces application. For example, new page templates can be created by an administrator and then these page templates can be used in multiple pages across spaces. Administrators can create and manage the navigation models available in the application as well as create and manage the resource catalog configuration of the application. Administrators can also create and manage new ADF skins and then use them in the application pages. Figure 7-20 shows the user interface to perform these operations.

The management of spaces, including editing and deleting spaces and making them available offline, can be done through this user interface, as shown in Figure 7-21.

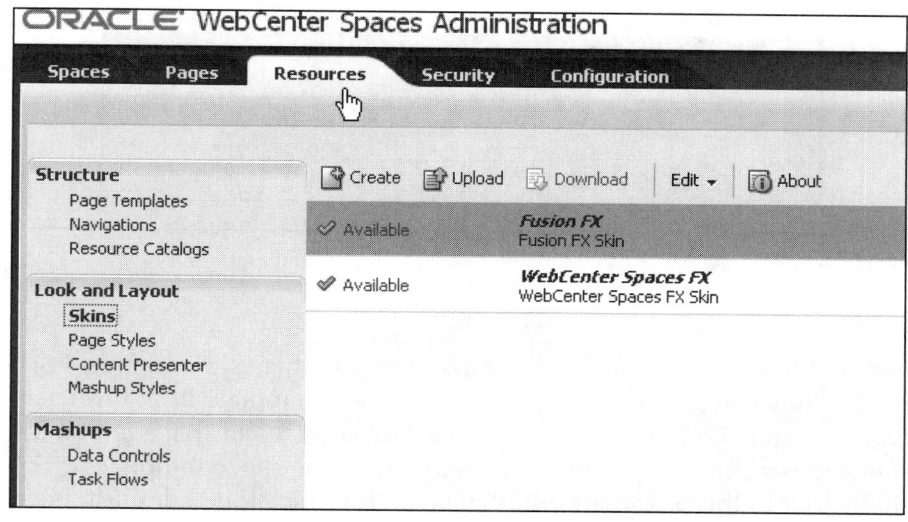

FIGURE 7-20. *Resource Management user interface*

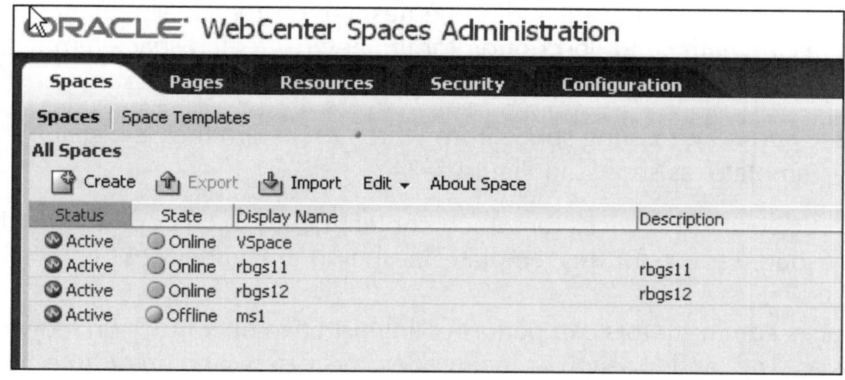

FIGURE 7-21. *Managing Spaces*

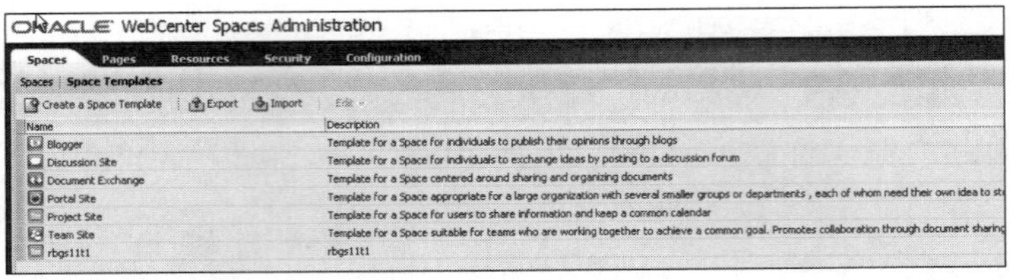

FIGURE 7-22. *Managing space templates*

Administrators can manage space templates in this user interface. For example, they can import a new space or a space template from this user interface. Figure 7-22 shows the user interface to manage space templates. Administrators can also remove access to any of the space templates available out of the box in an installed Spaces application. Administrators can create new space templates in this user interface. Note that moderators with the appropriate privileges can save specific spaces as space templates from the Spaces Administration user interface as well.

Administrators can create new space templates via the Create a Space Template Wizard. Here are the steps to follow:

1. Provide the setup-related properties. For example, set metadata such as the name and description for the newly created space template, as shown in Figure 7-23.
2. Choose an existing space from which to pattern the new space template, as shown in Figure 7-24.
3. Choose the services for which content needs to be copied from the source space for this template, as shown in Figure 7-25.

Spaces administrators can perform administrative operations on individual spaces as well, and for each space, moderators (users who are granted moderator privileges) can perform some configurations. Therefore, overall

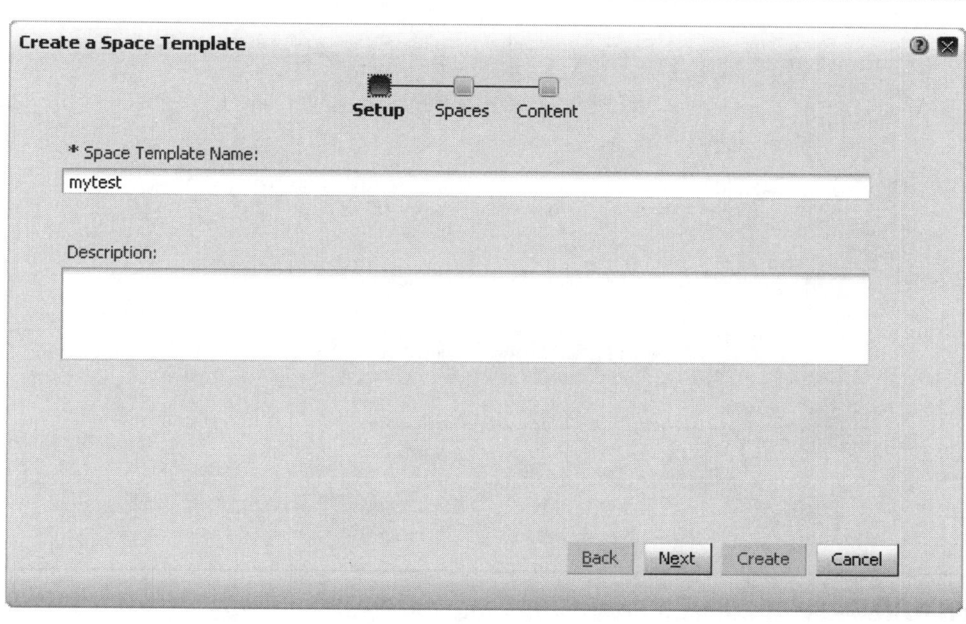

FIGURE 7-23. *Create a Space Template (Setup)*

there are three types of administrators: Fusion Middleware administrators, WebCenter Spaces application administrators, and individual space administrators (or moderators), each with different levels of administrative access.

Test-to-Production Migration of Spaces

This section describes key aspects of migrating a test Spaces instance to a production Spaces instance. This exercise involves configuration, metadata, and data migration. At the highest granularity, one can export the entire application, which is done in EM or via WLST commands. To export the entire application or to back up the entire application, several steps should be taken.

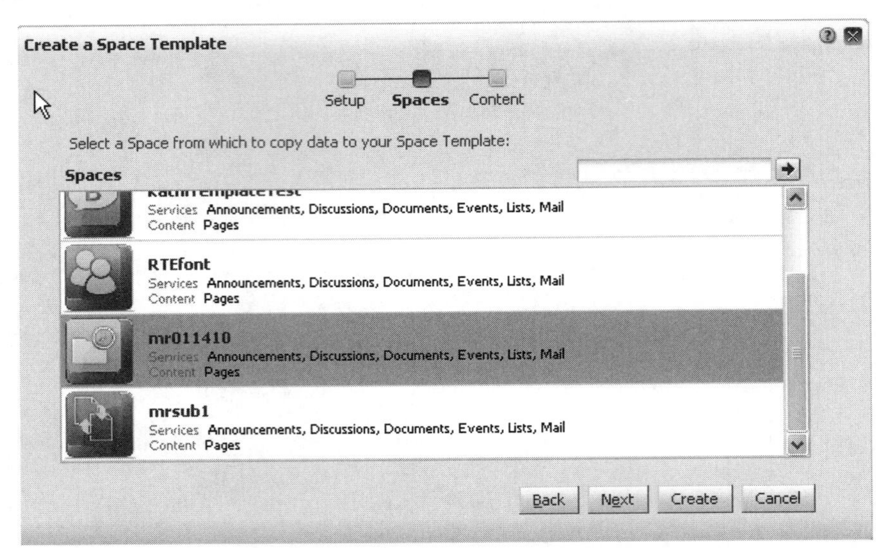

FIGURE 7-24. *Create a Space Template (Spaces)*

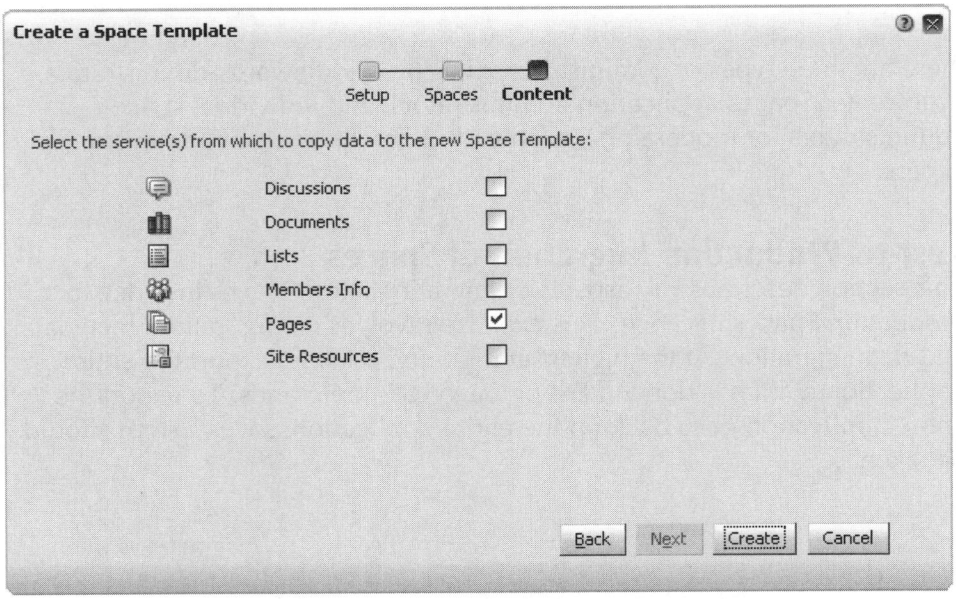

FIGURE 7-25. *Create a Space Template (Content)*

To begin, the administrator can export the application to an .ear file, which includes a .mar file for the metadata and the security policy information. This can be done from the EM or via the exportWebCenterApplication WLST command. The user interface in EM is shown in Figure 7-26, and the menu navigation to access this UI is shown in Figure 7-27.

The WLST command syntax to export the application is as follows:

```
exportWebCenterApplication(appName, fileName, [exportCustomizations],
[exportSecurity], [exportData])
```

Exporting the application using either of these mechanisms provides three options to the administrator:

- The *exportCustomizations* parameter determines whether to export the configuration customizations along with the rest of the application. Note that the metadata customizations and portlet customizations are always exported. Metadata customizations at the user layer, also known as "user personalizations," are not migrated automatically. If necessary, they can be migrated directly via the exportMetadata WLST command.

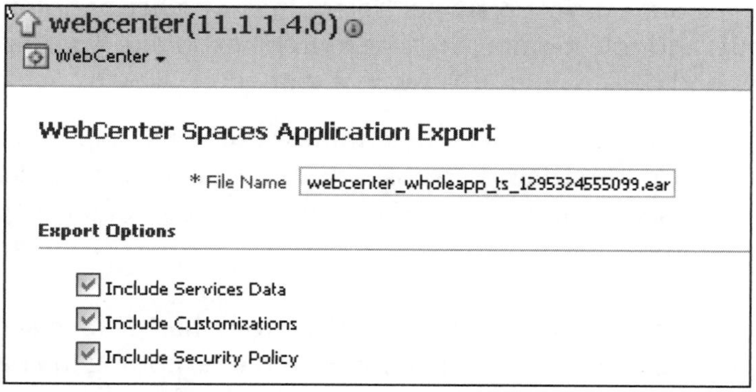

webcenter(11.1.1.4.0)
WebCenter
WebCenter Spaces Application Export
* File Name webcenter_wholeapp_ts_1295324555099.ear
Export Options
Include Services Data
Include Customizations
Include Security Policy

FIGURE 7-26. *Exporting the Spaces application via Enterprise Manager*

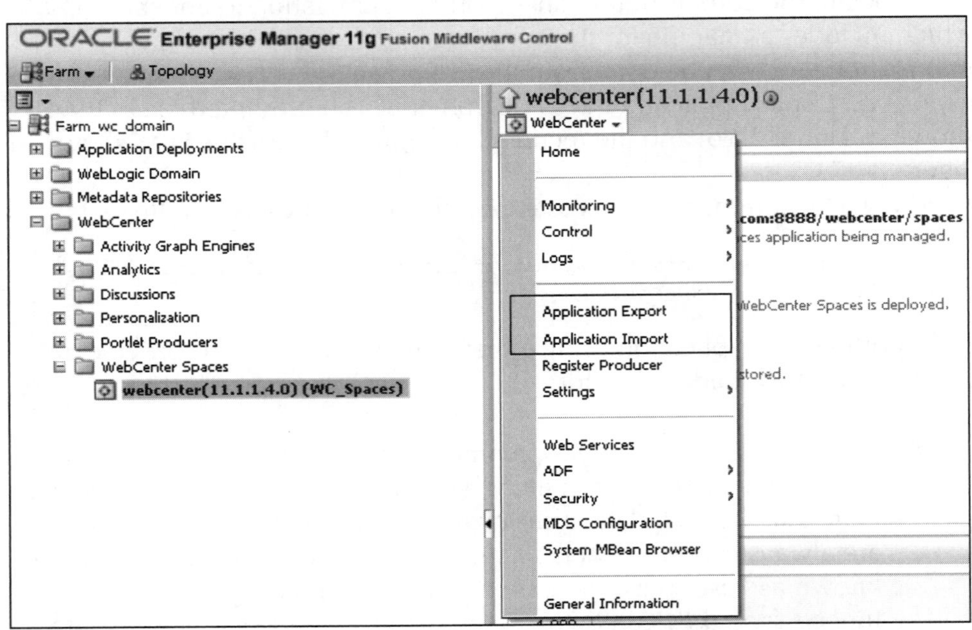

FIGURE 7-27. *Invoking application export and import operations via Enterprise Manager*

- The *exportSecurity* parameter determines whether or not the user details and role memberships need to be exported. The application roles and permissions are always exported.
- The *exportData* parameter determines whether to export data from the WebCenter database repository. Note that exporting data from backend servers is a separate step and is not part of this export operation.

Second, the administrator can export data from the backend servers used by the Spaces application as needed (for example, exporting the data from the associated discussion server to export the Discussions forums and threads associated with the spaces).

Third, the administrator can export the users, groups, and passwords from the identity management system, which is described in detail in Chapter 4.

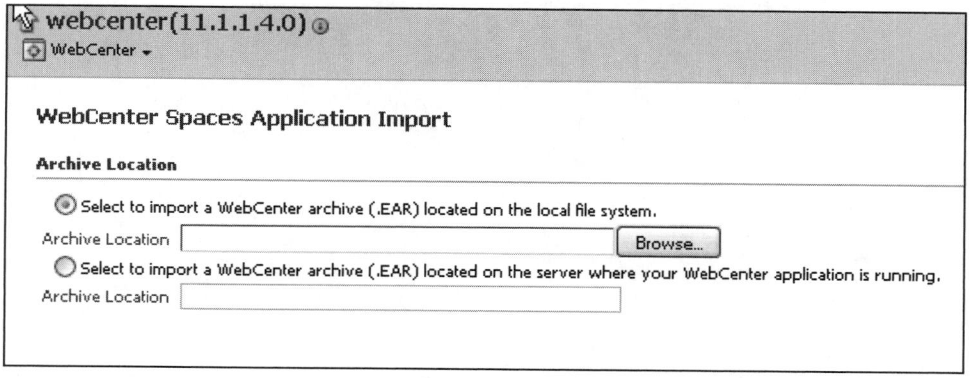

FIGURE 7-28. *Importing the Spaces application via Enterprise Manager*

Finally, the administrator can export user personalizations using the MDS WLST command exportMetadata, as mentioned in Chapter 6.

The archive exported from the Spaces application can then be imported to the target Spaces application. The user interface to perform this operation from EM is shown in the Figure 7-28. The menu option to invoke this UI was shown in Figure 7-27.

This can also be achieved via the following WLST command:

```
importWebCenterApplication(appName, fileName)
```

It is recommended that the version of the Spaces application from which the archive is exported be at the same major version as the application into which the archive is being imported. Importing the backend server data should be done prior to importing the application archive. Required users need to be created in the target identity store before the application archive import is done.

The user interface, as shown in Figure 7-29, can be used for cases where it is required to migrate only one or more spaces instead of the entire application. The WebCenter Spaces Administration pages provide mechanisms to export a specific space. The configuration link from the global region shows the Spaces administration link if the user has access to that functionality. Here is where the administrator can select one or more spaces from this user

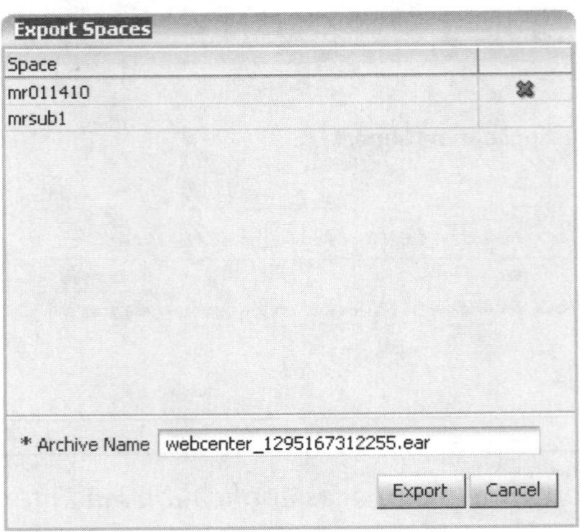

FIGURE 7-29. *Exporting spaces via the Administration user interface*

interface for exporting into an archive. The UI with this administrative option is shown in Figure 7-22. On the target system, from the same user interface the administrator can import the archive that will result in all those spaces being imported. If the same spaces already exist in the target application, the import process will identify this and provide an option either to cancel the import process or to overwrite the spaces already in the target application. Similar to how spaces can be exported and imported from the source instance to the target instance, space templates can also be exported and imported by the administrators from the same user interface.

Chapter Use Case

In this chapter's use case, we pick up where we left off in Chapter 6. In Chapter 3, we went through the steps to create the topology shown in Figure 3-2, with the pricing application deployed to its own cluster and its Web Services interface secured using OWSM. In Chapter 4, we configured this domain with a central LDAP server and set up Single Sign-On (SSO).

In Chapter 5, we deployed to this domain a SOA Suite composite that orchestrates the integration of the pricing application's Model Update web services with the corporate ERP system and exposes updated data through Oracle BAM. In Chapter 6, we deployed the Pricing WorkList ADF application, where the specialty product's product management team approves pricing changes. In this chapter, we will build a WebCenter Portal application that all the users in the enterprise can use to get and discuss information related to pricing. The topology of the target application is shown in Figure 7-30.

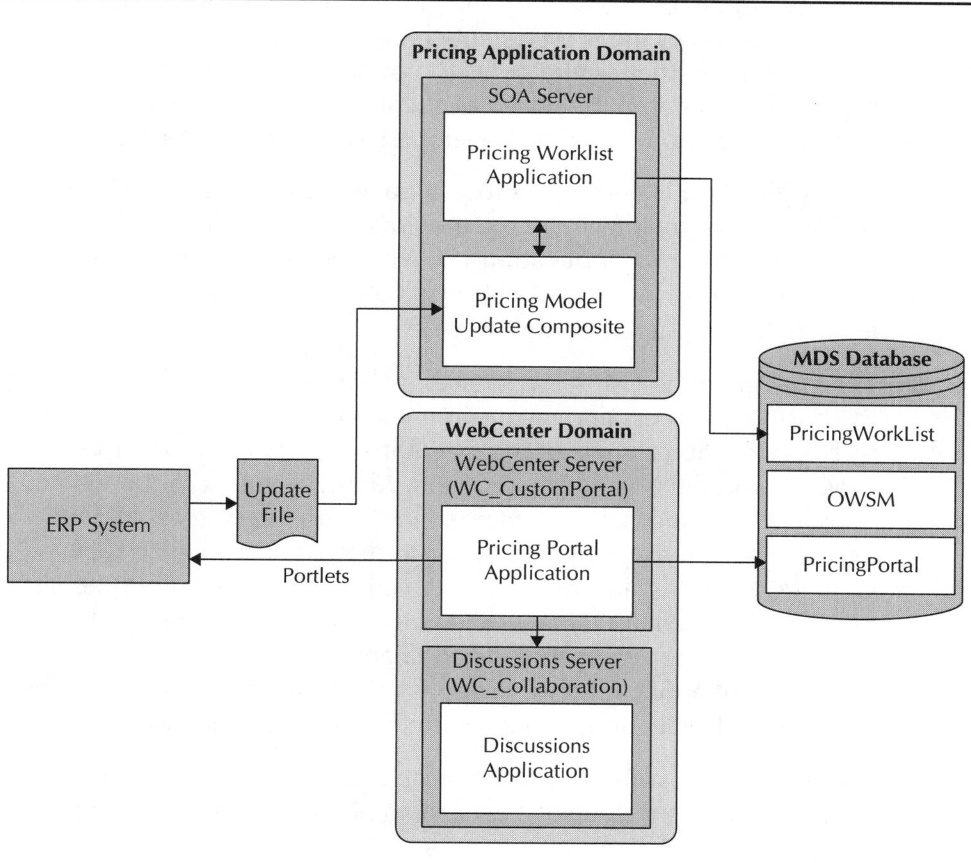

FIGURE 7-30. *Pricing Portal application topology*

Use Case Description

We first discuss the requirements of the portal application in this section. We then discuss how the application was developed and then proceed to discuss the deployment and administration aspects of the application.

After further discussions with the application's product development team, you have gathered the following key aspects about this portal application:

- The ERP system is already deployed and is a portlet producer application that exposes WSRP portlets so that they can be included in other portal applications. A key piece of functionality exposed is a portlet that shows the most recent changes done to the pricing models. One of the requirements for the portal application is to expose this portlet in the portal application pages. The pages in the PricingPortal application are developed to include this portlet.
- The application is developed so that pages can be customized by the senior product management team to include additional portlets exposed by the ERP application via WebCenter Composer. The resource catalog in the application is configured to show portlets from all the registered portlet providers.
- The change in the ERP system raises a change event that is read by the business process and results in invocation of the Pricing Update web service. Some such changes require approval from the specialty product's product management team. Changes that do not need any approval will automatically happen in the pricing system. All the users in the enterprise need a forum to discuss and analyze such changes. Similarly, for the changes that need approval, the specialty product management team would like to discuss them with others before approving. The development team developed the PricingPortal application to meet this requirement by integrating the WebCenter Discussions service with this portal application.

In further discussions with the development team, you understand that the following aspects relate to the deployment and administration of this application:

- The PricingPortal application is contained in its own EAR file named PricingPortal.ear.

- The connection to the production instance of the ERP portlet producer application needs to be set up after the application is deployed.
- The connection to the discussions server needs to be set up after the application is deployed.
- This application needs to be configured with an MDS repository to support portlet functionality and also to support the Composer-based customizations.
- All the product managers in the enterprise need access to the user interface pages in this application, and the senior product management team needs to be able to edit these pages in Composer.

After discussions with the development team, you formulate the strategy for deploying this application. As part of the setup of the environment, you already installed the WebCenter infrastructure, which created the servers illustrated in Figure 7-2. The servers we will use in the following steps are the WC_Collaboration and WC_CustomPortal servers in the wc_domain. An MDS repository, mds-CustomPortalDS, was also created during the installation. Following are the steps to prepare the application for deployment and to prepare the setup required by the functionality in the application:

1. Configure the application to use mds-CustomPortalDS and a partition PricingPortal as the target MDS repository. This is achieved by executing the following WLST commands prior to deploying the application:

```
PricingPortalArchive = getMDSArchiveConfig( fromLocation = '/home/
oracle/deployments/PricingPortal.ear')
PricingPortalArchive.setAppMetadataRepository
( repository = 'mds-CustomPortalDS', partition='PricingPortal',
type='DB', jndi='jdbc/mds/CustomPortalDS')
PricingPortalArchive.save()
```

2. Deploy this EAR file to the WC_CustomPortal server within the wc_ domain, as shown here:

```
deploy('PricingPortal', '/home/oracle/deployments/PricingPortal.ear',
targets='WC_CustomPortal')
```

3. Configure the application to use the discussions application owc_discussions already deployed to the WC_Collaboration server as part of the installation. The value for the default property is set to 1 so that this connection is used by the Discussions service in the PricingPortal application. The WebCenter Discussions forum server is preconfigured out of the box to have oracle/wss10_saml_token_service_policy as the WS-Security policy for its web service endpoint. So, we will use oracle/wss10_saml_token_client_policy as the security policy in the following commands:

```
createDiscussionForumConnection( appName= 'PricingPortal' , name=
'MyDiscussionServer', url = 'http://myenterprisehost1:8890/owc_
discussions', adminUser = 'weblogic', policyURIForAuthAccess =
'oracle/wss10_saml_token_client_policy', default=1)
```

   The value of the parameter *adminUser* needs to be a user account that is configured in the Discussions forum server as an administrator. By default, the user "weblogic" has this configuration. Also, the port used for the Discussions forum server is 8890, which is the default port used by the discussions server.

4. The ERP portlet producer is a WSRP producer. You know the WSDL URI for the producer and that it supports the oracle/wss10_saml_token_client_policy security policy. Also the name of the producer needs to be ERPProducer so that the portlet that is already added to one of the application pages is obtained from this producer. The following WLST command can be used to register this portlet producer:

```
registerWSRPProducer(appName='PricingPortal', name='ERPProducer',
url='http://myenterprisehost1:8080/erpApp/portlets/wsrp2?WSDL',
tokenType='oracle/wss10_saml_token_client_policy',
enforcePolicyURI=0)
```

5. The application user interface is configured to be accessible to the application role PricingPortalUsers, and this role has to be associated with the group PricingProductManagement in the identity store.

Also, the ability to edit these pages via Composer is granted to the application role PricingPortalAdmins, and this role needs to be associated with the group PricingProductSeniorManagement. These can be achieved via the WLST commands shown next.

```
grantAppRole(appStripe="PricingPortal", appRoleName=
"PricingPortalUsers",
principalClass="weblogic.security.principal.WLSGroupImpl",
principalName=  "PricingProductManagement")
grantAppRole(appStripe="PricingPortal", appRoleName=
"PricingPortalAdmins",
principalClass="weblogic.security.principal.WLSGroupImpl",
principalName="
PricingProductSeniorManagement")
```

After these steps, the application is now deployed and all of the dependencies are configured so that the full functionality of the portal application can be used by the product management team. These applications can be configured for Single Sign-On by following the techniques described in Chapter 4. Specific details on configuring the WebCenter discussion server for Single Sign-On are provided in the product documentation.

After your follow-up discussion with the development team to understand the upcoming requirements for the application, you anticipate the administration aspects of the portal application to evolve as follows:

- Registering new portlet producers with the application so that senior product management can add content from other portlet producers, not just the ERP application portlet producer, to the pages of the application.
- The application may need to be migrated to a different environment if the usage of the portal application goes beyond just the product management team to the entire enterprise. Any migration of this application from one environment to another includes migration of these aspects: the information for connecting to the portlet producer and the discussion server, the page customizations to include the ERP portlets, any other personalizations done by the users, and any migration of the discussions content from the discussions server.

Conclusion

This chapter described the WebCenter framework, including the WebCenter Composer technology and how it integrates with MDS, the WebCenter Enterprise 2.0 services, and the WebCenter Portal technology. This chapter also discussed the WebCenter Spaces application. Across all these areas, we discussed how an administrator can perform configuration changes on the application. Finally, we extended our use case discussion to include the deployment of the PricingPortal WebCenter application.

PART II

Deploying and Managing Enterprise Applications on Fusion Middleware

CHAPTER 8

Deploying Fusion Middleware Enterprise Applications

This chapter begins Part II of this book. The chapters in this section outline the detailed steps required for provisioning an end-to-end environment for the pricing application, which we progressively described within the use case sections of the previous chapters. In this first chapter, we begin with a review of the pricing application's functionality and architecture. We then continue with the installation steps for the Fusion Middleware software required by the pricing application, followed by the steps needed for the creation of the WebLogic Server domains and the deployment of the pricing application's different artifacts. Finally, we end this chapter with the steps required to scale out the topology to a two-node cluster.

Review of the Pricing Application

The pricing application is an enterprise application used by a mid-sized household goods manufacturing company to provide a pricing query service. The end users of this service are the company's sales force, which uses the service's web interface to determine the quoting price of a certain set of high-end specialty products, and the specialty product management team, which monitors the business parameters driving the pricing algorithm and, in the case of some special products, is also responsible for the approval of changes to these parameters. The price of these high-end products is subject to frequent change based on market conditions. The pricing application is therefore integrated with the corporate Enterprise Resource Planning (ERP) system to intercept events that affect its pricing model. Figure 8-1 illustrates the different components of the pricing application at a logical level.

Here's a description of the components depicted in Figure 8-1:

- **Pricing Query Web Interface** A web-based user interface used by the sales force to query the price of a specific pricing product. The interface is very simple and accepts a single product stock-keeping unit (SKU) number and returns as a result the suggested price for the product. The implementation of this interface is through a simple Java EE servlet-based web application deployed to WebLogic Server.

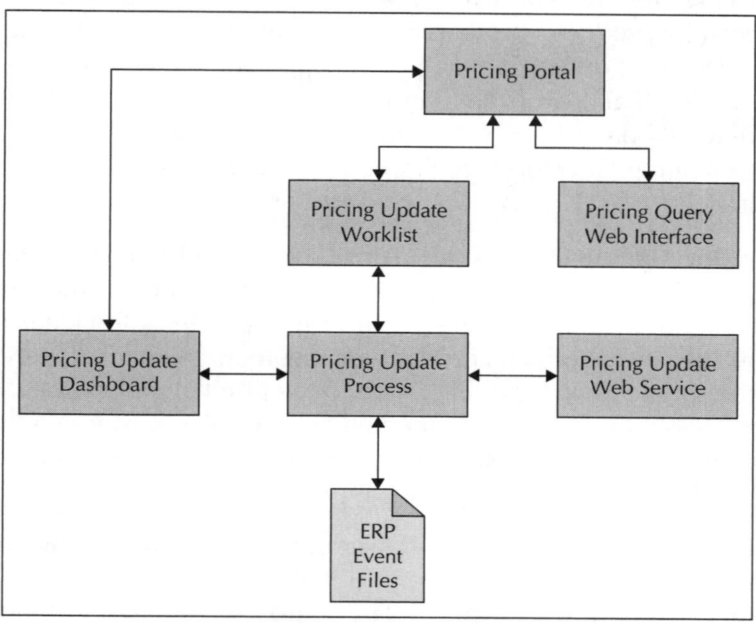

FIGURE 8-1. *Pricing Application logical view*

- **Pricing Update Web Service** A SOAP/HTTP-based web service that provides an operation that allows for the modification of the pricing application's business parameters. The Web Service is implemented as an EJB-based web service deployed to WebLogic Server.
- **Pricing Update Process** A business process that is executed every time changes occur to the company's ERP system that can affect the pricing application's business parameters. The process reads the change event and translates it to the parameters required by the Pricing Update web service. It then invokes the Web Service in order to ensure that the changes are reflected within the pricing application's business model. Depending on the nature of the changes involved, the process in some cases requests an approval from the specialty product's product management team before proceeding with the update of the pricing model. This process is implemented as an Oracle SOA Suite SCA composite.

- **Pricing Update Worklist** A web-based user interface used by the specialty product's product management team for processing approvals of updates to the pricing application's business model when such approvals are required, as deemed necessary by the Pricing Update process. It is implemented using the Oracle Application Development Framework (ADF) and has a rich user interface.
- **Pricing Update Dashboard** A web-based user interface with a single dynamically updated table showing all updates that are made to the pricing application's business model. This interface is used by the specialty product's product management team to actively monitor the changes being made to the pricing application's business model. It is implemented as an Oracle Business Activity Monitoring (BAM) dashboard on top of a BAM business object that is updated by the Pricing Update process.
- **Pricing Portal** A web-based user interface that brings together the interfaces of the Pricing Query web interface, Pricing Update worklist, and Pricing Update dashboard and also exposes the Pricing Update web service through a web interface. This interface is used by the specialty product's product management team as a central point of access to all of the user interfaces and functionality exposed by the different components of the pricing application. It is implemented as an Oracle WebCenter portal.

Together, these components compose the enterprise application known as the pricing application. In the next section, we go through the steps necessary to create an environment for hosting these different components.

Creating the Single-Node Topology

This section outlines the steps required for the creation of an environment to which the components of the pricing application can be deployed. This topology is referred to as a "single-node topology" because it does not include any cluster and no elements of it are replicated for reliability, scalability, or availability purposes. In the next section of this chapter we extend a part of this topology with a cluster in order to achieve scalability for certain elements of the application. Figure 8-2 shows the target topology we are aiming to create in this section.

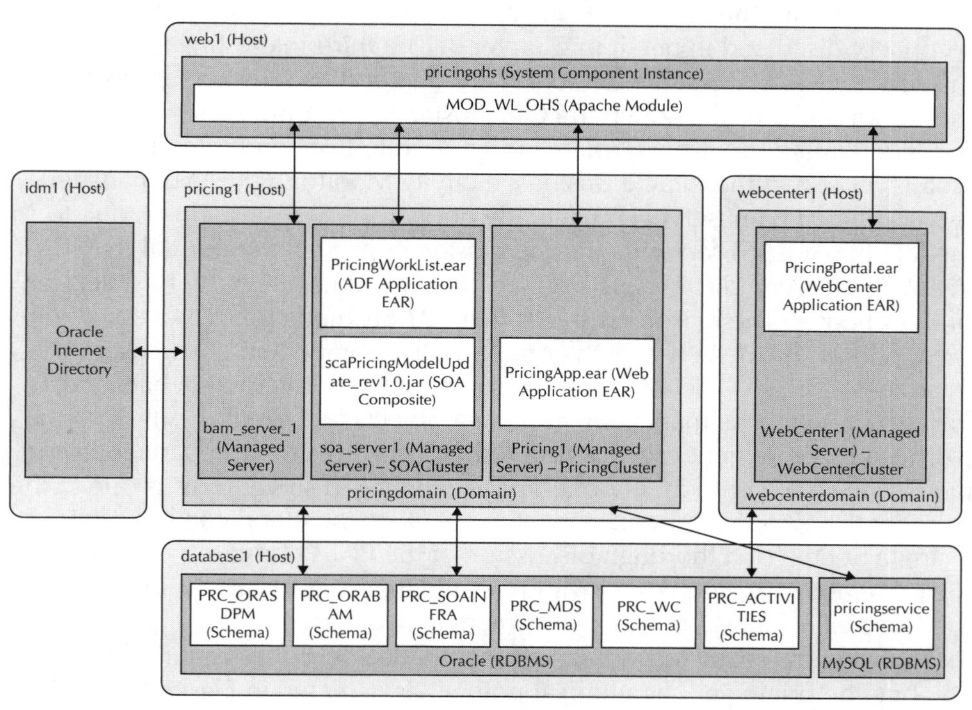

FIGURE 8-2. *Pricing application's single-node topology*

It is worth highlighting a few interesting elements of this topology. First, note that it is made up of two WebLogic Server domains: pricingdomain and webcenterdomain. The reason for this is that the IT department uses webcenterdomain as the single WebCenter domain for the deployment of multiple applications' WebCenter portals. Having such a separate domain allows for the delineation of the administrative responsibilities for this domain from other domains that are exclusively dedicated to a single enterprise application such as the pricingdomain. The second thing to note is that the two domains are using a single Metadata Services (MDS) schema. This allows for the simplification of the topology by reducing the need for multiple MDS schemas for different Fusion Middleware domains. The usage of a single MDS schema between multiple domains (and consumers in general) is possible because different applications can separate their metadata within the same MDS schema through the use of MDS partitions, a concept discussed in detail in Chapter 3. The third interesting element of this topology is that a single Oracle HTTP Server (OHS) instance is used to front both domains. Although the OHS instance can only be registered with a single domain to form a farm, it can be used to front multiple domains. Finally, note that the Oracle Business Activity Monitoring (BAM) managed server (named bam_server1) is actually not part of a cluster. This is due to the fact that a BAM server cannot be clustered through the normal WebLogic Server clustering steps, which we will cover in the next section of this chapter. The reason for this is that BAM is made up of two core components: BAM Web, which consists of the component's web user interfaces, and BAM Server, which consists of the component's backend infrastructure for the management of data objects and reports. Although the BAM Web component can be clustered, it first needs to be separated from the BAM Server component on a separate managed server. This is due to the fact that the BAM Server component is not clusterable and can only support a single node. For a thorough discussion of the BAM clustering process, please refer to "Oracle Fusion Middleware High Availability Guide" within the Oracle Fusion Middleware documentation library.

We are now ready to start describing the detailed steps required for creating the pricing application's topology, as depicted in Figure 8-2. Before doing so, however, it should be noted that for all steps outlined in this section of the book, the following assumptions apply:

- A database host (named database1 in Figure 8-2) containing an installation of the Oracle RDBMS and MySQL databases is already provisioned and available for use.
- All Fusion Middleware software being used by the pricing application has been downloaded and is available for use. Fusion Middleware software can be downloaded through the Oracle Technology Network or My Oracle Support. All products downloaded must be at the same exact patchset number. The patchset number is the fourth number within the Oracle Fusion Middleware product's version string. As an example, when a product's version string is 11.1.1.4, the patchset number is 4.
- A UNIX system is being used.

Besides these assumptions, all other elements required for creating the topology described by Figure 8-2 should be covered in this section.

Overall Flow of Events for the Creation of the Environment

In the sections that follow, we go through the steps required for the creation of the Fusion Middleware topology shown in Figure 8-2. These steps fall into two categories: the installation of the Fusion Middleware product binaries within a Middleware home directory and the creation of an environment based on these binaries on which the pricing application can execute (known as the configuration process). The following diagram illustrates the steps that fall into these two categories.

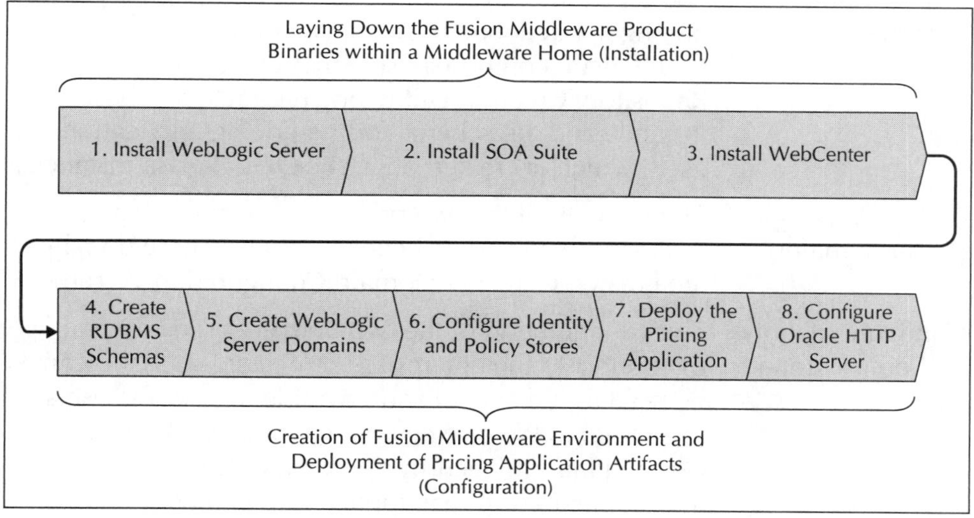

The Table 8-1 provides a summary of each of these steps.

Installing the Fusion Middleware Software

We will use a single user, named "oracle," to perform the installation of all software components described in this section.

Step	Description
Install WebLogic Server.	Installation of WebLogic Server on the pricing1 and webcenter1 hosts. This installation will also include the installation of the Sun Java Runtime Environment (JRE).
Install SOA Suite.	Installation of Oracle SOA Suite on the pricing1 host within the same Middleware home directory as WebLogic Server.
Install WebCenter.	Installation of Oracle WebCenter on the webcenter1 host within the same Middleware home directory as WebLogic Server.
Create RDBMS schemas.	The creation of the RDBMS schemas required by the pricing application. These consist of the Fusion Middleware component schemas created using the Repository Creation Utility on an Oracle database instance and the schema for the pricing application itself, which is created on a MySQL database instance.
Create WebLogic Server domains.	The creation of the two pricing application domains: pricingdomain and webcenterdomain. These domains are created using the Domain Configuration Wizard.
Configure identity and policy stores.	The configuration of the two domains' security realm to connect to the enterprise LDAP store so that it can be used as the central source of identity for the users logging in to the pricing application. The domain's Oracle Platform Security Services (OPSS) settings are also configured so that applications can use the same LDAP server as the authorization policy store.
Deploy the pricing application.	The deployment of the archives and configurations that make up the pricing application.
Configure Oracle HTTP Server.	The installation and configuration of an Oracle HTTP Server instance to front the web interfaces of the pricing application (spanning both domains) as a reverse HTTP proxy.

TABLE 8-1. *Pricing Application Installation and Configuration Step*

Installing WebLogic Server

The first product we need to install on the pricing1 and webcenter1 hosts is WebLogic Server. The WebLogic Server installation software is a wizard-based tool that guides you through the installation steps. For the pricing application, the following elements of the WebLogic Server installation process are important to note:

- Use /home/oracle/products as the Middleware home directory. This directory will also be used for as the Middleware home directory for the installation of all subsequent Fusion Middleware products. From now on, we will refer to it as the MW_HOME directory.
- If you are using My Oracle Support, complete the information requested by the Register for Security Updates window of the installation tool, as shown in the following screenshot. This information will enable the configuration of the Oracle Configuration Manager (OCM) as part of your installation. For more information on the purpose of OCM, see the gray box titled "Oracle Configuration Manager."

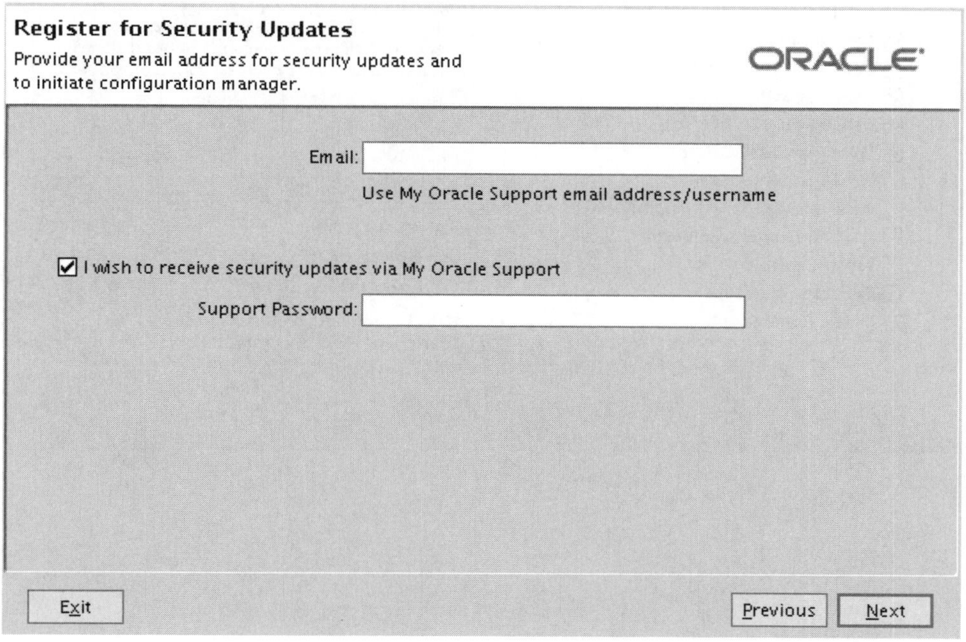

- Choose the custom installation option to ensure that only the components of WebLogic Server that are needed by the pricing application and Fusion Middleware layered products are installed, as shown in the following screenshot. These components are:
  - Core Application Server
  - Administration Console
  - Configuration Wizard and Upgrade Framework
  - WebLogic SCA
  - WebLogic JDBC Drivers
  - Third Party JDBC Drivers

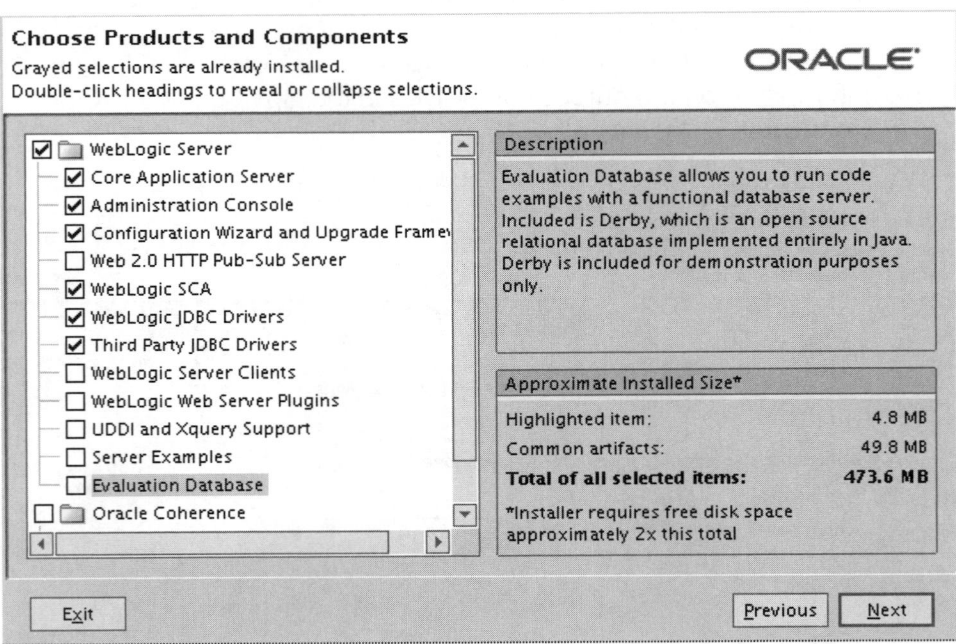

- Choose the Sun Java Runtime Environment (JRE) as the Java runtime to be installed. The WebLogic Server installation includes a copy of both the Sun and Oracle JRockit Java JREs. Optionally, you can skip installing any of these JREs and use a separately installed one, but in general it is a good idea to stick with the packaged JREs because these are the exact versions on which the version of the product being installed is certified.
- Accept the default installation directory of /home/oracle/products/wlserver_10.3. This will be your WebLogic Server ORACLE_HOME. As you can see, the WebLogic Server installation tool provides the flexibility of creating the WebLogic Server ORACLE_HOME within any path. However, the installation of the layered Fusion Middleware products requires that WebLogic Server be installed within the MW_HOME directory with the default name used by the installer.

Once you have completed the execution of the WebLogic Server installation tool, the WebLogic Server installation process is complete and you are now ready for the installation of Oracle SOA Suite.

Oracle Configuration Manager

All Fusion Middleware installation tools will attempt to configure the Oracle Configuration Manager (OCM) component. Users can decide whether to configure OCM by providing the information requested within the Register for Security Updates screen. If this information is not provided, OCM is not configured.

OCM is a low-footprint process (in terms of both CPU and memory usage) that is executed on a periodic basis on hosts where it is configured. Its task is to collect information about the Oracle products installed and configured on a given box and to send this information to a central server within My Oracle Support. The information is then used by Oracle in two ways: First, My Oracle Support uses the information to send out important notifications (in the form of e-mails) when security updates are found that are relevant to the installed

(continued)

products and their configuration. Second, some Oracle management tools, such as Oracle Enterprise Manager Grid Control, have built functionality on top of the data collected by OCM to simplify the management of Oracle products. As an example, Enterprise Manager Grid Control provides a feature that allows for the analysis of the configuration information collected by OCM for WebLogic Server domains and the comparison of this information across different collection snapshots in order to analyze the changes that have occurred over time.

For Fusion Middleware products, OCM collects three type of information. First, OCM goes through all Fusion Middleware WebLogic Server domains and collects a subset of the information stored in their config.xml file hierarchy. Second, OCM collects the content of the opmn.xml file from each configured system component instance directory. Finally, OCM collects information about the set of products installed within an MW_HOME (such as the product components and their versions).

Installing SOA Suite

With the installation of WebLogic Server completed, we are now ready to install SOA Suite via its installation tool, which is a wizard-based graphical user interface. The following elements of the SOA Suite installation process are important to note:

- The first thing the installer will query you for is the location of a Java Runtime Environment (JRE). Point the tool to the JRE directory installed within MW_HOME as part of your WebLogic Server installation.
- At the Install Software Updates screen, shown in the following screenshot, enter your My Oracle Support credentials. This allows the installer to connect to Oracle support to check for any critical patches that may have been released for the software you are

installing and, if so, download and install them as part of the installation process.

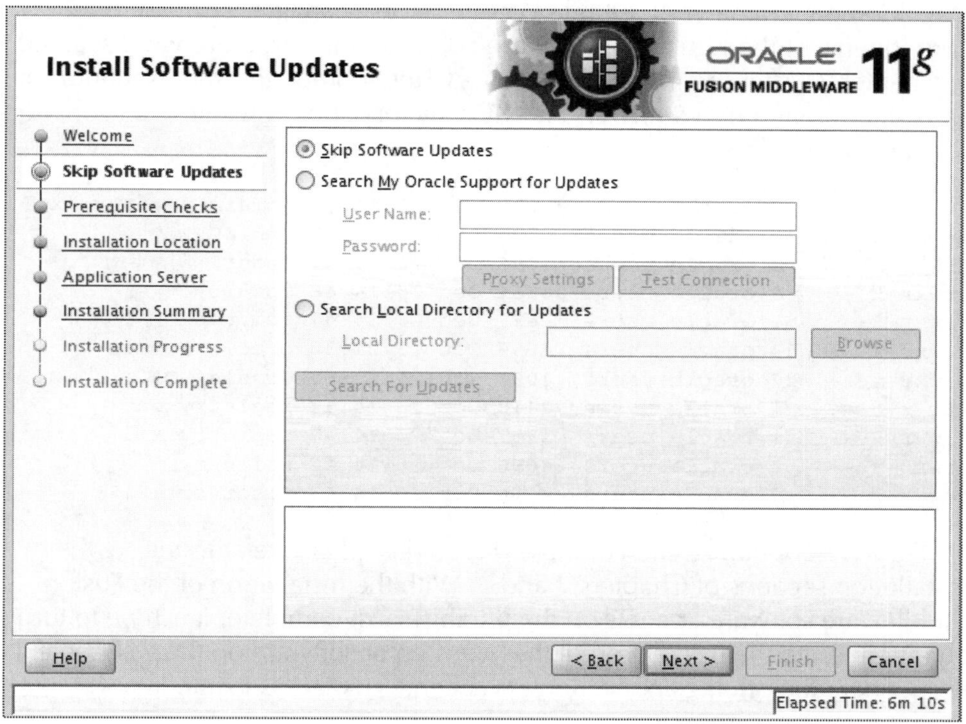

- Use the same MW_HOME used for the installation of WebLogic Server (that is /home/oracle/products).
- Use an Oracle home directory name of Oracle_SOA.
- When prompted to choose an application server, choose WebLogic Server. SOA Suite can also be installed on other application servers such as IBM WebSphere. However, a discussion of the architecture of SOA Suite on such third-party application servers is beyond the scope of this book.

The SOA Suite installation process installs the SOA Infrastructure components, Oracle Business Activity Monitoring, User Messaging Service, Enterprise Manager Fusion Middleware Control, Oracle Application Development Framework, Oracle Web Services Manager, and other components of the Fusion Middleware common infrastructure we discussed in Chapter 3. After the installation of SOA Suite completes, the execution of an ls -l command on your MW_HOME directory should result in a listing similar to the following:

```
-rw-rw----   1 oracle users   133 Oct 20 14:46 domain-registry.xml
drwxr-x---   7 oracle users  4096 Oct 20 14:47 jdk160_21
drwxr-x---   2 oracle users  4096 Oct 20 14:47 logs
drwxr-x---   6 oracle users 36864 Oct 20 14:46 modules
-rw-r-----   1 oracle users   623 Oct 20 14:47 ocm.rsp
drwxr-x---  33 oracle users  4096 Oct 25 21:30 oracle_common
drwxr-x---  27 oracle users  4096 Oct 24 13:52 Oracle_SOA
-rw-r-----   1 oracle users 72418 Oct 20 14:47 registry.dat
-rw-r-----   1 oracle users  1757 Oct 20 14:47 registry.xml
drwxr-x---   8 oracle users  4096 Oct 20 14:46 utils
drwxr-x---   9 oracle users  4096 Oct 20 14:47 wlserver_10.3
```

For a description of each of these directories, please refer to the installation sections of Chapters 2 and 3. With the installation of the Fusion Middleware software artifacts on the pricing1 host complete, it is time to turn our attention to the installation of the WebCenter software on the webcenter1 host, where the pricing application's webcenterdomain is located.

Installing WebCenter

The installation process for Oracle WebCenter is nearly identical to the installation process we just followed for Oracle SOA Suite. The same MW_HOME directory should be used and the WebCenter Oracle Home directory name to use should be Oracle_WC. Before installing WebCenter, you first need to install WebLogic Server on the webcenter1 machine as described in detail in Chapter 2. After you have completed the WebCenter installation process, you are done with the Fusion Middleware installation required on the webcenter1 host.

Configuring the Initial Environment

With all of the software components needed by the pricing application installed, we can now turn our attention to the creation of the environment on which the application is to be deployed. This task is also sometimes referred to simply as the *configuration* phase. As discussed in detail in Chapters 2 and 3, Fusion Middleware products have a clear separation of installation and configuration: The software's binaries are laid down on disk as part of the installation process. The individual configurations of the components encapsulated within the installed binaries are then created in the form of domains and system components. Domains encapsulate the configuration of WebLogic Server entities such as managed servers and clusters. System components encapsulate the configuration of instances of non–Java-EE-based components such as instances of the Oracle HTTP Server. In this section we begin by configuring the pricing application's environment, then move on to deploy the deployment archives that constitute the various parts of the application, and finally review how to automate the different elements of this process.

Creating the Schemas

The first step in configuring the environment is to ensure that the database schemas needed by the applications are created. The pricing application's environment needs two types of database schemas—those needed by the Fusion Middleware products and one schema needed by the Pricing Update web service and query components deployed on the Pricing1 managed server, as shown earlier in Figure 8-2. As discussed in more detail in Chapter 3, database schemas needed by Fusion Middleware products are created by the Repository Creation Utility (RCU). You can download the RCU from the Oracle Technology Network, and it will allow you to create the schemas required by the latest available versions of all Fusion Middleware products. To create the schemas needed by the two WebLogic Server domains located on the pricing1 host, run the RCU as follows:

- After downloading and running RCU, select the Create option. After this you will be prompted to provide information about your database instance. Although Fusion Middleware products can also use IBM DB2 and Microsoft SQL databases, for the pricing application we will be using an Oracle RDBMS database. The RCU requires the credentials of a system user. The reason for this is that as part of the creation of Fusion Middleware schemas in a database, RCU also creates a table called SYSTEM.SCHEMA_VERSION_REGISTRY (if the table already exists, RCU just maintains it). This table is used to maintain state and version information regarding all other Fusion Middleware schemas created within that database instance. This information is, in turn, used by Fusion Middleware management tools to facilitate life-cycle capabilities such as upgrade and patching.

- The Select Components screen of the RCU is where you choose the schemas you would like to create. This screen presents the list of all component schemas on which any Fusion Middleware products, including the common infrastructure components, may have a dependency. The pricing application only has components built on top of Oracle SOA Suite and WebCenter. Therefore, all you need to select are the AS Common Schemas, SOA and BPM Infrastructure, and the WebCenter Suite set of schemas, as shown in the following screenshot. A couple important notes should be made with regard to this screen. First, you should deselect the Audit Services and Enterprise Scheduler Services schemas (listed under AS Common Schemas) because the pricing application does not use the Oracle Platform Security Services audit service (as covered in Chapter 4 in detail), nor does it have any dependencies on the Enterprise Scheduler Services schema, which is an internal component used by Oracle Fusion Applications products that use Fusion Middleware. Second, you should select the Create a New Prefix option and specify a prefix of **PRC** so that all schemas are created (as shown within the Schema Owner column) with the value PRC_ as their prefix. This RCU feature allows multiple Fusion Middleware domains to share a single RDBMS database instance because multiple schemas, with different names, can be created for the same component.

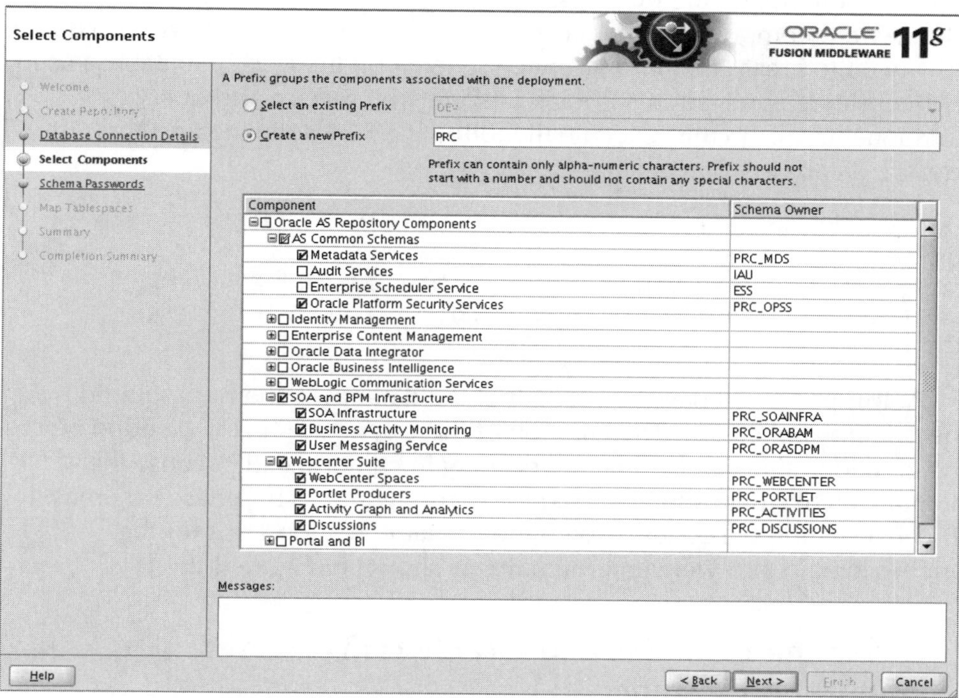

- On the Schema Passwords screen, choose the Use One Password for All option and set a password of **welcome1** for all schemas. RCU also allows you to enter a different password for each schema password separately, but we will not use that option.
- Finally, the Map Tablespaces page allows you to tune detailed schema properties such as the specific data files that each tablespace should use and their size settings. This screen is designed for DBAs to fine-tune the schema settings at creation time. For the pricing application, we can just use the default tablespace settings.

After completing the RCU session, you have created all Fusion Middleware component schemas needed by the pricing application. You now need to create the pricingservice schema on the MySQL database used by the pricing application's Pricing Update web service and query components. To do this, execute the following SQL script against the MySQL database instance:

```
CREATE DATABASE pricingservice;
USE pricingservice;
CREATE TABLE PRICEMODEL (productSku SMALLINT NOT NULL,
marketConditionIndex INT, revenueIndex INT, PRIMARY
KEY(productSku));
```

At this point you have created all of the database schemas required by the pricing application. The creation of these schemas has to be done before the creation of the WebLogic Server domain can proceed because the domain's JDBC data sources need to be configured to use these schemas. In the next section we continue with the domain creation steps for the pricingdomain and webcenterdomain, as shown in Figure 8-2.

Creating the Domains and Oracle HTTP Server Configuration Instance

As shown in Figure 8-2, the components of the pricing application are deployed onto two domains. The first, named pricingdomain, is used to host the following components:

- The pricing application's web UI (the query interface) and Model Update web service. Both of these are contained within a single EAR file named PricingApp.ear. We will deploy this EAR file to its own dedicated managed server, which will need to be extended with the Fusion Middleware common infrastructure Java Required Files (see Chapter 3 for details) so that we can secure its web services using the Oracle Web Services Manager (OWSM).
- The pricing application's SOA Suite composite, which contains the logic for communicating with the corporate Enterprise Resource Planning (ERP) system in order to receive product update events, to

request approval for the submission of a change to the pricing model if needed, and invoke the pricing application's Model Update web service. The composite is contained within a SOA Archive (SAR) JAR file named sca_PricingModelUpdate_rev1.0.jar. We will deploy this EAR file to a SOA infrastructure managed server.

- The pricing application's custom ADF-based worklist application, which is used by end users to approve or reject update events to the pricing model. This application is contained in its own EAR file named PricingWorkList.ear. We will also deploy this EAR file to the SOA infrastructure managed server.

The second domain of the pricing application, named pricingwebcenter, is used to host the Pricing WebCenter–based portal that brings together the different interfaces of the pricing application for use by the specialty products product management group. This application is contained in its own EAR file named PricingPortal.ear. Each of these domains will be configured on their own host machines, respectively named pricing1 and webcenter1. In the next sections we will review the process for creating these two domains.

Creating the Pricing Domain As we reviewed in Chapter 2 and 3, Fusion Middleware domains are created through the configuration wizard. We will create the domain using the same user, named "oracle," as we used for the installation process. Note that if you don't use the same user and the user used for running the configuration wizard does not have write access to the WebLogic Server ORACLE_HOME directory, then the configuration wizard will end with an error indicating that it was unable to complete the domain creation process. This is due to the fact that the configuration wizard attempts to modify the WebLogic Server Node Manager properties in order to prepare its configuration for the management of the domain being created. This step is not necessary, and the error can be safely ignored. In Chapter 11, we will cover in detail the steps required for configuring the node manager for the pricing application domains. For the purpose of this section's steps, it is sufficient that the user creating the domain have read access to the MW_HOME directory and its content. To use the configuration wizard to create the pricingdomain, follow these instructions:

1. Run the configuration wizard from the ~/products/wlserver_10.3/common/bin/config.sh directory.
2. Select the Create a New WebLogic Domain option as opposed to Extend an Existing WebLogic Domain.
3. On the Select Domain Source window, select the Oracle Enterprise Manager, Oracle SOA Suite, Oracle Web Services Manager, and Oracle Business Activity Monitoring templates, as shown in the following screenshot. These domain configuration templates allow for the creation of all the managed servers (and the deployment of all artifacts) necessary for this domain.

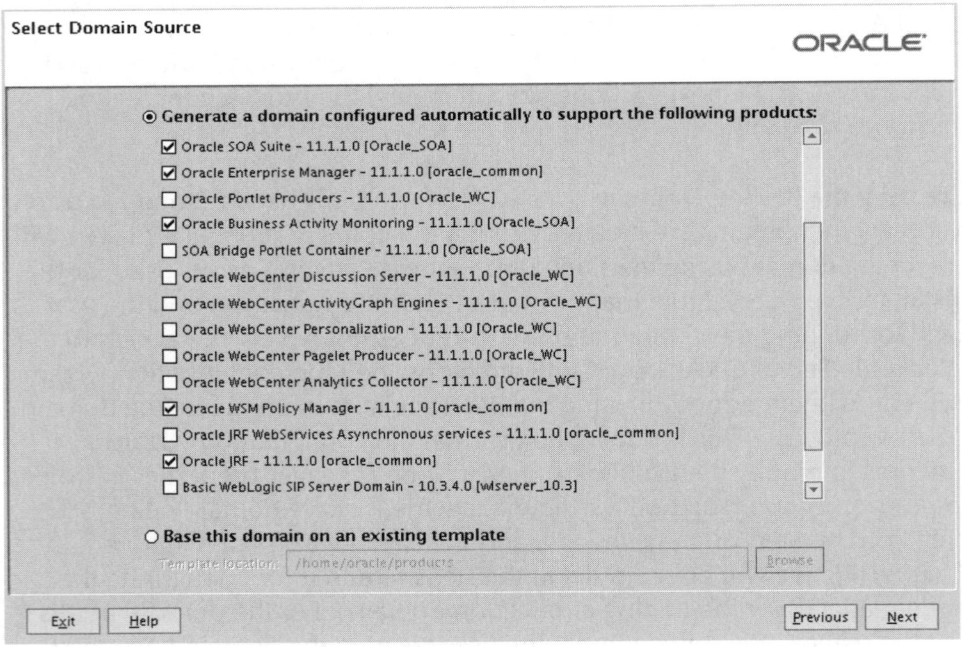

Select Domain Source

ORACLE

Generate a domain configured automatically to support the following products:

- [x] Oracle SOA Suite - 11.1.1.0 [Oracle_SOA]
- [x] Oracle Enterprise Manager - 11.1.1.0 [oracle_common]
- [ ] Oracle Portlet Producers - 11.1.1.0 [Oracle_WC]
- [x] Oracle Business Activity Monitoring - 11.1.1.0 [Oracle_SOA]
- [ ] SOA Bridge Portlet Container - 11.1.1.0 [Oracle_SOA]
- [ ] Oracle WebCenter Discussion Server - 11.1.1.0 [Oracle_WC]
- [ ] Oracle WebCenter ActivityGraph Engines - 11.1.1.0 [Oracle_WC]
- [ ] Oracle WebCenter Personalization - 11.1.1.0 [Oracle_WC]
- [ ] Oracle WebCenter Pagelet Producer - 11.1.1.0 [Oracle_WC]
- [ ] Oracle WebCenter Analytics Collector - 11.1.1.0 [Oracle_WC]
- [x] Oracle WSM Policy Manager - 11.1.1.0 [oracle_common]
- [ ] Oracle JRF WebServices Asynchronous services - 11.1.1.0 [oracle_common]
- [x] Oracle JRF - 11.1.1.0 [oracle_common]
- [ ] Basic WebLogic SIP Server Domain - 10.3.4.0 [wlserver_10.3]

Base this domain on an existing template

Template location: /home/oracle/products Browse

Exit Help Previous Next

4. When the wizard prompts you for the domain name and directory, enter the following information:
   - Enter **pricingdomain** as the domain name.
   - Enter the domain directory as **/home/oracle**.
   - Enter the application directory as **/home/oracle/pricingdomainapplications**.

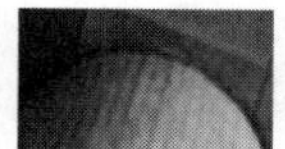

NOTE
The domain directory does not have to be within the MW_HOME directory of the installation. In fact, it is often best to keep the domain directory of your applications separate from the MW_HOME installation directory because, as we will see in Chapter 9, the MW_HOME directory's structure should be configured as a read-only directory for security purposes, whereas the domain directory is often written to by the WebLogic Server managed servers and the Fusion Middleware layered products.

5. Choose an administrative user name of **weblogic** and a password of **welcome1**.
6. In Configure Server Start Mode and JDK window, select the Production start mode and select the Sun JDK.
7. Within the Configure JDBC Component Schema window, enter the information listed next, as illustrated in the following screenshot. Note that this is the window that prompts for the information required for configuring the JDBC data sources of the domain being created.
   - Set the password for all component schemas to **welcome1**.
   - Set the hostname for all component schemas to **database1**.

- Set the other required information as per the set of schemas created through the RCU and shown in the following screenshot. Note that you need to change the prefix to PRC from DEV. Also note that you should set the schema name for the OWSM and SOA Suite Metadata Services schemas to be the same because both these components will share a single MDS schema.

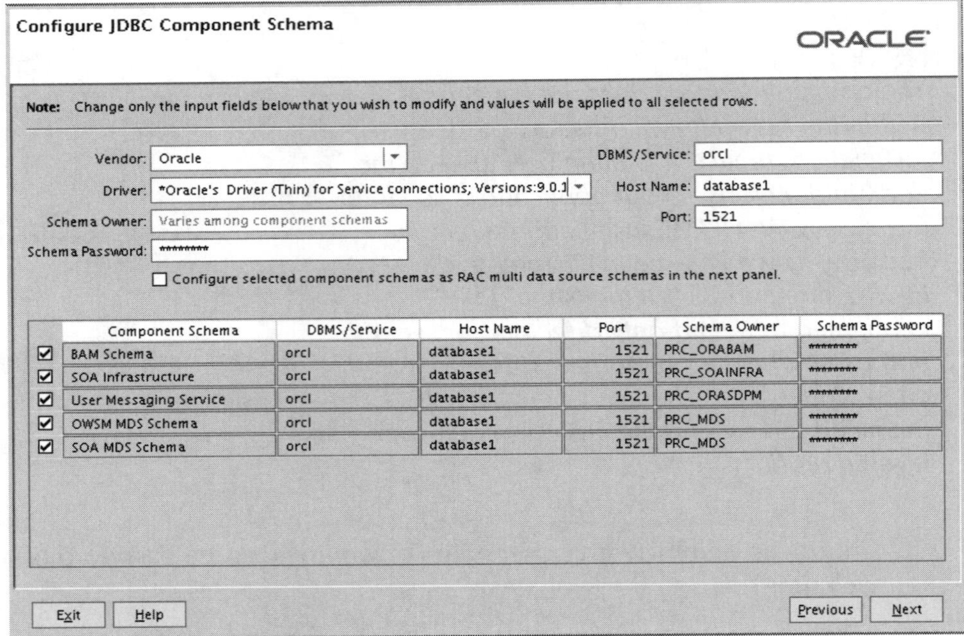

8. Within the Select Optional Configuration, select the Managed Servers, Clusters and Machines option.

9. Create an additional managed server named Pricing1 and a cluster named PricingCluster. Target Pricing1 to PricingCluster. For the managed servers, don't use SSL, and set the port number of the Pricing1 server to 7011.

10. Create another cluster named SOACluster and target the soa_server1 managed server to it.

11. Create a single machine named pricing1 and target all managed servers to this machine.
12. Skip the Create HTTP Proxy Applications screen. This screen is used to designate a managed server within the domain to serve as a reverse proxy for HTTP requests to the other servers and clusters within the domain. We will instead use the Oracle HTTP Server for this purpose.

In the final screen of the configuration wizard, you are asked to confirm the creation of the domain after which point the wizard proceeds to create the domain directory. When this process completes, you should be able to browse to the domain's config directory (~/pricingdomain/config) and open the config.xml file, which is the master XML file containing all of the domain's configuration information. The content of this file should reflect the information you entered within the configuration wizard session. As a validation point, make sure that within the config.xml file all four servers within the domain—that is, the administration server (AdminServer), the pricing services server (Pricing1), the SOA infrastructure server (soa_server1), and the Oracle Business Activity Monitoring server (bam_server1)—are listed within the <server> and <cluster> elements, as per the following listing:

```
<server>
  <name>AdminServer</name>
  <listen-address></listen-address>
  <server-diagnostic-config>
    <name>AdminServer</name>
    <diagnostic-context-enabled>true</diagnostic-context-enabled>
  </server-diagnostic-config>
</server>
<server>
  <name>bam_server1</name>
      <machine>pricing1</machine>
  <listen-port>9001</listen-port>
  <listen-address></listen-address>
  <server-diagnostic-config>
    <name>bam_server1</name>
    <diagnostic-context-enabled>true</diagnostic-context-enabled>
  </server-diagnostic-config>
</server>
```

```
<server>
  <name>soa_server1</name>
  <machine>pricing1</machine>
  <listen-port>8001</listen-port>
  <cluster>SOACluster</cluster>
  <listen-address></listen-address>
  <server-diagnostic-config>
    <name>soa_server1</name>
    <diagnostic-context-enabled>true</diagnostic-context-enabled>
  </server-diagnostic-config>
</server>
<server>
  <name>Pricing1</name>
  <listen-port>7011</listen-port>
  <cluster>PricingCluster</cluster>
  <listen-address></listen-address>
</server>
<cluster>
  <name>SOACluster</name>
  <cluster-messaging-mode>unicast</cluster-messaging-mode>
  <cluster-broadcast-channel></cluster-broadcast-channel>
</cluster>
<cluster>
  <name>PricingCluster</name>
  <cluster-messaging-mode>unicast</cluster-messaging-mode>
  <cluster-broadcast-channel></cluster-broadcast-channel>
</cluster>
```

The next step in putting together the pricingdomain is to ensure that the Pricing1 server is enabled with the Java Required File (JRF) components. As described in detail in Chapter 3, JRF enables the Fusion Middleware common infrastructure components on plain WebLogic Server managed servers. To do this, we run the WLST tool from the SOA Oracle home ~/products/Oracle_SOA/common/bin directory and use the applyJRF command in WLST offline mode, as follows:

```
applyJRF('Pricing1','/home/oracle/pricingdomain',true)
```

Next, we copy the MySQL JDBC JAR file to the domain's ~/pricingdomain/lib directory to ensure that the JDBC driver is available to the Pricing1 managed server's classpath for use by the applications within the PricingServiceEAR.ear deployment archive that we will be deploying later. After this step, we are ready to start all of the servers within the domain. Before doing so, it is useful to configure each server so that its startup does not require the manual input of the admin user credentials for its execution. To do this, create a file named boot.properties with the following content:

```
username=weblogic
password=welcome1
```

Then navigate to the domain ~/pricingdomain/servers directory and for each managed server create a directory in the following path <managed server>/security, where <managed server> is a placeholder for the actual name of the managed server (for example, Pricing1). Once these directories are created, copy the boot.properties file you just created in each of the managed server security directories. This will ensure that the managed servers can start without prompting for these credentials every time. Note that upon startup the server encrypts the content of the boot.properties file password. You are now ready to start the domain's servers. To do so, run the following commands in their own shell scripts (in Chapter 11 we will go through the steps required for starting servers through node manager, and thus without the need for executing these commands manually from shell scripts):

```
~/pricingdomain/bin/startWebLogic.sh
~/pricingdomain/startManagedWebLogic.sh Pricing1
~/pricingdomain/startManagedWebLogic.sh bam_server1
~/pricingdomain/startManagedWebLogic.sh soa_server1
```

You can now verify that all servers have properly started by opening a browser window and navigating to the WebLogic Server administration console at the http://pricing1:7001/console URL. Log in using the weblogic/welcome1 credentials and navigate to the Environment | Servers screen through the left panel tree. You should see the following screen.

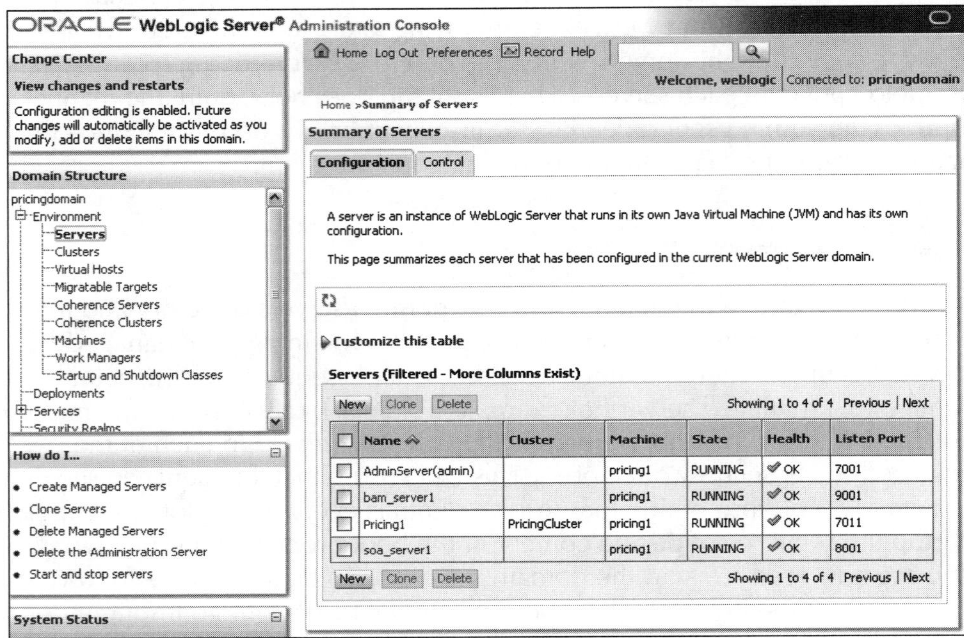

To complete the configuration of the pricingdomain, we need to take care of one other piece of business. The applications within the PricingServiceEAR.ear deployment archive also require a set of custom WebLogic Server Java EE JMS and JDBC resources. The resources required by this archive are described in detail within the use case of Chapter 2. You can run the following script from WLST to ensure that these resources are created:

```
#
# WLST online script which creates the
# WebLogic Server domain resources needed
# by the pricing application. Assumes that the domain has a managed server
# named Pricing1 which is targeted to a cluster named PricingCluster
#
connect('weblogic','welcome1','t3://pricing1:7001')
edit()
```

```
startEdit()

#
# Create the XA JDBC data source and target it to the PricingCluster
#
cd('/')
cmo.createJDBCSystemResource('pricingDS')
cd('/JDBCSystemResources/pricingDS/JDBCResource/pricingDS')
cmo.setName('pricingDS')
cd('/JDBCSystemResources/pricingDS/JDBCResource/pricingDS
/JDBCDataSourceParams/pricingDS')
set('JNDINames',jarray.array([String('jta.pricingDS')], String))
cd('/JDBCSystemResources/pricingDS/JDBCResource/pricingDS
/JDBCDriverParams/pricingDS')
cmo.setUrl('jdbc:mysql://database1:3306/pricingservice')
cmo.setDriverName('com.mysql.jdbc.jdbc2.optional.MysqlXADataSource')
set('Password', 'welcome1')
cd('/JDBCSystemResources/pricingDS/JDBCResource/pricingDS
/JDBCConnectionPoolParams/pricingDS')
cmo.setTestTableName('SQL SELECT 1\r\n\r\n\r\n\r\n')
cd('/JDBCSystemResources/pricingDS/JDBCResource/pricingDS
/JDBCDriverParams/pricingDS/Properties/pricingDS')
cmo.createProperty('user')
cd('/JDBCSystemResources/pricingDS/JDBCResource/pricingDS
/JDBCDriverParams/pricingDS/Properties/pricingDS/Properties/user')
cmo.setValue('oracle')
cd('/SystemResources/pricingDS')
set('Targets',jarray.array([ObjectName('com.bea:Name=PricingCluster,
Type=Cluster')], ObjectName))

#
# Create the non-XA JDBC data source and target it to the PricingCluster
#
cd('/')
cmo.createJDBCSystemResource('pricingDSNonXA')
cd('/JDBCSystemResources/pricingDSNonXA/JDBCResource/pricingDSNonXA')
cmo.setName('pricingDSNonXA')
cd('/JDBCSystemResources/pricingDSNonXA/JDBCResource/pricingDSNonXA/
JDBCDataSourceParams/pricingDSNonXA')
set('JNDINames',jarray.array([String('nonjta.pricingDS')], String))
cd('/JDBCSystemResources/pricingDSNonXA/JDBCResource/pricingDSNonXA/
JDBCDriverParams/pricingDSNonXA')
cmo.setUrl('jdbc:mysql://database1:3306/pricingservice')
cmo.setDriverName('com.mysql.jdbc.Driver')
set('Password', 'welcome1')
```

```
cd('/JDBCSystemResources/pricingDSNonXA/JDBCResource/pricingDSNonXA/
JDBCConnectionPoolParams/pricingDSNonXA')
cmo.setTestTableName('SQL SELECT 1\r\n\r\n\r\n\r\n')
cd('/JDBCSystemResources/pricingDSNonXA/JDBCResource/pricingDSNonXA/
JDBCDriverParams/pricingDSNonXA/Properties/pricingDSNonXA')
cmo.createProperty('user')
cd('/JDBCSystemResources/pricingDSNonXA/JDBCResource/pricingDSNonXA/
JDBCDriverParams/pricingDSNonXA/Properties/pricingDSNonXA/Properties/user')
cmo.setValue('oracle')
cd('/JDBCSystemResources/pricingDSNonXA/JDBCResource/pricingDSNonXA/
JDBCDataSourceParams/pricingDSNonXA')
cmo.setGlobalTransactionsProtocol('None')
cd('/SystemResources/pricingDSNonXA')
set('Targets',jarray.array([ObjectName('com.bea:Name=PricingCluster,
Type=Cluster')], ObjectName))


#
# Create the JMS Pricing server and target it to the Pricing
managed server
#
cd('/')
cmo.createJMSServer('PricingJMSServer')
cd('/Deployments/PricingJMSServer')
set('Targets',jarray.array([ObjectName('com.bea:Name=Pricing1,
Type=Server')], ObjectName))

#
# Create the JMS module and map it to the PricingCluster
#
cd('/')
cmo.createJMSSystemResource('PricingJMSModule')
cd('/SystemResources/PricingJMSModule')
set('Targets',jarray.array([ObjectName('com.bea:Name=
PricingCluster,
Type=Cluster')], ObjectName))

#
# Create a JMS connection factory and a JMS queue within the JMS
module
# Target the factory to the cluster and the queue to the JMS server
using
```

```
# sub-deployments
#

#
# First create the model and its sub-deployments
#
cd('/')
cd('/SystemResources/PricingJMSModule')
cmo.createSubDeployment('ConnectionSD')
cmo.createSubDeployment('PricingJMSSD')


#
# Now create the JMS connection factory
#
cd('/JMSSystemResources/PricingJMSModule/JMSResource/
PricingJMSModule')
cmo.createConnectionFactory('PricingCF')
cd('/JMSSystemResources/PricingJMSModule/JMSResource/
PricingJMSModule/
ConnectionFactories/PricingCF')
cmo.setJNDIName('myenterprise.pricing.pricingeventscf')
cd('/JMSSystemResources/PricingJMSModule/JMSResource/
PricingJMSModule/
ConnectionFactories/PricingCF/SecurityParams/PricingCF')
cmo.setAttachJMSXUserId(false)
cd('/JMSSystemResources/PricingJMSModule/JMSResource/
PricingJMSModule/
ConnectionFactories/PricingCF')


#
# Finally, create the JMS Queue
#
cmo.setSubDeploymentName('ConnectionSD')
cd('/JMSSystemResources/PricingJMSModule/JMSResource/
PricingJMSModule')
cmo.createQueue('PricingQ')
cd('/JMSSystemResources/PricingJMSModule/JMSResource/
PricingJMSModule/
Queues/PricingQ')
```

```
cmo.setJNDIName('pricingmodel.events')
cmo.setSubDeploymentName('PricingJMSSD')
cd('/SystemResources/PricingJMSModule/SubDeployments/PricingJMSSD')
set('Targets',jarray.array([ObjectName('com.bea:Name=
PricingJMSServer,
Type=JMSServer')], ObjectName))

activate()
```

With the execution of this script, you have completed the creation of the pricingdomain and are now ready for the creation of the webcenterdomain, which is described in the next section.

Creating the WebCenter Domain Now that the pricingdomain is fully configured, it is time to move to the webcenter1 machine to configure the WebCenter domain on which the pricing application's portal is to be deployed. Because we are not using any of the WebCenter added services such as spaces and composer and because we only want to use the WebCenter core framework services needed by the pricing portal application, we need to first configure a simple domain that contains only Enterprise Manager, Oracle Web Services Manager, and the Java Required Files Fusion Middleware shared infrastructure components and then extend this domain with the WebCenter custom portal template. The reason for this is that the WebCenter custom portal template, which as the name suggests is used for the configuration of resources needed by custom portals, is a domain extension template and can only be applied to an existing domain to extend its capabilities. As of this writing, WebCenter did not have a domain configuration template for the creation of new domains only for supporting custom portals; therefore, we have to revert to this technique. To create the WebCenter domain, proceed as follows:

1. Run the configuration wizard from the ~/products/wlserver_10.3/common/bin/config.sh directory.
2. Select the option Create a New WebLogic Domain.
3. On the Select Domain Source window, select the Oracle Enterprise Manager, Oracle Web Services Manager, and Oracle Business Activity Monitoring templates. These domain configuration templates allow for the creation of a domain that can be extended with the WebCenter custom portal template later.

4. When the wizard prompts you for the domain name and directory, enter the information:
   - Enter **webcenterdomain** as the domain name.
   - Enter the domain directory as **/home/oracle**.
   - Enter the application directory as **/home/oracle/webcenterdomainapplications**.
5. Choose an administrative user name of **weblogic** and a password of **welcome1**.
6. In Configure Server Start Mode and JDK window, select the Production start mode and select the Sun JDK.
7. The Configure JDBC Component Schema window will request the information for a single MDS schema to be used for the configuration of the data source needed by the domain's Oracle Web Services Manager (OWSM) components. We will be sharing the same MDS schema between this domain and the pricingdomain. Therefore, you should enter exactly the same information for the schema as you entered for the MDS data sources when creating the pricingdomain.
8. Within the Select Optional Configuration area, don't select any of the options.
9. Proceed to create the domain and complete the configuration wizard session.
10. Run the configuration wizard again.
11. Select the Extend an Existing WebLogic Domain option.
12. On the Select a WebLogic Domain Directory page, select the directory of the domain you just created (that is, ~/webcenterdomain).
13. On the Select Extension Source page, select the Extend My Domain Using an Existing Extension Template option and browse to the /home/oracle/Oracle_WC/common/templates/applications directory to select the oracle.wc_custom_portal_template_11.1.1.jar domain extension template file.

14. Within the Configure JDBC Component Schema window, enter the information listed here (and as illustrated within the following screenshot):

- Set the password for all component schemas to **welcome1**.
- Set the hostname for all component schemas to **database1**.
- Set the other required information as per the set of schemas created through the RCU and shown in the following screenshot. Note that you do not need to reenter the schema information for the OWSM MDS schema, which you configured in the first configuration wizard session as part of the webcenterdomain creation process. Also note that you should set the Custom Portal MDS Schema name to be the same as the single MDS schema used throughout the domain configuration process because all of the pricing application's domains and Fusion Middleware components are sharing a single MDS schema. This sharing greatly simplifies the domains' management processes.

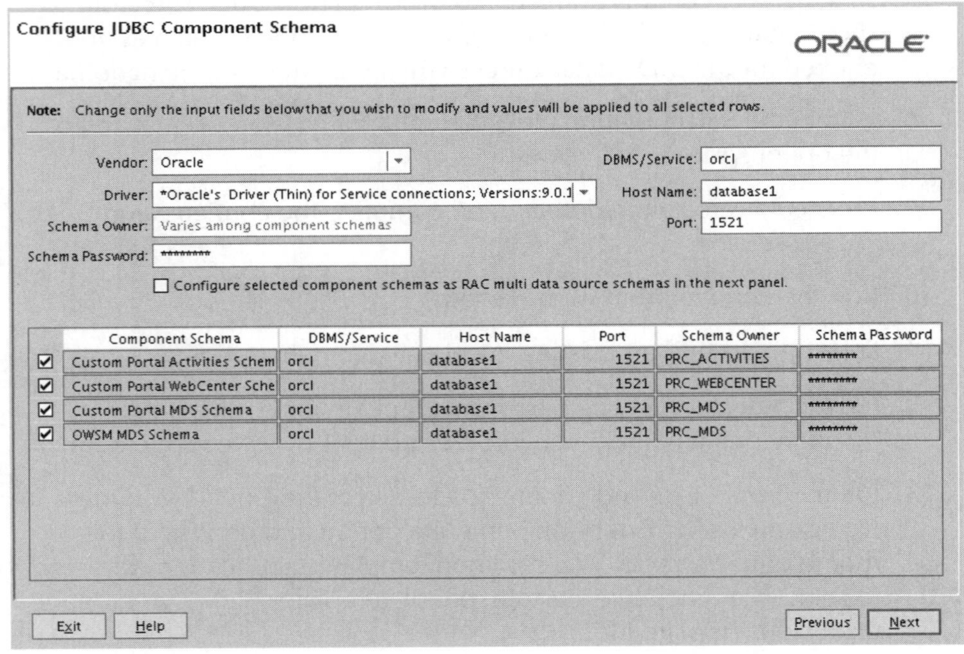

15. Within the Select Optional Configuration area, select the Managed Servers, Clusters and Machines option.
16. On the Configure Managed Servers page, change the name of the default managed server shown to WebCenter1 and choose a listen port of 7022. This is the managed server that will contain the entire WebCenter infrastructure necessary for the deployment of the pricing portal application.
17. On the Configure Clusters page, create a single cluster named WebCenterCluster and leave all of its settings at their default values. On the next screen, assign the WebCenter1 managed server to this cluster.
18. On the Configure Machines screen, create a machine named webcenter1 and assign all servers to this machine on the next screen.
19. Confirm the extension of the domain and let the configuration wizard session complete.

When you have completed the execution of the configuration wizard, as described in the preceding steps, you should be able to browse to the domain's config directory (~/webcenterdomain/config) and open the config.xml file to verify its content, as we did with the pricingdomain. In this case, make sure that the file contains the following snippet for the configuration of the administration server and the WebCenter1 managed server:

```
<server>
  <name>AdminServer</name>
  <machine>webcenter1</machine>
  <listen-address/>
  <server-diagnostic-config>
    <name>AdminServer</name>
    <diagnostic-context-enabled>true</diagnostic-context-enabled>
  </server-diagnostic-config>
</server>
<server>
  <name>WebCenter1</name>
  <machine>webcenter1</machine>
  <listen-port>7022</listen-port>
  <cluster>WebCenterCluster</cluster>
  <listen-address/>|
</server>
```

```
<cluster>
    <name>WebCenterCluster</name>
    <cluster-messaging-mode>unicast</cluster-messaging-mode>
    <cluster-broadcast-channel></cluster-broadcast-channel>
</cluster>
```

After you have verified the domain configuration, you are ready to start the domain's servers. Follow a process similar to the one described at the end of the last section to populate the server's boot.properties files and to get them started.

Creating the Oracle HTTP Server Configuration Instance We now move on to the installation of the Oracle HTTP Server (OHS) on the web1 host. Unlike the components of a WebLogic Server domain, the installation and configuration of OHS can happen within the same session. This is due to the fact that OHS is not a WebLogic Server–based component and its configuration is managed as a system component instance, as described in detail in Chapter 2. To install the latest patchset of OHS (11.1.1.4 at the time of this writing), the installation of the previous patchset version is first required. For example, to install the third patchset of OHS, you first need to install the first patchset of OHS 11*g*R1 (11.1.1.2), followed by the installation of the second patchset (11.1.1.3) and finally by the installation of the latest patchset. Note that when you install OHS, you can choose to configure an instance of it as well or only install the bits. Once you have started the installation for OHS, keep the following notes in mind:

- For the purpose of the steps covered in this section, choose the install and configure option. This will allow for the same session of the installer to not only lay down the OHS bits but also to create an OHS system component instance we will configure to act as a reverse proxy for all HTTP requests for the pricing application's web interfaces.
- Choose ~/products as the Middleware home directory and Oracle_WT as the Oracle home directory.
- When running the update installers from newer patchsets, enter the same Middleware home and Oracle home paths as you used as part of the installation of the previous patchset installers.

- On the configure components page, select Oracle HTTP Server and make sure that the Associate Selected Components with WebLogic Server Domain check box is selected.
- When prompted to specify WebLogic Server domain information, provide the information for the pricingdomain, which we created in the previous section. This will allow the installation tool to register the system component instance (which it creates as part of this install and configure session) with the domain for management through the Enterprise Manager console.
- On the Specify Component Details window, enter the following information:
  - For Instance Home Location, enter **~/pricinginstance**.
  - For Instance Name, enter **pricinginstance**.
  - For OHS Component Name, enter **pricingohs**.
- On the Configure Ports screen, select the Auto Port Configuration option. This will automatically use port 7777 as the OHS non-SSL listen port and port 4443 as the SSL listen port.

Once you have completed the execution of the Web Tier installation tool, you will have an instance of OHS configured and ready to start. To start this instance, navigate to the ~/pricinginstance/bin directory and run OPMN as follows:

```
opmnctl startall
```

This command starts all components under the instance; in our case, that is the single OHS system component instance we just configured. With the OHS instance configured and started, we are ready to move on to the configuration of the environment for the pricing application using all of the Fusion Middleware products we just installed.

Configuring the Identity and Policy Store

Before deploying the pricing application, we will complete our domain by setting up the proper identity store and policy store for the environment. As discussed earlier in the book, the out-of-the-box identity store and policy store for Oracle Platform Security Services are both file based. We will configure both identity and policy stores to point to the IT department's enterprise LDAP directory store—which in this case will be an instance of Oracle Internet Directory (OID). We will assume that an 11*g* Oracle Internet Directory instance already exists. This assumption does mimic most corporate scenarios where application owners and identity management infrastructure owners belong to different IT departments. The steps listed within this section use the pricingdomain as an example, but it is important to note that they need to also be executed with the webcenterdomain.

Configure LDAP Identity Store with Oracle Internet Directory In order to set up the Oracle Internet Directory authenticator, you need to first identify a few pieces of the key information about your directory:

- **User Base DN** This is the distinguished name in OID under which all the users reside (for example, "dc=users, dc=acme, dc=com").
- **Group Base DN** This is the distinguished name in OID under which all the groups reside (for example, "dc=groups, dc=acme, dc=com").
- **Principal** This is the distinguished name in OID used by WebLogic Server to connect to OID.
- **Credential** This is the password for the principal listed previously to connect to OID.
- **User Search Scope** This is the search scope to indicate whether the user lookup will be done at one level under the user base DN or for the entire subtree under the user base DN.

The following WLST script configures a WebLogic Server authentication provider within the domain with an existing OID installation:

```
#
# Connect to the pricing application domain.
#
connect('weblogic','welcome1','t3://pricing1:7001')
edit()
startEdit()

# Create an OracleInternetDirectoryAuthenticator
```

```
# in the default realm called
# 'OID_Authenticator'.  The following must be run from
# the DomainMBean root.
cmo.getSecurityConfiguration().getDefaultRealm()
.createAuthenticationProvider('OID_Authenticator',
'weblogic.security.providers.authentication.OracleInternetDirectory')

# Now, traverse to the newly created OID_Authenticator
cd('SecurityConfiguration/pricing1/Realms/myrealm
/AuthenticationProviders/OID_Authenticator')

# First, set the connection information of OID.  Assume the host name
is
# 'OIDhost'; port is "389" (default value);
# login principal is "cn=orcladmin"
# with password "welcome1".  It is worth noting

# that the login principal should
# ideally be a user other than "cn=orcladmin" but a newly
# created user with less
# but sufficient privilege to perform the required operations for
the
# authenticator.
cmo.setHost('OIDhost')
cmo.setPort('389')
cmo.setPrincipal('cn=orcladmin')
cmo.setCredential('welcome1')

# Now, configure the user and group base DN
cmo.setUserBaseDN('dc=users,dc=acme,dc=com')
cmo.setGroupBaseDN('dc=groups,dc=acme,dc=com')


# Set the Authenticator control flag as 'SUFFICIENT'.
# With this option, if
# the login succeeds, return control to the application.

# If it fails and other
# authentication providers are configured,
# authentication proceeds down the
# LoginModule list.
cmo.setControlFlag('SUFFICIENT')
```

```
# The rest of the parameters can stay as default.
# The default values have
# been defined specifically for Oracle Internet Directory.
# Now save and activate.
save()
activate()
```

At this point, you must restart the admin server and all the managed servers for the changes to take effect.

Configure LDAP Policy Store with Oracle Internet Directory In order to use Oracle Internet Directory as your OPSS policy store, a root distinguished name or a root node must be identified in the directory under which the policy store metadata will be created. We will create this root node in OID with the following LDIF (LDAP Data Interchange Format) file. We will name it opssroot.ldif. Here, we assume the root distinguished name to be "cn=opssroot":

```
dn: cn=opssroot
cn: opssroot
objectclass: top
objectclass: orclContainer
```

The root node does not need to be at the top level of the LDAP tree. It is important, however, to ensure that the connecting DN eventually used in the policy store configuration has read and write access to the subtree. To do this, we use a set of LDAP administrative command-line tools, which you can find within the OID Oracle home directory under ORACLE_HOME/bin. Begin by creating the root node with the following ldapadd command using "cn=orcladmin":

```
> ldapadd -h ldap_host -p ldap_port -D cn=orcladmin
-w password -c -v -f opssroot.ldif
```

To verify the creation of the node, use the following ldapsearch command:

```
> ldapsearch -h ldap_host -p ldap_port -D cn=orcladmin
-w password -b "cn=opssroot" objectclass="orclContainer"
```

The command should return the distinguished name in the output, along with the attributes as defined in the preceding LDIF file. To complete this setup, the oidstats.sql utility script for Oracle Internet Directory must be run using sqlplus. The file can be found at ORACLE_HOME/ldap/admin/oidstats.sql within the Oracle Internet Directory installation.

Once the root node has been created, we can use the reassociateSecurityStore WLST command to set up both the policy and credential stores to use the Oracle Internet Directory as specified. It should be noted that the admin user specified here to connect to the LDAP should ideally be a user other than "cn=orcladmin" with less but sufficient privileges to perform the required operations under "cn=opssroot":

```
reassociateSecurityStore(domain='pricing1',admin='cn=orcladmin',
password='password',ldapurl='ldap://ldap_host:ldap_port',
serverType='OID',jpsroot='cn=opssroot')
```

After executing this command, you must restart the admin server and all the managed servers within the domain for the change to be activated.

Deploying the Pricing Application Artifacts

With the creation of the pricing application's domains completed, we are now ready to deploy the different artifacts that constitute the pricing application. The development team has packaged these artifacts in a single directory, and they are now placed within the ~/development directory. An ls -l command on this directory reveals its content to be the following:

```
-rw-r--r--  1 oracle users  994075 Oct 30 17:48
PricingBAMExport.xml
-rw-r--r--  1 oracle users   14138 May 30 10:33
PricingServiceEAR.ear
-rw-r--r--  1 oracle users 2617015 Nov  9 20:47 PricingWorklist.ear
-rw-r--r--  1 oracle users 2617015 Nov  9 20:47 PricingPortal.ear
-rw-r--r--  1 oracle users   71002 Nov  9 10:40 sca_PricingUpdate_
                                                        rev1.0.jar
```

All of these artifacts are available for download on the Oracle Press site (http://community.oraclepressbooks.com/downloads.html) so that you can follow through the remaining steps described in this section.

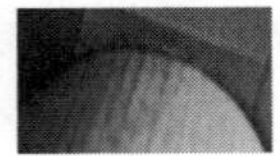

DOWNLOAD
The artifacts of the pricing application referred to in this chapter are available for download on the Oracle Press site at http://community .oraclepressbooks.com/downloads.html.

Let's quickly review each of these artifacts in turn:

- **PricingBAMExport.xml** An XML file containing the exported content of an Oracle Business Activity Monitoring (BAM) repository. This content consists of the BAM data objects and reports created by business analysts and updated by the pricing update process. The content was created by issuing a BAM ICommand export command (described in detail in Chapter 5).
- **PricingServiceEAR.ear** An enterprise application deployment archive containing a custom-made Java EE application that implements the Pricing Query web interface and the Pricing Update web service. These components are described in detail in the Chapter 2 use case.
- **PricingWorklist.ear** An enterprise application deployment archive containing the ADF application for the custom worklist used by the pricing application. This application is described in detail in the Chapter 6 use case.
- **PricingPortal.ear** An enterprise application deployment archive containing a WebCenter-based portal application that integrates the pricing application's different UIs. This application is described in detail in the Chapter 7 use case.
- **sca_PricingUpdate_rev1.0.jar** Oracle SOA Suite archive containing a Service Component Architecture (SCA) composite for the integration of the pricing service with the corporate ERP system, BAM, and the pricing worklist application. This composite is described in detail in the Chapter 5 use case.

The way that these artifacts must be targeted to the different servers and clusters within the domain is illustrated in Figure 8-2. In the next sections, we go over the steps required in deploying each of these artifacts.

Deploying the Custom Pricing Application Because the custom pricing application is packaged within a WebLogic Server enterprise application archive (EAR) file, you can deploy it to WebLogic Server through the WLST deploy command. For the pricing application's EAR file, the WLST command is the following:

```
deploy('pricingService','/home/oracle/deployments/
PricingServiceEAR.ear',
targets='PricingCluster', securityModel='CustomRoles')
```

Note the use of the CustomRoles security model. The reason for using this model is that it allows the roles defined within the deployment descriptors of the application to be defined externally as part of the WebLogic Server security realm and mapped to the enterprise LDAP users and groups without the modification of the deployment descriptor's content. The custom pricing application declares a single role, named "sales," within its deployment descriptor. Using the CustomRoles security model for deployment allows us to define a global role of the same name at the domain's security realm and map this role to the Sales group within the corporate LDAP server that you integrated with the domain in the previous section. Here's the WLST script to create the global role and map it to the Sales group:

```
domainConfig()
cd('SecurityConfiguration/pricingdomain/Realms/myrealm/RoleMappers
/XACMLRoleMapper')
cmo.createRole(None,'sales',None)
cmo.setRoleExpression(None,'sales','Grp(Sales)')
```

The pricing application is now ready to be used. You can test it by navigating to the URL of the Query Service web application at http://pricing1:7011/PricingServiceWeb and logging in using the credentials of a user within the Sales group.

Importing the Business Activity Monitoring Objects It is now time to prepare the BAM server with the data objects needed to keep track of the updates made to the pricing application's model. The entity that updates the BAM server's data objects is the SOA composite, which we will be deploying in the next section. To create the objects, we just import into the BAM repository an export file, named PricingBAMExport.xml, provided by the business analysis team. This export file was produced after the analysts created the business objects and reports they needed on a design-time BAM server.

To export the file, begin by editing the content of the BAMICommandConfig.xml file (which you can find in the ~/products/Oracle_SOA/bam/config/ directory) to point it to the domain BAM server, as follows:

```
<?xml version="1.0" encoding="UTF-8" standalone="yes"?>
<BAMICommand>
  <ADCServerName>pricing1</ADCServerName>
  <ADCServerPort>9011</ADCServerPort>
  <Communication_Protocol>t3</Communication_Protocol>
<SensorFactory>oracle.bam.common.statistics.noop.
SensorFactoryImpl</SensorFactory>
<GenericSatelliteChannelName>invm:topic/oracle.bam.messaging.
systemobjectnotification</GenericSatelliteChannelName>
</BAMICommand>
```

After you have modified this file, you use the BAM ICommand tool (which you can find in the ~/products/Oracle_SOA/bam/bin/ directory) to execute an import command against the BAM server. The command to perform the import is as follows:

```
icommand -cmd import -file ~/deployments/PricingBAMExport.xml
-preserveowner
```

Once the import is done, the BAM data objects that are updated by the pricing application's SOA suite composite are now available for update. However, you still need to associate the BAM web application roles with their associated enterprise groups within the domain LDAP server. To do this, you need to associate the Report Viewer role with the SpecialtyProductGroup group, and the Report Creator and Report Architect roles with the SpecialtyProductManagement group. This will ensure that all staff within the specialty product team can view all reports created from the pricing application's BAM data objects, and only the specialty product's product management team can create new reports or data objects. Here's the code:

```
grantAppRole(appStripe="oracle-bam#11.1.1", appRoleName="Report
Viewer",
principalClass=
"weblogic.security.principal.WLSGroupImpl",principalName="
SpecialtyProductGroup")
```

```
grantAppRole(appStripe="oracle-bam#11.1.1", appRoleName="Report
Creator",
principalClass=
"weblogic.security.principal.WLSGroupImpl",principalName="
SpecialtyProductManagement")
grantAppRole(appStripe="oracle-bam#11.1.1", appRoleName="Report
Architect",
principalClass=
"weblogic.security.principal.WLSGroupImpl",principalName="
SpecialtyProductManagement")
```

You can now verify whether the import of the pricing application's BAM objects succeeded by using the BAM Architect user interface at the http://pricing1:9001/OracleBAM URL and logging in with the credentials of a user under the SpecialtyProductManagement group. Choose the BAM Architect option, and then under the DataObjects panel you should be able to find a folder named Pricing with a data object named PricingUpdateProcessEvent, as shown here.

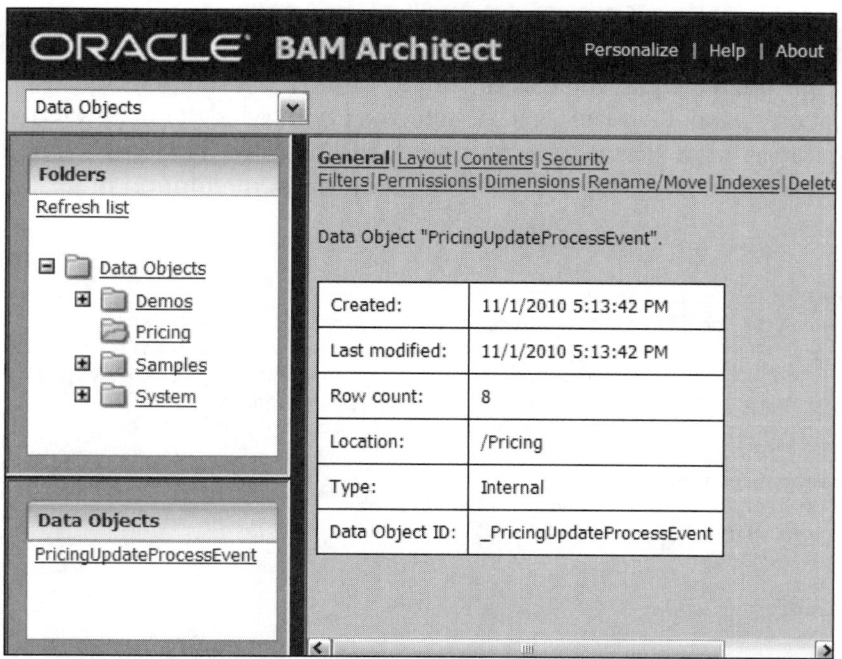

Deploying the SOA Suite Composite Application The next piece of the pricing application we are going to put in place is the pricing update SOA Suite composite. This composite contains the BPEL process that integrates with the corporate ERP system to receive pricing model change events. The process then orchestrates the process for events that require approval from the specialty products product management, the update of the pricing application's model through the invocation of its web service, and the update of the BAM pricing data object. The composite is packaged within a SOA Suite archive file that is delivered in a JAR format. The WLST command for deploying this type of file is named sca_deployComposite, and for the pricing application's composite the deployment command is as follows:

```
sca_deployComposite('http://pricing1:8001','/home/oracle/deployments/
sca_PricingUpdate_rev1.0.jar',configplan='/home/oracle/deployments/
PricingModelUpdate_cfgplan.xml')
```

Note the use of the SOA Suite configuration plan named PricingModelUpdate_cfgplan.xml. This plan allows for the modification of specific elements of the composite to adjust for differences between environments. In our case, we have received the composite from development, which has been using a value of localhost for all URI references to the pricing application's Model Update web service. The PricingModelUpdate_cfgplan.xml configuration plan allows us to modify all instances of localhost within the composite to pricing1. Here's the content of this configuration plan:

```
<?xml version="1.0" encoding="UTF-8"?>

<SOAConfigPlan xmlns:jca=
"http://platform.integration.oracle/blocks/adapter/fw/metadata"
               xmlns:wsp="http://schemas.xmlsoap.org/ws/2004/09/policy"
               xmlns:orawsp="http://schemas.oracle.com/ws/2006/01/policy"
               xmlns:edl="http://schemas.oracle.com/events/edl"
               xmlns="http://schemas.oracle.com/soa/configplan">
  <wsdlAndSchema name="*">
    <searchReplace>
      <search>http://localhost:7002</search>
      <replace>http://pricing1:7011</replace>
    </searchReplace>
  </wsdlAndSchema>
</SOAConfigPlan>
```

With the composite deployed, we need to make sure the file system directory exists that the composite's file-adapter-based service polls for updates from the ERP system. The path of the directory that needs to be created on the system is /myerp/erp-in. If you do not have access to the system's root directory to create this path, you can always modify the path being polled by the composite through the configuration plan. Of course, we are using this directory only for the sake of our example, and a real ERP system is not in the picture. However, to test the composite, you can drop test XML files into this directory and wait (the polling cycle used by the composite's service is 15 seconds) until they are picked up and processed by the composite. Here is a sample test XML snippet you can use for this purpose:

```
<EnvChangeEventType>
   <productSKU>101010</productSKU>
   <currentMonthlyOverallUnitDemand>121</currentMonthlyOverallUnitDemand>
   <previousMonthlyOverallUnitDemand>92</previousMonthlyOverallUnitDemand>
   <currentPrice>212<currentPrice>
</EnvChangeEventType>
```

Deploying the Application Deployment Framework Custom Application

The pricing application has a custom-built SOA Suite human workflow worklist application used by the specialty products product management group to approve sensitive changes to the application's pricing model. The application was built using Oracle Application Development Framework (ADF), as discussed in detail in the Chapter 6 use case. It is delivered for deployment as an EAR file that we can deploy to the SOA Suite server within the domain using the WebLogic Server WLST deploy command, as follows:

```
deploy('PricingWorkList','/home/oracle/deployments/PricingWorkList.ear',
targets='soa_server1')
```

For any ADF application that does not require an MDS database repository, the preceding command will be sufficient. However, as described in Chapter 6, our PricingWorkList application uses an MDS repository to support personalization and customizations. This requires providing the MDS repository information at the time of deployment. When the deployment is from JDeveloper or Enterprise Manager, the UI will provide options to select an already registered MDS repository as the target repository for this application. If the deployment is via WLST commands, offline WLST commands are provided to save the appropriate configuration before deploying the application using the aforementioned deploy command. Because the MDS repository mds-owsm is already registered with our target server and has the JNDI name jdbc/mds/owsm, we will use this repository to deploy the PricingWorkList application via the following commands:

```
PricingWorkListArchive = getMDSArchiveConfig(fromLocation='/home/oracle/
deployments/
PricingWorkList.ear')

PricingWorkListArchive.setAppMetadataRepository(repository='mds-
owsm',partition='PricingWorkList',type='DB',jndi='jdbc/mds/owsm')

PricingWorkListArchive.save()

deploy('PricingWorkList','/home/oracle/deployments/PricingWorkList.ear',
targets='soa_server1')
```

The application uses the role PricingAnalysts internally to control access to its functionality. Therefore, after deployment we need to associate this application role with the appropriate group (SpecialtyProductManagement) from the enterprise LDAP server. We do this through the following WLST command:

```
grantAppRole(appStripe="PricingWorkList",appRoleName="PricingAnalysts",
principalClass="weblogic.security.principal.WLSGroupImpl",
principalName="SpecialtyProductManagement")
```

After the deployment of the application is complete, you can verify that it has been successful by checking the application's URL at http://pricing1:8001/PricingWorklist http://pricing1:8001/PricingWorkListRoot/faces/PricingWorkList.jspx. At this point, you have completed the deployment of all artifacts required for the pricingdomain. You can verify the health of the domain by navigating to the Enterprise Manager page (at http://pricing1:8001/em) where you should see a screen similar to the following.

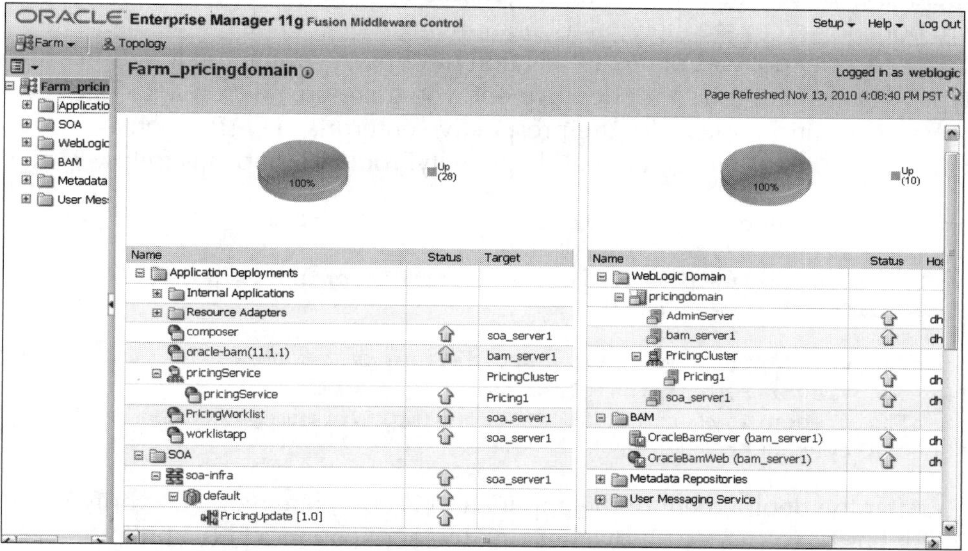

Deploying the WebCenter Portal Application The final piece of the deployment puzzle for the pricing application is the WebCenter portal, which exposes the different interfaces of the application in an integrated and personalized user interface. The application is delivered as an EAR file that we deploy to the WebCenter server, within its dedicated webcenterdomain, using the following WebLogic Server WLST deploy command. Similar to the PricingWorkList application, this application requires an MDS repository, and hence the steps to deploy this application are as follows:

```
PricingPortalArchive = getMDSArchiveConfig(fromLocation='/home
/oracle/deployments/PricingPortal.ear')

PricingPortalArchive.setAppMetadataRepository(repository=
'mds-owsm',partition='PricingPortal',type='DB',jndi='jdbc/mds/owsm')

PricingPortalArchive.save()deploy('PricingPortal','/home/oracle/
deployments/PricingPortal.ear',targets='PricingWebCenter1')
```

The Pricing portal uses two different application roles: PricingAnalysts and PricingViewers. PricingAnalysts are allowed to see all portlets within the portal, including the worklist and the pricing model update interface. PricingViewers are not allowed to see the worklist and pricing model update interface. The OPSS security policies of the application have been configured to ensure this type of access control. After deployment, you therefore need to associate these application roles with their respective enterprise LDAP groups—SpecialtyProductManagement and SpecialtyProductGroup—as follows:

```
grantAppRole(appStripe="PricingPortal",appRoleName=
"PricingAnalysts",principalClass=
"weblogic.security.principal.WLSGroupImpl",principalName=
"SpecialtyProductManagement")

grantAppRole(appStripe="PricingPortal",appRoleName=
"PricingViewers",principalClass=
"weblogic.security.principal.WLSGroupImpl",principalName=
"SpecialtyProductGroup")
```

After the deployment of the application is complete, you can verify that it has been successful by checking the application's URL at http://webcenter1:8001/PricingPortal.

Configuring the Oracle HTTP Server

With all of the WebLogic Server–based components of the pricing application deployed, it is time to configure the OHS instance we created in the previous section. To do this, you need to open the file ~/pricinginstance/config/OHS/pricingohs/mod_wl_ohs.conf and enter the following set of <Location> directives, one for each context root that needs to be accessed by entities external to the components of the pricing application:

```
<Location /PricingServiceWeb>
  SetHandler weblogic-handler
  WebLogicHost pricing1
  WebLogicPort 7012
</Location>
```

```
<Location /PricingWorklist>
  SetHandler weblogic-handler
  WebLogicHost pricing1
  WebLogicPort 8001
</Location>

<Location /PricingPortal>
  SetHandler weblogic-handler
  WebLogicHost webcenter1
  WebLogicPort 7022
</Location>

<Location /OracleBAM >
  SetHandler weblogic-handler
  WebLogicHost pricing1
  WebLogicPort 9001
</Location>
```

These directives allow for the routing of all HTTP requests incoming to the OHS 7777 and 4443 ports to be matched against the values specified within the <Location> directives. If the target URL of the request begins with the value specified within this directive (for example, /OracleBAM), then OHS routes the request to the host and port specified by the WebLogicHost and WebLogicPort directives. After entering these directives, you need to restart the OHS instance for them to take effect. To do this, navigate to the ~/pricinginstance/bin directory and perform an opmnctl stopall command followed by an opmnctl startall command. This will ensure that the OHS server is restarted and that it is now serving as the single reverse proxy to all of the pricing application web user interfaces across the pricingdomain and webcenterdomain.

Extending a Cluster for Scalability

In this section, we discuss the steps required in transforming the PricingCluster within the pricing application's existing topology with an additional managed server. Before listing these steps, however, it is worth exploring the possible reasons behind such a change. In general, the purpose of a WebLogic Server cluster is to allow for a replication of application logic across multiple managed servers in order to allow for scalability and high availability. To achieve the goal of increased availability, we would need to look beyond the

PricingCluster alone, and all elements of the pricing application's topology would need to be examined. Furthermore, the nature of the changes we would need to make would go beyond clustering and include elements such as the failover of singleton services (such as the JMS servers used by the components of the pricing application) and the availability of the hardware devices used by the application's environment. The details of the configurations required for increasing availability for Fusion Middleware environments are beyond the scope of this book and are described in "Fusion Middleware High Availability Guide" within the Oracle Fusion Middleware documentation library.

Scalability, on the other hand, is sometimes possible to achieve through the clustering of only certain specific elements of an enterprise application. Using the pricing application as an example, imagine that the usage of the application's Pricing Query web interface is some order of magnitude higher than that of its other interfaces, such as the update process, Business Activity Monitoring reports, and the Pricing portal. The reason for this could be that the Query service is available to the entire sales force that uses it on a regular basis, whereas the application's other interfaces are used only by select groups (or end systems such as the corporate ERP) with relatively low frequency. In such a case, it would make sense to extend the PricingCluster with an extra managed server residing on another machine with extra processing and memory resources in order to allow it to process more concurrent requests for the Pricing Query service and thus improve its performance. This process is sometimes referred to as a "scale-out process" and would achieve the scalability goal that the application's nature demands in this case. We will use this PricingCluster example within the rest of this section to provide a concrete example of how such a scale-out process can be performed within a Fusion Middleware environment. It is important to note, however, that these steps are tailored for the scale-out of a cluster of the same exact nature as the PricingCluster (that is, plain WebLogic Server managed server with the Java Required Files common infrastructure applied). The scale-out of managed servers with other Fusion Middleware layered products requires considerations specific to those products' needs. For a detailed discussion of each Fusion Middleware layered product's specific clustering needs, please refer to "Oracle Fusion Middleware High Availability Guide" within the Oracle Fusion Middleware documentation library.

Extending the WebLogic Server Pricing Cluster

At this point we are ready to proceed with extending the pricing application's PricingCluster. As shown in Figure 8-2, this cluster consists of the Pricing1 managed server and has the pricing application's Pricing Query interface (a web application) and Pricing Update web service (a WebLogic Server web service application) deployed within a single EAR file named PricingApp.ear. After we have completed the extension of this cluster, the pricing application's environment will appear as shown in Figure 8-3.

As you can see, the new managed server of the PricingCluster is being added to the webcenter1 host. The reason for this is that the number of users for the Pricing portal application deployed on this host is very low, and as a result the machine has extra capacity that can be used to extend the PricingCluster.

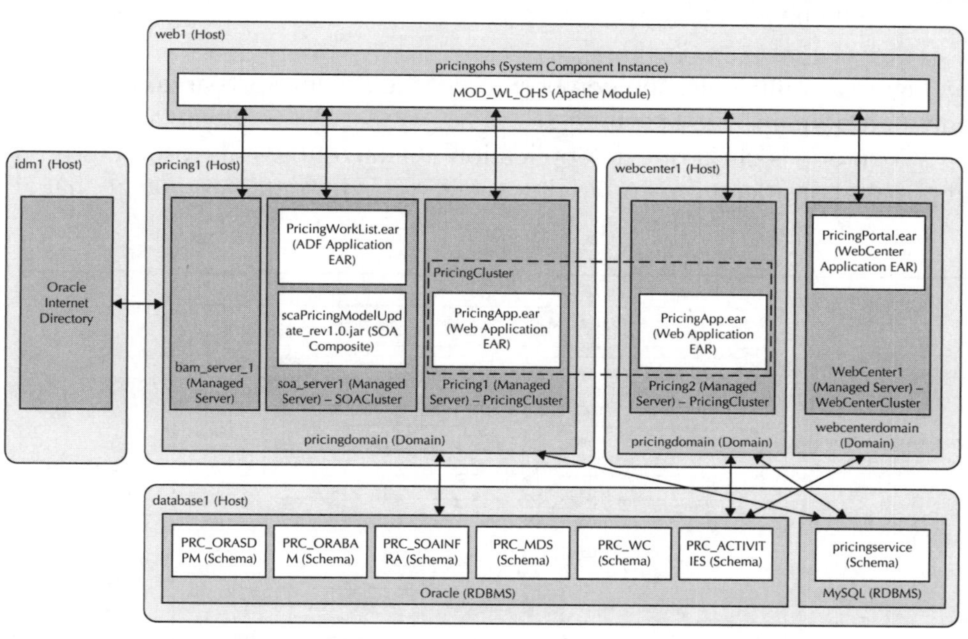

FIGURE 8-3. *Pricing Application's Scaled-out Topology*

Until now we have been able to look at the deployment artifacts of the pricing application as black boxes and did not need to have a detailed knowledge of their internal architecture. To ensure that the PricingApp.ear business logic can properly function on a multinode clustered topology, however, we need to take a closer look at the content of this archive. As we discussed in the use case section of Chapter 2, this archive is made up of the following components:

- A servlet-based web application that provides the query interface. This application uses a stateless session bean Enterprise Java Bean (EJB) to query the database through a JDBC data source configured at the domain configuration level.
- A POJO-based web service that uses a JMS queue to communicate update messages to a Message Driven Bean (MDB) EJB. The MDB dequeues the messages and updates the content of the pricing model schema accordingly.

Figure 8-4 illustrates the composition of the PricingApp.ear components and their domain-level resources.

When one is clustering an application, the targeting of its resources is an important consideration. For PricingApp.ear, it is important to realize that all

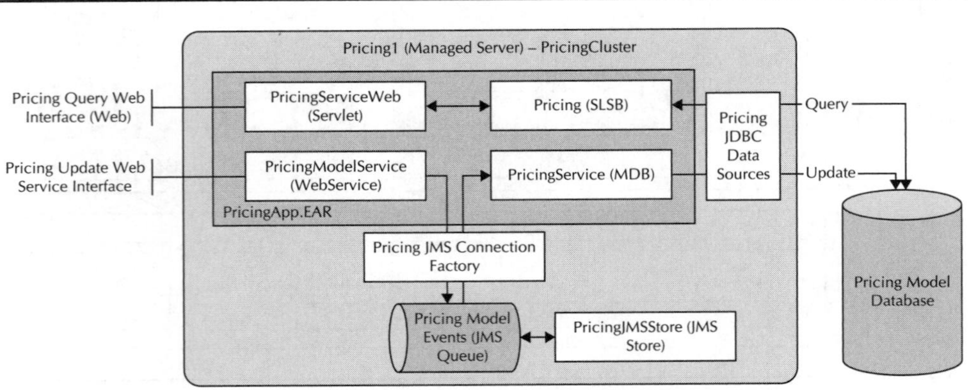

FIGURE 8-4. *PricingApp.ear components on a single node*

of the WebLogic Server resources it depends on are targeted to the cluster PricingCluster1, except for the JMS Queue and Server used by the application's web service. The reason for this is that WebLogic JMS servers are singleton resources, and although JMS queues (and topics) can be clustered, the pricing application's environment does not take advantage of clustered JMS destinations. Therefore, the expansion of the cluster will lead to the replication of all cluster targeted components of the application, except for the JMS resources just mentioned. Figure 8-5 illustrates the composition of the PricingApp.ear components and their domain-level resources after the PricingCluster is expanded.

The good news is that despite the fact that the cluster does not replicate the JMS resources, the intended scalability is achieved because the business logic of the PricingApp.ear components and its two public interfaces—namely, the Pricing Query web interface and the Pricing Update web service interface—are still replicated across the cluster nodes. It is important to note, however, that in this clustered configuration, the Pricing1 managed server is effectively a single point of failure; therefore, reliability is not achieved by the environment.

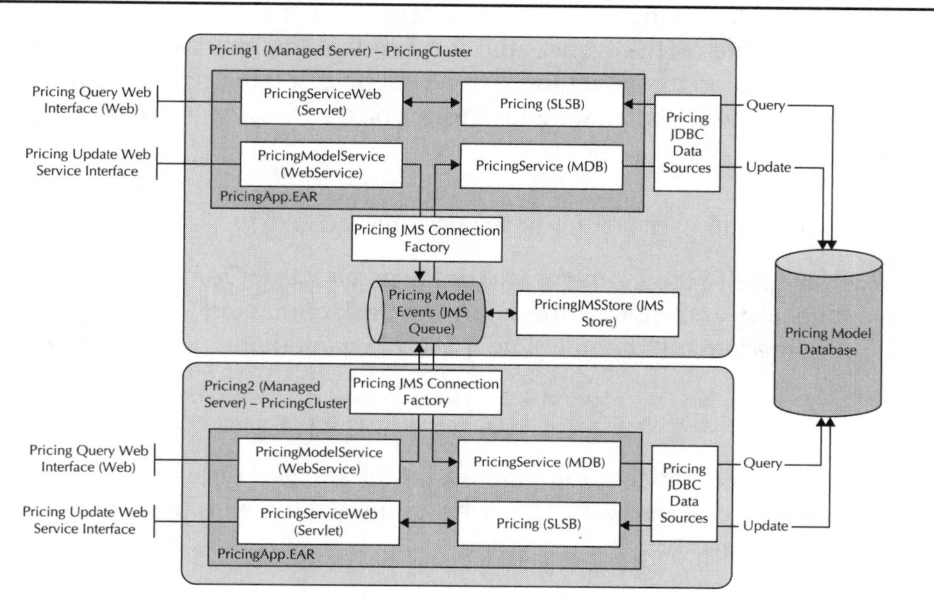

FIGURE 8-5. *PricingApp.ear components in a two-node cluster*

To extend the PricingCluster, begin by adding a new managed server, named Pricing2, to the cluster. This can be done through the WebLogic Server admin console or by executing the following WLST script from the pricing1 host:

```
connect('weblogic','welcome1')
edit()
startEdit()
cd('/')
cmo.createServer('Pricing2')
cd('/Servers/Pricing2')
cmo.setListenAddress('')
cmo.setListenPort(7014)
cmo.setCluster(getMBean('/Clusters/PricingCluster'))
activate()
```

Note the use of a different port number (7014 instead of 7012) than the port used by the Pricing1 managed server. Because the two managed servers are running on different machines, we could have used the same port value; however, it is a good practice to use different ports to allow the second managed server to be started on the same machine as the first managed server, if this is ever needed. Once the new managed server has been created and added to the cluster, it is necessary to create the domain's directory structure on the webcenter1 host so that the new managed server can be executed on that machine. The WebLogic Server pack and unpack commands are designed exactly for this purpose. To use them, perform the following steps:

1. Start as the user oracle on the pricing1 host.
2. Navigate to the /home/oracle/products/Oracle_SOA/common/bin directory and execute the following pack command to package the pricingdomain's content into a JAR file named pricingdomainpack.jar:

   ```
   pack.sh -domain=/home/oracle/pricingdomain -template=/home/oracle/
   pricingdomainpack.jar -template_name=pricingapptemplate
   ```

3. Transfer the pricingdomainpack.jar file created through the pack command to the webcenter1 host and place it within the /home/oracle directory.

4. Log in as the user oracle on the webcenter1 host and start by installing SOA Suite as per the "Installing SOA Suite" section of this chapter. This step is needed because pricingdomain is in a SOA Suite domain and therefore you need SOA Suite installed on a machine in order to be able to scale out a managed server to it.

5. Still on webcenter1, navigate to the /home/oracle/products/Oracle_SOA/common/bin directory and execute the unpack command to transform the content of the pricingdomainpack.jar into a domain directory named pricingdomain:

```
pack.sh -domain=/home/oracle/pricingdomain -template=/home/
oracle/pricingdomainpack.jar -template_name=pricingapptemplate
```

At this point you are ready to start the second managed server on the webcenter1 host. To do this, execute the startManagedWebLogic.sh command with an extra argument that indicates the URL of the domain's administration servers, as follows:

```
startManagedWebLogic.sh Pricing2 http://pricing1:7001
```

With this step we have completed the extension of the PricingCluster cluster. The scale-out process is, however, still not complete because you still need to make sure all the clients of the services we just extended are aware of the fact that they are clustered and can therefore take advantage of it. We will perform this configuration in the next section.

Configuring the Clients

As shown earlier in Figure 8-5, the query and update interfaces of the PricingApp.ear archive are now available on the two nodes of the cluster. We must take some special measures to ensure that the client applications that use these interfaces can take advantage of the cluster's replication of these interfaces. Specifically, we need to ensure that the WebLogic Server mod_wl_ohs module of the Oracle HTTP Server (OHS) instance fronting the domain is configured to serve both nodes of the cluster and that the SOA Suite composite that accesses the query interface uses the OHS instance to access the update interface. Because consumers of the web-based query interface access it through its OHS exposed endpoint, the configuration of OHS will automatically ensure that requests to the query interface are load-balanced for this web application.

Configuring the Web Tier

We need to modify the mod_wl_ohs directives we configured in the "Configuring the Oracle HTTP Server" section. Currently, for the Pricing Query web interface, the OHS module configuration file (at ~/pricinginstance/config/OHS/pricingohs/mod_wl_ohs.conf) contains the following directives:

```
<Location /PricingServiceWeb>
  SetHandler weblogic-handler
  WebLogicHost pricing1
  WebLogicPort 7012
</Location>
```

These directives route all requests that begin with /PricingServiceWeb to the pricing1 host's 7012 port. We need to modify these directives to tell the mod_wl_ohs module to use the cluster endpoints of the PricingCluster domain instead. We do this by modifying the directives as follows:

```
<Location /PricingServiceWeb>
  SetHandler weblogic-handler
  WebLogicCluster pricing1:7012,webcenter1:7014
</Location>
```

The WebLogicCluster directive is followed by the endpoints (host name/IP and port number) of the cluster's managed servers. This directive ensures that incoming requests that begin with /PricingServiceWeb are sent to one of the cluster endpoints in a round-robin fashion. With this directive configured, end users can now access the pricing application Query web interface using the URL http://web1:7777/PricingServiceWeb. Their request will be load-balanced across the two cluster nodes, thus allowing for this interface to serve a higher number of concurrent users. To allow the PricingApp.ear archive's web service interface to also be accessible in the same fashion, all we need to do is to add a similar directive but using the web service's context root prefix, as follows:

```
<Location /PricingModelWebService>
  SetHandler weblogic-handler
  WebLogicCluster pricing1:7012,webcenter1:7014
</Location>
```

Configuring the SOA Composite

As part of the deployment of the pricing application's SOA Suite composite, we used a configuration plan that pointed the composite's reference to the pricing application's web service to the pricing1:7012 endpoint. With the extension of the PricingCluster, we need to ensure that the composite's access to the web service is also load-balanced between the pricing1 and webcenter1 nodes of the cluster. Because we exposed the web service's endpoint through a WebLogicCluster directive on the OHS instance in the previous section, the rerouting of the composite's reference comes down to simply applying a new SOA Suite configuration plan that uses the OHS endpoint instead of the direct pricing1 endpoint, as follows:

```
<?xml version="1.0" encoding="UTF-8"?>

<SOAConfigPlan xmlns:jca="http://platform.integration.oracle
/blocks/adapter/fw/metadata"
               xmlns:wsp="http://schemas.xmlsoap.org/ws/2004/09/
policy"
               xmlns:orawsp="http://schemas.oracle.com/ws/2006/01/
policy"
               xmlns:edl="http://schemas.oracle.com/events/edl"
               xmlns="http://schemas.oracle.com/soa/configplan">
  <wsdlAndSchema name="*">
    <searchReplace>
      <search>http://localhost:7002</search>
      <replace>http://web1:7777</replace>
    </searchReplace>
  </wsdlAndSchema>
</SOAConfigPlan>
```

To apply this configuration plan, all we need to do is undeploy the composite and then redeploy it by running the following WLST commands:

```
sca_undeployComposite('http://pricing1:8001','PricingUpdate', '1.0')
sca_deployComposite('http://pricing1:8001',
'/home/oracle/deployments/sca_PricingUpdate_rev1.0.jar',
configplan='/home/oracle/deployments/PricingModelUpdate_cfgplan.xml')
```

We have now completed the scaling out of the pricing application's PricingApp.ear component, and the application's topology is as shown earlier in Figure 8-3.

Conclusion

This chapter described the detailed end-to-end process for the creation of an environment hosting all of the components of an enterprise application that uses a variety of the different Fusion Middleware products, as we described in the first section of this book. The process began with the installation of the Fusion Middleware software, the configuration of this software to achieve a desired topology, and the deployment of the application's artifacts on top of this topology. The process also included the steps for the extension of a WebLogic server cluster that is part of this topology into two nodes to accommodate increasing usage needs for the applications deployed on this cluster. Throughout the description of this process, we included the configuration file snippets, command-line examples, and WLST scripts needed for performing the tasks at hand.

CHAPTER 9

Securing Fusion Middleware Enterprise Applications

ith the components of the pricing application deployed, the next important task is to ensure that the environment created in the previous chapter is properly secured. In this chapter, we start by securing the WebLogic Server hosts at the operating system and file system levels. We then look at hardening the environment by enabling Secure Sockets Layer (SSL) on the different interfaces exposed by the pricing application's components and enabling Single Sign-On for the authentication of all of the application's web interfaces. Finally, we end the chapter by configuring the components of the application with the Fusion Middleware audit framework to enable the generation of audit reports that allow for the analysis of changes to important security aspects of the environment.

Securing the Pricing Application

The security considerations of the production environment of an enterprise application must be planned carefully and in advance. In this chapter, we will go through the most important areas of consideration for securing the environment of the pricing application, as described in Chapter 8. We will also identify the specific steps required for addressing these considerations. The topology of the application's environment will remain the same as that depicted in Figure 8-3 in Chapter 8, with only one major change: To allow for the configuration of Single-Sign-On (SSO) for the application's web interfaces, we will assume the existence of a new host, named "idm2," that contains an existing installation of the Oracle Access Manager (OAM) product, which we reviewed in Chapter 4. After we have completed the application of the steps outlined in this chapter, the pricing application's environment will be as shown in Figure 9-1.

Prior to beginning a discussion of the steps required to achieve the topology shown in Figure 9-1, it is important to note that the securing of IT environment's IDM shared infrastructure (that is, the Oracle Internet Directory and Oracle Access Manager configuration itself) and data tier (in our case, the Oracle and MySQL RDBMS installations) is just as crucial as securing of the application's middleware components. A secured IDM and RDBMS layer builds the foundation for a secured middleware and application deployment.

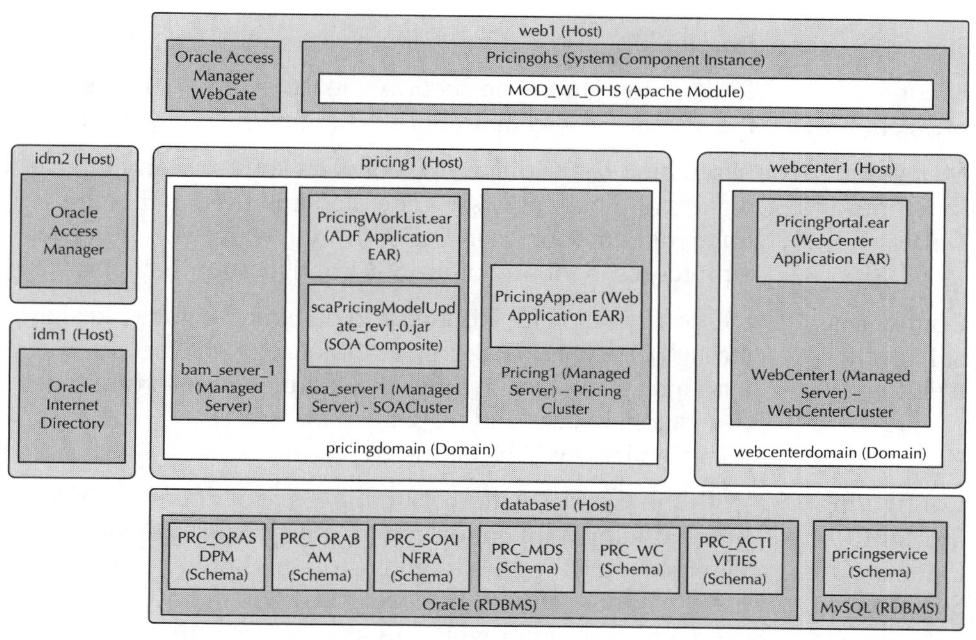

FIGURE 9-1. *Pricing application's secured topology*

This chapter, however, focuses on the security of the pricing application's Fusion Middleware components and assumes that the RDBMS and IDM shared infrastructures used by the application have themselves been secured.

Overall Flow of Events for Securing the Deployment

The sections of this chapter go through some of key steps for securing the pricing application's environment. Although these steps are discussed in a particular sequence, they can be carried out separately because they are mostly independent considerations, unless mentioned otherwise. Table 9-1 provides a summary of these steps.

Step	Description
Securing the physical host	Recommendations on security measures implemented on the operating system and file system of the UNIX host.
Managing keystores and wallets	Discussion of the difference between keystores and Oracle wallets and how they are generated and used across the different components in Fusion Middleware. This step is a prerequisite for any of the SSL configuration sections.
Configuring SSL for the web tier	SSL configuration for inbound and outbound communication through Oracle HTTP Server. In this chapter, the focus is on inbound SSL protection only. The entire process—from wallet generation, import, and registration to OHS SSL configuration—will be discussed.
Configuring SSL for Oracle Platform Security Services and Oracle Internet Directory	With the Oracle Platform Security Services configurations of the pricing application relying on Oracle Internet Directory (OID) as the identity store and policy store, the LDAP channel should be secured by SSL in any production environment. This step assumes that OID has already been configured in SSL mode. We will go through the process of obtaining the certificate from OID as well as setting the keystore for OPSS and switching on SSL from Fusion Middleware. In addition, we discuss some best practices on Oracle Internet Directory access control to further protect the OPSS data residing in the directory.
Configuring Single Sign-On	Setting up Single Sign-On for the pricing application with Oracle Access Manager. The main objective is to configure our Oracle HTTP server to be protected by Oracle Access Manager. In this step we go through the entire WebGate installation process and how to register it with Oracle Access Manager and the OHS instance.
Configuring the audit framework	Converting the out-of-the-box file-based audit repository to a production-grade Oracle RDBMS audit repository. In this step we also discuss setting up Oracle Business Intelligence Publisher to generate reports on audit data in the audit repository.

TABLE 9-1. *Pricing Application Security Configuration Steps*

Securing Physical Host

In Chapter 8, we performed the installation of all of the pricing application's Fusion Middleware components through a single user with ID, "oracle." Here are some important considerations concerning how to grant and protect access to the physical hosts of any Fusion Middleware deployment:

- **Accounts on the host** You should not create too many user accounts on any Fusion Middleware hosts. A general recommendation is to create two sets of users—one set with system privileges on the operating system, and the other set with sufficient privileges to install, deploy, and maintain Fusion Middleware components—acting as Fusion Middleware administrator with restricted access.
- **File access permissions** It is important to configure file access on the operating system carefully. Examples of sensitive file system data used by Fusion Middleware components that would benefit from restricted access include the LDAP data files used by the embedded WebLogic Server LDAP server as well as any private keystores, certificates, and Oracle wallets. There are other persistent stores in the local file system for various other components within Fusion Middleware. Whenever possible, you should adhere to production guidelines by switching to external repositories, such as using an external LDAP server as an identity store and using databases for MDS's repository and the Fusion Middleware security audit framework. Although such measures will minimize the amount of sensitive data stored in the file system, they do not remove all such occurrences. As a result, for the remaining file system elements of a Fusion Middleware environment, you should leverage the UNIX file system's access permissions: At a minimum, you should consider using umask 066 to deny read and write permissions to Group and Others on your MW_HOME directory (which is /home/oracle/products, based on Chapter 8) and limiting access to only the administrative users you have identified for installing, deploying, and maintaining Fusion Middleware, as described in the previous section. In doing so, you protect your WebLogic Server product installation, the Fusion Middleware component installation (SOA, WebCenter, and so on), the MW_HOME

product installations, and your domain directories containing configuration files, security files, log files, and other resource files.

- **Root user usage** Do not run Oracle HTTP Server on UNIX systems as the root user. This ensures protection against attempts to inject malicious operations executed by the web server. The root user has access to the entire file system, including many key files dealing with operating system user access. The root user also has access to many of the system ports (< 1024) commonly used by important inbound and outbound protocols and system services.
- **Unencrypted passwords** When WLST is being used, a username and clear text password are required for certain commands, such as the following:
  - **connect()** Used to connect to a WebLogic Server instance
  - **startServer()** Used to start the admin server
  - **nmConnect()** Used to connect to the node manager for invoking node manager commands via WLST

In general, you should avoid using clear text passwords in commands and WLST scripts because they may be easily viewed by others and sometimes captured by process listings on the operating system if the password is used in the command line. Instead, wait for the interactive prompts for better security.

WLST allows users to create a user configuration file for storing their username and encrypted password that can be referenced in commands that require this information. Once you have logged in to WLST, you can use the storeUserConfig command to store the login credentials of the current session, as follows:

```
wls:/pricingdomain/serverConfig> storeUserConfig("/home/oracle/my.secure",
"/home/oracle/my.key")
```

This creates your encrypted credentials in the my.secure file with an associated my.key file containing the decryption key. These files must be protected with proper file access, as discussed before. Once created, these user configuration files may be used in any WLST commands that support them. For example, here's how to perform a connect() command using these files:

```
wls:/offline >  connect(userConfigFile="/home/oracle/my.secure",
userKeyFile="/home/oracle/my.key")
```

Securing Communication with SSL

Secure Sockets Layer (SSL) provides a mechanism for two systems connecting over the network to authenticate against each other and establish a secure channel for communication by encrypting the data exchanged between the two parties. It is the most widely used transport-level data-communication protocol providing support for authentication, confidentiality, message integrity, and secure cryptographic key exchange between client and server. Here are the key aspects of SSL:

- **Data encryption** Ensures that the data exchanged between the two parties is encrypted and can only be read by the intended recipient. SSL supports many different encryption algorithms, and the choice of algorithm is determined by the two parties in the initial SSL handshake when the secure channel is being established.
- **Data integrity** Ensures that the message received has not been tampered with. The recipient of the message needs to verify that the message was prepared and sent by the intended sender and that it was not altered en route by any other party. In addition to the encrypted message, the client also sends a message digest generated by a hash function using the message. The server will use the same pre-negotiated hash function to generate a digest from the received message and match it with the incoming digest to verify the integrity.
- **Authentication** Ensures that the parties are who they claim to be. This is done by exchanging certificates, which are digital identities issued by trusted certificate authorities.

In one-way SSL, the recipient presents a certificate to the sender for verification, but the sender is not required to present a certificate to the recipient. In this case, the sender must ensure that the recipient is what it claims to be by authenticating the recipient using the certificate. For example, the channel between the end-user browser and the OHS in our pricing application setup can be protected by one-way SSL. In this case, the sender is the browser and OHS is the recipient of the message. OHS presents a certificate to the browser for verification so that end users know they are indeed accessing the correct URL for the application.

In two-way SSL, both the sender and recipient present a certificate to each other. Using the same example, the end-user browser must now also present a certificate so that the pricing application can also authenticate the end user.

Figure 9-2 shows a simplified version of our pricing application topology. The figure highlights the key communication channels and components where SSL is relevant.

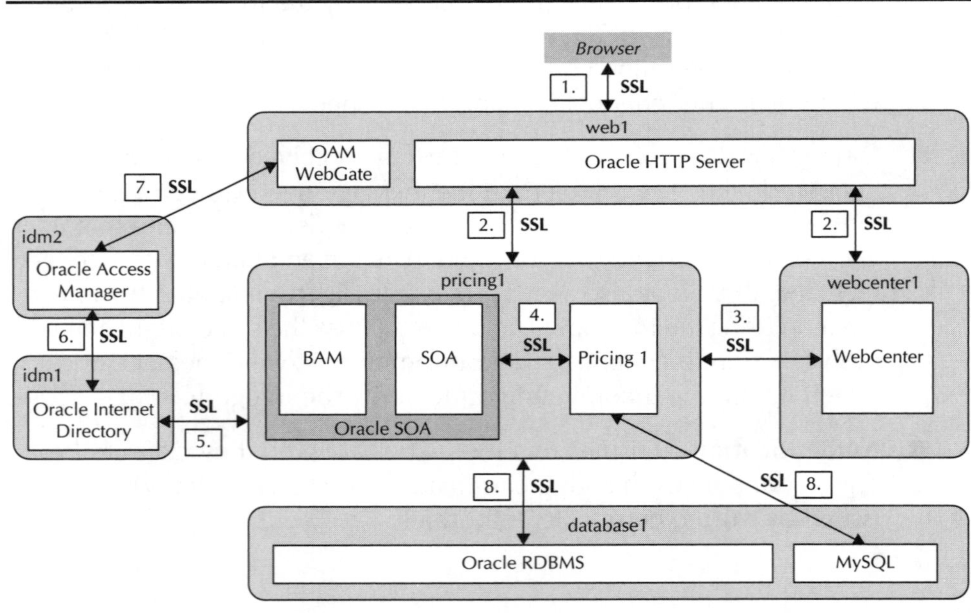

FIGURE 9-2. *Simplified pricing application topology*

Here's a description of each of the communication channels (as enumerated in Figure 9-2) of the pricing application's environment that can be protected using SSL:

1. **Inbound HTTP** Inbound HTTP traffic coming from the end-user browser. When SSL is set up, HTTPS will be used between the browser and the OHS endpoint.
2. **Outbound HTTP** Outbound HTTP traffic from OHS to WebLogic Server. This channel is typically behind the firewall.
3. **Oracle WebCenter** Traffic between Oracle WebCenter and other components in Fusion Middleware, such as Oracle WebCenter Spaces connection to WebLogic Server portlets and Oracle WebLogic Communication Services.
4. **Oracle SOA** Traffic to and from SOA composites and web services.
5. **OPSS and WebLogic Server with Oracle Internet Directory** LDAP traffic between WebLogic Server and OPSS against Oracle Internet Directory as the identity and policy store.
6. **Oracle Access Manager and Oracle Internet Directory** LDAP traffic between Oracle Access Manager and Oracle Internet Directory where user authentication and authorization queries are frequent.
7. **Oracle Access Manager and WebGate** Oracle WebGate Interaction with Oracle Access Manager.
8. **Database** Traffic between Fusion Middleware components and their data sources.

We will be covering only the configuration of SSL for the inbound HTTP traffic (item 1) as well as the traffic between OPSS and OID (item 5) in detail in this chapter. However, the steps required for configuring security for the other communication channels shown in Figure 9-2 are very similar to the steps we will be describing as part of our discussion. The sections that follow assume that an Oracle Internet Directory instance is available on the idm1 host and has already been configured for one-way SSL, which is sometimes referred to as SSL mode 1.

A detailed description of SSL is beyond the scope of this book. The "Fusion Middleware Administrator's Guide" in the Oracle Fusion Middleware documentation library does contain a section devoted to Secure Sockets Layer.

Keystore and Wallet Management

In preparation for setting up SSL between the various components, we need to first have the required private keys and certificates properly registered before they can be configured for usage. Fusion Middleware supports two types of keystores for keys and certificates:

- **JKS-based keystore and truststore** This is the default JDK implementation of Java keystores and is used by all Java components and applications in Fusion Middleware and within WebLogic Server, including:
  - Oracle Virtual Directory
  - Oracle SOA Suite
  - Oracle WebCenter
- **Oracle Wallet** This is used by system components, including Oracle HTTP Server, Oracle WebCache, and Oracle Internet Directory. Originally designed to support Oracle products written in C, an Oracle wallet is a container that stores your credentials, such as certificates, trusted certificates, certificate requests, and private keys. It can be created to reside on the file system or stored in LDAP directories such as Oracle Internet Directory.

Configuring SSL for the Web Tier

As shown earlier in Figure 9-2, the Oracle HTTP Server (OHS) within the pricing application's web tier handles two types of traffic. The first consists of inbound requests coming from the end users' browsers (in larger deployments, a load balancer or Oracle WebCache may be placed in front of OHS, but for the purpose of the remainder of this chapter we assume that browsers are directly hitting OHS). The second consists of outbound traffic requests that go to WebLogic Server. We will look at configuring one-way SSL for the inbound traffic into OHS through HTTPS—an SSL-enabled HTTP protocol with support for data encryption and identity authentication with a web server.

Creating a Self-Signed Wallet

For the purpose of this exercise, we will create a self-signed wallet for testing. In a production environment, you should never use a self-signed certificate. A trusted certificate should be purchased from a well-known certificate authority (CA) such as VeriSign. However, the steps to create the wallet with a trusted certificate are very similar to what's outlined here.

We will use the orapki command-line tool to create the initial wallet. You can find orapki under the MW_HOME/oracle_common/bin directory in all Fusion Middleware installations. Because we are securing OHS, perform this on host web1. On a UNIX system, set your ORACLE_HOME environment variable to the installation directory of OHS before running the tool, which in the case of the pricing application's web tier is ~/products/Oracle_WT. Start by using the following command to create an empty wallet:

```
$ ./orapki wallet create -wallet ./root -pwd <password>
```

The password here will be used later on to access the wallet. The ./root element of the command specifies the directory under which the wallet will be created. You have now created an empty wallet under the directory root from where the command is run, as shown here:

```
$ ls root
ewallet.p12
```

The next step is to add a self-signed certificate to this wallet with the following DN:

```
cn=root_test,cn=US
```

Typically, the DN in a certificate is used to identify the issuer. Because this is a self-signed certificate, we are going to set it to some arbitrary value. We will set the keysize to be 1024 and the expiration date to be a year from the creation date. The keysize defines the length of the encryption key used in the encryption algorithm. In the same directory as before, run the following command:

```
$ ./orapki wallet add -wallet ./root -dn "cn=root_test,c=US" -keysize 1024
-self_signed -validity 3650 -pwd <password>
```

We now have a self-signed wallet that we can use. In a production environment, after purchasing the certificate from a well-known CA, you can use the orapki command to add the trusted certificate to the wallet.

Importing the Wallet for the OHS Instance

Once you have the wallet created, you need to import the wallet and associate it with the component where it will be used. To do so, we will use Enterprise Manager. For components where SSL configuration is relevant, there is a wallet management page corresponding to that component. To access the OHS Wallet Management page of Enterprise Manager, right-click the OHS node within the tree pane and select Security | Wallets, as shown next.

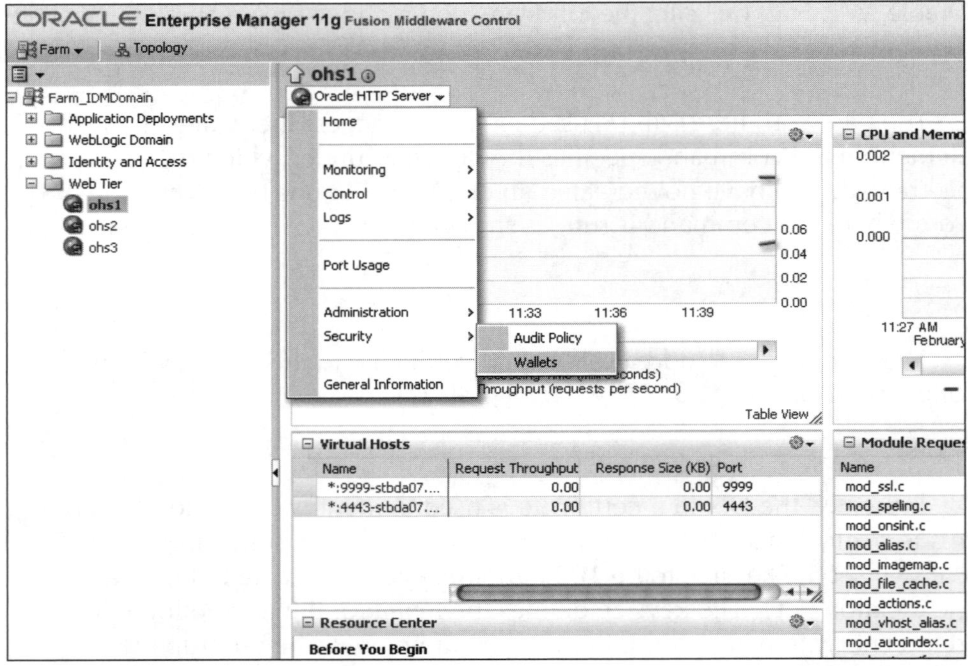

The wallet page allows you to create and delete wallets, create wallets with self-signed certificates, as well as import and export wallets. This particular page is associated with this OHS instance only. If you need to manage wallets for another component, you must navigate to that component instance to access the corresponding wallet management page. To import a wallet, perform the following steps from the OHS wallet page:

1. Click on Import to access the Import Wallet page, shown here.

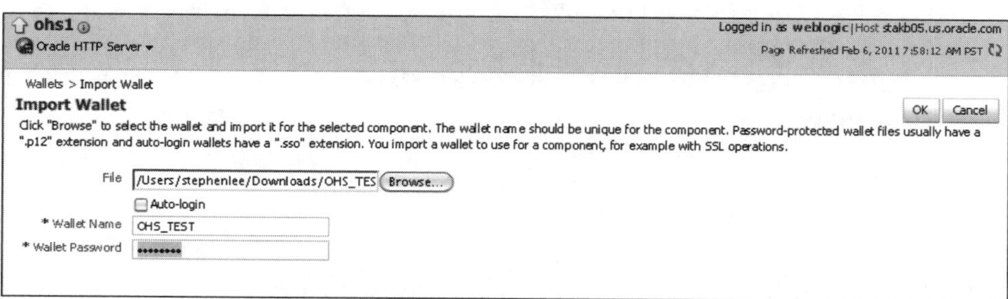

2. Use the Browse button to locate the wallet created in the previous section in the file system.
3. Our wallet is password-protected. Make sure the Auto-login box is unchecked.
4. Enter a wallet name of your choice (in this example, OHS_TEST) and a password for the wallet.
5. Click OK.

After following these steps, you are now ready to use the OHS_TEST wallet to configure SSL for inbound OHS requests.

Enabling SSL for Inbound Requests to Oracle HTTP Server

We will continue to use Enterprise Manager to enable SSL for inbound OHS requests. To do so, perform the following steps:

1. Navigate back to the OHS instance.
2. From the component drop-down, select Administration | Virtual Hosts.
3. By default, you should see two ports. We will select port 4443 to be set up with the wallet for one-way SSL.

4. From the Configure drop-down, select SSL Configuration, as shown here.

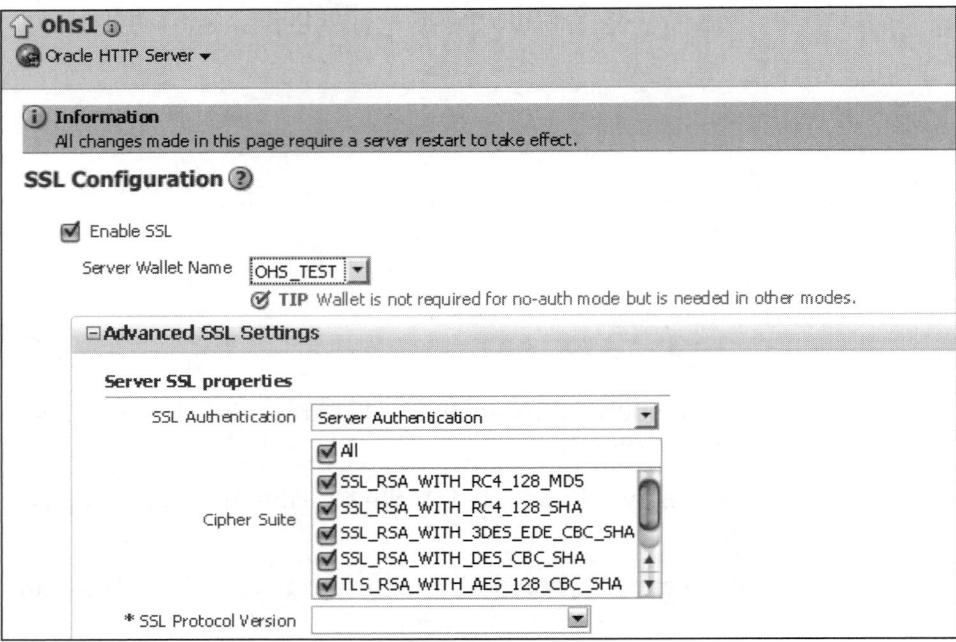

5. Check the Enable SSL box.

6. In the Server Wallet Name drop-down, select the wallet name (OHS_TEST in this case).

7. Leave the rest of the settings at their default values and click OK to apply the changes.

8. The changes do not take effect until the OHS instance is restarted. Navigate back to the OHS instance and select Control | Restart.

You now have SSL enabled with one-way authentication. Open a browser session and connect to https://web1:4443/PricingServiceWeb to test this out. If you wish to change the SSL port, you can do the following:

1. Navigate back to the OHS instance in Enterprise Manager.

2. Select Administration | Ports Configuration from the drop-down, and a list of active ports will be shown.

3. Select the Listen port being used for HTTPS (in this case, 4443).
4. Click Edit to change the port number.
5. Restart OHS as instructed before.

Configuring SSL for Oracle Platform Security Services with Oracle Internet Directory

In Chapter 8, we configured both the domain identity store as well as the policy and credential stores of the Oracle Platform Security Services to point to an existing Oracle Internet Directory. In this section we will configure all the LDAP channels against Oracle Internet Directory to use one-way SSL. In many directory deployments, both non-SSL and SSL ports will be configured. The non-SSL port is often used for white pages and address book lookups involving only nonsensitive data. The SSL port is set up for LDAP queries involving sensitive data such as passwords and authorization-related data.

The assumption here is that Oracle Internet Directory is already configured to be listening for one-way SSL LDAP requests. For more information on SSL for Oracle Internet Directory, refer to the "Administrator's Guide for Oracle Internet Directory" in the Oracle Fusion Middleware documentation library.

Retrieving Certificate Authority Information from Oracle Internet Directory

Because Oracle Internet Directory (OID) is already running in one-way SSL mode, it has already been configured with an Oracle wallet containing the certificate authority (CA) information. Assuming you have access to host idm1, where the Oracle wallet resides, go to MW_HOME/oracle_common on idm1 and use the following orapki command to extract the certificate needed by the LDAP clients (in this case, OPSS and WebLogic Server).

```
$ orapki wallet export -wallet <wallet file name> -dn "<CA DN>" -cert
serverTrust.cert
```

Here, serverTrust.cert is the file you want the certificate to be exported to. If you do not have access to the OID host—which could very well be the case in a real IT environment where the shared IDM infrastructure is often administered by a separate group—then you should provide these instructions to your IDM administrator so that he can extract the certificate for your LDAP client.

Importing the Certificate into WebLogic Server

The LDAP connection for OPSS is established through WebLogic Server, whether the connection is for the identity store or for the policy and credential stores. We need to use the OID certificate we exported in the previous section and create the appropriate keystore for WebLogic Server. A keystore, as discussed earlier, is similar to an Oracle wallet and is used by all the nonsystem components in Fusion Middleware. Because we have multiple WebLogic Server domains on multiple hosts, the steps in this section need to be repeated for both the pricingdomain and the webcenterdomain. In the following description, we use pricingdomain as the example:

1. Copy serverTrust.cert to the WebLogic Server host.
2. Generate myKeys.jks, a keystore file with the CA in serverTrust.cert, imported using the following keytool command (keytool can be found in JAVA_HOME/bin):

```
$ keytool -import -v -trustcacerts -alias trust -file
serverTrust.cert -keystore myKeys.jks -storepass <keyStorePassword>
```

3. Now log in to the WebLogic Server admin console to configure a custom identity and custom trust keystore, as shown next. Click on Lock & Edit to enable editing if it is currently locked.

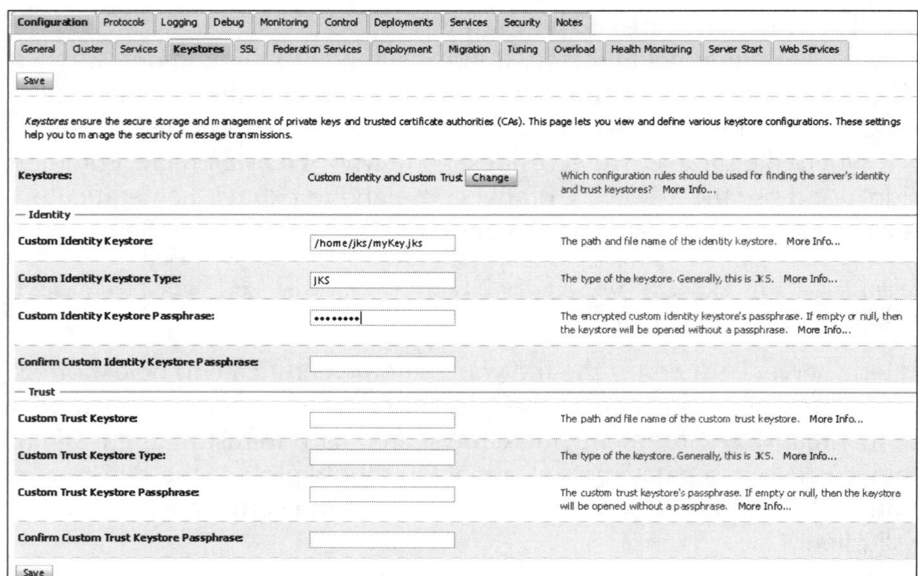

4. Navigate to Environment | Servers. Select the administration server in pricingdomain.
5. Select the Keystores tab.
6. Click Change to change the keystore to Custom Identity and Custom Trust. Then click Save.
7. Under the Identity section, enter the following:
   - For Custom Trust Keystore, enter the absolute path of myKey.jks, generated earlier.
   - For Custom Identity Keystore Type, enter **JKS**.
   - For Custom Identity Keystore Passphrase, enter the keystore password.
8. Modify the ~/pricingdomain/startWebLogic.sh script by including the following in the admin server startup script:

```
-Djavax.net.ssl.trustStore=<absolute path of myKey.jks>
```

9. Restart the WebLogic admin server.

Repeat these steps for the admin server in webcenter1 domain as well.

Configuring LDAP Authenticator for SSL

With the keystore now imported, we need to revisit the configuration for the WebLogic Server security realm authentication provider (OracleInternetDirectoryAuthenticator), which we configured in Chapter 8. The configuration of this authentication provider now needs to point to the Oracle Internet Directory SSL port. The *SSLEnabled* flag for the provider should also be set to true. The following WLST script can be used to perform these changes:

```
#
# Connect to the pricing application domain.
#
connect(userConfigFile="/home/oracle/my.secure",
userKeyFile="/home/oracle/my.key")
edit()
startEdit()
```

```
# Traverse to the OID_Authenticator created in chapter 8
cd('SecurityConfiguration/pricing1/Realms/myrealm/
AuthenticationProviders/OID_Authenticator')

# First, set the port to the SSL port.  Here we will set it to 636 which
# is the standard LDAP SSL port.  Next, we will set SSLEnabled to true

cmo.setPort(636)
cmo.setSSLEnabled(true)
```

After executing this script, you must restart your WebLogic Server instances for the changes to take effect. You must perform this step on both the pricingdomain and webcenterdomain.

Configuring the OPSS Policy and Credential Stores for SSL

Similarly, we will now configure the OPSS policy and credential stores to enable one-way SSL against Oracle Internet Directory. To do this, we will use the same WLST reassociateSecurityStore command as we used in Chapter 8. The only difference is that the LDAP URL will be modified to the following format:

```
ldaps://ldap_host:ldap_ssl_port
```

Note the change from ldap:// to ldaps://, which now points to the OID server's SSL port. The rest of the command should be the same:

```
reassociateSecurityStore(domain='pricing1',
admin='cn=orcladmin',password='password',
ldapurl='ldaps://ldap_host:ldap_SSL_port',
serverType='OID',jpsroot='cn=opssroot')
```

After executing this command, you must restart your WebLogic Server instances for the changes to take effect on both domains of the pricing application.

Other SSL Considerations

We have completed SSL configuration for inbound HTTP requests and all the LDAP channels in our pricing application setup. As shown earlier in Figure 9-2, there are many other areas where SSL can be configured to provide added security. For example, the Pricing Update web service can be protected by one-way SSL, in which case all the web service clients calling this service will be required to create a keystore containing the appropriate certificate. The channel between Oracle HTTP Server and WebLogic Server can be protected with SSL. If the databases are configured in SSL mode, configuration will be needed to make sure the data sources created in WebLogic Server are SSL-enabled with the appropriate keystores created.

It should be noted that although enabling SSL increases the security of your deployment, it may have an impact in performance, particularly with the choice of the keysize. A larger keysize results in a more secure encryption at the expense of reduced performance.

Securing Oracle Platform Security Services Access to Oracle Internet Directory

So far, the connection from the pricing application's OPSS component within the WebLogic Server domain to the OID LDAP server is established using the *cn=orcladmin* user. As mentioned briefly in Chapter 8, it is generally recommended that instead a dedicated LDAP Distinguished Name (DN) be used for each client application. In a production environment, the credentials for *cn=orcladmin* are typically only used by LDAP directory administrators and should not be used by client applications to access the LDAP server. A client application-specific DN can be given just enough privileges to access the directory and to perform the necessary authentication, authorization, and user/group lookups for OPSS. Furthermore, the use of such a DN allows us to protect the OPSS directory subtree to be seen only by this DN. This will prevent other LDAP users from tampering with application policies and credentials stored in OPSS. It also avoids improper usage and exposure of the *cn=orcladmin* super user.

We will address these concerns by implementing an access control list (ACL) to restrict access to the OPSS context and the entire the OPSS subtree in OID. An ACL allows you to specify who would be allowed to access the information and what types of operations (read, write, delete, and so on) are allowed on the OID objects. The control list is specified at an LDAP node level, and its restrictions apply to all entries in the LDAP subtree under that node. In this case, we will create an ACL for our *cn=jpsRootNote* where the OPSS policy store resides.

We begin this process by first creating an LDIF file that specifies the ACL. Here is an example of such a file:

```
dn: cn=jpsRootNode
changetype: modify
add: orclACI
access to entry by dn="cn=myAdmin,cn=users,dc=acme,dc=com"
(browse,add,delete) by * ( none )
access to attr=(*) by dn="cn=myAdmin,cn=users,dc=acme,dc=com"
(search,read,write,compare) by * (none)
```

We name this file opssacl.ldif. In this ACL, we assume that user *cn=myAdmin* is the LDAP DN to be used to connect to the OPSS store. Use the following ldapmodify command to add this ACL. The command can be found under the ORACLE_HOME/bin directory of your Oracle Internet Directory installation in the idm1 host.

```
$ ldapmodify -h idm1 -p 389 -D cn=orcladmin -w <password>
-c -v -f opssacl.ldif
```

To have this ACL take effect, the next step is to modify the configuration of the OID security authentication provider configuration of the pricingdomain and webcenterdomain of the pricing application by changing the LDAP DN from its current value of *cn=orcladmin* to *cn=myAdmin,cn=users,dc=acme,dc=com*. It is important not to make this domain change before performing the ACL change at the OID level.

Configuring Single Sign-On

The next step in securing the pricing application's environment is to configure Single Sign-On (SSO) to ensure that a single authentication session is required for all web interfaces of the pricing application. Our assumption is that the Oracle Access Manager product has been installed and configured on the idm2 host, as shown earlier in Figure 9-1. With this assumption in place, the process of configuring SSO consists of installing and configuring an instance of the Oracle Access Manager WebGate component within the pricing application's web tier. Recall from Chapter 4 that WebGate is the policy-enforcements agent that is typically deployed on the web tier to filter HTTP requests to ensure authentication before they reach the application. The following sections outline the steps for installing and configuring WebGate with Oracle HTTP Server.

Installing WebGate

This section outlines the steps for the installation of WebGate on the pricing application's web1 host.

1. Download the WebGate installer onto your Oracle HTTP Server host. You can find it on the Oracle Technology Network (OTN).
2. Because WebGate is a C++ implemented component, you will also need to have the correct GNU Compiler Collection (GCC) libraries downloaded and made available on your host. For the list of versions and additional information on GCC libraries required, please refer to the "Installing Third-Party GCC Libraries" section in the *Oracle Fusion Middleware Installation Guide for Identity Management* book in the Fusion Middleware documentation library.
3. Unzip the executable. This should result in a directory named Disk1. Go to Disk1 and launch the Oracle Installer using .runInstaller.
4. When prompted for the JRE/JDK location, enter **~/products/jdk<version>** from your OHS installation.
5. Proceed with the Oracle Universal Installer. For the directory locations, we use ~/products as the MW_HOME and ~/products/Oracle_OAMWebGate1 as the ORACLE_HOME.
6. When prompted for the GCC libraries location, specify the folder containing the GCC libraries and proceed.
7. Under $MW_HOME, you should now see Oracle_OAMWebGate1 if you took the default values during the installation.

Creating and Registering a WebGate Instance

We will now create a WebGate instance on host web1 for the OHS. Here are the steps to follow:

1. Go to ~/products/Oracle_OAMWebGate1/webgate/ohs/tools/deployWebGate and then run the following commands (this

command will modify the OHS instance configuration we created in Chapter 8 to ensure that it is registered with WebGate):

```
$ ./deployWebgateInstance.sh
-w ~/pricinginstance/config/OHS/pricingohs
-oh ~/products/Oracle_OAMWebGate1
Copying files from WebGate_Oracle_Home to WebGate_instancedir
$ export LD_LIBRARY_PATH=$LD_LIBRARY_PATH:~/products/Oracle_WT/lib
$ cd ~/products/Oracle_OAMWebGate/webgate/ohs/tools/setup/
InstallTools
$ ./EditHttpConf -w ~/pricinginstance/config/OHS/pricingohs
 -oh ~/products/Oracle_OAMWebGate1 -o webgate.conf
```

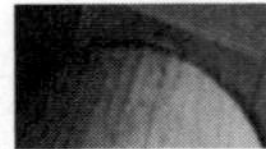

NOTE
Steps 2 through 7 listed next need to be carried out on the Oracle Access Manager host, idm2.

2. Go to ORACLE_HOME/oam/server/rreg/input in the OAM installation directory and modify OAM11GRequest.xml by setting values for these parameters:

   - **<serverAddress>** Set this to the OAM Admin Server URL, which is http://idm2/7001.
   - **<agentBaseUrl>** Set this to the OHS URL, which is http://web1:7777.
   - **<hostIdentifier>** Set this to RREG_web1 to identify the OHS host.
   - **<agentName>** Set this to RREG_web1_agent1 to identify the agent.
   - **<applicationDomain>** Set this to RREG_PricingDomain to identify the domain.
   - **<logoutCallbackUrl>** Set this to /oam_logout_success.

   Save the changes.

3. Go to $ORACLE_HOME/oam/server/rreg/bin. Open oamreg.sh and set OAM_REG_HOME to $ORACLE_HOME/oam/server/rreg.
4. Change the file permission of oamreg.sh by using chmod777 oamreg.sh.
5. Make sure JAVA_HOME in the environment is set to $MW_HOME/<jdk directory>.
6. Go to $ORACLE_HOME/oam/server/rreg and execute the following command:

   ```
   $ ./bin/oamreg.sh inband input/OAM11GRequest.xml
   ```

   When prompted for the agent username and password, enter the administrator names for OAM server. When prompted for the WebGate password, enter **N** and proceed. When prompted for URIs file, enter **N** and proceed.
7. When finished, go to $ORACLE_HOME/oam/server/rreg/output/RREG_web1_agent1. Copy cwallet.sso and ObAccessClient.xml to the OHS machine web1 and make them available under ~/pricinginstance/config/OHS/pricingohs/webgate/config/.
8. Restart OHS on web1 with the following command:

   ```
   $ cd ~/pricinginstance/bin
   $ ./opmnctl stopall
   $ ./opmnctl startall
   ```

At this point, you have completed the WebGate registration. You should now be able to access the pricing application's web interfaces using the http://web1:7777/ URL prefix, which should redirect you to the OAM login page.

Securing Web Services

As discussed in Chapter 3, our pricing application exposes a single operation (modifyModel) that is used to modify the pricing model for a given product. It is used solely by components behind the firewall. Therefore, we will not be focusing on data-encryption-related policies.

We will apply the binding_permission_authorization_policy using Fusion Middleware Control. The binding_permission_authorization_policy ensures that the subject has permission to perform the operation with our PricingModelWebService. Here are the steps:

1. From the left pane of Fusion Middleware Control, under WebLogic Domain, expand pricingdomain and select Pricing1.
2. From the WebLogic Server menu, select Web Services.
3. From the list of policies, select the one with the endpoint called PricingModelWebService and click on the endpoint.
4. Under Directly Attached Policies, click on the Attach/Detach button to open the policy attachment page, shown here.

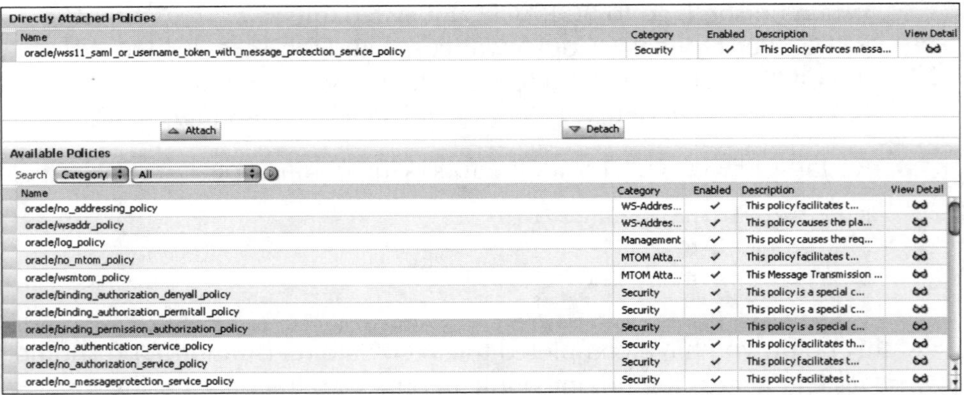

5. Select oracle/binding_permission_authorization_policy and click Attach. The policy should now show up under the Direct Attached Policies section.
6. Click OK.

Now that the binding_permission_authorization_policy is attached, we need to create the oracle.wsm.security.WSFunctionPermission. Here are the steps:

1. In Fusion Middleware Control, navigate to the pricingdomain.
2. From the WebLogic Domain menu, select Security | Application Policies.

3. Select soa_server1/soa_infra under Select Application Name to Search and click on the search button next to the Permission search field. This will show all existing permissions.
4. Click Create.
5. On the Create Application Grant page, click Add under Permissions.
6. Under Customize, enter the following:
   - **Permission Class** oracle.wsm.security.WSFunctionPermission
   - **Resource Name** com.myenterprise.pricing/modifyModel#
   - **Permission Actions** invoke (always)
7. Click OK.
8. Back on the Create Application Grant page, click on Add Application Role under Grantee and select [authenticated-role] on the pop-up to grant all authenticated users permission to invoke this web service.

Configuring Audit

In Chapter 4, we configured audit for the OPSS credential store framework by enabling audit on some of the credential-related operations. Out of the box, Fusion Middleware audit framework uses a file-based repository. In a production environment, it is strongly recommended that an RDBMS-based audit repository be used. The obvious advantage of the RDBMS-based audit repository is the ability to centralize the audit data across the entire domain in a single protected repository. With the RDBMS-based repository, Fusion Middleware audit framework supports integration with Oracle Business Intelligence Publisher (BI Publisher). A comprehensive set of BI Publisher reports is shipped out of the box. The audit database schema is also published in the Fusion Middleware Documentation library, allowing customers to easily create their own custom reports on top of the data collected. Lastly, an RDBMS-based repository can better handle and manage the volume of production audit data through features such as database partitioning and data backup.

Installing the Audit Schema

The first task in setting up an RDBMS-based repository for audit is to install the RDBMS schema. Technically, you may install the audit schema in an RDBMS containing other component schemas. This may be useful in a development or test environment. However, in a production environment, it is recommended that you use a dedicated database instance for audit purposes due to the potential high volume of data and the need for a backup strategy, which may differ from the other operational stores being used for other components.

Like all other Fusion Middleware product schemas, the audit schema is created by the Repository Creation Utility (RCU). You can download RCU from the Oracle Technology Network to obtain the latest available version of the tool containing the latest versions of the schemas across all the Fusion Middleware products. RCU can be run locally or remotely from where the RDBMS is located. You can reuse the RCU installed in Chapter 8. Here are the steps to follow:

1. Run RCU.
2. Select the Create option.
3. Enter your database instance information. For the purpose of this exercise, you should use the Oracle RDBMS set up on host database1 for the other components. If you are choosing a different instance, ensure it is an Oracle RDBMS database.
4. RCU requires the credentials of a system user.
5. On the Select Components screen, choose Audit Services from the list of schemas.
6. As in Chapter 8, select the option to create a new prefix (we will continue to specify "PRC_").
7. On the Schema Passwords screen, choose the Use One Password for All option and set a password of **welcome1** for all schemas, as we did in Chapter 8.
8. On the Map Tablespaces screen, accept the default tablespaces settings.

Once your RCU session is complete, you need to proceed to configure the appropriate data sources within the WebLogic Server domains that contain components that must use the single RDBMS-based audit repository. The configuration of WebLogic Server data sources can be performed through the WebLogic Server Administration Console, as per the following steps (you need to perform these steps for both the pricingdomain and the webcenterdomain of the pricing application):

1. Connect to the Oracle WebLogic Server administration console.
2. Under Domain Configurations, find JDBC and click on the Data Sources link.
3. When the Data Sources page appears, select New to create a new data source to start the wizard and then enter in the following information:
   - For Name, enter a name such as **Audit Data Source-0**.
   - For JNDI Name, enter **jdbc/AuditDB**.
   - For Database Type, select Oracle and then click Next.
   - For Database Driver, select Oracle's Driver (Thin XA) Versions: 9.0.1, 9.0.2, 10, 11. Click Next. On the Transaction Options page, click Next again.
   - Enter the appropriate DB connection information based on where you have installed your audit schema. The Database User Name is PRC_IAU in this case and the password is welcome1. Click Next.
   - On the summary page, click Test Configuration to test the connection.

Configuring the Audit Repository

Now that we have the data source set up, we need to configure Fusion Middleware audit framework to switch from the existing file-based repository to leverage the newly created audit schema in a database. The configuration for Java EE, OPSS, Oracle SOA Suite, Oracle WebCenter, and ADF components is slightly different from the configuration for system components. We need to perform both sets of configurations in order to set up audit for OPSS, Oracle SOA Suite, and Oracle HTTP Server (system component) for our pricing application.

Configuring the Audit Repository for Java EE and Oracle Platform Security Services

We start with Java EE and OPSS Audit configuration using Enterprise Manager. Follow these steps:

1. Log in to Enterprise Manager and select the pricingdomain under WebLogic Domain.
2. From the WebLogic Domain menu, go to Security | Audit Store as shown here.

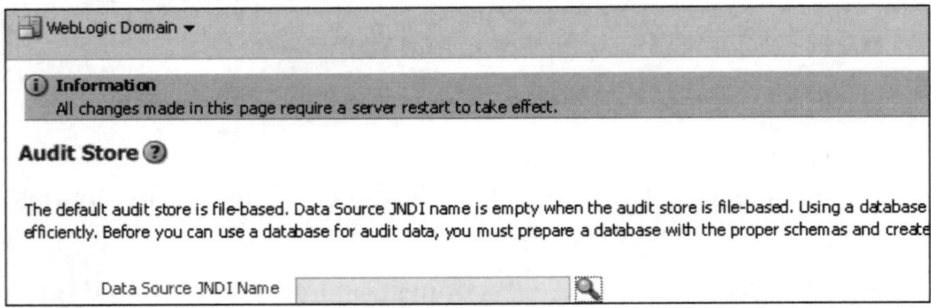

3. Use the Browser button to look up an existing data source. Enterprise Manager is able to list out only those data sources with the appropriate audit schema installed. You should see jdbc/AuditDB listed based on what we have just created. Select this data source. Click OK and then click Apply to complete the configuration.
4. You must now restart all the Oracle WebLogic servers in the domain to complete the setup. This enables Audit Loader Startup Class in Oracle WebLogic Server to reread the configuration.

Configuring the Audit Repository for System Components

For system components, Oracle Process Manager and Notification Server (OPMN) is used to process audit events and push them to the audit repository. For our setup, we are focusing on Oracle HTTP Server (OHS). Perform the following on the web1 OHS host.

1. Locate ~/products/Oracle_WT/instances/pricinginstance/config/OPMN/opmn.xml and open the file.
2. Locate the rmd-definitions element:

```
<rmd-definitions>
      <rmd name="AuditLoader" interval="15">
          <conditional>
            <![CDATA[({time}>=00:00)]]>
          </conditional>
          <action value="exec $ORACLE_HOME/jdk/bin/java
-classpath
                $ORACLE_HOME/modules/oracle.osdt_11.1.1/
osdt_cert.jar:
                $ORACLE_HOME/modules/oracle.osdt_11.1.1/
osdt_core.jar:
                $ORACLE_HOME/jdbc/lib/ojdbc5.jar:
                $ORACLE_HOME/modules/oracle.iau_11.1.1/fmw_
audit.jar:

$ORACLE_HOME/modules/oracle.pki_11.1.1/oraclepki.jar
                -Doracle.home=$ORACLE_HOME
                -Doracle.instance=$ORACLE_INSTANCE
                -Dauditloader.jdbcString=
jdbc:oracle:thin:@host:port:sid
                -Dauditloader.username=username

oracle.security.audit.ajl.loader.StandaloneAuditLoader"/>
          <exception
             value="exec /bin/echo PERIODICAL CALL For Audit
Loader FAILED"
         />
      </rmd>
</rmd-definitions>
```

3. Replace *jdbcString* with the database JDBC connection string for your audit repository. Replace *username* with the audit schema name, which in this case is PRC_IAU. The interval value by default is set to a very high number. Change it to a reasonable value, such as 15, as here. This means that OPMN will attempt to execute Audit Loader to push new audit data to the database once every 15 seconds. Audit Loader is the Java class listed in the RMD definition in the preceding code.

4. Save and exit the file.

5. We now need to create a password secret store for the Audit Loader containing the RDBMS password. Make sure your environment has $ORACLE_HOME and $ORACLE_INSTANCE set to ~/products/ and ~/products/Oracle_WT/instances/pricinginstance, respectively. Now execute the following in the command line:

```
$ java -classpath
     $ORACLE_HOME/modules/oracle.osdt_11.1.1/osdt_cert.jar:
     $ORACLE_HOME/modules/oracle.osdt_11.1.1/osdt_core.jar:
     $ORACLE_HOME/jdbc/lib/ojdbc5.jar:
     $ORACLE_HOME/modules/oracle.iau_11.1.1/fmw_audit.jar:
     $ORACLE_HOME/modules/oracle.pki_11.1.1/oraclepki.jar
     -Doracle.home=$ORACLE_HOME -Doracle.instance=$ORACLE_
INSTANCE
     -Dauditloader.jdbcString=
jdbc:oracle:thin:@host:port:sid
     -Dauditloader.username=username
     -Dstore.password=true
     -Dauditloader.password=welcome1
     oracle.security.audit.ajl.loader.StandaloneAuditLoader
```

The *auditloader.password* should be your PRC_IAU password, which is welcome1. The *jdbcString* should be your audit repository DB connect string.

6. Reload OPMN with the following two commands:

```
$ $ORACLE_INSTANCE/bin/opmnctl validate
$ $ORACLE_INSTANCE/bin/opmnctl reload
```

7. To validate that everything is working correctly, check the content in $ORACLE_INSTANCE/diagnostics/logs/OPMN/opmn/rmd.out. The output should look like this:

```
<date> <time> global:AuditLoader
```

Configuring the Audit Policy

In Chapter 4, we showed a simple audit policy to monitor credential store activities. The configuration of the audit policy is identical with an RDBMS-based repository. Using Enterprise Manager, it is very easy to modify the policy as described in Chapter 4 to add additional events and fine-tune each event itself.

Setting Up Business Intelligence Publisher

Now that we have an RDBMS-based repository, we can now set up Business Intelligence (BI Publisher) to view the audit data. With a file-based audit, there is no viewing option for the data other than looking directly into the local audit files on each machine. With RDBMS-based audit configured, we can now configure the powerful Oracle BI Publisher for reports. As part of the Oracle Business Intelligence Enterprise Edition, BI Publisher offers flexible reporting displays, report filtering, report scheduling, report export (to PDF, Excel, and so on), and customized report support.

To begin the configuration of BI Publisher with the audit framework, begin by installing the 10*g* Oracle Business Intelligence product as follows (at the time of writing, only 10*g* Oracle Business Intelligence Publisher is certified with the Fusion Middleware IDM audit framework):

1. Download and complete the Oracle BI Publisher 10*g* installer. BI Publisher need not reside in the hosts of our pricing application. In a production environment, this would typically be deployed separately. A single BI Publisher instance can be used for multiple audit repositories from multiple different domains. BI Publisher can be deployed using different Java EE containers. For this use case, we will assume that you have installed it with WebLogic Server.

2. Locate AuditReportTemplate.jar in your Middleware Home under $MW_HOME/oracle_common/modules/oraclee.iau_11.1.1./reports and copy this file to the BI Publisher host.

3. In your BI installation, navigate to the $ORACLE_HOME/XMLS/Reports folder.
4. Unjar AuditReportTemplate.jar into your Reports folder. You should now see a folder called Oracle_Fusion_Middleware_Audit, containing all the out-of-the-box report templates from all the Fusion Middleware products that are audit-enabled.
5. Set up the data source in BI Publisher to establish the connection to the audit repository by following these steps:
   - Make sure a data source is set up in WebLogic Server, similar to the steps described for configuring the audit repository for Java EE and OPSS. We will assume that the data source with the JNDI name "jdbc/Audit" has been created.
   - Log in to BI Publisher and navigate to the Admin tab.
   - Click on JNDI Connection and Add Data Source.
   - Specify Name as **Audit** (this can be any value you choose).
   - Specify JNDI Name as **jdbc/AuditDB** (matching your WebLogic Server data source).
   - Test your connection and click Apply to save your changes.

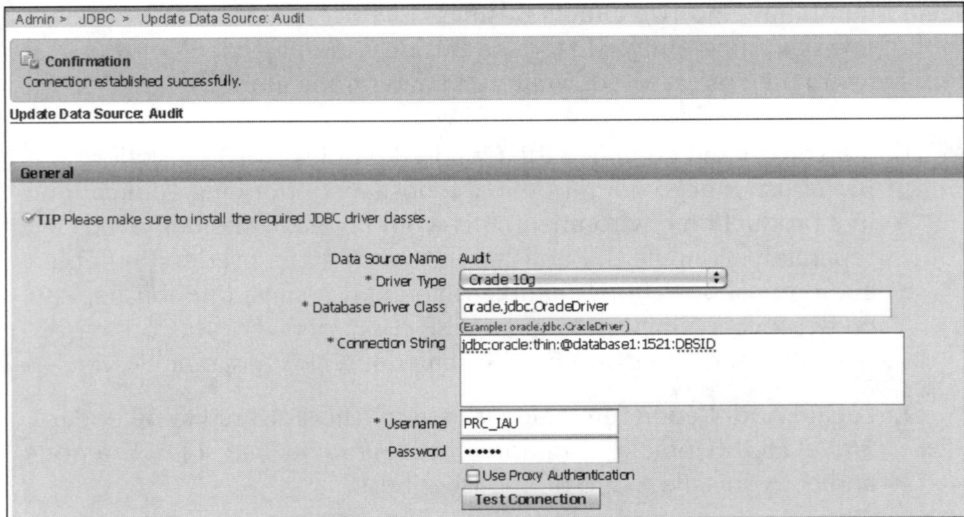
Admin > JDBC > Update Data Source: Audit
Confirmation
Connection established successfully.
Update Data Source: Audit
General
TIP Please make sure to install the required JDBC driver classes.
Data Source Name: Audit
* Driver Type: Oracle 10g
* Database Driver Class: oracle.jdbc.OracleDriver
(Example: oracle.jdbc.OracleDriver)
* Connection String: jdbc:oracle:thin:@database1:1521:DBSID
* Username: PRC_IAU
Password: ••••••
Use Proxy Authentication
Test Connection

You should now be able to access the reports in BI Publisher under the Oracle_Fusion_Middleware_Audit folder. Note that the report templates for all the products are available here; however, you will only see report results for components in your domain where audit has been enabled. For example, let's access the Credential Management report under OPSS. Follow these steps:

1. Log in to BI Publisher.
2. Under the Reports tab, click on Shared Folders and select Oracle_ Fusion Middleware Audit.
3. Navigate to the Component Specific folder and select Oracle Platform Security Services. Then select Oracle Platform Security Services and click on Credential Management to access the report, shown next. The report shows you the events being audited for Credential Management based on your audit policy configurations. The events are shown based on the default time range.

Credential Management						
User ID	Component Name	Application Name	Timestamp	Map	Key	Message
weblogic			1/11/2009 5:58:46 PM	initiatorMap	initiatorKey	Setting credential succeeded.
weblogic			1/11/2009 5:58:46 PM	mapSimpleServlet	keySimpleServlet	Setting credential succeeded.
weblogic			1/11/2009 5:58:46 PM	*	*	Deleting all credentials from the store succeeded.
weblogic			1/11/2009 5:58:46 PM	*	*	Deleting all credentials from the store succeeded.

Conclusion

This chapter has highlighted some of the common security considerations around a typical Fusion Middleware environment. We have taken some initial steps in securing our pricing application, starting with securing the physical hosts for each server. We began our infrastructure hardening by introducing keystores and Oracle wallets for setting up Secure Sockets Layer (SSL). We then proceeded with SSL configuration for Oracle HTTP Server, followed by securing the LDAP channels with SSL between OPSS and Oracle Internet Directory. We also looked at how to secure OPSS artifacts being stored in Oracle Internet Directory that are serving as the identity and policy stores for OPSS. Web access to our pricing application was protected by the installation and registration of Oracle Access Manager WebGate with Oracle Access Manager. We finished by configuring a production-grade RDBMS-based audit repository for storing our audit data, and we completed the Oracle BI Publisher installation and configuration against the audit repository for audit reporting.

CHAPTER 10

Optimizing Fusion Middleware Enterprise Applications

n this chapter we explore some of the most important aspects for optimizing the performance of a Fusion Middleware environment. Now that we have reviewed the steps for the deployment of the pricing application's components as well as the creation of a secure environment in the last two chapters, the next natural provisioning step in our path is the optimization of the environment to allow the application to make effective use of available hardware resources and to achieve its intended performance goals. We will discuss the optimization of the entire Fusion Middleware stack, starting from the Java Virtual Machine and moving up to the layered Fusion Middleware products. For each layer we will review the relevant performance optimization concepts as well as, wherever applicable, their relevance to the pricing application.

Performance Optimization

For the purpose of this chapter, we will define performance optimization as the application of configuration changes designed to ensure that the overall latency and/or throughput of an enterprise application's interfaces are improved. We will also be using the short term *optimization* instead of the full term *performance optimization* interchangeably in this context throughout. Additionally, we will be approaching optimization from a middleware point of view alone. Specifically, the optimization of the hardware and operating system layers on which the middleware executes, although important, are beyond the scope of this chapter. Finally, in line with the book's theme, we will be approaching optimization mainly from an environmental point of view instead of an application development point of view. Also, it is important to note that a large part of how any software application performs is a function of how much performance has been a consideration in its development and design.

To optimize the performance of an enterprise application, it is important to establish two important quality of service parameters for each of its interfaces. First, what is the interface's highest acceptable response time? Second, what is the maximum request frequency that the interface is expected to process? The answers to these questions can then form the basis of your performance optimization tests—that is, tests designed to exercise a set of interfaces with their maximum request frequency. While running such tests, it is then possible to measure the interface's response time to see whether it is able to achieve the desired goals. If it is, the interface can be considered to be sufficiently tuned to achieve its desired quality of service goals. If it is not, the addition of more hardware resources and tuning of the interfaces might be required. In the remainder of this chapter we will review the possible areas of tuning that you may consider for achieving quality of services goals for applications deployed to a Fusion Middleware environment.

Structure of Remaining Sections

The remainder of this chapter is organized into three sections, each mapping to a specific layer of the Fusion Middleware stack, as illustrated in Figure 10-1.

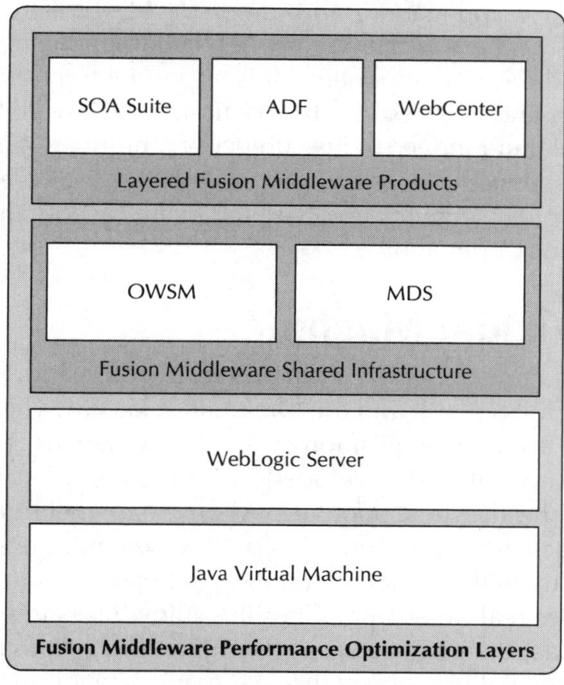

FIGURE 10-1. *Fusion Middleware performance optimization layers*

Within each section that follows, we will review the most fundamental performance optimization concepts that map to each of the layers shown in Figure 10-1 and, where applicable, describe how they apply to the pricing application's environment. It is important to note that each of the upper-layer products has dependencies on the lower layers, and a complete optimization of applications built on top of the Fusion Middleware stack requires the tuning of all layers.

Optimizing the Java Virtual Machine and WebLogic Server

The Java Virtual Machine (JVM) and WebLogic Server layers expose a number of important optimization knobs. Because all layered Fusion Middleware components are Java applications and run on WebLogic Server managed servers, the tuning of these two layers is essential in optimizing the execution of all Fusion Middleware components. It is important to note that a thorough discussion of JVM and WebLogic Server optimization is well beyond the scope of this book (and indeed is the subject of a number of articles and books). In this discussion we instead discuss some of the core principles that the optimization of these layers involves and examine how these principles apply to the pricing application.

The Java Virtual Machine

WebLogic Server can support two different implementations of the JVM: the Oracle Java HotSpot VM and the Oracle JRockit VM. The HotSpot VM comes to Oracle from the acquisition of Sun Microsystems. This JVM is the evolution of the original JVM developed by Sun as part of its launch of the Java language and is the most popular JVM on the market today. The JRockit VM comes to Oracle from the acquisition of BEA Systems. JRockit was designed from the ground up with the optimization of enterprise application servers in mind and provides real-time capabilities that allow users to specify quality of service goals that are guaranteed at execution time. Although these two VMs have fundamental implementation differences that impact the specifics of their tuning, the principles described in this section generally apply to both. When specific differences between the two VMs exist, the text explicitly points them out.

The optimization of the JVM can be broadly categorized into two parts. The first is the optimization of the way in which the JVM processes the Java programs that it executes. The second is the optimization of the way the JVM dynamically manages memory on behalf of the application. Let's look at each of these in turn.

Code Generation

One of the main benefits of the Java programming language is that it does not have to be compiled for a specific platform. This is unlike a language such as C/C++, where the application code must be compiled into assembly code that is specific to each operating system and CPU combination (together known as a platform). Java programs, on the other hand, are "write once, run everywhere." In other words, they can be written independently of the platform on which they are meant to execute. This benefit is made possible by the virtue of the Java Virtual Machine (JVM), which in effect is a virtual, software-based platform. Instead of compiling into assembly code directly, Java programs compile into .class files that contain instructions known as bytecode, and they execute the logic of the associated Java objects on the virtual platform offered by the JVM. The compiled bytecode can therefore run on any physical platform for which a JVM exists. Whereas in a straight-to-machine-code-compilation language such as C/C++, the compiler is responsible for ensuring that the assembly code it generates is optimized for execution on the target platform, for a virtual-machine-based language such as Java, there is no machine code compiler and the JVM is instead the entity that needs to ensure the bytecode is mapped to assembly code in an efficient manner. An important aspect of the optimization of a JVM is therefore ensuring that the settings it exposes for controlling its bytecode execution capabilities are properly configured.

The most straightforward approach to implementing a JVM is to translate bytecode into machine code by executing the bytecode through a simple interpreter. Such interpreters are written in a straight-to-assembly-compilation language such as C++, and their main task is to examine each bytecode instruction of a Java program in sequence and to perform the required operations to accomplish the task of the bytecode. This is, in fact, exactly how early implementations of the Sun JVM worked. This approach, however, is far from optimal because each bytecode instruction leads to the generation of a large number of machine instructions (including the overhead of the interpreter logic itself), and code that is repeatedly executed must go through this translation process every time. Given the inefficiencies of the pure interpreter approach, today's JVMs have evolved to include more sophisticated adaptive bytecode execution techniques that allow for the detection of Java methods with high frequency use known as hot methods. Hot methods are then selectively compiled into machine code as part of the execution of the bytecode—a process also known as Just-in-Time (JIT) compilation—and cached for reuse the next time the method is called. Adaptive bytecode execution typically requires an initial performance hit, because the JVM needs to first identify hot methods and incur the one-time cost of compiling them into bytecode. As a result, during this initial calibration period, the performance of the JVM will not be optimal, but over a long period of time it will achieve significant performance gains. This type of behavior is well suited for server-side applications that are run for long periods of time.

When the JRockit JVM is used, adaptive bytecode generation capabilities are always on. This is because JRockit has been designed from the core to be optimized for server-side applications.

For the HotSpot JVM, the adaptive bytecode generation capabilities can be controlled through the *-server* and *-client* parameters. When the *-server* parameter is used, the JVM will maximize its hot-method-detection algorithms. The overhead of the logic involved in detecting these hot methods will cause the JVM to start with a suboptimal performance. However, this performance will improve over time as hot methods are compiled into assembly code and cached for directed execution the next time a call to them is encountered. When the *-client* parameter is used, the JVM does not pursue the same degree of hot method detection and instead focuses on achieving a quicker startup time. Obviously, for server-side Fusion Middleware components, the execution of WebLogic Server managed server JVM instances within production or staging environments requires the use of the *-server* parameter. The execution of these servers on development and evaluation environments, on the other hand, can benefit from a *-client* flag because long-term runtime efficiencies are typically not a goal, whereas fast startup times usually are. In fact, this is exactly how the Fusion Middleware domain configuration wizard configures the startup parameters of the domains it creates when the HotSpot JVM is chosen: When the wizard is used to create a domain in development mode, the server's Java startup parameters are configured to use the *-client* command-line parameter.

On the other hand, when the wizard is used to create a domain in production mode, the server's Java startup parameters are configured to use the *-server* command-line parameter.

Memory Management

The tuning of the memory management settings of a JVM can be divided into two broad categories: the optimization of the way in which the garbage collection (GC) is performed (known as the GC scheme), and the sizing of the JVM processes' memory for dynamic object allocation.

Parallel and Concurrent Garbage Collection Schemes The Java Virtual Machine uses a garbage collection scheme for managing the memory that is dynamically allocated by the Java programs it executes. This scheme puts the responsibility of deallocating the memory allocated by the Java program's objects on the Java Virtual Machine. This is in contrast to languages such as C/C++, where instructions for the deallocations of memory must be explicitly specified within the application code itself as part of development. If deallocation instructions are not specified, the program will have a memory leak that over time can lead to out-of-memory exceptions. The benefit of the garbage collection scheme is obvious: By freeing software developers from the need to worry about memory management concerns in their code, they can instead focus on the application's business logic, thus improving their productivity and the quality of their program. This benefit, however, comes with a performance cost because the detection and deallocation of unused memory, which is the actual process known as garbage collection, requires JVM logic to be executed.

The exact nature of this performance cost depends on the type of GC algorithm used by the JVM. Modern GC algorithms can be roughly divided into two categories: parallel and concurrent. Parallel GC algorithms consist of the JVM stopping the execution of all application logic and concurrently using as many threads as possible (and therefore all available CPU resources) to detect the unused memory within the application's memory and deallocating it. Concurrent GC algorithms, on the other hand, attempt to minimize the complete halting of the application logic's execution as much as is possible by performing the garbage collection logic in parallel within threads that run concurrently with the application logic threads. The tradeoff between parallel and concurrent GC algorithms is between throughput and latency. *Throughput* can be roughly described as the percentage of CPU time spent on executing application logic, whereas *latency* refers to the response time of the application. Generally speaking, parallel GC algorithms allow for better throughput at the cost of latency. This is because in such algorithms, garbage collection logic is only executed at specific times with the goal of minimizing the overall GC cycles as a percentage of application execution cycles within the lifetime of the JVM process. However, when the GC does interrupt the application, it does so with full force by taking over all CPU resources to complete the garbage collection as quickly as possible, but with the side effect of completely interrupting the application logic and thus leading to high latency during the time of the GC execution. Concurrent GC algorithms, on the other hand, allow for low latency at the expense of throughput. This is because in such algorithms the application execution logic is never entirely halted for long periods of time as the GC process mostly executes concurrently with the application logic. However, the concurrent execution of the GC and the extra work required in ensuring that memory management can be performed while application logic is also executing leads to a constant usage of CPU resources. This, in turn, means that over time, the application logic will have a lesser percentage of the available CPU resources for its execution and therefore a lower overall throughput.

Both the HotSpot and JRockit JVMs have a number of command-line parameters that control their garbage collection scheme. A complete description of these parameters is beyond the scope of this book; therefore, the reader is referred to associated performance-tuning guides for each of these JVMs, which can be found through a simple Internet search. Instead, we will highlight some of the main command-line parameters that control the garbage collection schemes used for each JVM.

The JRockit JVM provides a rich set of command-line parameters that allow for the control of its GC scheme. The simplest of these options is the *-XgcPrio* command-line parameter. This command-line parameter can take one of three subparameters, as follows:

- ***XgcPrio:pausetime*** Used to indicate that the JVM should minimize latency and results in the usage of a mostly parallel GC algorithm. This parameter can be used in conjunction with the *-XpauseTarget:<pause time>* parameter to indicate the maximum GC pause time the JVM should try to achieve. If the *-XpauseTarget* parameter is not used, a default of 200 ms is used.

- ***XgcPrio:throughput*** Used to indicate that the JVM should maximize the throughput of the application and leads to the usage of a mostly concurrent GC algorithm.

- ***XgcPrio:deterministic*** Used for real-time systems where it is important for the JVM to do its best to guarantee a specific maximum pause time. This parameter works like the *XgcPrio:pausetime* parameter, except that the JVM strives even harder to achieve the specified maximum pause time and therefore might incur a higher throughput hit. This parameter can also be used with the *-XpauseTarget:<pause time>* parameter. If it's not provided, a default of 30 ms is used.

For the HotSpot JVM, the *-XX:UseParallelGC* command-line parameter is used to indicate to the JVM that a parallel GC scheme should be used. The *-XX:+UseConcMarkSweepGC* command-line parameter is, on the other hand, used to indicate to the JVM that a concurrent GC scheme should be used. Note that when the JVM is executed on a single CPU core system, the use of *XX:+UseConcMarkSweepGC* by itself is discouraged because this command line leads to the JVM always running a thread, which would contend with the application's own thread for a share of the CPU cycles. The HotSpot JVM does provide a set of command-line options—known as independent mode—to allow for an effective execution of a concurrent scheme on single-core systems. The description of these options is, however, beyond the scope of this book.

Heap Size The area within a process's memory space where an application's objects are allocated is known as the heap. The size of the heap can be set for each instance of a JVM, and usually this size has a significant impact on the performance of Java applications. As a general rule of thumb, as the heap size grows, so does the overhead of GC for the JVM process no matter what GC algorithm is used. However, most server-side applications have a need for large heap spaces as they often have to manage large amounts of application state that needs to be stored in memory for improved latency. The tradeoff between decreased GC overhead with low heap sizes and better latency with larger ones is usually resolved by finding the "right" heap size for an application to achieve a balance. This size can be found through performance testing.

It should also be noted that modern JVM heaps are partitioned into different areas for managing objects based on the amount of time of their existence. New objects are created within a special partition known as Eden for HotSpot and the Nursery for JRockit, and over time they are promoted to other areas reserved for longer living objects. This type of internal heap structure is part of a scheme known as generation GC, and the sizing of the different heap partitions plays an important role in the performance of the JVM for any given application. However, a discussion of the sizing of such internal heap partitions is beyond the scope of this book, and we will limit our discussion to the more fundamental issue of the sizing of the overall heap space.

Even when the optimal heap size for an application's JVM process is found, there often is a need to scale the application to allow for the processing of more requests or to allow it to cache more objects in memory in order to decrease latency. In such cases, the way to achieve this scalability is through clustering: By adding new JVM nodes and ensuring that additional CPU cores are available for these JVMs to use, we can achieve scalability beyond a single JVM's GC and heap size limits. This clustering can be performed at the level of WebLogic Server by scaling out a managed server cluster, as described in Chapter 8, or at the level of a Coherence data grid cluster, as we briefly reviewed in Chapter 2. In fact, the need for such clustering for scale-out is becoming more and more important as the prominence of 64-bit machines increases. The reason for this is that the maximum possible available heap size for each operating system process is beyond the possible amount of actual memory that can possibly be provisioned on any machine and therefore for all intents and purposes can be considered unlimited. As already mentioned, due to the GC overhead that would be incurred, a single JVM process cannot be used to take advantage of the large amounts of memory that can be available to a 64-bit system. Therefore, even on a single host, the ability to scale out the application logic to multiple JVM processes (each optimally configured with a manageable heap size) is crucial from a performance optimization perspective. Such a scale-out of an application to multiple JVMs on the same host is also known as vertical clustering. Of course, to perform such a scale-out, we need to ensure that the machine's CPU resources do not become a bottleneck. Fortunately, the trend for today's enterprise application systems is toward machines with multiple CPUs, each with multiple cores, thus facilitating the ability to create vertical JVM clusters that can take advantage of a 64-bit system's vast process heap space.

This thought process leads us to the natural question of how many JVM processes are optimal per CPU core. Unfortunately there is no hard-and-fast rule to answer this question because the answer very much depends on the nature of the application and the type of platform being used. However, as rule of thumb, a good starting point is to have a single JVM per core and to carry out performance tests by adding and removing JVM instances until an optimal cluster size is achieved.

NOTE
To size the number of JVMs for a given system, start with a single JVM per CPU core and then execute performance tests to lower or increase the number of JVMs until an optimal number is found.

It is worth noting that it is not always necessary to ensure that a machine's available memory is completely used through vertical clustering. As an example, on a machine with 16GB of memory and eight CPU cores, performance tests might determine that the optimal JVM sizing is to have 10 JVMs with a heap size of 1GB each, for a total of 10GB used by the application's vertical cluster. This would leave 6GB of memory not used by the application.

With the understanding of heap size and its effect on JVM performance and scale-out in mind, let's look at how the total heap size of the HotSpot and JRockit JVMs is configured. For both JVMs, the parameters used to control the initial and maximum heap size, respectively, are *-Xms* and *-Xmx*. The following command line would therefore lead to a JVM instance with an initial heap size of 512Mb and a maximum heap size of 1Gb:

```
java -Xms512M -Xms1024
```

In cases where the application would try to obtain more heap space than 1Gb, an out-of-memory exception would be thrown. The reason for separating the parameter used to size the heap into initial and maximum heap sizes is to allow for faster JVM startup because larger initial heap sizes will lead to a slower startup time. However, the progressive allocation of space performed by the JVM to expand the heap size beyond the initial size, as required by the executing application, leads to increased latency.

Given that for server-side applications, increased startup time is usually not an issue, the recommendation is generally to set the initial and maximum heap size of the JVM to the same value in order to ensure that heap extension latencies are never incurred as part of the execution of the application logic.

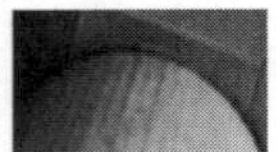

NOTE
Set the values of the initial and maximum heap sizes to be the same on all WebLogic server managed servers to ensure that heap-expansion-related latencies are not introduced.

WebLogic Server

This section outlines some of the most important elements for ensuring that WebLogic Server managed servers are configured for optimal performance. The elements discussed in this section cover only aspects of the performance optimization as they relate to external configuration parameters and do not address development-time optimization strategies. For a detailed discussion of optimization for WebLogic Server environments and applications, please refer to the *Oracle Fusion Middleware Performance and Tuning for Oracle WebLogic Server* book within the Fusion Middleware documentation library.

Production Mode

One of the most important aspects of WebLogic Server optimization is to ensure that a domain is configured with the production mode runtime flag enabled. This flag ensures that server instances are configured for maximizing performance at the expense of higher startup times and the disabling of development environment flexibilities. As an example, the production mode flag ensures that the value of *pageCheckSeconds* within the weblogic.xml deployment descriptor of all deployed applications is overridden so that servers do not continuously have to check for updates to the application's JSP files in order to perform recompilation. Although this type of check is convenient at development time, it incurs a performance cost that can be avoided in production because JSPs are typically not modified without redeployment in production. To ensure that the server's production mode runtime flag is enabled, use the following WLST offline command after having issued a readDomain command:

```
set('ProductionModeEnabled','true');
```

NOTE
Always ensure that a domain's production mode is enabled in nondevelopment environments to improve performance.

Work Managers

One of the most important areas of optimization for any multithreaded software application is its threading model. The threading model of all WebLogic Server deployed applications is controlled by the container itself, and the application code is not allowed—based on Java EE rules—to spawn its own threads. Instead, incoming application requests to a WebLogic Server instance are executed within the context of a WebLogic Server execute thread. Each server has a single pool of execute threads from which all requests are assigned their thread and all deployed applications compete for their share of the available execute threads. As described in detail in Chapter 2, the WebLogic Server entity used to manage the way in which requests are dispatched to threads is known as a Work Manager. Because the WebLogic Server thread pool is self-tuning, in cases when only a single deployment archive is deployed to a WebLogic Server instance, the tuning of Work Managers is not necessary because the deployed application will have access to all of the execute threads within a server instance. The consideration for explicit Work Manager configuration, however, can become important when multiple applications are deployed to the same server. In such cases, the default WebLogic Server behavior is to ensure that each application is treated equally in getting its fair share of execute threads. Therefore, in cases where the deployed applications have different quality of service requirements, the configuration of the application's Work Managers with appropriate request classes might be necessary to ensure that each application is assigned threads by WebLogic Server according to the quality of service policies its usage demands.

JDBC Data Sources

For a JDBC data source, the number of connections within the data source's connection pool is one of the most important parameters. This is due to two reasons: First, the creation of new connections is an expensive operation that leads to increased latency for requests that encounter this need. Second, if all connections are being used when a request is in need of accessing the data source, the request's thread blocks until a new connection pool is available, which once again leads to increased latency. The connection pool settings of WebLogic Server data sources have three parameters that can be used to avoid these issues. The first, called Initial Capacity, configures the initial set of connections within the data source's thread pool. These connections are created at server startup time to allow incoming requests to access the database through them, without the need for the creation of a new connection. The second parameter, called Capacity Increment, defines the number of new connections created every time a request needs a connection and the connection pool does not have one to offer. The final parameter, called Maximum Capacity, sets the upper bound to the number of connections that can exist within the thread pool. If the pool's connection count reaches this number, no new connections will be created, and new requests that need a connection will block until other requests return their connections to the pool.

To ensure that all threads always have access to a pre-created connection within the connection pool, we would ideally set the Initial Increment parameter to the maximum number of execute threads the server can have. However, this is not possible because the number of execute threads available on the server is defined by the WebLogic Server self-tuning execute thread. Therefore, the best way of determining the optimal initial capacity of a connection pool is through performance testing: It is usually best to start with a relatively high value (say, 100) and see if the connections are ever exhausted under stress and then increase the number if they are. Similarly, to ensure that request threads will never run into cases where they have to block as a result of reaching the maximum capacity of a connection pool, we would optimally set the maximum capacity to the maximum number of execute threads. However, again, because this number cannot be defined at the self-tuning thread pool level, we find ourselves in a bind.

The solution is to turn on the connection pool's *PinnedToThread* setting. When set to true, this setting ensures that every time an execute thread requires a new connection, one is created and associated with the actual execute thread itself for later use. When this setting is used, the connection pool's maximum capacity configuration is ignored and the connection pool's maximum number of connections is effectively the same as the maximum number of execute threads that are ever created for the server. The server will still, however, use the Capacity Increment configuration to increase the number of connections every time the pool's connections are exhausted. It is therefore still important to ensure that the increment value is set appropriately. If this value is too small, new connections would need to be created too often at peak times when the pool is exhausted. If the value is set to too large, the latency for the first connection that encounters the exhausted pool will be very high whereas subsequent requests will benefit from the expanded pool size. There is no hard-and-fast rule on the appropriate setting for Capacity Increment, and its optimal value depends on the nature of the application: Is a high latency for some requests at peak time acceptable to achieve quicker response on subsequent requests? If so, you would set the increment to a higher value (say, 20), whereas if you would like to evenly distribute the latency cost of having hit the maximum pool size across a number of requests, you can keep the value low (say, 5).

A second important parameter in determining the performance of JDBC data sources is its connection pool's Statement Cache Size setting. This parameter allows for the caching of prepared SQL statements that applications execute through the data source. Once again, the optimal value of this parameter depends on the nature of the application and is best determined through performance testing: The number of prepared statements used by the application and the frequency with which they are used will derive the optimal value.

Java Message Service (JMS)

Although a detailed discussion of WebLogic Server JMS tuning is out of the scope of this book, it should be noted that the core elements for tuning JMS resources boil down to the proper configuration of the JMS server's persistent store and the JMS paging, quotas, and thresholds configurations—as described in the "Paging, Quotas, and Thresholds" section of Chapter 2—based on the needs of the applications using these resources. For a detailed discussion of this topic, refer to the "Tuning WebLogic JMS" section of the *Fusion Middleware Performance and Tuning for Oracle WebLogic Server* book within the Fusion Middleware documentation library.

Optimizing the Pricing Application's Java Virtual Machine and WebLogic Server Configurations

In this section we look at how the JVM and WebLogic Server optimization concepts we reviewed in the last section can be applied to the pricing application's environment. To properly apply these concepts, we need to have more details on the hosts on which the application's domains are created. To have some numbers to work with, let's assume that a sizing exercise had deemed that the pricing1 and webcenter1 hosts each need to be two quad-core CPUs with 16Gb of memory.

Tuning the Java Virtual Machine Parameters

We begin by ensuring that the JVMs of all managed servers are executing in *-server* mode to ensure that their code generation algorithm is optimized for a server-side production environment, as we described in the previous section. Because as part of the domain-creation process of the pricing application we used the production mode offered by the domain configuration wizard as well as a HotSpot JVM, all of the managed servers of all domains within the pricing application environment shown in Figure 8-3 should be using the *-server* parameter. We have therefore already taken the appropriate step to ensure that the JVMs of the pricing application are optimized from a code-generation point of view and don't need to do anything else to optimize the environment for this purpose.

When considering the JVM memory configurations for the domains of the pricing application, we need to take a closer look at the nature of each deployed application. Using Figure 8-3 to examine each component in turn, we can see that the Pricing Query web interface of the PricingApp.ear deployment archive is the most heavily used component of the pricing application. It is the one with the most users (the entire company sales force will be using it), and it is also expected to be used on a frequent basis.

Therefore, ensuring that the JVMs of the managed servers to which PricingApp.ear is deployed (that is, the JVMs of the PricingCluster) are configured to consistently ensure low latency is very important. The Pricing Update process, on the other hand, does not have any human user interface and there is no need for this processes to complete with low latency on a consistent basis. We could therefore use a high-throughput JVM configuration for this SOA Suite composite. However, the SOA Suite SCA component for this process is deployed to the same managed server (soa_server1) as the pricing application's ADF worklist application—which, by the virtue of being a web application, should ideally not suffer from high latencies incurred by JVM garbage collection. The same thing could also be said for the bam_server1 and WebCenter1 managed servers because they both host web applications. We should note, however, that the consistent low latency requirement for these web applications is not as high as those for the Pricing Query web interface because they are not used by the same high number of users and as frequently. Taking all of this information in, we arrive at a reasonable conclusion that the proper JVM garbage collection (GC) configuration for the pricing application's managed servers would be to use a concurrent GC scheme on the PricingCluster managed servers and a parallel GC scheme on all other managed servers. At least, we could start with such a configuration as the basis for our performance tests and modify them according to our results. However, to set different JVM parameters for different servers within the same domain, it is best to make use of the WebLogic Server node manager. We will be configuring the node manager for the pricing application in the next chapter, but we should make a note that we need to ensure that the managed servers of the pricing application's domains need to use the following JVM parameters:

- soa_server1 should use *-XX:+UseParallelGC* to ensure a parallel garbage collection scheme.
- All other managed servers should use *-XX:+UseConcMarkSweepGC* to ensure a concurrent garbage collection scheme.

We should also note that the use of the concurrent garbage collection strategy is possible because on both machines that host the application's domains, spare CPU core capacity exists that can be used to execute the concurrent garbage collection thread for the JVM. To be specific, because we have four JVM processes (bam_server1, soa_server1, Pricing1, and the admin server) on the pricing1 host and a total of eight cores, we can safely assume that the system can always use a single core for the dedicated execution of the concurrent garbage collection. The situation is the same on the webcenter1 host, where we have three JVM processes and again a total of eight cores.

Now that we have figured out the best initial GC settings, we can turn our attention to finding the optimal heap size for the domain's managed servers to start with. The managed servers within a domain created using the SOA Suite domain creation wizard will have a default initial heap size setting of 512Mb and a maximum setting of 1024Mb (1Gb). To optimize the performance of the server, we know that we can at the very least modify the initial size to be the same as the maximum size in order to avoid heap expansion at runtime. However, given the total of 16Gb of memory available on each host, we can probably start with a higher heap size per managed server of 2Gb. To do this, open the ~/pricingdomain/bin/setSOADomainEnv.sh file and look for the following line:

```
DEFAULT_MEM_ARGS="-Xms512m -Xmx1024m"
```

Then modify it as follows:

```
DEFAULT_MEM_ARGS="-Xms2048m -Xmx2048m"
```

With the initial memory settings for our managed servers determined, the system is ready for a first round of performance testing to tune these initial settings so that they can be optimized for peak loads. To do this, you need to simulate peak loads by ensuring that each of the interfaces of the pricing application is being exercised with the same rate of requests as it would in production. To do this, you can use tools such as Apache JMeter, which allows you to create simulated loads on different types of interfaces, including HTTP web interfaces, SOAP/HTTP web services, and JMS interfaces. Once you have created these simulations, you need to have a good way to monitor the JVM's memory usage and the time spent on garbage collection. Fortunately, both the HotSpot and JRockit JVMs come with such tools. For JRockit, this tool is named JRockit Mission Control. For HotSpot, the tool is JConsole and can be executed from the JRE installation directory's bin directory. The following screenshot shows the memory pane of the HotSpot JConsole while monitoring a WebLogic Server instance JVM.

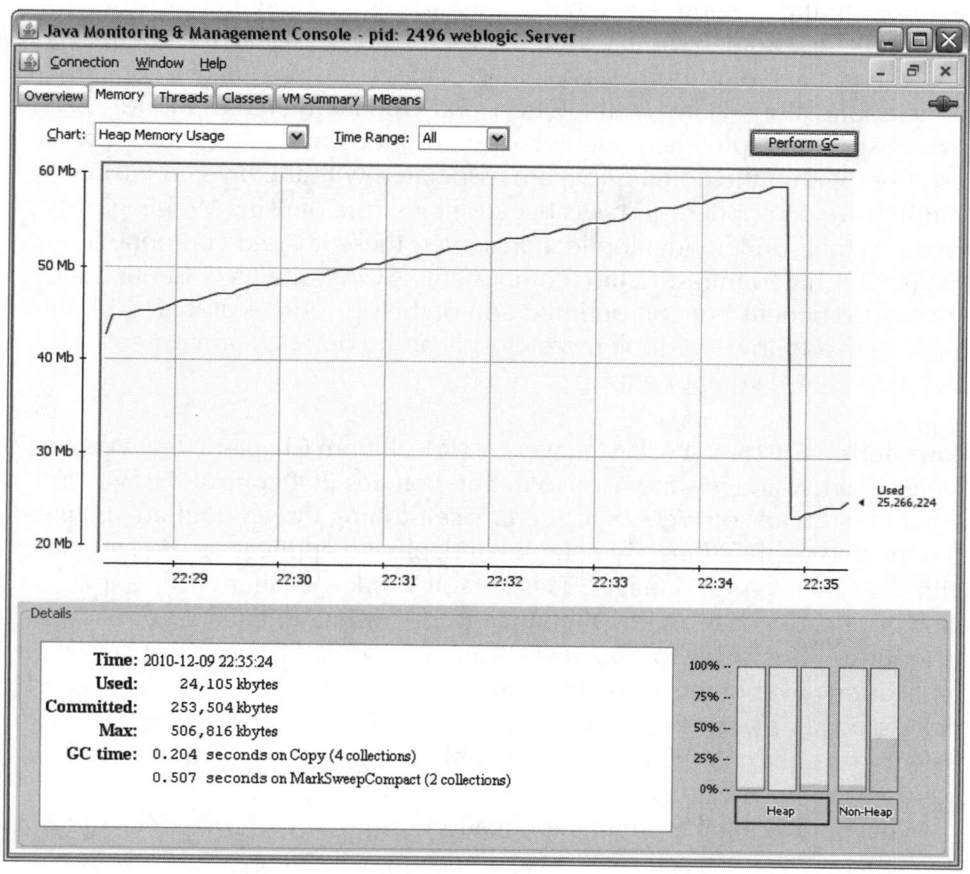

JConsole allows you to monitor a wide array of JVM metrics, including the total heap size of the JVM as well as the frequency and length of garbage collections. During performance testing, you want to make sure the JVM does not operate near its maximum heap size, but also is not leaving much of the heap size free at most times. You are also looking to analyze the garbage collection pattern of the JVM and ensure that it is behaving as intended based on the high throughput or low latency goals you had in mind when choosing the garbage collection scheme.

Tuning the WebLogic Server Parameters

In this section we will review the WebLogic Server areas of optimization we reviewed in the previous section and tune the environment of the pricing application accordingly. In this exercise, we not only consider the optimization of WebLogic Server resources associated with the custom Java EE components of the application—namely, the Query and Update interfaces of the PricingApp.ear deployment archive—but also look at the WebLogic Server resources within the domain that are associated with the layered Fusion Middleware components. This is because by virtue of using WebLogic Server as their underlying application server, these layered components—that is, the shared infrastructure components, SOA Suite, WebCenter, and ADF—also benefit from an optimization of their resources at this level. In sections that follow, we look more closely at the optimization aspects specific to these components.

Considering Custom Work Managers Recall from Chapter 2 that WebLogic Server Work Managers are used to define policies that control the way in which the threads of WebLogic Server's self-tuning thread pool are assigned to deployed applications. By default, all deployed application are associated with their own Work Manager. This default Work Manager ensures that each application has an equal chance of obtaining an execute thread for its requests. This behavior, however, can be modified to prioritize some applications over others through the definition of new Work Managers and their association with request classes that specify the details of the thread assignment policy WebLogic Server should use for deployed applications that use the Work Manager.

When analyzing the pricing application's topology, shown in Figure 8-3 of Chapter 8, we can see right away that only one managed server could benefit from explicit Work Manager request class policies, and that is the soa_server1 server. The reason is that only this server has deployed to it more than a single deployment archive of the pricing application. These archives are PricingWorklist.ear and scaPricingModelUpdate_rev1.0.jar, with the first containing the ADF custom worklist application of the pricing application (which we discussed within the use case of Chapter 6) and the second containing the Pricing Update BPEL process within a SOA Suite SCA composite (as we discussed within the use case of Chapter 5). Based on the requirements of the pricing application, we know that the BPEL processes of the pricing update applications do not have a high priority for execution, and if the managed server is ever saturated with requests, it should prioritize the thread assignment to requests bound for the worklist web application instead of those bound for the BPEL process. To do this, we can use a fair-share request class that ensures that on average about 20 percent of the fair share of the server's execute threads are assigned to requests bound for the BPEL process and that about 80 percent are assigned to those bound to the worklist application. We can configure the domain with such a request class in two ways. The first is to define a fair-share request class and associate it with the worklist application. To do this, we would have to create a domain-level request class and modify the PricingWorklist.ear's weblogic-application.xml deployment descriptor to point to it. We can create the fair-share request class using the following WLST online script:

```
cd('/SelfTuning/pricingdomain')
cmo.createFairShareRequestClass('PricingWorklistRequestClass')
cd('/SelfTuning/pricingdomain/FairShareRequestClasses
/PricingWorklistRequestClass')
set('Targets',jarray.array([ObjectName('com.bea:Name=soa_server1,
Type=Server')], ObjectName))
cmo.setFairShare(200)
```

As you can see, we are setting the value of the request class to 200. This is because this value is relative to the fair-share value of other deployed applications. By default, deployed applications have a fair-share value of 50; therefore, by ensuring that the worklist application has a fair-share value of 200, we are setting a policy that ensures that 80 percent of the time (that is, 200 / 250) the worklist application receives its fair share of the execute threads when compared to the other applications' 20 percent (50 / 200). To complete the configuration of this request class, we need to ensure that the worklist application is referring to it. To do this, we need to make sure the application's weblogic-application.xml deployment descriptor contains the following snippet:

```
<work-manager>
  <name>pricing-worklist</name>
  <fair-share-request-class>
    <name>priority-application-share</name>
  </fair-share-request-class>
</work-manager>
```

If we are unable to modify the deployment descriptor directly, a deployment plan, as described in Chapter 2, can be used instead. The second way of configuring the fair-share requirements of the domain is to define the fair-share request class and associate it with the SOA infrastructure application that contains all of the SOA Suite service engine logic and is therefore effectively the WebLogic Server deployment archive that executes SOA Suite deployed SCA SOA Archive (SAR) files. The SOA infrastructure application uses a Work Manager named wm/SOAWorkManager that is defined within all SOA Suite domains. Therefore, to ensure that the pricing application's SCA archive gets a 20-percent fair share of the server execute threads, we can configure a request class and associate it with the wm/SOAWorkManager as follows:

```
cd('/SelfTuning/pricingdomain')
cmo.createFairShareRequestClass('SOAInfraRequestClass')

cd('/SelfTuning/pricingdomain/
FairShareRequestClasses/SOAInfraRequestClass')
set('Targets',jarray.array([ObjectName('com.bea:Name=soa_server1,
Type=Server')], ObjectName))
cmo.setFairShare(12)

cd('/SelfTuning/pricingdomain/WorkManagers/wm/SOAWorkManager')
cmo.setResponseTimeRequestClass(None)
cmo.setFairShareRequestClass(getMBean('/SelfTuning/pricingdomain/
FairShareRequestClasses/SOAInfraRequestClass'))
```

As you can see, we are using a fair-share value of 12 in this case because 12/(50+12) is approximately 20 percent, and that is the percentage of the execute threads we want WebLogic Server to use for the SOA infrastructure application on this managed server.

Tuning the JDBC Connection Pools To tune the configurations of the JDBC data sources of the pricing application's domains, we can start by making sure that each data source has its *PinnedToThread* setting enabled and that its initial capacity is set to a reasonable value from a performance point of view. As we discussed in the previous version, ideally we would be setting the initial capacity of each connection pool to the maximum number of threads that could be using the data source. However, without performance testing we would be unable to know for sure what this value is.

Therefore, a good starting point is to increase the initial capacity of each connection pool to its maximum capacity. This works out well because for the layered Fusion Middleware components, the default maximum capacity has been set to a reasonable maximum value. To do this, you can use WLST to execute the following script against both the pricingdomain and webcenterdomain of the pricing application.

DOWNLOAD
The following script is available for download on the Oracle Press site at http://community.oraclepressbooks.com/downloads.html.

```
#
# WLST online script which goes through a domain's data sources and
# for each sets the connection pool's initial capacity to the maximum
# capacity configured and also turn on the PinnedToThread flag for each.
# The script's connect command needs to be modified with the target server
# coordinates.
#

connect('weblogic','welcome1','t3://pricing1:7001')
edit()
startEdit()
cd('JDBCSystemResources')

dslist = ls('','true','c')

for ds in dslist:
    path = ''
    path += '/JDBCSystemResources/' + ds + '/JDBCResource/' +
ds + '/JDBCConnectionPoolParams/' + ds
    cd(path)
    maxCapacity = get('MaxCapacity')
    set('InitialCapacity',maxCapacity)
    set('PinnedToThread','true')

activate()
```

Once we have set these initial values on all of the domain data sources, you can begin another round of performance testing to check their effect on the overall performance of the application. As part of this performance test, you need to have a good way to monitor the set of active connections for each data source. Fortunately, the WebLogic Server admin console allows you to easily monitor this information. To do this, log in to the admin console and navigate from the left pane's Environment | Servers node to the managed server you would like to monitor. When you are at the managed server page, click the Monitoring tab and then the JDBC sub-tab. If you follow these steps for the Pricing1 managed server, you should see a screen similar to the following.

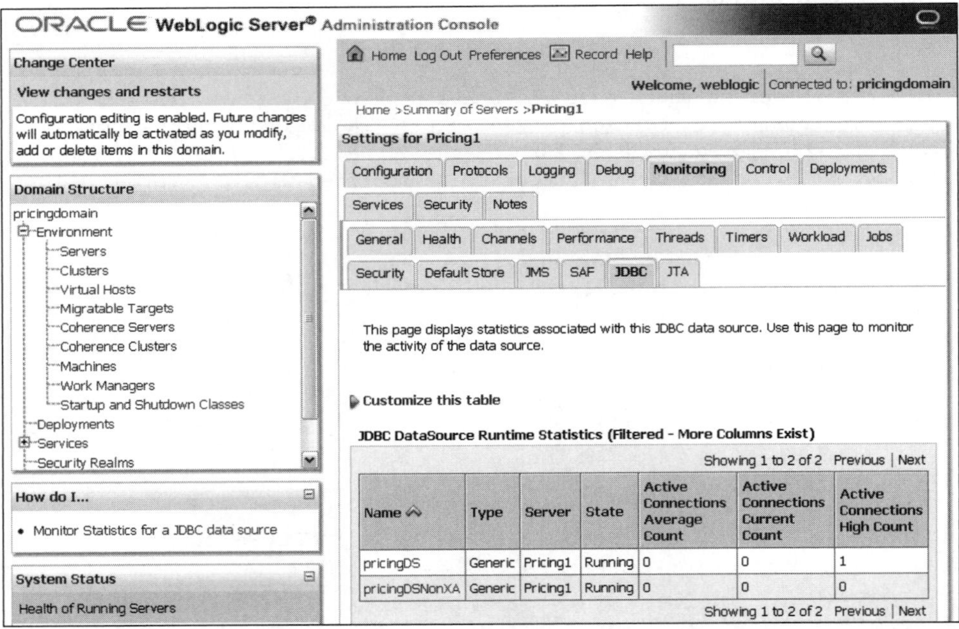

As you can see, this page allows you to monitor the current count of active connections for each data source (Active Connections Current Count field) as well as the highest count ever achieved since the connection pool was initiated (Active Connections High Count field) at server startup. During performance testing, the monitoring of these two pieces of information will allow you to determine whether you have the right settings for your connection pool's capacity parameters or whether you need to tune them further to improve performance. Effectively, if you are consistently hitting an Active Connections High Count value that is higher than the connection pool's initial capacity, this is usually a good sign that you need to increase the initial capacity setting and think about a proper value of the capacity increment, as we discussed in the previous section.

Optimizing the Fusion Middleware Shared Infrastructure

Now that we have completed our overview of the optimization of the JVM and WebLogic Server layers, we can turn our attention to the Fusion Middleware shared infrastructure components, which we covered in Chapter 3. Specifically, we will consider the optimization of two components within this layer: Oracle Web Services Manager (OWSM) and Metadata Services (MDS).

Oracle Web Services Manager

As we reviewed in detail in Part I, OWSM is a component used for decorating the web services interfaces of Fusion Middleware applications with security and management policies. The optimization of MDS therefore is most important for applications that have web services using OWSM policies. The first area of optimization we will look at for OWSM concerns its Policy Enforcement Point's (PEP) polling setting. As we reviewed in Chapter 3, all deployed web services within a WebLogic Server domain are associated with OWSM agents. OWSM agents discover changes regarding their policy attachments by periodically polling the domain's OWSM policy manager service that is deployed to a single managed server within the domain. This polling is performed through an entity known as the PEP, and a single PEP instance exists per managed server instance within a domain. The frequency at which the domain's PEPs poll the policy manager service is determined by the value of the OWSM *cache.tolerance* parameter. This parameter has a default value of 60,000 ms (1 min). Every time a PEP within the domain issues a polling request, the policy manager will potentially have to access the database. The PEP polling also consumes CPU and networking resources on both the client managed server as well as the managed server on which the policy manager resides. As a result, setting the value of the *cache.tolerance* parameter to a higher value—say, 600,000 (10 min)—is a worthy performance improvement consideration for environments where web services policies are not frequently modified. You can modify this value through Enterprise Manager by selecting the domain node within the tree pane and navigating to Web Services| Platform Policy Configuration and then selecting the Policy Cache tab. Here's the Enterprise Manager screen for modifying the *cache.tolerance* value.

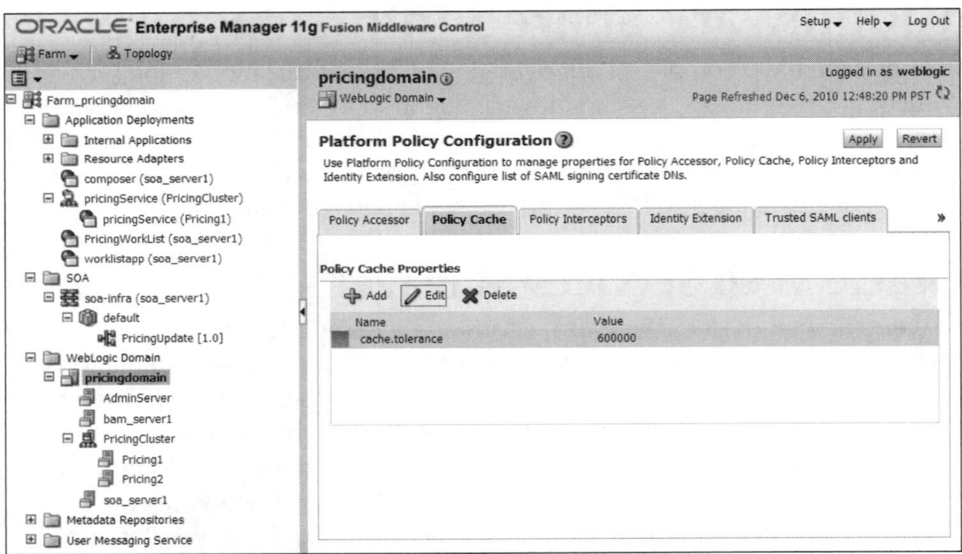

The second area of optimization worth mentioning concerns the logging assertions contained within OWSM predefined policies. By default, many OWSM predefined policies have a pair of logging assertions that ensure that the content of the web service's incoming request and outgoing response messages are logged to the domain's log file. As an example, the WS-Security *wss10_message_protection_service_policy*'s default assertions consist of a logging assertion for the request message, followed by the actual WS-Security assertion, which ensures message protection properties on the incoming requests, and finally another logging assertion for the response message.

The logging assertions can be configured to log different elements of the SOAP message, as follows:

- ***all*** Logs the entire content of the message, including attachments
- ***header*** Logs only the SOAP header of each message
- ***soap_body*** Logs only the SOAP body of each message
- ***soap_envelop*** Logs both the SOAP header and body of each message

By default, the assertions of predefined policies are configured with an *all* value, meaning that the entire content of both request and response messages for the web services using them are logged on each invocation. Because each time a message's content is logged the server has to access the file system, this can easily become a bottleneck for web services that have a high request frequency. Therefore, a simple way of optimizing web services that have OWSM policy attachments is to modify the definition of the policies they use to delete surrounding logging assertions. Alternatively, the level of the logging being performed could be decreased to *header* but the optimization obtained through such a change would be minimal because the file system access would still be required. To delete the logging assertions of specific policy attachments, you need to use to the policy's definition page within Enterprise Manager, as illustrated next.

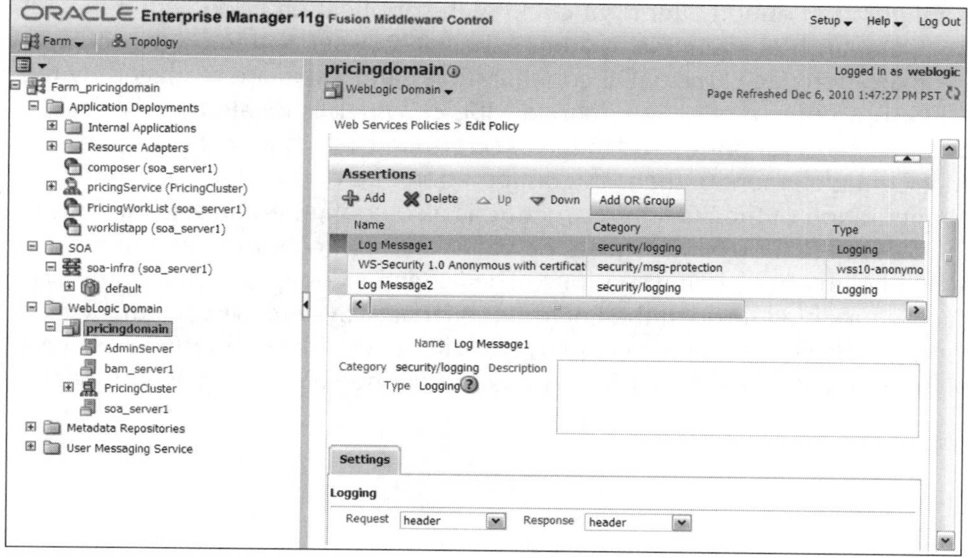

To open to this page, right-click the domain node within the Enterprise Manager tree pane, navigate to Web Services | Policies, and then select the policy you would like to modify and click Edit. Use the Assertion section of the Edit Policy page to delete the logging assertions or modify their request and response message logging levels.

Because the pricing application's component's web services interfaces have no OWSM policies attached in their production settings, we do not need to consider any of the performance optimization aspects covered in this section.

Metadata Repository Services

As we reviewed in the first part of the book, the Fusion Middleware Metadata Services (MDS) repository is used by Fusion Middleware layered components as well as SOA Suite, ADF, and WebCenter applications to centrally store and manage certain metadata information. MDS uses an in-memory cache to improve the performance of access requests to this metadata at runtime, and the configuration of this cache is an important consideration for all Fusion Middleware environments where SOA Suite, ADF, or WebCenter components are deployed. The initial parameters for this cache are specified on a per-application basis within the deployment descriptors of the deployed applications that use MDS (for example, adf-config.xml for ADF applications). Using Enterprise Manager, you can modify a deployed application's MDS parameters by choosing the MDS Configuration option after right-clicking the application node within the left tree pane and selecting the Systems MBeans browser option on the MDS configuration page. The MDS configuration parameters are managed by the MDSAppConfig application defined MBean, which is located within the oracle.adf.share.config | <managed-server-name> | <application-name> | ADFConfig element of the JMX configuration tree of the domain. The configuration of the SOA infrastructure is also configured through such an MDS configuration MBean with the value of <application-name> in the MBean path above being soa-infra. The MBean's configuration parameters can be modified through the Enterprise Manager System MBeans Browser or through WLST. In the next chapter, we will review in detail how WLST can be used to browse and modify application-defined MBeans. The following is a screenshot of the System MBeans Browser opened on the pricing application's MDS MBean configuration page.

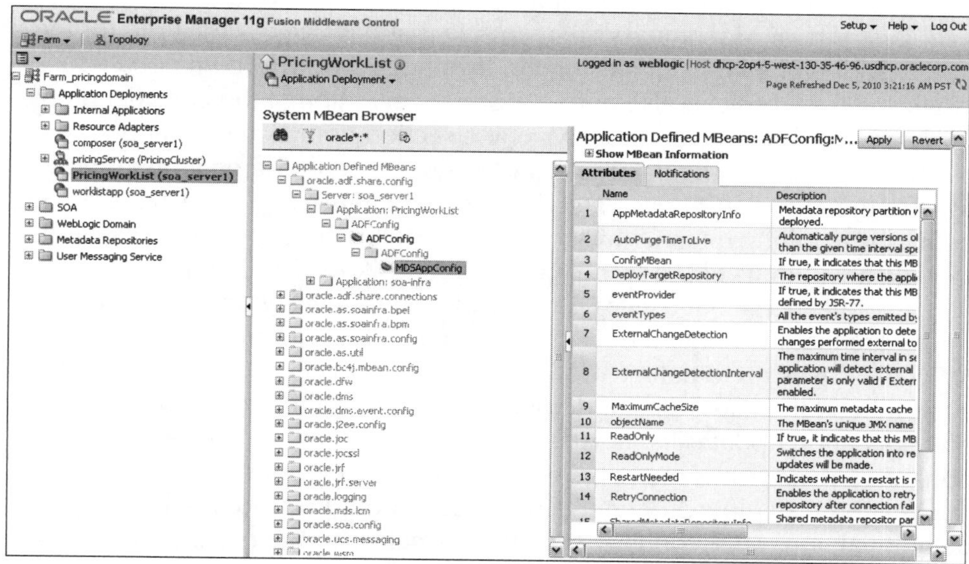

Two MDS cache parameters are important to consider when tuning the MDS cache for any application. The first is the *MaximumCacheSize* parameter, which controls the size of the in-memory cache (in kilobytes) that MDS uses for any given application. It is important to match the size of this cache to the size of the MDS metadata managed by the application. As an example, if an ADF application uses WebCenter personalization capabilities—which as we saw in Chapter 7 are managed through MDS—and the application is expected to be highly personalized by a large number of users, then increasing the size of the cache from its default value (the actual initial value will be –1, which MDS internally maps to a default value of 10MB) to a larger value (say, 200MB) could make sense. The same would be true if a large number of SOA Suite composites—which as we saw in Chapter 5 also have their definitions stored within MDS—are deployed to the same server. In that case, increasing the size of the MDS cache for the SOA infrastructure application could improve performance. Ultimately, however, the only way to know if performance improvements can be achieved by increasing the size of the MDS cache is through extensive performance testing with different cache sizes. Also note that the sum of the size of the MDS caches for all deployed applications should not exceed the total Java Virtual Machine (JVM) heap size that has been configured for the managed server's JVM. Increasing the JVM heap size to accommodate for larger MDS caches can also help performance, although the considerations we reviewed in the Java Virtual Machine section of this chapter apply.

The second caching parameter that should be considered when tuning MDS is the *ExternalChangeDetectionInterval* parameter. This parameter defines the polling interval (in seconds) for MDS to check for changes to its metadata within its file- or schema-based repository. This is only relevant when applications that use MDS are deployed to a WebLogic Server cluster. To ensure that the content of each managed server's in-memory cache of MDS data stays up to date, MDS polls the repository content on a periodic basis to read the latest data and to update its cache content accordingly. If an application updates its metadata frequently at runtime and requires that consistent metadata is seen across all managed servers to which the application is deployed, then this parameter should be modified from its default value of 30 seconds to something smaller in order to ensure that metadata changes are more quickly propagated across the WebLogic Server cluster. However, it is important to note that setting this value too low for many different applications within the domain will have a negative impact on performance. A good example of a scenario where the tuning of this parameter is useful is for ADF applications that support user personalizations. In such cases, it is usually important that the same personalizations are honored and shown even if the user's requests are routed to different managed servers within a WebLogic Server cluster. As a result, ensuring that the value of this parameter is decreased for such applications might be appropriate.

Finally, another important aspect of MDS optimization is the maintenance of older versions of MDS metadata. The MDS runtime can be configured to automatically purge older versions of its metadata content through the application's MDS configuration MBean *AutoPurgeTimeToLive* parameter. This parameter affects performance in two ways: If its value is set too low, the purging process can occur too often, thus using server resources and negatively affecting its deployed application's performance. On the other hand, if its value is set too high, the amount of unpurged metadata can extend to a point where it will also negatively affect the usage of the overall metadata repository. The default value of the *AutoPurgeTimeToLive* parameter is 0, which means that the MDS auto-purge feature is not enabled. Once again, finding the optimal value for this parameter depends on the nature of the application and can be optimally determined only through performance testing.

In the context of the pricing application, the optimization of the parameters discussed in this section should be considered for all components that make use of MDS. These components are the ADF-based Worklist application, the WebCenter-based Pricing portal, and the Pricing Update SOA Suite process. However, because the interfaces of these components are expected to have low-frequency usage and neither of these components is clustered, the default values for the MDS parameters discussed in this section should suffice.

Optimizing the Layered Fusion Middleware Components

We now turn our attention to the optimization of parameters specific to the Fusion Middleware layered products we reviewed in the first part of this book—namely, Oracle SOA Suite, ADF, and WebCenter. The areas of optimization outlined in this section are not exhaustive but should cover the most significant elements of performance optimization for each product.

SOA Suite

As we reviewed in detail in Chapter 5, the Fusion Middleware SOA infrastructure audits the execution path and state of deployed SCA composites. This information is then exposed through the SOA Suite pages of Enterprise Manager for monitoring and diagnostics purposes. The level of audit information details captured by the SOA infrastructure has a significant impact on the performance of SOA Suite managed servers. This is due to the fact that a higher level of audit detail leads to more interactions with the database by the SOA infrastructure for each composite instance that is being executed. The increased database interaction has a negative effect on the throughput of the SOA infrastructure service engines. The SOA infrastructure's level of audit can be modified through Enterprise Manager's SOA Infrastructure Common Properties page. This page can be reached by right-clicking the soa-infra node of the left pane tree and navigating to SOA Administration | Common Properties, as shown here.

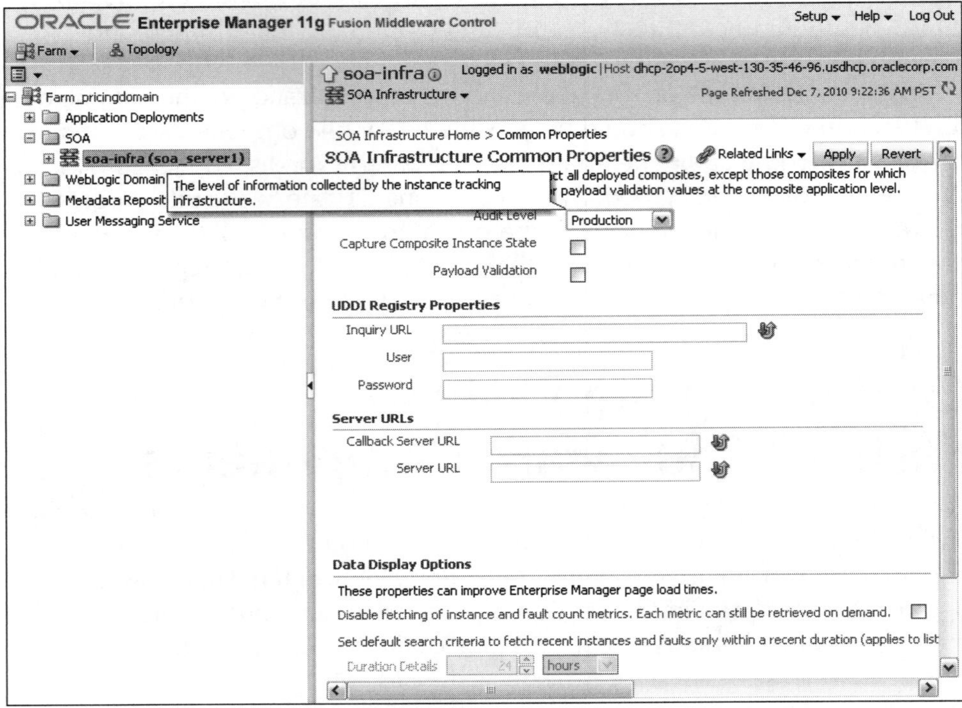

The settings of the first three parameters on this screen all have important implications on the performance of the SOA infrastructure. Let's review each in turn. The first parameter, Audit Level, controls the level of information audited by each composite instance. The possible values of this parameter and their descriptions are as follows:

- **Off** No audit information at all is tracked. This option brings the most performance gain at the expense of the ability to analyze and diagnose the execution of composites.
- **Production** Audit information is tracked for everything except the message payload details for Mediator components and for BPEL assign activities. This option will lead to some performance gains and allows for tracking of composite instances.

- **Development** All information for all composites is collected. This audit level has obviously the highest performance cost and should only be used within development and test environments.

The second parameter is Capture Composite Instance State. The setting of this parameter controls whether or not the SOA infrastructure engine keeps track of the state of composite instances. If the parameter is set, then composite instances are associated with a state of *running, completed, faulted, recovery needed, stale, terminated, suspended,* or *state not available,* depending on their status. If the parameter is not set, these state transitions are not maintained for composite instances and their state will always be set to *unknown*.

The last parameter within the top section of the SOA Infrastructure Common Properties page is Payload Validation. It is not associated with instance audit tracking but is important to understand from a performance point of view nonetheless. This parameter controls whether the SOA infrastructure performs a validation test on incoming XML messages using their associated schemas. For interfaces with a high request frequency, such a validation can have a significant performance cost; therefore, setting the value of the Payload Validation parameter to false in such cases should be considered. Finally, it should be noted that all three of the SOA infrastructure configuration parameters we just discussed are managed by the soa-infra application-defined MBean, which is located within the oracle.as.soa-infra.config | <managed-server-name> | SOAInfraConfig | soa-infra element of the JMX configuration tree of the domain. Therefore, these settings can also be modified through the Enterprise Manager System MBeans Browser as well as through WLST. In the next chapter, we will review in detail how WLST can be used to browse and modify such application-defined MBeans.

Application Development Framework

A number of aspects of an ADF application's model, view, and controller layers need special consideration from ADF developers from a performance optimization perspective. One example of this is the functionality of partial page rendering, which allows for the enhancement of an ADF application's browser rendering performance. The tuning of the SQL statement within an application's view objects is another such aspect. However, given the post-development scope of this book, we will not be discussing such development-time optimization concerns and instead focus on the post-deployment performance optimization concerns.

One of the most important sets of post-deployment performance-optimization-related parameters of an ADF application that uses the ADF Business Component (ADFBC) features is those related to the settings of its application modules. As we reviewed in Chapter 6, an application module is the transactional component that allows the ADF view UI components to access data. For each application module, the ADF infrastructure maintains an application module pool. This pool is a collection of instances of a single application module type that are shared by multiple active user sessions between HTTP requests. The performance of application module pools can be monitored through Enterprise Manager. During performance testing, if the monitoring of the application module performance parameters shows that the number of incoming requests is higher than the application module pool size, the size of the pool should be increased. Likewise, if the number of free application module instances within the pool is too low, this is an indication that the size of the pool should also be increased. To monitor the parameters of an ADF application's application module pools, you can use the Enterprise Manager ADF Performance page, which can be reached by navigating from the tree pane to the deployed ADF application node and selecting ADF | ADF Performance Summary. On this page, the Application Module Pools tab shows the list of application module pools and any related performance information, such as the number of free instances within each pool and the average and maximum time to serve a request. Within this page, the application module pool can be monitored and modified accordingly.

Because the pricing application's ADF-based Update Worklist component does not use any ADFBC features, we do not need to perform any application module optimizations on it.

Before concluding the ADF section of this chapter, we should note that for the monitoring of general performance parameters of an ADF application, such as the number of active sessions, the average request processing time, and the number of requests per minute, the Enterprise Manager's Performance Summary page can be used. This page can be reached by navigating on the left tree pane of a deployed ADF application node and selecting

Performance Summary. The following is a screenshot of the Performance Summary page for the pricing application's ADF-based worklist application.

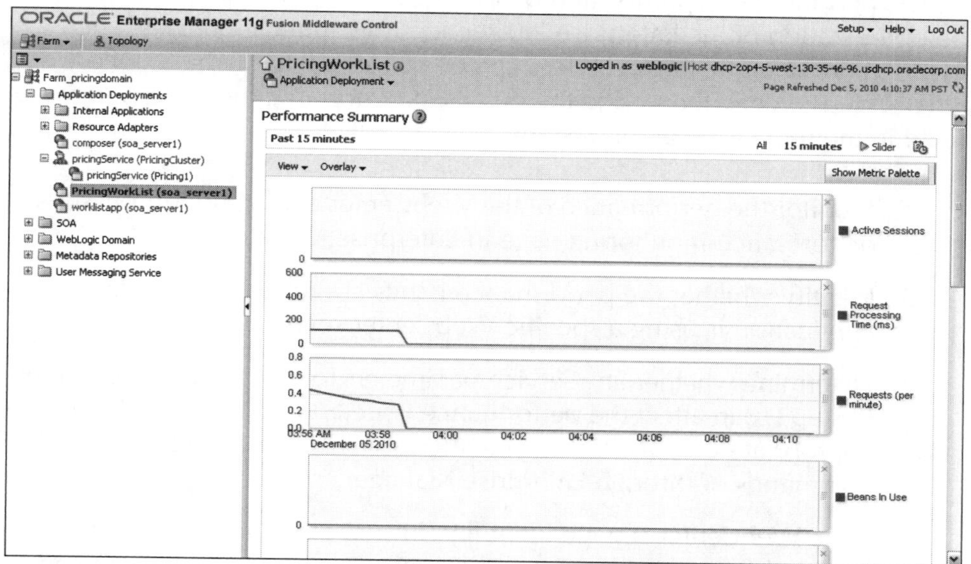

WebCenter

In this section we review the aspects of a WebCenter application that may need special consideration from administrators from a performance optimization perspective. As discussed in Part I of this book, all WebCenter applications are built using ADF features, and as such the ADF performance optimization discussion in the previous section is very relevant to all WebCenter applications. Moreover, a typical WebCenter application and its Enterprise 2.0 services use JDBC data sources to access data and MDS metadata within RDBMS schema repositories. Hence, the JDBC optimizations discussed in earlier sections will also enhance the performance of WebCenter applications. Similarly, the WebLogic Server and JVM optimizations we discussed earlier also apply to WebCenter managed servers. Finally, because WebCenter applications can create and update metadata at runtime within the MDS repository—either for the management of Spaces customizations,

Group Space metadata, or ADF resources—the MDS optimizations discussed in this chapter also apply to the optimization of a WebCenter environment.

The performance optimization of a WebCenter application consists of the optimization of the Enterprise 2.0 services the application uses. The analysis and tuning of these services can be performed through the following general steps. We will describe the details of performing these steps in more detail in the remainder of this section.

1. Monitor the performance of the WebCenter application through the performance-monitoring page in Enterprise Manager.
2. Identify whether the performance issues are related to how the application is using a specific WebCenter service.
3. Determine whether any service parameters for the service(s) identified in step 2 can affect the performance issue and, if so, make the appropriate modifications using the service's associated WLST commands or through Enterprise Manager.
4. If the WebCenter service identified in step 2 has an associated backend server, as explained in Chapter 7, check the backend server connection and its properties, determine whether any modifications can be made to improve performance and, if so, make the appropriate modifications using the server's associated WLST commands.

The WebCenter Service Metrics page of Enterprise Manager shows the performance metrics of each service used within a WebCenter application. Navigate to the home page of the WebCenter application in EM and then from the Application Deployment menu choose the WebCenter | Service Metrics menu option to access this page. This page shows the performance metrics for the application's Enterprise 2.0 services and its operations. The service-level metrics include the status, the number of invocations, the percentage of successful invocations, and the average response time in milliseconds per invocation. The per-operation metrics include the maximum response time for any invocation since startup. Together, these metrics enable the identification of performance bottlenecks within the application.

Table 10-1 shows some of the most important WebCenter Enterprise 2.0 services, their associated backend servers, and some possible performance optimization questions that should be considered. Although a thorough discussion of each of these services is beyond the scope of this book, in the next section we use the WebCenter Discussions service as an example to illustrate how service properties and the application's backend server connections can be modified to address performance issues.

Service	**Backend Server**	**Performance Optimization Considerations**
Document Library Service, Content Presenter Service	Content Server Connection	Is the content server down? Are there any network connectivity issues between the application and the content server? Configuration of the content server properties needs to be checked.
Announcements or Discussions Service	Discussions and Announcements Server	Is the discussions server down? Are there any network connectivity issues between the application and the discussions server? Configuration of the discussions server properties needs to be checked.
Lists Service	WebCenter repository for List data and MDS repository for List metadata	Are there issues with the WebCenter repository connectivity or the MDS repository connectivity? Note that an issue with any of these connection points will result in a negative effect on the performance of various parts of the application, not just the Lists service. For example, if the connectivity to the MDS repository is slow, the loading of pages and the page service will also be impacted.

TABLE 10-1. *WebCenter Discussion Service Properties Optimizations*

Optimizing the WebCenter Discussions Service

As we reviewed in detail in Chapter 7, the WebCenter Discussions service enables users to publish and store discussions in WebCenter applications, and the WebCenter Announcements service enables moderators and administrators to create and expose announcements on WebCenter application pages. The Discussions service and the Announcements service require a connection to the WebCenter Discussions server. Both services use the same server connection and their performance metrics are displayed in the Enterprise Manager WebCenter Service Metrics page, as shown here.

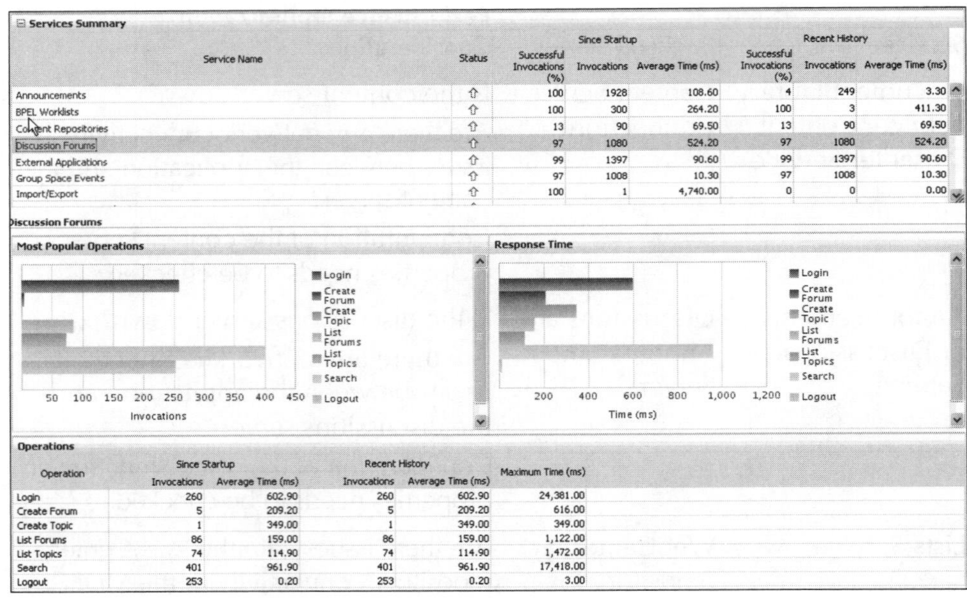

Services Summary

Service Name	Status	Since Startup: Successful Invocations (%)	Since Startup: Invocations	Since Startup: Average Time (ms)	Recent History: Successful Invocations (%)	Recent History: Invocations	Recent History: Average Time (ms)
Announcements	⇧	100	1928	108.60	4	249	3.30
BPEL Worklists	⇧	100	300	264.20	100	3	411.30
Content Repositories	⇧	13	90	69.50	13	90	69.50
Discussion Forums	⇧	97	1080	524.20	97	1080	524.20
External Applications	⇧	99	1397	90.60	99	1397	90.60
Group Space Events	⇧	97	1008	10.30	97	1008	10.30
Import/Export	⇧	100	1	4,740.00	0	0	0.00

Operations

Operation	Since Startup: Invocations	Since Startup: Average Time (ms)	Recent History: Invocations	Recent History: Average Time (ms)	Maximum Time (ms)
Login	260	602.90	260	602.90	24,381.00
Create Forum	5	209.20	5	209.20	616.00
Create Topic	1	349.00	1	349.00	349.00
List Forums	86	159.00	86	159.00	1,122.00
List Topics	74	114.90	74	114.90	1,472.00
Search	401	961.90	401	961.90	17,418.00
Logout	253	0.20	253	0.20	3.00

The Discussion service's connection has a number of properties that affect its performance. These properties can be set via Enterprise Manager or through the WLST setDiscussionForumConnection command. As an example, the timeout property specifies the length of time (in seconds) that the Discussion and Announcement services wait for a response from the Discussions server before issuing a connection timeout message. The service default (10 seconds) applies if the value set is –1. The minimum value for this property is 0 seconds, and the maximum value is 45 seconds. A short timeout setting means that if the server has long response times as a result of high loads, the service will show timeout messages to users. On the other hand, too long a timeout setting means that in genuine fault cases when the server has crashed and is not available, the service will take too long to report the issue to the user. The timeout property is stored within the WebCenter application's connections.xml descriptor, as shown by the following snippet:

```
<StringRefAddr addrType="connection.time.out"
   <Contents>15</Contents>
</StringRefAddr>
```

Another Discussions service property that may have an impact on application performance is the maximum number of topics fetched by the service and displayed within the page. This setting can be configured via the *topics.fetch.size* property, which can be set via the following command:

```
setDiscussionForumServiceProperty(appName='PricingPortal',
property='topics.fetch.size', value='30')
```

If this property is set to a high value, it can have a negative effect on the rendering time of application pages that use the Discussions service.

Conclusion

In this chapter we reviewed the areas of performance optimization for each layer of the Fusion Middleware stack. We started from the Java Virtual Machine and moved up to the ADF, SOA Suite, and WebCenter layers. Wherever applicable, we also considered how each potential area of performance optimization specifically applies to the pricing application's environment.

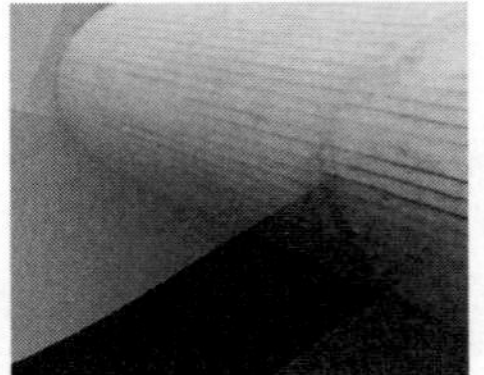

CHAPTER 11

Monitoring and Diagnosing Fusion Middleware Enterprise Applications

ne of the most important aspects of managing any enterprise application is the ability to effectively troubleshoot issues. Troubleshooting is not only important for a production environment, where every second of application downtime can have a significant negative impact on the organization's profitability, but it is also enormously important for development and testing environments, where the effective resolution of issues can greatly improve the efficiency of the development and testing processes. Of course, the best way to deal with issues is to make sure you can avoid them in the first place, and that is where the monitoring capabilities of a system come into play: Through monitoring of key metrics, it is sometimes possible to detect conditions that might cause system failures and to take preventative actions.

In this chapter, we review both the monitoring and diagnostics management capabilities provided by Oracle Fusion Middleware components. We begin the chapter with a review of the Fusion Middleware logging infrastructure. We then continue by exploring the WebLogic Diagnostics Framework, a WebLogic Server layer component that provides a rich set of diagnostics and monitoring capabilities. Finally, we end the chapter with a closer look at the WebLogic Server node manager component, which can be used to remotely manage, monitor, and diagnose WebLogic Server–based Fusion Middleware components.

Understanding Fusion Middleware Logging

The simplest, and sometimes most effective, way of analyzing a Fusion Middleware environment's health and failure conditions consists of examining the environment's log files. To do so, however, requires a good understanding of the Fusion Middleware logging infrastructure—that is, the way log files are generated—as well as the format of the content of the log files. There are two categories of log files within a Fusion Middleware environment: log files generated by WebLogic Server, and log files generated directly by Fusion Middleware layered components. The former is managed by the WebLogic Server logging infrastructure, whereas the latter is managed through the Oracle Diagnostics Logging (ODL) framework, which we reviewed in Chapter 3. The analysis of both types of log files is important because issues may arise from WebLogic Server resources used by Fusion Middleware layered components (in which case the WebLogic Server logs would be the main source of information for diagnosing the problem) or they may be caused directly by malfunction at the layered component level (in which case the analysis of the ODL log files becomes necessary). In this section we review both of these logging infrastructures and their relationship to each other.

WebLogic Server Logging Infrastructure

All servers within a WebLogic Server domain, including the administration server, output their logs to a file within the \servers\<server-name>\logs\<server-name>.log (where <server-name> is the name of the server instance) subdirectory of the host's DOMAIN_HOME directory. The administration server is special: In addition to outputting its own log information to the domain's \servers\AdminServer\logs\AdminServer.log file, it also maintains a domain-wide log file, with the same name as the domain name, within the same directory. All managed servers within a domain periodically send their logs (by default of severity NOTICE or higher) to the administration server, which in turn writes them to the single domain-wide log file. As such, the domain-wide log file is an important tool in monitoring the status of the entirety of a distributed WebLogic Server domain. In cases where a managed server is unable to reach the administration server, it buffers its log content so that it can be sent when the communication between the two servers is reestablished. Figure 11-1 illustrates the flow of a WebLogic Server's log data.

Many of the characteristics of the default WebLogic Server logging behavior just described are configurable. As an example, the path (including directory

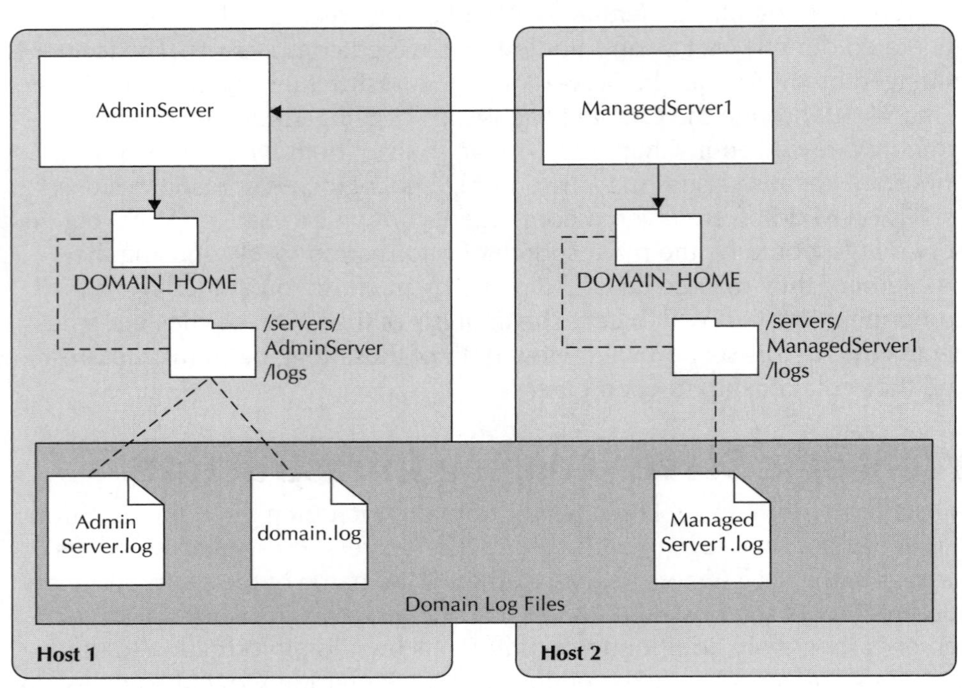

FIGURE 11-1. *WebLogic Server domain log flow*

and filename) to which each server's logging information is outputted can be modified and the cutoff level for the logs sent by managed servers to the administration server can be changed. The modification of server-specific logging parameters can be performed through WLST online by navigating to the /<domain-name>/serverConfig/Servers/<server-name>/Log/<server-name> MBean path of each server and modifying the appropriate MBeans attributes. Domain-wide logging configurations can be modified via WLST by navigating to the /<domain-name>/serverConfig/Log/<domain-name> MBean path. Both categories of log configurations can also be modified through the Administration Console. The following screenshot shows the Administration Console window that allows for the modification of domain-wide logging parameters.

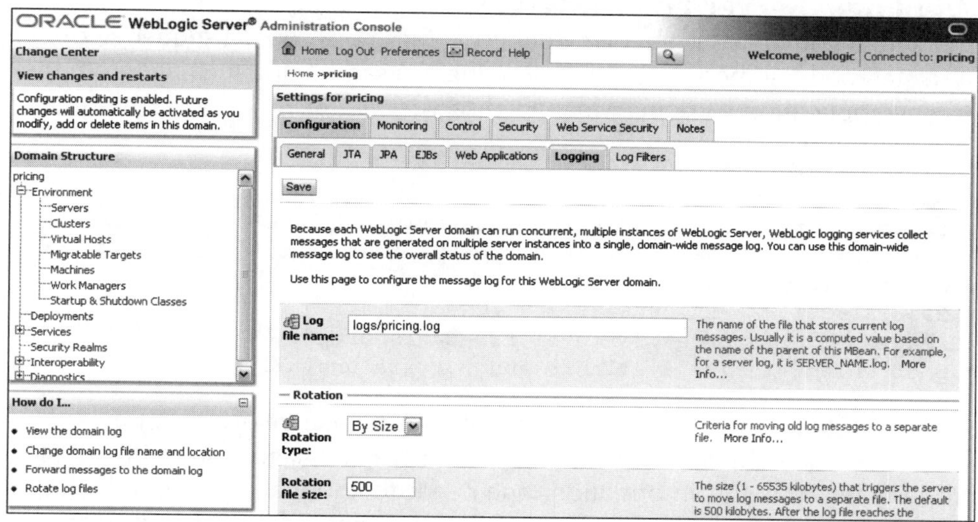

An important aspect of the management of a domain's logging configuration is the way in which log files are rotated and archived. Log file rotation ensures that the domain's files do not grow indefinitely. By default, all the logging parameters of a WebLogic Server domain (for all servers as well as for the domain-wide log file) are configured to rotate the log file each time its size reaches 500KB. At that point, the active log file to which the server is outputting its log is renamed to <server-name>.log{N}, where {N} is an auto-incremented sequence number. The default WebLogic Server configuration is to maintain up to seven previous rotations of each log file before deleting them. The logging configuration can also be modified (for each server and the domain) to trigger rotation based on time (that is say, every 24 hours) instead of based on the log file's size. Furthermore, by default, the directory to which log files are rotated is the same as the directory in which the active log files reside, although this configuration can also be modified to allow for a separation of rotated log files from the active one.

WebLogic Server Log Messages

The actual content of WebLogic Server log files consists of a sequence of time-stamped log messages. The following is a sample log message from the pricing application's Pricing1 managed server log file:

```
####<Jan 1, 2011 9:55:59 AM PST> <Info>
<Common> <pricing1> <soa_server1>
<weblogic.work.j2ee.J2EEWorkManager$WorkWithListener@139e28e>
<anonymous> <BEA1-06168D81DFA00A734575>
<0000IoTkuarFw000jzwkno1D5VG1000002>
<1293818159511> <BEA-000628>
<Created "1" resources for pool "SOADataSource",
out of which "1" are available and "0" are unavailable.>
```

As should be obvious from this sample message, a great deal of information is embedded within every single log message, and to be able to properly interpret this information, one needs to know exactly how the log message is formatted. The following string decomposes the content of a WebLogic Server log message into its different elements.

```
####<TIME-STAMP><SEVERITY><SUBSYSTEM><SERVER-HOST><SERVER-NAME>
<THREAD-ID><USER-ID><DIAGNOSTICS-CONTEXT-ID>
<RAW-TIME-STAMP><MESSAGE-ID><MESSAGE-CONTENT>
```

Table 11-1 describes each element of a WebLogic Server log message in detail.

Log Message Element	Description
TIME-STAMP	The time and date when the message was logged, as obtained from the logging server's operating system.
SEVERITY	Indicates the severity of the condition being reported as a log message. The value of this element can be one of the following (listed in the order of increasing severity): ■ **TRACE** Used to follow an application method's request path using the WebLogic Diagnostics Framework. Messages of this severity are only logged when diagnostics instrumentation is enabled, as described in more detail in the "Using the WebLogic Diagnostics Framework" section of this chapter.

TABLE 11-1. *WebLogic Server Log Message Elements*

Log Message Element	Description
	■ **DEBUG** Contains detailed information that is typically only relevant when application issues are being debugged. ■ **INFO** Contains information about regular (expected) operations of the server subsystem or deployed applications that are not of significant importance. ■ **NOTICE** Contains information about regular (expected) operations of the server subsystem or deployed applications that are of significant importance. ■ **WARNING** Contains information regarding an operational event that indicates an issue with the server subsystem or application operations that might have failure consequences. ■ **ERROR** Contains information regarding an operational event that indicates an issue that has caused the failure of a server subsystem or an application. ■ **CRITICAL** Contains information regarding an operational event that indicates an issue that has caused the failure of a server subsystem or an application. The severity of the failure is higher than that reported by an ERROR message. ■ **ALERT** Contains information regarding an operational event that indicates an issue that has caused the failure of a server subsystem. The failure has caused a complete termination of operations to the affected subsystem and applications that depend on it can no longer expect to be functional. ■ **EMERGENCY** The server has entered an unstable state that makes it dysfunctional.
SUBSYSTEM	Indicates the WebLogic Server subsystem logging the message. As an example, a value of "JDBC" would indicate that the server's JDBC data source management subsystem is logging the message.
SERVER-HOST	The DNS name of the host on which the WebLogic Server instance logging the message is executing.
SERVER-NAME	The name of the WebLogic Server instance (admin or managed) logging the message.

TABLE 11-1. *WebLogic Server Log Message Elements* (continued)

Log Message Element	Description

THREAD-ID	The ID of the thread within the WebLogic Server instance that performed the logging of the message. If the thread in question is a WebLogic Server execute thread (as reviewed in detail in the "WebLogic Server Request Management" section of Chapter 2), the format of this field will be similar to the following:
	`[ACTIVE] ExecuteThread: '14' for queue:`
	`'weblogic.kernel.Default (self-tuning)`
	This indicates the state of the thread (in this case, "ACTIVE"), the thread number, and the execute queue from which the thread was obtained (in this case, the default self-tuning execute queue of the server is indicated).

USER-ID	The user ID of the authenticated subject associated with the request that has led to the generation of the log message. If the log message is being generated by a WebLogic Server component outside of the context of a user request or if the request has no authenticated subject, then the value of this field is set to <anonymous>.
TRANSACTION-ID	The ID of the JTA transaction that was active at the time the message was logged. The field is empty if the message was not executing within a JTA transaction context.
DIAGNOSTIC-CONTEXT-ID	An ID that correlates related set of messages. The correlation is performed using the WebLogic Diagnostics Framework's instrumentation component, as described in more detail in the "Using the WebLogic Diagnostics Framework" section of this chapter.
RAW-TIME-VALUE	The epoch timestamp (that is, the number of seconds elapsed since midnight Coordinated Universal Time of January 1, 1970, not counting leap seconds) when the message was logged, as obtained from the logging server's operating system.
MESSAGE-ID	A unique six-digit identifier for the type of message being logged. All WebLogic Server subsystem-generated (as opposed to custom-application-generated) messages have a BEA prefix and have a numerical suffix in the range of 0–499999.
MESSAGE-CONTENT	The actual text that describes the conditions of the subsystem or application in the context of this log message.

TABLE 11-1. *WebLogic Server Log Message Elements* (continued)

WebLogic Server Logging Diagnostics Tools

An understanding of the composition of WebLogic Server log messages is critical in troubleshooting issues within an environment. However, the sheer number of log messages created within the domains of an enterprise application can sometimes complicate the direct analysis of log files. The WebLogic Server Administration Console provides a Summary of Log Files page that allows for the central analysis and filtering of the domain's log files, as shown in the following screenshot. Using this page, users can view and filter the domain logs as well the log entries of a specific managed server.

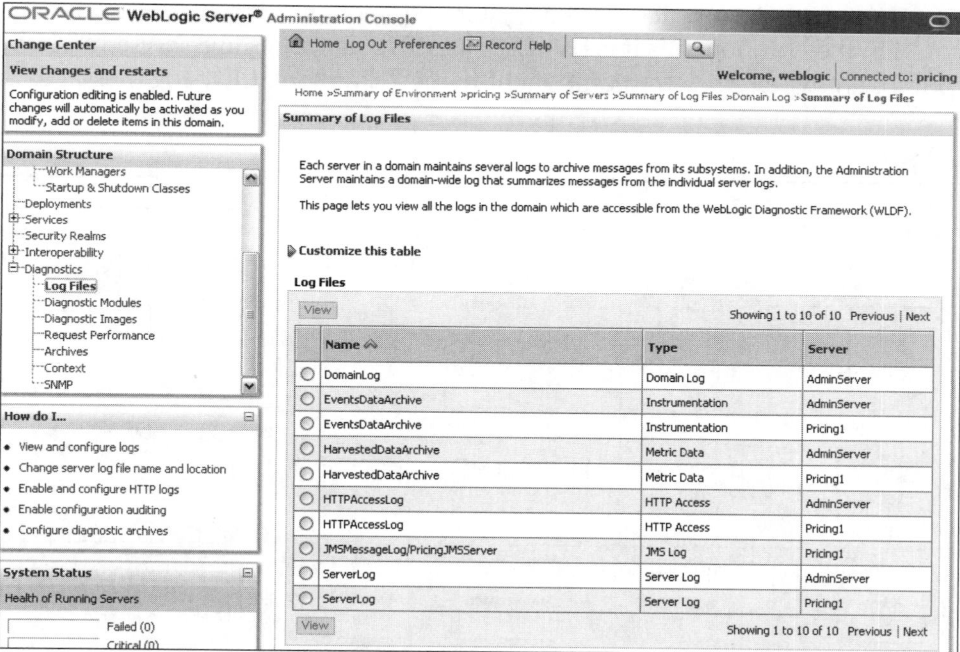

This page is accessible by navigating to the Diagnostics | Log Files node of the console's Domain Structure tree, and it allows for the remote analysis of log files through the Administration Console. Its use is especially convenient for environments to which access to local file systems, for a direct analysis of server files, is not easily obtainable.

Oracle Diagnostics Logging

As discussed in Chapter 3, the Oracle Diagnostics Logging (ODL) framework is a Fusion Middleware shared infrastructure component that provides a standard logging service. Each layered Fusion Middleware component, be it Java EE-based (such as the SOA Infrastructure) or non–Java EE-based (such as the Oracle HTTP Server) uses ODL for its logging. Figure 11-2 shows how ODL extends the WebLogic Server log flow described in the previous section and illustrated in Figure 11-1.

For Java EE components, log messages are by default placed within the DOMAIN_HOME's /servers/<server-name>/logs directory within a file named <server-name>-diagnostics.log. For system components, log messages are stored in the component's INSTANCE_HOME /diagnostics/logs/<system-component-type>/<system-component-name> directory. ODL log messages

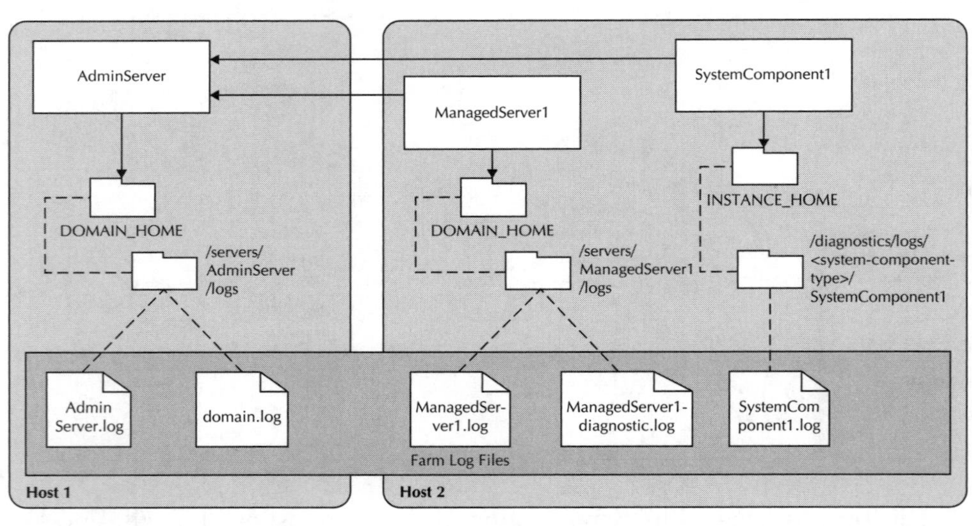

FIGURE 11-2. *Fusion Middleware Oracle Diagnostics Logging flow*

of severity ERROR or higher are also sent to the administration server and captured within the WebLogic Server domain-level log file. This integration allows the domain log file to serve as the single source of analysis for troubleshooting issues within the entire Fusion Middleware farm.

NOTE
The WebLogic Server domain-wide log file contains the error messages for all Java EE and system components within a Fusion Middleware farm and, as such, can serve as a good source of first-level analysis.

Just like the WebLogic Server logging infrastructure, ODL provides the ability to define either time-based or size-based log file rotation policies. We will review how these policies can be modified later in this section.

Oracle Diagnostics Logging Log Messages

Just like WebLogic Server log files, the content of ODL log files consists of a sequence of time-stamped log message. The following is a sample log message from the pricing application's soa_server_1 Oracle SOA Suite managed server log file:

```
[2010-11-29T15:40:39.627-08:00] [soa_server1] [NOTIFICATION]
[SOA-20167] [oracle.integration.platform] [tid:
weblogic.work.j2ee.J2EEWorkManager$WorkWithListener@61b34a]
[userId: <anonymous>]
[ecid: 0000ImPzbmUFw000jzwkno1Cx3ZC000003,0] [APP: soa-infra]
[arg: 7] Done deploying composites. took 7 seconds.
```

As should be obvious from this sample message, ODL log message entries have some overlapping fields with WebLogic Server log messages. The following string decomposes the content of an ODL log message into its different elements:

```
[TIME-STAMP] [COMPONENT-INFO] [SEVERITY] [MESSAGE-
ID] [SUBSYSTEM] [THREAD-ID]
[USER-ID] [EXECUTION-CONTEXT-ID] [LOG-CONTEXT-ARGUMENTS] [MESSAGE-
CONTENT]
```

Table 11-2 details each element of an ODL log message.

Log Message Element	Description
TIME-STAMP	The time and date when the message was logged, as obtained from the logging server's operating system.
COMPONENT-INFO	Indicates the Fusion Middleware component that is logging the message. In some cases the source component of the log message will use its WebLogic Server managed server name for the value of this field.
SEVERITY	Indicates the severity of the condition being reported as a log message. The value of this element can be one of the following (listed in the order of increasing severity): ■ **TRACE** Used to display detailed internal information that is generally used for troubleshooting purposes. ■ **NOTIFICATION** Contains information about regular (expected) operations of the Fusion Middleware component that are not of significant importance. ■ **WARNING** Contains information regarding an operational event that indicates an issue with the Fusion Middleware component's operations that might have failure consequences. ■ **ERROR** Contains information regarding an operational event that indicates an issue that has caused the failure of a Fusion Middleware component subsystem. ■ **INCIDENT_ERROR** Contains information regarding an operational event that indicates an issue that has caused the failure of a Fusion Middleware component. The failure has caused a complete termination of operations to the affected component, and services that depend on it can no longer expect to be functional.

TABLE 11-2. *ODL Log Message Elements*

Log Message Element	Description
MESSAGE-ID	A unique five-digit identifier for the type of message being logged. All Fusion Middleware component generated messages have a unique prefix (for example, "SOA") appended to their message ID.
SUBSYSTEM	Indicates the Fusion Middleware component subsystem that is logging the message. As an example, a value of "oracle.mds" would indicate that the server's Metadata Services repository management subsystem is logging the message.
THREAD-ID	Same exact value as the equivalent WebLogic Server log element, as described earlier in this chapter.
USER-ID	The user ID of the authenticated subject associated with the request that has led to the generation of the log message. If the log message is being generated by an internal subsystem outside of the context of a user request or if the request has no authenticated subject, then the value of this field is set to <anonymous>.
EXECUTION-CONTEXT-ID	Described in detail in the "Cross-Component Request Tracking" section, which follows.
LOG-CONTEXT-ARGUMENT	Additional contextual arguments provided by the component. This information is meant for analysis by Oracle support.
MESSAGE-CONTENT	The actual text that describes the conditions of the subsystem or application in the context of this log message.

TABLE 11-2. *ODL Log Message Elements* (continued)

Cross-Component Request Tracking

As we reviewed in the previous section, each ODL message generated by a Fusion Middleware component contains within it an Execution Context ID (ECID). This is a globally unique ID that is assigned to incoming user requests within a Fusion Middleware domain. As the request traverses different Fusion Middleware components, all ODL log messages generated by the components as a result of processing the request will contain the request's ECID. This allows for a better root-cause analysis of environmental issues such as when an error condition is found; the path of the requests that led to the error can be traced by filtering the log files of the domain for the ECID of the ODL error message. We can use an example to illustrate the value of ECIDs. Assume that the pricing application's Oracle Business Activity Monitoring (BAM) server is being used to host multiple BAM reports designed to receive data object updates from a SOA composite as well as another system through JMS. If error messages suddenly start showing up within the BAM server's ODL logs, determining whether SOA composite requests or JMS requests are leading to the error becomes simple through the use of ECIDs. All one has to do is to filter the logs of all servers within the domain for the specific ECID contained within the BAM server's ODL message. If the notification messages that match this ECID show the SOA Infrastructure as the source subsystem, then one can be sure it is the SOA composite generated BAM events causing the issue. Otherwise, the JMS source is likely the root of the issue. The ECID also allows for the pinpointing of the specific SOA log message, perhaps identifying a specific composite instance, that caused the error. This information can be used to further examine the state of the specific composite that was at the source of the issue.

Oracle Diagnostics Logging Tools

As we reviewed in Chapter 3, the Enterprise Manager log-viewing capabilities consist of the ability to query ODL log messages—at either the farm, domain, server, system component, or layered component specific artifact (for example, SOA composite) level—and to filter them based on date range, message type, message content, and/or subsystem. The configuration of each Fusion Middleware component's logging can also be modified through Enterprise Manager. The following screenshot shows the Enterprise Manager log configuration page, which can be accessed by right-clicking a node within the left tree pane and selecting the Log Configuration option.

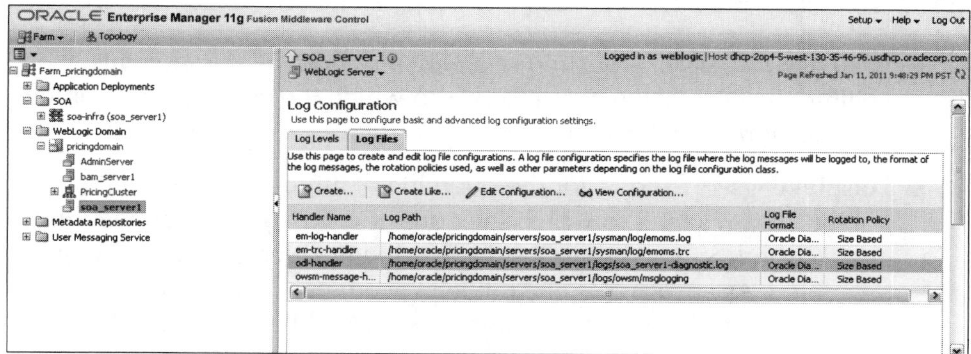

This page also allows for the modification of the configuration of the ODL logging for each Fusion Middleware component. For each component, the page allows for the modification of logging attributes, such as the directory in which the ODL log files are generated, the minimum severity that should be logged for the component, and log file rotation properties. The next screenshot shows the log file editing page.

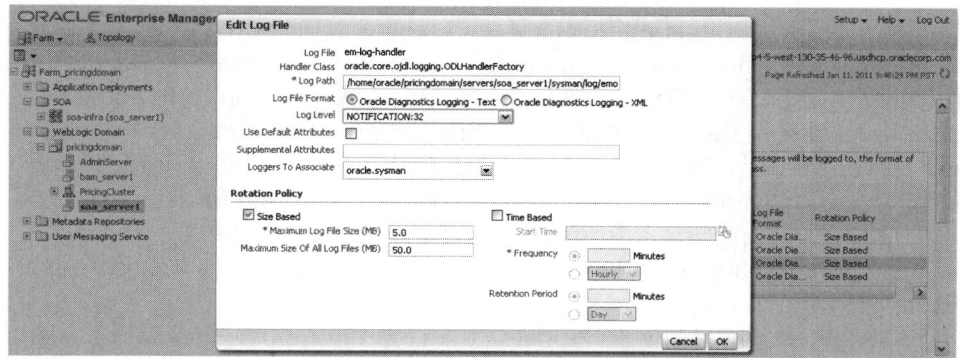

Beyond the graphical user interfaces exposed within Enterprise Manager, ODL also provides a set of WLST commands for diagnosing an environment's log files. The full list of such commands can be obtained by executing the following WLST command:

```
help('fmw diagnostics')
```

However, the following two commands are worth singling out because they can be very useful in troubleshooting issues within a Fusion Middleware environment:

- **listLogs()** Lists the location of all log files from all components within the farm of the admin server to which the current WLST online connection is established.
- **displayLogs()** Allows for the querying of all log files within the farm of the admin server to which the current WLST online connection is established. Specific search strings or log file element criteria can be specified. As an example, the following command lists all log messages, from all components of the target Fusion Middleware farm, that contain the word "Error":

```
displayLogs('Error')
```

Using the WebLogic Diagnostics Framework

The WebLogic Diagnostics Framework (WLDF) is a WebLogic Server module that provides a set of capabilities to facilitate the collection and analysis of diagnostics information for a domain's servers and its deployed applications. Through the configuration of WLDF, specific pieces of monitoring data can be collected from the Java Virtual Machine, application code, server logs, and server MBeans. WLDF can be an invaluable tool for diagnosing issues within a Fusion Middleware environment because it allows for the collection of detailed and specific information about a WebLogic Server domain and its deployed applications without the need for any additional coding. Figure 11-3 shows the high-level architecture of WLDF.

As shown in Figure 11-3, the data collected through WLDF can be used through the following output channels:

- **Diagnostics images** This WLDF feature allows for the dumping of the server state within a domain into a ZIP file. The ZIP file consists of a set of image files that contain a snapshot of the state of the server's components (JVM, deployed applications, JDBC data

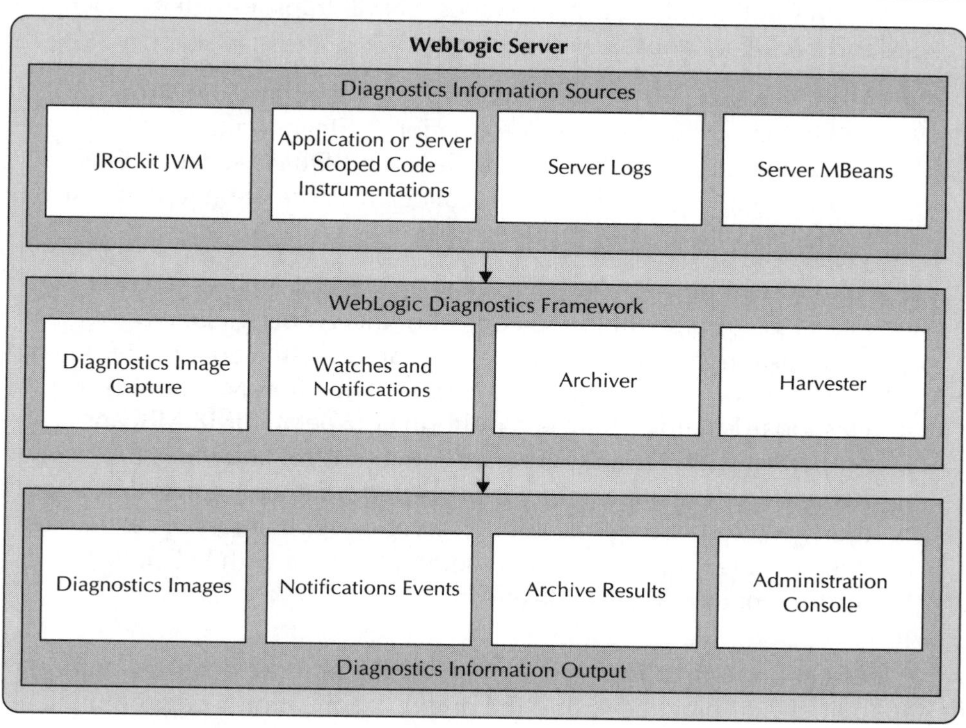

FIGURE 11-3. *WebLogic Diagnostics Framework architecture*

sources, and so on) at the time of the capture. This feature is primarily used for interaction with Oracle support because it allows for the consolidation of all server information that might be relevant to support the analysis of issues with a particular Fusion Middleware environment.

- **Notification events** The WLDF watches and notification feature allows for the creation of watch conditions on a server's log information, MBeans values, and instrumentation events. When these conditions are met, they can lead to the triggering of asynchronous notification events. Notification events can be emitted as JMX notifications, JMS messages, SNMP traps, e-mail messages, and WLDF diagnostics image dumps.

- **Archive results** The WLDF archiving capabilities allow for the collection of a server's log information, MBeans values, and instrumentation events within a file or an RDBMS schema. This capability allows for the WLDF collected information to be persisted for historical analysis purposes.
- **Administration Console** WLDF provides two web-based user interfaces—both within the context of the WebLogic Server Administration Console—that allow for the visual analysis of domain metrics information. The first interface, known as Monitoring Dashboards, allows for the monitoring of specific JMX MBeans properties within graphs. The second interface, known as the Request Performance page, displays performance information about the execution of requests within server or application code that has been enabled for fine-grained method tracking with WLDF's instrumentation capabilities.

In the sections that follow, we explore WLDF in more detail by putting its capabilities into practice within the pricing application's environment.

Diagnostics Images

A WLDF diagnostics file is a ZIP file that contains a set of .img (image) files—one for each subsystem of a server. Each contains information regarding the state of the subsystem it represents. In effect, a diagnostics file contains the detailed information that represents a snapshot of the status of a server at the point in time when the file was created. The creation of a diagnostics file can be triggered for any WebLogic Server instance within a domain through the Administration Console (see the following screenshot) or through WLST commands—for the specific commands and their syntax, use the following WLST command:

```
help('diagnostics')
```

As we will see in the next section, WLDF watches can also act as a trigger for the creation of a diagnostics file.

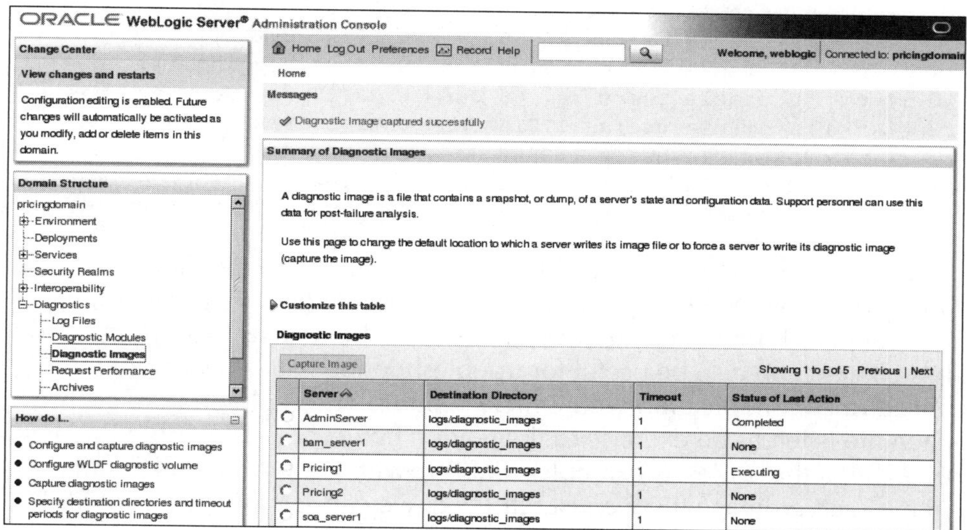

WLDF diagnostics files are often captured as a way to provide information about a particular server's environment to Oracle support when an issue is being investigated. Let's take a closer look at the content of a diagnostics file for the Pricing1 managed server. After triggering a diagnostics file capture through the Administration Console, we should find a diagnostics ZIP file within the domain's /servers/Pricing1/logs/diagnostics_images directory (note that this is the default location where the file is placed, but it can be changed for each diagnostics capture). Examining the content of this ZIP file, we can see that it consists of the following .img files:

```
-rw-r--r--  1 oracle users 765526 Jan  6 22:03 APPLICATION.img
-rw-r--r--  1 oracle users    167 Jan  6 22:04 Cluster.img
-rw-r--r--  1 oracle users  20135 Jan  6 22:04 configuration.img
-rw-r--r--  1 oracle users    223 Jan  6 22:04 CONNECTOR.img
-rw-r--r--  1 oracle users  27177 Jan  6 22:04 Deployment.img
-rw-r--r--  1 oracle users    169 Jan  6 22:04
HarvesterImageSource.img
-rw-r--r--  1 oracle users  27440 Jan  6 22:04 image.summary
-rw-r--r--  1 oracle users    181 Jan  6 22:04
InstrumentationImageSource.img
-rw-r--r--  1 oracle users   1878 Jan  6 22:04 JDBC.img
```

```
-rw-r--r--  1 oracle users  39455 Jan  6 22:04 JMS.img
-rw-r--r--  1 oracle users  11820 Jan  6 22:04 JNDI_IMAGE_
SOURCE.img
-rw-r--r--  1 oracle users   1751 Jan  6 22:04 JTA.img
-rw-r--r--  1 oracle users  26358 Jan  6 22:04 JVM.img
-rw-r--r--  1 oracle users   7108 Jan  6 22:04 Logging.img
-rw-r--r--  1 oracle users     66 Jan  6 22:03 PathService.img
-rw-r--r--  1 oracle users  17716 Jan  6 22:04 PERSISTENT_STORE.img
-rw-r--r--  1 oracle users    586 Jan  6 22:04 SAF.img
-rw-r--r--  1 oracle users    161 Jan  6 22:04 WatchSource.img
-rw-r--r--  1 oracle users   5685 Jan  6 22:04 WORK_MANAGER.img
```

Although the information within each .img file is designed for consumption by Oracle support (and in the case of the configuration.img files, contains binary data and therefore cannot be read as text), some of the file's content can also be useful for troubleshooting issues outside of the context of communication with Oracle support. The exploration of each image file is left as an exercise to the reader; however, it is worth pointing out a few of these files as examples. Starting with the JVM.img file of the Pricing1 server image file we just retrieved, we can see the following XML snippet listing the managed server JVM's memory and thread count information at the time when the diagnostic file was produced:

```
  ...
  <web:heap-memory-used-bytes>265518392</web:heap-memory-used-
bytes>
  <web:heap-memory-max-bytes>1037959168</web:heap-memory-max-bytes>
  <web:heap-memory-init-bytes>536870912</web:heap-memory-init-
bytes>
  <web:heap-memory-committed-bytes>518979584
</web:heap-memory-committed-bytes>
  <web:non-heap-memory-used-bytes>113211320
</web:non-heap-memory-used-bytes>
  <web:non-heap-memory-max-bytes>570425344</web:non-heap-memory-
max-bytes>
  <web:non-heap-memory-init-bytes>134381568
</web:non-heap-memory-init-bytes>
  <web:non-heap-memory-committed-bytes>145063936
</web:non-heap-memory-committed-bytes>
  <web:thread-count>52</web:thread-count>
  <web:peak-thread-count>52</web:peak-thread-count>
  <web:total-started-thread-count>69</web:total-started-thread-
count>
  <web:daemon-thread-count>49</web:daemon-thread-count>
  ...
```

Furthermore, the JTA.img file contains information about the global transactional configuration of the server (such as the default transaction timeout settings) as well as the configuration of each of the transactional resources, including the JDBC data source of the pricing application, within the domain. The JDBC.img and JMS.img files contain similar information, respectively, for the JDBC and JMS resources configured within the domain. Prior to concluding our discussion of the content of the WLDF diagnostics file, it is worth noting that the names of the .img files contained within a diagnostics image ZIP file are also the values that should be used as the first argument of the following WLDF WLST command:

```
saveDiagnosticImageCaptureFile(imageName, outputFile=None)
```

This command allows for the targeted capture of the content of a single .img file from a running server.

Diagnostics Modules

WebLogic Server allows for the configuration of diagnostics modules that can be targeted to specific server instances in order to enable a certain diagnostics capability. Diagnostics modules can be defined and targeted through the Administration Console, as illustrated in the following screenshot.

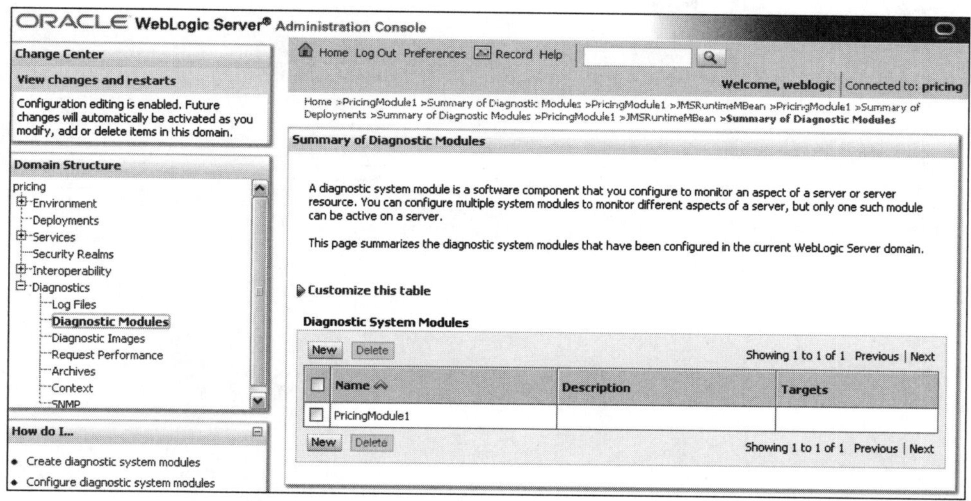

A diagnostics module is composed of a set of JMX metrics harvesters, watches and notifications, and instrumentation diagnostics monitors. JMX metrics harvesters are the simplest elements of a diagnostics module. Each harvester defined within a module allows for the collection of a specific JMX MBean instance. Harvesters collect the values of the specified attributes of the JMX MBean instances they are configured with. The value of harvested metrics is persisted within the server's WLDF archive location: Each WebLogic Server instance is associated with a single WLDF archiver that determines the location of the harvested metrics. By default, each server's archiver is configured to harvest its metrics within a file named WLS_DIAGNOSTICS{N}.dat (where {N} is an incrementing integer value). Each server's archiver configuration can be modified through the Administration Console, as shown next.

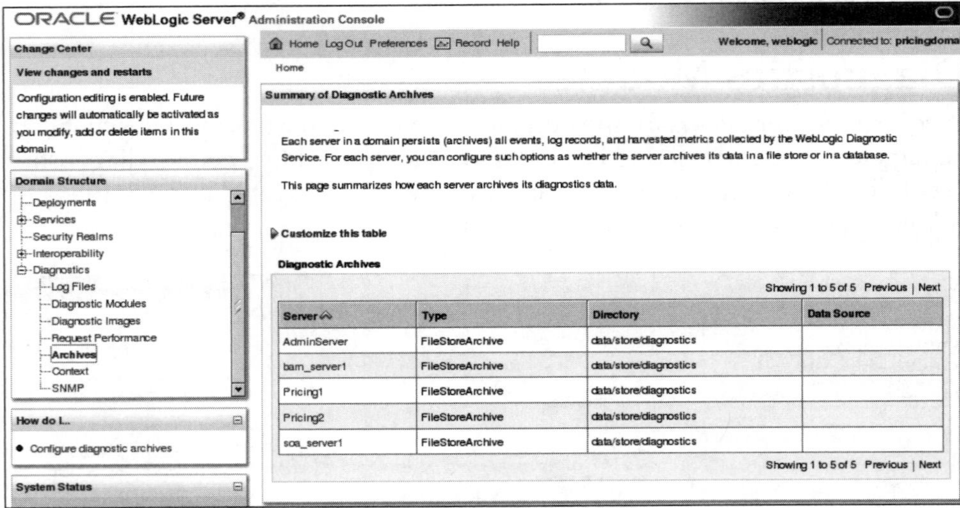

Archivers can be configured to store harvested metrics within a file—as per the default configuration—or within an RDBMS schema, in which case they would need to be configured with the JDBC data source that is pointing to the RDBMS instance that contains an appropriate WLDF schema. Furthermore, for each option, purging policies can be defined that ensure the archived metrics do not cause an overflow of storage space. The instructions for the creation of an RDBMS WLDF schema to serve this purpose are beyond the scope of this book but are described in detail within the book *Oracle Fusion Middleware: Configuring and Using the Diagnostics Framework for Oracle WebLogic Server* in the Fusion Middleware documentation library.

A WLDF module's watches and notifications allow for the configuration of policies that lead to the creation of asynchronous events to notify external systems or end users of a certain condition within the server. A WLDF notification configuration contains the information that describes a communication channel by which such events should be emitted. WLDF allows for the configuration of notifications that lead to the generation of an e-mail message (through the specification of the coordinates of a Simple Mail Transfer Protocol server), a JMS message (through the specification of a JMS destination's JNDI attributes), a JMX notification, a Simple Network Management Protocol (SNMP) trap, or a WLDF diagnostics image file (as described in the previous section). Notifications generated by WLDF can have an associated severity that can be configured within the module. The available values for the severity that can be associated with WLDF notifications are the same as the set of severity types described earlier in the "WebLogic Server Log Messages" section of this chapter. A WLDF watch configuration contains the information that specifies the conditions that should be watched for in order to trigger a specific event, as specified by a notification configuration. The types of events that can be watched for include changes in the value of specific server MBean attributes, the execution of an instrumentation monitor (which will be described in detail shortly), and the occurrence of a specific log message within the server log. The following screenshot shows the Administration Console screen that allows for the configuration of watches and notifications within a WLDF module.

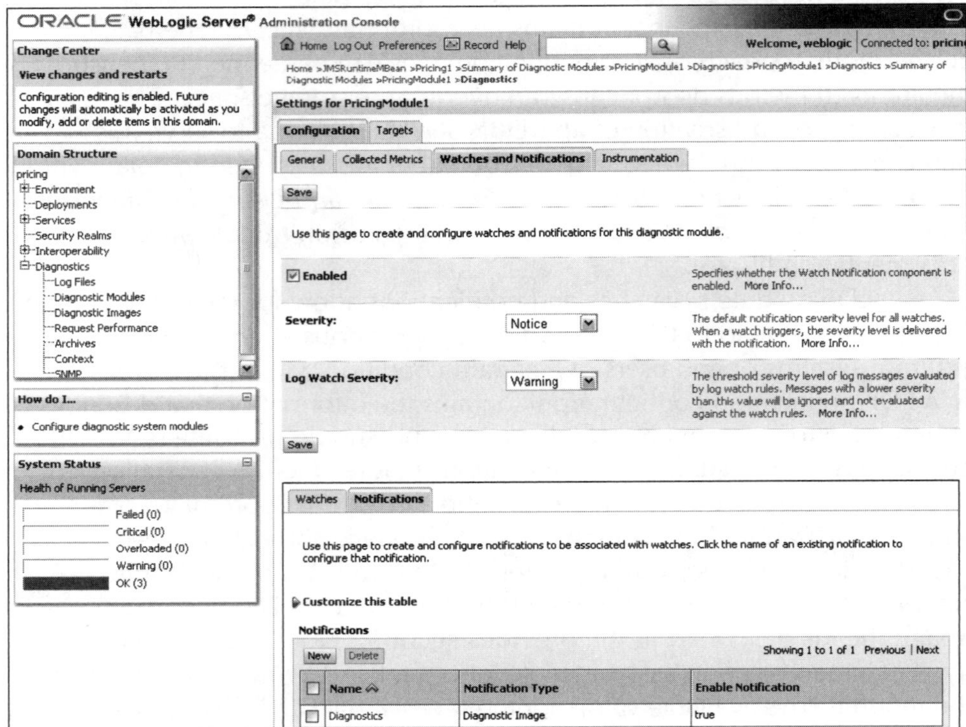

The final component of a diagnostics module is an instrumentation diagnostics monitor. Such monitors can be configured to inject a piece of Java code that performs a specific monitoring action within the methods of deployed applications or within the server infrastructure's request execution logic. WebLogic Server comes with a large set of predefined monitors that are documented within the "WLDF Instrumentation Library" appendix of *Configuring and Using the Diagnostics Framework for Oracle WebLogic Server* in the Fusion Middleware documentation library. Instrumentation monitors can be either application scoped or server scoped. Application-scoped monitors are executed within the context of the deployed application's logic: As an example, the instrumentation monitor JMS_After_AsyncMessage_Received is an application-scoped monitor. When enabled, it injects the monitoring code after all occurrences of the JMS MessageListener.onMessage() method invocation within the application code. Server-scoped monitors, on the other hand, are executed within the context of the WebLogic Server container services: As an example, JDBC_Before_Commit_Internal is a server-scoped monitor that, when enabled, injects monitoring code within the WebLogic Server JDBC subsystem to ensure that monitoring logic is executed prior to any JDBC transactions being committed. The nature of the monitoring logic performed as a result of an instrumentation monitor's enablement is determined by the action associated with the monitor as part of its configuration. Any one of the following types of monitoring instrumentation actions can be configured:

- **TraceAction** Generates a trace instrumentation event. The event contains detailed information about the state of the monitor's execution point, such as a timestamp, the identity of the authenticated subject, and the executing Java class and method names. As discussed earlier in this section, such events can be acted upon by watches and notification components of a WLDF module. This event also leads to the generation of a log message with a TRACE severity and content describing the monitor's context.
- **TraceElapsedTimeAction** Generates the same information as TraceAction, except that the event is generated once before and once after the target location of the instrumentation monitor.
- **TraceMemoryAllocationAction** This action can only be used when the underlying server's JVM is Oracle JRockit. It is very similar to TraceElapsedTimeAction, except that the information within the event also includes the incremental amount of memory allocated by the method as part of its execution.
- **DisplayArgumentsAction** Generates the same information as TraceAction, except that the event is also captured by the server's WLDF archiver.
- **StackDumpAction** Generates the same information as TraceAction, with the addition of the thread's full stack trace. The information is also captured by the server's WLDF archiver.

- **ThreadDumpAction** Generates the same information as TraceAction, with the addition of the stack trace and state for all of the threads that currently exist within the JVM.
- **MethodInvocationStatisticsAction** This is the only action that does not emit an instrumentation event. Instead, it generates method invocation statistics that it exposes within the server's InstrumentationRuntimeMBean JMX MBean. As a result, the generated information is available for use by the WLDF module's harvesters as well as watches and notifications components. This allows for the creation of WLDF notification policies that can combine method performance statistics and metrics from other server MBeans.

It is worth mentioning that beyond our discussion of instrumentation monitors so far, WLDF also makes available a special instrumentation monitor named DyeInjection. This monitor allows for the tracking of requests with certain specific characteristics. A discussion of the DyeInjection monitor is, however, beyond the scope of this book, and the reader is instead referred to the "Configuring the DyeInjection Monitor to Manage Diagnostic Contexts" section of the book *Configuring and Using the WebLogic Diagnostics Framework* in the Fusion Middleware documentation library.

Configuring the Pricing Application with a Diagnostics Module

We'll now bring the features of a WLDF module together by applying them to the pricing application's environment. Let's assume that we are noticing an issue with the pricing application's Pricing Update web service that, in some rare occasions, does not seem to persist pricing model changes that are sent to it through the Pricing Update SOA composite. You suspect that the issue is either with the JMS server (which might be overloaded and is therefore losing messages) or with the JDBC module (which is not properly committing transactions to the database). Therefore, to diagnose the problem, you decide to create a diagnostics module to enable the following WLDF diagnostics capabilities:

- The creation of a metrics collection harvester on the pricing application JMS server's Runtime MBean's *ConnectionsCurrentCount* attribute. This will allow you to have a historical view of the total connections on this server through the collection of this information within the server's archiver file.
- The creation of a WLDF instrumentation monitor of type JDBC_After_Commit_Internal with a TraceAction. This will allow you to emit instrumentation events after any JDBC transaction commit is performed by the server. To capture the complete state of the server after this event, you further configure a watch configuration that is activated whenever TraceAction events by the *PricingEventMDB* class are emitted (given your knowledge that the database transaction is performed by the pricing application's Message Driven Bean named PricingEventMDB). To complement the watch event, you associate it with a notification that triggers a server diagnostics image capture. This will allow you to have a complete view of the server state whenever the *PricingEventMDB* class has attempted to commit a JDBC transaction.

Needless to say, you would not configure such a WLDF module within a production environment because the generation of a diagnostics image on every JDBC commit will have a significant performance impact on your application. However, for example's sake, let's assume you are able to configure such a module within your staging environment where the lack-of-commit issue is reproduced through the execution of your test beds. You can perform the configuration of this WLDF module through the domain's Administration Console, as described in the previous section. When this is completed, the result of the configuration will be an XML file, with the same name as the module, within the domain's /config/diagnostics directory. The content of this file for our example would be as follows:

```
<?xml version='1.0' encoding='UTF-8'?>
<wldf-resource xmlns=
"http://xmlns.oracle.com/weblogic/weblogic-diagnostics"
xmlns:sec="http://xmlns.oracle.com/weblogic/security"
xmlns:wls="http://xmlns.oracle.com/weblogic/security/wls"
xmlns:xsi="http://www.w3.org/2001/XMLSchema-instance"
xsi:schemaLocation=
"http://xmlns.oracle.com/weblogic/weblogic-diagnostics
 http://xmlns.oracle.com/weblogic/weblogic-diagnostics
/1.0/weblogic-diagnostics.xsd">
  <name>PricingModule1</name>
  <instrumentation>
    <enabled>true</enabled>
    <wldf-instrumentation-monitor>
      <name>JDBC_After_Commit_Internal</name>
      <description></description>
      <dye-mask></dye-mask>
      <action>TraceAction</action>
    </wldf-instrumentation-monitor>
  </instrumentation>
  <harvester>
    <enabled>true</enabled>
    <sample-period>300000</sample-period>
    <harvested-type>
      <name>weblogic.management.runtime.JMSRuntimeMBean</name>
      <harvested-attribute>ConnectionsCurrentCount</harvested-
attribute>
      <harvested-instance>com.bea:Name=Pricing1.jms,
ServerRuntime=Pricing1,Type=JMSRuntime</harvested-instance>
      <namespace>ServerRuntime</namespace>
    </harvested-type>
  </harvester>
  <watch-notification>
    <watch>
      <name>InstrumentationEventsWatch</name>
      <enabled>true</enabled>
      <rule-type>EventData</rule-type>
      <rule-expression>(CLASSNAME = 'PricingEventMDB')</rule-
expression>
      <alarm-type>None</alarm-type>
```

```
      <notification>Diagnostics</notification>
    </watch>
    <image-notification>
      <name>Diagnostics</name>
      <enabled>true</enabled>
      <image-directory>logs\diagnostic_images</image-directory>
      <image-lockout>1</image-lockout>
    </image-notification>
  </watch-notification>
</wldf-resource>
```

We should note that for this diagnostics module to take effect, it needs to be properly targeted to the appropriate servers. In our example, we can target the module to the PricingCluster, because that is the target of the pricing application components for which this WLDF module is designed.

Administration Console Monitoring

The final component of WLDF we will explore is the WLDF monitoring user interface exposed through the Administration Console. This interface is referred to as a monitoring dashboard and can be accessed on the administration server at the console/dashboard context root, as shown next.

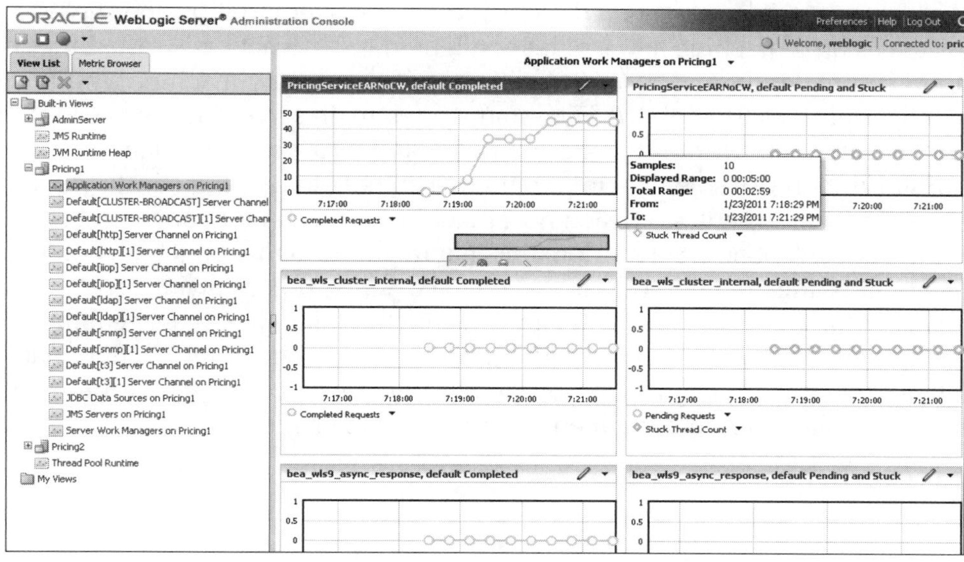

The monitoring dashboard allows for the display of JMX metrics with different chart types. Metrics are displayed within views that define the set of MBeans that should be charted. The WLDF dashboard comes with a set of preexisting views configured with groups of metrics that are relevant for the monitoring of specific server subsystems. These preexisting views are shown within the dashboard's Built-in Views tab, and examples include the Application Work Managers view, which shows the number of completed and pending requests on all deployed applications within a server. Users can also create new views in the View List that they can customize—by dragging and dropping specific MBeans attributes—within the Metrics Browser tab.

Configuring and Using Node Manager

As we discussed in Chapter 2, node manager is a management agent installed as part of the WebLogic Server installation process. Node manager can be configured on each machine hosting WebLogic Server instances to provide remote management and diagnostics capabilities. Although the Administration Console alone can be used to remotely shut down the servers, only through the configuration of node manager can one remotely start the managed servers of a domain. Node manager monitors the server instances on a machine and can be configured to automatically restart them upon failure. Furthermore, it is possible to connect to any machine's node manager process through WLST to start/stop domain servers as well as to obtain status and log information without going through the domain Administration Console. It is important to also note that a single instance of node manager executes on each host machine and can be configured to monitor all WebLogic Server domains that might be active on it. As should be obvious, the configuration of a WebLogic Server domain with node manager has many benefits and can enhance the reliability, manageability, and diagnosability of a Fusion Middleware environment. In the section that follows, we go through the step-by-step instructions for configuring the pricing application's environment with node manager.

Configuring Node Manager within the Pricing Application Environment

In this section we go through the step-by-step instructions for configuring a node manager process on the pricing1 and webcenter1 hosts of the pricing application's topology, as shown in Figure 8-3 of Chapter 8. The configuration of node manager allows us to remotely manage and diagnose the WebLogic Sever instances within the application's pricingdomain and webcenterdomain. Figure 11-4 shows the interaction of the two node manager servers on the two hosts with the pricing1 domain's Pricing1 and Pricing2 managed servers.

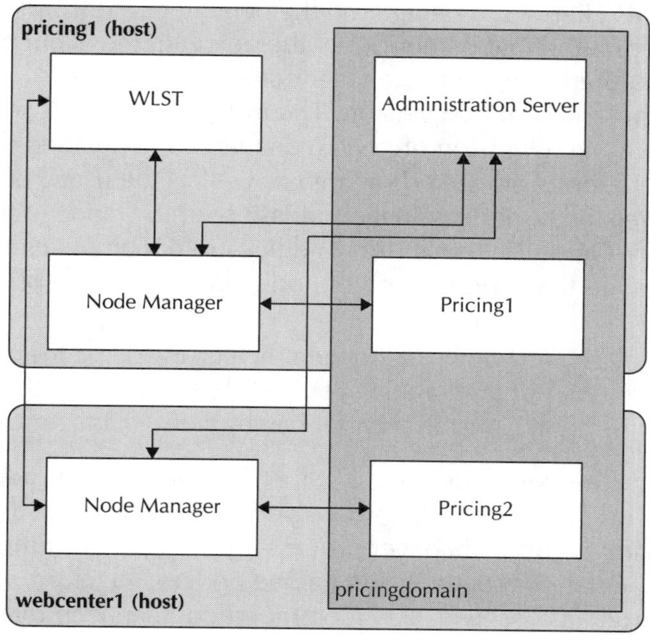

FIGURE 11-4. *Node manager configuration for the pricingdomain*

When node manager is configured on a host, it can be used by WLST as well as the Administration Console. Both of these clients communicate with WLST by first authenticating themselves through a special set of credentials that must be configured on a per-domain basis. As we will see in the steps outlined next, these credentials are configured with node manager by specifically enrolling a domain with it. Once a domain has been enrolled with node manager, clients (WLST and Administration Console) can issue commands to the process, which in turn directly communicates with the domain's servers in order to execute them.

Step-by-Step Configuration of Node Manager

The steps outlined in this section describe the tasks that are essential in getting node manager configured. It should be noted, however, that these steps do not include the configuration of SSL security between node manager and its clients and depend on the default, demonstration, SSL security configuration that comes out of the box with the WebLogic Server installation. Furthermore, node manager comes in two flavors: a Java-based as well as a shell-script-based version. The instructions in this section apply only to the Java-based version of node manager. For a detailed description of the configuration of advanced security as well as the usage of the shell-script-based version of node manager, please refer to "Node Manager Administrator's Guide" in the Fusion Middleware documentation library.

We begin with the configuration of node manager on the pricing1 host:

1. Begin by shutting down all domain servers, including the administration server of the pricingdomain. You can do this through the domain's Administration Console without having node manager configured.
2. Execute the startNodeManager.sh script within the /products/wlserver_10.3/server/bin WebLogic Server installation directory. This will start the node manager process for the very first time, and as a result initiate a properties file named nodemanager.properties within the /products/wlserver_10.3/common/nodemanager/ directory. The properties in this file can be used to configure the node manager instance on this host.

3. We will only need to modify a single configuration for the pricing1 node manage instance, and that is the *StartScriptEnabled* property. By default, the value of this property is set to *false,* which means that Node Manager will not use the domain's /pricingdomain/bin start scripts to start server instances. When this is the case, all customized Java properties and classpath settings must be configured explicitly within the domain configuration for each server. Fusion Middleware layered components such as Oracle SOA Suite have a large set of such Java properties and classpath dependencies that are all captured within the domain's startup scripts. To avoid having to migrate these settings from the startup scripts to the server's associated domain configurations, it is therefore best to configure node manager to use those same scripts when starting the servers, thus preserving the settings of their required Java properties and classpaths. To do this, open the file named /products/wlserver_10.3/common/nodemanager/nodemanager.properties and set the *StartScriptEnabled* property to *true.*

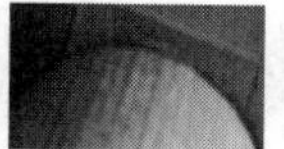

NOTE
The management of Fusion Middleware WebLogic Server environments requires server instances to be started through their domain-based start scripts. As a result, when configuring node manager, you must ensure that the StartScriptEnabled *property is set to* true.

4. We need to configure the credentials that will be used by node manager clients to authenticate themselves in order to issue management commands for the pricingdomain. To do this, start the administration server of the domain back up by using its start script. Once the admin server is started, log in to the Administration Console of the domain and navigate to the Domain (domain name) | Security | General page and open the Advanced area, as shown next.

Within the area, set the NodeManager Username field to *weblogic* and the NodeManager Password field to *welcome1*.

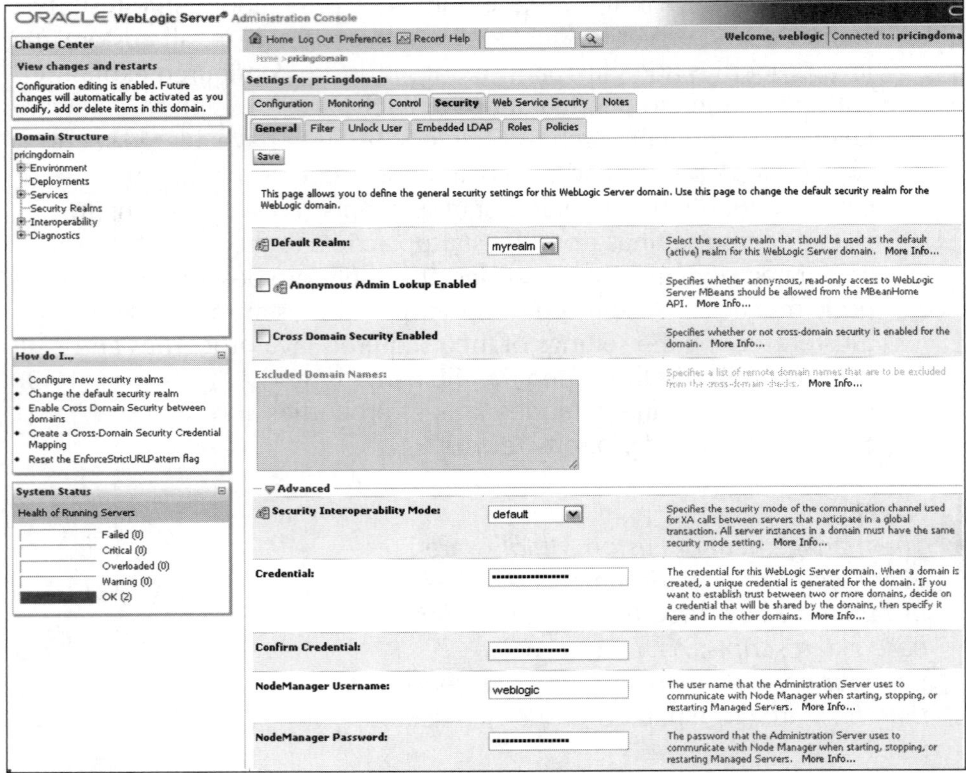

5. We now need to introduce node manager to the pricing1 domain. To do this, run WLST, connect to the pricingdomain, and execute the following command:

```
nmEnroll('/home/oracle/pricingdomain')
```

This command performs the following steps:

- It registers the domain directory with node manager by placing an entry for it within the nodemanager.domains file of the products/wlserver_10.3/common/nodemanager directory. Node manager keeps track of the directory of all domains it is aware of within this file.

- It connects to the domain's administration server to obtain the credentials we configured in the last step—that is, the credentials that need to be used by node manager clients that want to manage this domain—and stores them in encrypted form within the nm_password.properties file in the /pricingdomain/config directory. If the credentials configured within the domain do not match those within this file, node manager clients will not be able to connect to node manager to manage this domain.

6. Shut down the node manager instance started in step 2 and start it back up again so that it can re-read the pricingdomain's information now that it has been enrolled.

We have now completed the configuration of node manager on the pricing1 host and can start using it through WLST or the Administration Console. At this point, you can start the servers from the Administration Console or by running WLST from any machine, connecting to the node manager remotely, and issuing specific WLST commands. However, before using WLST in this way, you need to start each server at least once using the Administration Console. This is due to an existing issue with node manager functionality that will hopefully be fixed within an upcoming Oracle Fusion Middleware release. Once you have done that, here are some steps you can follow to test out your configuration using WLST:

1. Start WLST from any machine and connect to the pricingdomain.
2. Execute the following command to connect to the node manager instance on the pricing1 host:

```
nmConnect('weblogic','welcome1','localhost','5556','pricingdomain',
'/home/oracle/pricingdomain','ssl')
```

3. Now that you are connected to the node manager, you can start and stop servers through WLST. You can start the domain's managed servers by issuing the following commands:

```
nmStart('Pricing1','/home/oracle/pricingdomain')
nmStart('soa_server_1','/home/oracle/pricingdomain')
nmStart('bam_server_1','/home/oracle/pricingdomain')
```

4. You can also obtain the status of each server by issuing the following command:

```
wls:/pricingdomain/serverConfig> nmServerStatus('Pricing1')
RUNNING
```

Other WLST commands that you can use once you have established a connection to node manager include nmKill (to stop servers) and nmServerLog (to retrieve the log messages of a specific server). One of the important advantages of having node manager configured is that all of these commands can be executed remotely (that is, from a different server than the server on which the managed servers are running) without needing access to the Administration Console. This provides more flexibility in managing a Fusion Middleware environment and troubleshooting any issues that might arise.

The steps outlined in this section lead to the configuration of node manager within the pricing1 host and the registration of the pricingdomain with it. To complete the picture, we would also need to configure node manager on the webcenter1 host and register both the pricing1 and webcenter1 domains on that host with it. This process consists of repeating steps 4 through 6 for both domains on the webcenter1 host.

Conclusion

In this chapter we reviewed three important areas concerning the monitoring and diagnostics capabilities of Fusion Middleware. We began with a detailed discussion of the two Fusion Middleware logging infrastructures: the WebLogic Server logging service and the Oracle Diagnostics Logging (ODL) service. We discussed how these two logging services relate to each other as well as the structure and content of the log messages they produce. We then continued by exploring the WebLogic Diagnostics Framework, a comprehensive set of services that facilitate the analysis and monitoring of WebLogic Server–based components. Finally, we ended the chapter with a detailed look at the way in which the WebLogic Server node manager component functions and the steps associated with configuring it within the pricing application's environment.

CHAPTER 12

Virtualizing Fusion Middleware Enterprise Applications

erver virtualization provides the ability to use a single physical host computer for the execution of multiple, isolated, purely software-based computers, known as virtual machines. Although the concept of server virtualization has existed for a long time, going as far back as the heydays of mainframe computing, in recent time it has gained more momentum as a tool that allows for the simplification of IT operations. Today, server virtualization allows organizations to consolidate their physical hardware infrastructures by running multiple, isolated, virtual machines on the same physical machines. Furthermore, virtualization also simplifies administration of development, staging, and sometimes even production environments by facilitating the provisioning of new virtual machines. This chapter contains a high-level review of the Oracle products designed to enable server virtualization: Oracle Virtual Machine, Oracle JRockit and WebLogic Server Virtual Edition, Oracle Virtual Assembly Builder, and, finally, Oracle Exalogic. The aim of this chapter is not to describe the features of these products at a level of detail that would provide a complete understanding of their end-to-end usage—such a treatment would require a book onto itself—but rather to provide an overview description that allows the reader to gain an understanding of the main capabilities each product offers. In our description of each of these products, we will also review, where relevant, the application of the product to the pricing application in order to better illustrate the practical application of the product's capabilities.

Oracle Virtual Machine

The Oracle Virtual Machine (OVM) is the product that acts as the cornerstone for all Oracle Fusion Middleware virtualization capabilities. The core component of OVM consists of a hypervisor that is installed on a physical machine instead of a platform operating system. The hypervisor is the runtime environment for virtual machine instances. It manages the physical machine's hardware resources and exposes them to all running virtual machine instances as virtual hardware resources according to their required specifications.

The hypervisor is also the resource that ensures that each virtual machine instance's operating system—known as a *guest* operating system—can execute in complete isolation from the operating system of the other virtual machines executing on the same physical host. Each virtual machine consists of an operating system image and a set of metadata specifying the hardware requirements that the hypervisor must meet when the virtual machine is instantiated. Figure 12-1 shows a sample topology of OVM on a single physical server with two virtual machines that have different operating systems: Oracle Enterprise Linux (OEL) and Solaris. Other than the hypervisor, OVM also provides a optional Virtual Machine Manager (VM Manager) that exposes a web-based user interface with functionality for the management of an OVM environment. This includes functions for the life-cycle management of virtual machine instances. The VM Manager itself can execute on the OVM hypervisor as a virtual machine instance and also on a separate machine outside of the OVM servers it managers. The VM Manager is also generally intended for use in environments where multiple OVM servers exist because it allows for their central management.

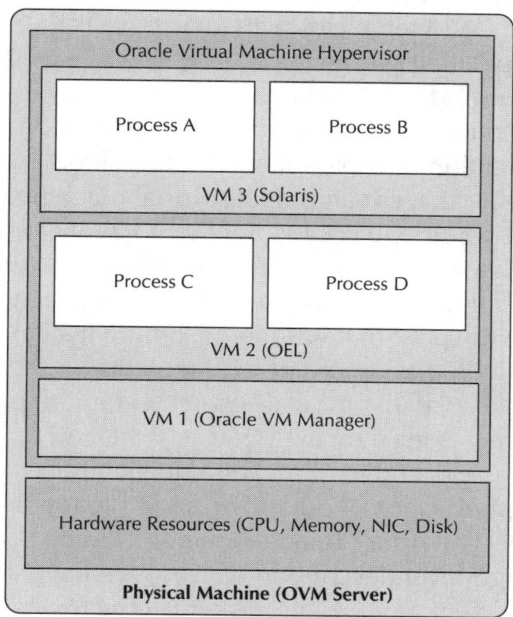

FIGURE 12-1. *Virtualization of a single physical machine with OVM*

The provisioning of a new virtual machine instance within an OVM server can be done in two ways. The first is through a command-line tool named virt-install, which prompts for the required properties of the virtual machine as well as a pointer to an actual operating system image. The tool then creates a virtualized guest on the OVM server. The second way of creating virtual guest instances is through the registration of an OVM template. This can be done with the VM Manager or through the virt-install command-line tool. An *OVM template* is a package that contains the guest operating system image for a specific type of virtual machine as well as metadata regarding its virtual hardware specification (for example, the amount of memory, number of CPUs, network interface cards, and disk volumes). Once a template is registered, new virtualized guest instances that are based on the template can be created on the OVM server. OVM templates can contain more than just a blank operating system image, and templates with preinstalled applications can be used to simplify the life-cycle management of an enterprise application and its dependencies. In fact, Oracle provides a number of predefined OVM templates that contain preinstalled and preconfigured versions of a number of its Applications, Fusion Middleware, and Database products. Oracle also provides predefined OVM templates with images for the Oracle Enterprise Linux and Solaris operating systems.

OVM also allows for the aggregation of multiple OVM server machines into a single server pool. A *server pool* is a group of OVM servers that can be used for the execution of a user-defined set of virtual machines. Using a server pool, the VM Manager can migrate virtual machine instances from one physical server within the pool to another to allow for load-balancing and high-availability capabilities. As an example, upon virtual machine startup, when a server pool is configured, the VM Manager chooses an OVM server within the pool that has the maximum available hardware resources. One of the more important requirements for the creation of a server pool is the need for all physical servers within the pool to use a shared file system that is used by the OVM to store and manage the running virtual machine's images and to allow for a quick failover between different servers within the pool. Figure 12-2 shows a sample topology of OVM on two physical servers with four virtual machines forming a server pool.

Although the high-level description of OVM we have covered so far should provide sufficient grounds for the remaining topics covered in this chapter, a detailed discussion of the product is beyond the scope of this book. For a detailed description of OVM and VM Manager, please refer to

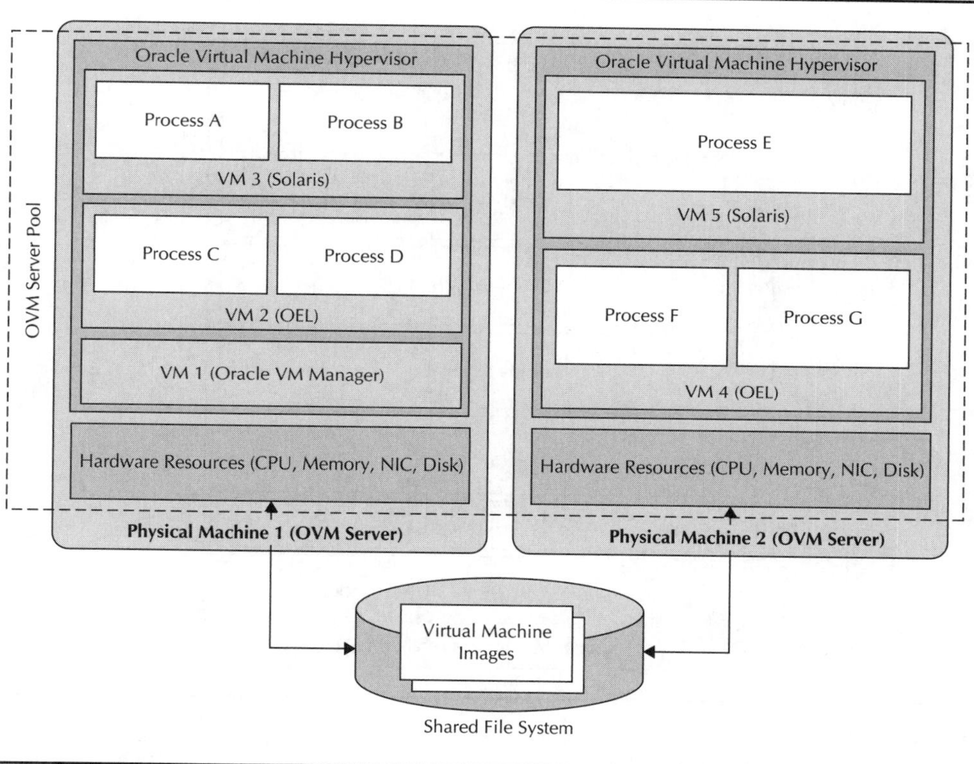

FIGURE 12-2. *Virtualization of two physical machines with OVM to form a server pool*

the *Oracle Virtual Machine User Guide* and *Oracle Virtual Machine Manager User Guide* books within the Oracle document library.

Pricing Application on Oracle Virtual Machine

The use of the OVM to virtualize the pricing application's environment, as shown in Figure 8-3, could take a number of forms, depending on the specifications of the physical servers available and the IT organizational requirements. At one extreme, one could create a virtual instance for every single machine shown in Figure 8-3 of Chapter 8 (for a total of five, not including the OVM VM Manager instance) and deploy them on a single physical OVM-enabled server, as illustrated in Figure 12-3.

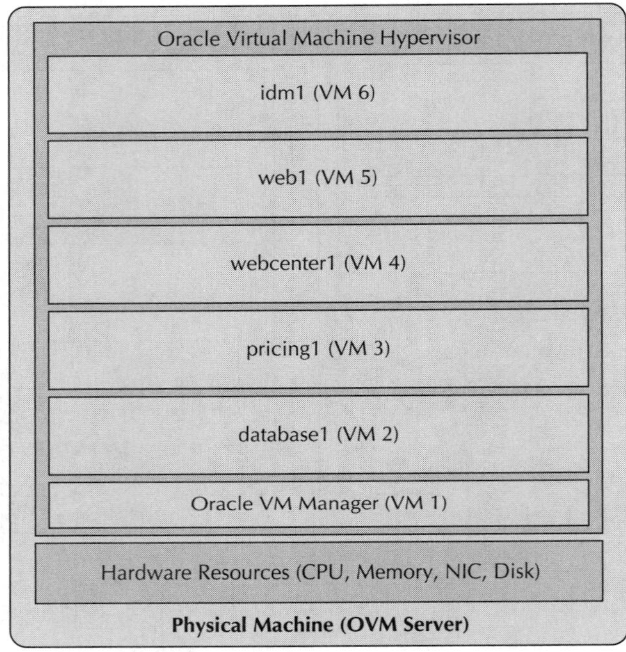

FIGURE 12-3. *Sample single-server OVM deployment of pricing application*

However, this would require a large server to suit the needs of the five virtual machines' guest operating systems as well as the running applications. Furthermore, this topology would not be beneficial to the application's PricingCluster because a failure of the single physical server would lead to the failure of the application despite the cluster's two nodes. Finally, from an organizational point of view, it is probably not desirable to host the idm1 host on the same OVM server as the pricing applications because this server contains the shared IDM infrastructure components that are serving the needs of all of the organization's enterprise applications, and their coupling with the pricing application's physical server will probably not make sense for performance and maintenance reasons. For all of these

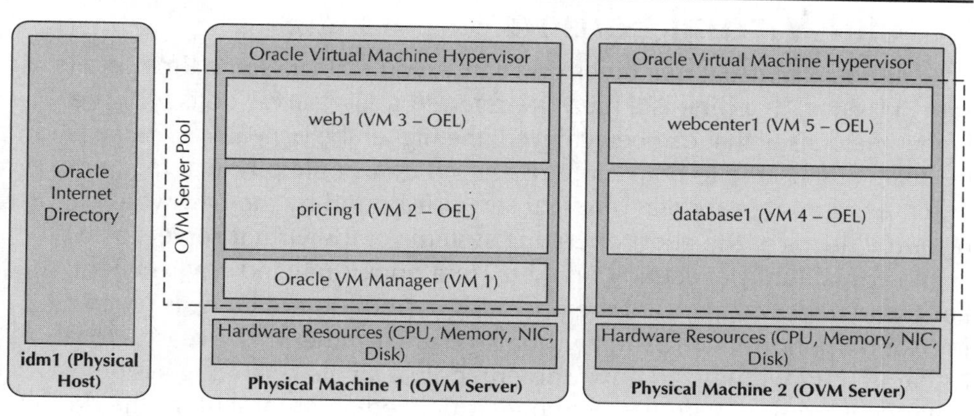

FIGURE 12-4. *Sample two-server virtualization of pricing application*

reasons, one could consider a topology that is closer to the one shown in Figure 12-4. In this topology, we are consolidating what used to be four physical servers onto two by virtue of virtualization. Again, the adequacy of this topology will need to be measured against the particular environmental requirements. For example, even this topology might not be adequate because the database and web tiers might be managed by separate groups who would like to ensure that they are executing these layers on their own physical systems.

JRockit and WebLogic Server Virtual Edition

In this section we review Oracle JRockit and WebLogic Server Virtual Editions. These products allow for the deployment of Java and WebLogic Server applications on an OVM server without the need for a guest operating system.

JRockit Virtual Edition

The number of virtual machines one can execute at the same time on the same physical machine is a measure referred to as "server density." The higher the density that can be achieved, the higher the benefits of virtualization because one is able to reap more usage out of a single physical machine. The maximum density of a physical server is bound by the hardware resource needs of the guest operating systems of the virtual servers as well as the applications executing on them. In a nonvirtualized environment, the hardware resource needs of the operating system do not have as much impact on performance as in a virtualized environment. The reason for this is that in a nonvirtualized environment, only a single operating system instance is present, whereas within a virtualized environment, as the density increases, so does the number of host operating systems. As a result, the overall operating system footprint on a single machine from a hardware resource utilization point of view becomes more significant.

To address this issue, Oracle has introduced a version of the JRockit JVM, named Virtual Edition (VE), that is designed to execute on an OVM hypervisor without the need for a host operating system. JRockit VE therefore allows applications written in Java to execute directly on an OVM virtualized server's hypervisor just as a guest operating system would. The elimination of the need for a guest operating system allows for a significant improvement in virtualization density. This is due to the fact that JRockit VE virtual machines no longer have a need to allocate physical resources for guest operating system usage. Furthermore, the execution of the JVM directly on the hardware, as opposed to going through the operating system, introduces additional efficiencies because it eliminates an extra level of processing. Using JRockit VE, one can create an OVM virtual machine template, which is also referred to as an "image." Once the OVM template for a specific Java application is created, it can be used as with any other templates for the instantiation of virtual machines within an OVM server. Figure 12-5 illustrates the runtime environment of an OVM server that is hosting a set of Java applications running on JRockit VE.

JRockit VE application images are created using a command-line tool, known as the imaging tool, which is included with JRockit VE. Once such an image is created, it can be imported as a template into an OVM server environment using the OVM Manager. The JRockit imaging tool accepts as

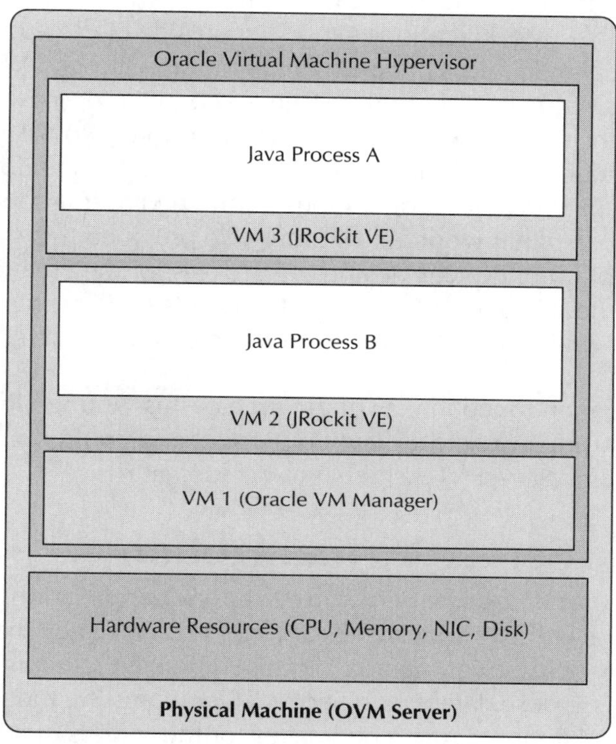

FIGURE 12-5. *Virtualization of a single physical machine with OVM using JRockit VE*

input an XML configuration file. This configuration file includes pointers to the JAR files and dependencies of the Java application that needs be included into the image as well as information about the image's virtual environment, including the amount of memory and CPU resources from the host OVM server that should be dedicated to it. To allow for the execution of Java applications without the need for an operating system, JRockit VE includes within its runtime environment a built-in file system and it also allows the Java application to access external NFS mounts. The built-in file system is used to store the JRockit JVM binaries as well as the Java application's own JAR files. This file system can be accessed when the virtual machine is running using SSH. The file system is, however, not directly accessible by applications executing outside of the application's JRockit VE virtual machine. For cases where multiple JRockit VE JVMs need to access the same set of files, they should be configured to use a shared NFS mount point at image creation time. Furthermore, JRockit VE virtual machine instances also include a virtual network stack that allows for the Java application's network IO operations to proceed as if an operating system layer existed that would have otherwise provided this stack. For a detailed description of JRockit VE and the process for the creation and deployment of new images, please refer to "User's Guide for Oracle JRockit Virtual Edition" within the Oracle Fusion Middleware documentation library.

It should be mentioned that as of the time of this writing, JRockit VE was not available through Oracle as its own product and could only be obtained through WebLogic Server VE, which we will look at next.

WebLogic Server Virtual Edition

Given the fact that WebLogic Server itself is a Java application, its servers can also execute within a JRockit VE runtime. In fact, Oracle has released a version of WebLogic Server, named Virtual Edition (VE), that is designed exactly for this purpose. WebLogic Server VE contains the tooling required for creating JRockit virtual machine images for the servers of a WebLogic Server domain and executing them within an OVM environment. Figure 12-6 illustrates the runtime of a sample WebLogic Server VE-based domain within an OVM environment containing two separate physical servers.

Within a virtualized domain, each WebLogic Server instance—that is, the domain administration server and all managed servers—must execute within its own JRockit VE image, which in turn means that each instance will be treated as a its own virtual machine instance from an OVM point of view. Each server instance stores its WebLogic Server binary and domain directory content within its internal JRockit VE image file system. The propagation of configuration changes and application deployments within the domain is managed by the administration server in the same fashion as a non-VE domain, as we discussed in detail within Chapter 2. Each managed server virtual machine must also be enabled with a special version of the node manager. Conceptually, this can be thought of as an embedded node

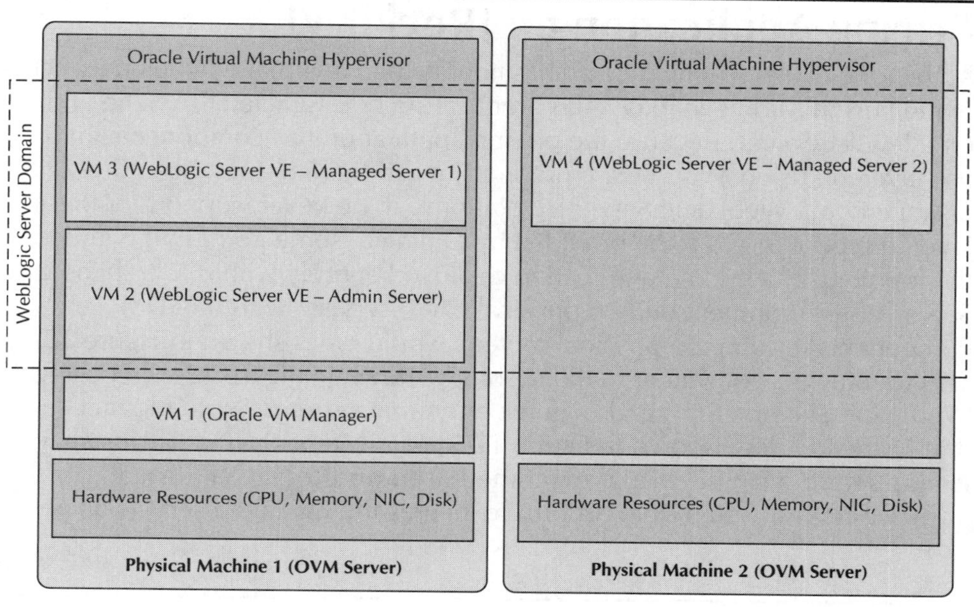

FIGURE 12-6. *Sample WebLogic Server VE-based domain across two physical servers*

manager interface within the JVM process itself that allows for the remote management and control of the virtual server instance's life cycle through the admin console and WLST. This special type of node manager is named a Virtual Machine Monitor (VMM) node manager. A VMM is another name for hypervisor, and the VMM node manager is so named because it provides its functionality through the OVM hypervisor.

WebLogic Server VE allows for the creation of virtualized domains either from scratch or by converting an existing domain (created within a physical environment) into its virtual version. The latter is a process known as Physical-to-Virtual (P2V). The creation and configuration of the JRockit VE images that constitute a full WebLogic Server domain are facilitated through a tool known as the WebLogic Server VE imaging tool. For a detailed description of WebLogic Server VE and the process for the creation and deployment of VE-based domains, please refer to "WebLogic Server on JRockit Virtual Edition Installation and Configuration Guide" within the Oracle Fusion Middleware documentation library.

Pricing Application on JRockit VE

At the time of this writing, Oracle has not released a virtual edition equivalent of the Fusion Middleware layered products such as Oracle SOA Suite and Oracle WebCenter. Because the pricing application has components that use layered Fusion Middleware products, it can therefore not be entirely executed on a WebLogic Server VE platform. If, however, support for these layered products was to be provided by Oracle at some point in the future, the topology of a pricing application deployed entirely within a WebLogic Server VE environment on two physical OVM servers, with the IDM components residing on physical servers, would be as shown in Figure 12-7. This topology is equivalent to the topology shown in Figure 12-4 but using WebLogic Server VE instead of guest operating systems. Note the fact that in the topology shown in Figure 12-7, each WebLogic Server instance is mapped to a single virtual machine based on JRockit VE instead of a full operating system that, in turn, executes the managed servers as per

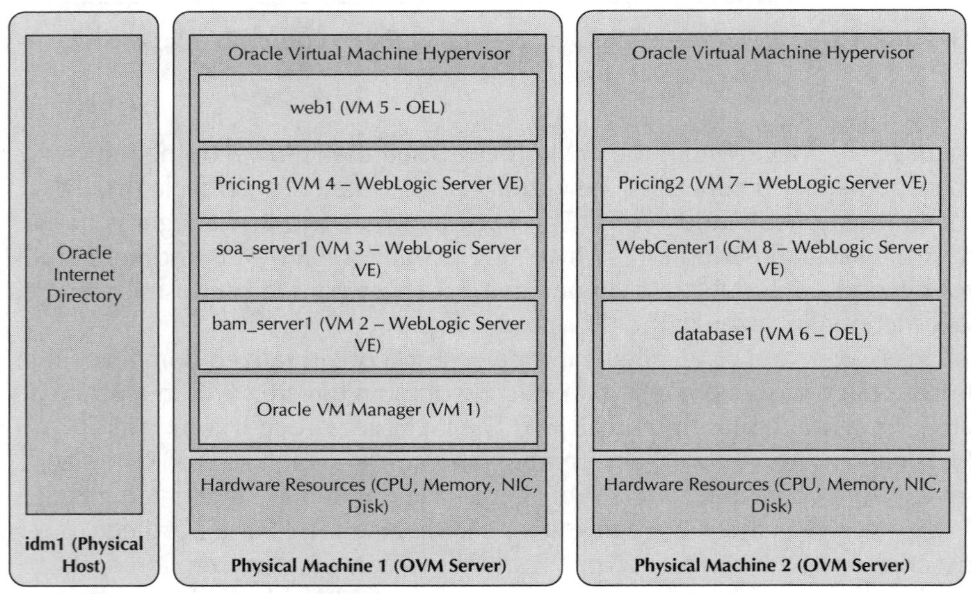

FIGURE 12-7. *Sample topology of the pricing application on JRockit Virtual Edition*

the topology shown in Figure 12-4. Non-Java components of the topology (that is, the OHS server and RDBMS instance) are however still executing as operating system-based virtual machines. The IDM components are kept on a physical server with the same underlying assumption that they share resources and are managed by a separate group within the organization.

Comparing Figure 12-4 with 12-7, we can see that the use of WebLogic Server VE would reduce the need for two guest operating system layers.

Oracle Virtual Assembly Builder

As stated in the previous section, WebLogic Server VE already provides a tool that allows for the migration of an existing, non-VE–based domain into an OVM template that uses WebLogic Server VE. This tool has to be executed on every managed server of the domain to create the associated VE templates for registration and instantiation within an OVM server. Furthermore, if the entire stack was to be virtualized, all components not supported by WebLogic Server VE—such as the Oracle HTTP server at the Web Tier layer, which is not a Java process—would need to be mapped to their own operating system-based virtual machines. Given the fact that an enterprise application typically consists of multiple managed servers, is composed of multiple WebLogic Server domains, and may contain some non-Java processes, the process of creating a purely OVM-based version of its environment can quickly become very complicated. More complication is added by the fact that after virtualization, the dependencies between each virtual machine need to be revisited to ensure that all of the references between the components within separate virtual machines are properly maintained. As an example, if the mod_wl_ohs module of an OHS server instance is configured to route requests to a specific managed server's IP address within the physical environment, the IP address of this managed server can change within the OVM environment and would require an OHS reconfiguration on the virtual machine hosting the OHS instance. Wouldn't it be nice if we instead had a way of migrating an entire physical environment for an existing application (such as the one used by the pricing application and depicted in Figure 8-3) into the associated OVM virtual machines and capture the dependencies between each virtual machine's Fusion Middleware components as metadata that can be tailored for specific instances of the topology? This is, in fact, exactly what the Oracle Virtual Assembly Builder (OVAB) product allows us to achieve.

OVAB allows for the introspection of an existing environment either through a command-line tool, named abctl, or through a graphical user interface named OVAB Studio. These tools allow users to specify the set of Fusion Middleware products that are installed within an environment and point to the coordinates of their running instances (for example, the directories and administrator credentials of the WebLogic Server domains that form the environment). Using this information, OVAB generates an entity known as a "software appliance" for the components within the environment. OVAB allows for the creation of appliances for WebLogic Server domains, Fusion Middleware system components, or Oracle RDBMS instances. A software appliance consists of XML metadata that describes the configuration state of a specific instance of the component for which it was created as well as information about the external inbound and outbound interfaces associated with the component. Examples of interfaces captured by OVAB within an appliance include OHS virtual host endpoints and WebLogic Server JDBC data sources. The description of an appliance's interfaces includes information such as the interface's transport protocol and endpoint IP address/port.

Appliances are stored within a repository known as the OVAB catalog. Using the OVAB Studio tool, users can use the set of appliances within the OVAB catalog as building blocks for the creation of OVAB assemblies. An assembly consists of a group of appliances, metadata that describes the relationship between their interfaces (such as an OHS appliance's reference to an application deployed on another WebLogic Server managed server appliance to signify a routing relationship), as well as metadata that describes the relationship between the appliances and components that might be external to the assembly (such as an external LDAP server). It should be noted that in some cases, the introspection of a physical environment leads directly to the generation of an assembly. Notably, the introspection of a WebLogic Server domain leads to the generation of an assembly with associated appliances for each of the server instances within the domain.

After the creation of an assembly through the OVAB Studio, users can deploy the assembly to an OVM environment. This deployment process begins by using OVAB to convert the assembly into its associated OVM templates—one template is created for each WebLogic Server instance, system component instance, and Oracle RDBMS instance. The OVAB-assembly-to-OVM-template conversion tooling allows users to specify whether the template should be Oracle WebLogic Server VE-based or based on a virtual machine with a full guest operating system. Once the OVM templates of an assembly are generated, they can be registered with an OVM environment's VM Manager and instantiated as described in the "Oracle Virtual Machine" section of this chapter. OVAB Studio can also be used to facilitate the deployment of templates to an OVM environment by providing wizards that allow for the creation of connections to OVM environments for later reuse as well as the registration of templates with such environments. OVAB thus allows the end-to-end process for the deployment of an N-tier system topology embodied within an assembly to be performed with only a few clicks of the mouse. A more detailed discussion of OVAB is beyond the scope of this book, and the reader is instead referred to the *Oracle Virtual Assembly Builder User's Guide* book within the Oracle documentation library for further information regarding this product.

Oracle Exalogic

Oracle Exalogic is a preassembled hardware system delivered with a set of Fusion Middleware components. The hardware system is designed from the ground up to serve as a platform for the deployment, execution, and management of enterprise applications. The release of Exalogic follows that of Oracle Exadata, which is a preassembled hardware system delivered with Oracle Relational Database software and designed to deliver optimal performance. A number of Fusion Middleware components have been extended with features that allow them to take optimal advantage of the Exalogic hardware architecture. Furthermore, Exalogic can serve as a powerful virtualization platform when combined with the capabilities of OVM and OVAB. In this section, we review the Exalogic hardware and software capabilities and end with an exploration of the system's potential as a virtualization platform.

Exalogic Hardware

Each Exalogic rack consists of a set of compute node racks, a clustered, high-performance disk storage subsystem, and a high-bandwidth interconnect that allows for communication between the compute nodes, the disk storage, as well as with external Exalogic or Exadata systems. Each rack also provides 10GB and 1GB Ethernet connection ports for communication with external systems. Figure 12-8 illustrates the hardware configuration of an Exalogic rack.

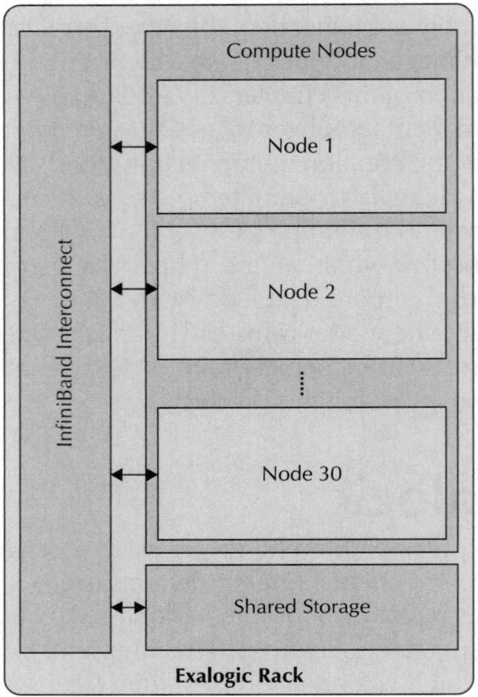

FIGURE 12-8. *Exalogic rack hardware configuration*

At the time of this writing, Oracle had just released the first version of Exalogic. In this 1.0 version, two models of Exalogic are available: X2-2 and T3-1B. The difference between these models lies in the type of supported compute nodes. For the X2-2 model, each compute node consists of two 2.93GHz Intel Xeon six-core CPU chips, 96Gb of 1333MHz memory, and 32Gb of Flash memory. Each compute node of the T3-1B system consists of four 1.6GHz SPARC quad-core CPU chips, 130Gb of 1333MHz memory, and as with the X2-2, 32Gb of Flash memory. An Exalogic box is available with either an 8 (quarter rack), 16 (half rack), or 30 (full rack) compute node configuration. Although the compute nodes are designed to provide a scalable platform for the execution of enterprise applications, each Exalogic box also contains a 40Tb ZFS Storage 7320 appliance shared file system to satisfy the applications' persistent storage needs. From a networking point of view, each Exalogic box provides a 40Gb/second InfiniBand networking backbone that is used by the applications executing on its compute nodes to communicate with each other, the file system, and with other Exalogic or Exadata systems connected to the box via a special InfiniBand port.

Exalogic Software

Exalogic systems come with a set of software components that have been optimized for their hardware configuration. This starts at the operating system layer, which (as of the time of this writing) consisted of either Oracle Enterprise Linux or Solaris. Any software application built on any one of these operating systems is therefore capable of executing within Exalogic and thus takes advantage of it as a pure high-performance and preconfigured hardware platform. The more significant part of the advantages brought by Exalogic, however, stems from synergies offered at the Fusion Middleware level. A set of Fusion Middleware components that Oracle collectively refers to as the Exalogic Elastic Cloud Software (from now on referred to simply as Elastic Cloud) introduce features to take advantages of the Exalogic architecture in order to optimize their performance. In general, the optimizations introduced within the Elastic Cloud version of the Fusion Middleware stack address performance areas that are only apparent when the stack is executing within the high-capacity compute nodes and networking environment of an Exalogic system. Elastic Cloud, therefore, really refers to these special optimizations that allow the Fusion Middleware stack to provide improved performance, in most cases without any required tuning, when executing within an Exalogic environment. The Elastic Cloud elements currently consist solely of the Fusion Middleware components falling within the Application Grid category (as per the review of the different categories of Fusion Middleware products described in Chapter 1). Here are some of the significant areas of optimizations that are part of Exalogic's Elastic Cloud Software and are currently at the WebLogic Server level:

- **InfiniBand-based optimizations** InfiniBand allows for the transmission of significantly larger packets than is possible over an Ethernet network. To take advantage of this fact when executing on an Exalogic platform, the WebLogic Server network interface infrastructure has been modified to allow for the grouping of outgoing packages into larger chunks and, on the other side of the wire, the redistribution of these chunks back into smaller ones. Given the high performance cost of socket read/write operations, the higher package size permitted by InfiniBand combined with this WebLogic Server feature allows for a significant improvement in performance for all network communication between WebLogic Server instances. Furthermore, the WebLogic Server networking infrastructure has been modified to take advantage of JRockit-level optimizations (as a result, these optimizations are only available when JRockit is used as a JVM). This allows different WebLogic Server instances to access each other's memory space directly through the InfiniBand network interface. These optimizations allow for significant improvement of performance for features that require a high level of chatter between multiple WebLogic Server managed servers, such as cases where HTTP session replication is used to provide high availability for web applications.

- **GridLink optimizations** As we reviewed in Chapter 2, the WebLogic Server GridLink feature provides an alternative approach for the integration of WebLogic Server–based applications with Real Application Cluster (RAC) Oracle database instances. The GridLink capabilities of WebLogic Server, which present an optimization of the multi-data-source model of RAC integration as per our review in Chapter 2, are only available for use within an Exalogic environment. Furthermore, the GridLink JDBC data source has been modified to take advantage of the InfiniBand optimizations discussed in the previous point when the target Oracle database RAC topology is executing within an Oracle Exadata system connected to the Exalogic system.
- **Self-tuning thread pool optimizations** When executing within an Exalogic environment, the WebLogic Server self-tuning thread pool algorithm (as we reviewed in detail in Chapter 2) has been altered to take advantage of the high number of cores available on each compute node. In default execution, the self-tuning thread pool increases its size by one thread at a time when such an expansion is required. However, when executing within an Exalogic environment, the self-tuning thread pool is configured to increase the size of the pool by 24 threads at a time when an expansion is required. This higher increment value leads to a better usage of the underlying CPU cores of the Exalogic compute nodes.

Exalogic Virtualization Platform

At the time of this writing, none of the Exalogic machine models provided support for OVM. However, when such functionality is introduced by Oracle, the potential of Exalogic as a virtualization platform is easy to foresee. The compute nodes of an Exalogic rack can form OVM server pools and allow for the execution of multiple guest operating system and/or JRockit VE instances. Furthermore, the communication between the virtual machine instances is enabled through the Exalogic system's InfiniBand network, thus allowing for the high-bandwidth and low-latency communication it facilitates. Figure 12-9 illustrates a sample topology that could execute on an OVM-enabled Exalogic rack.

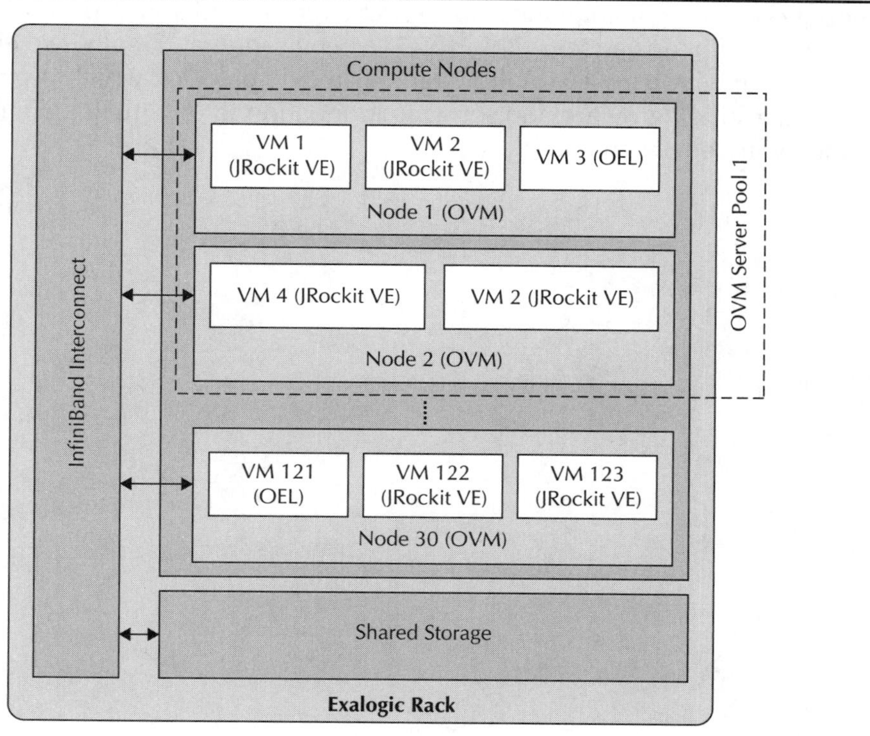

FIGURE 12-9. *Sample OVM-enabled Exalogic topology*

Conclusion

In this chapter we reviewed the core set of Oracle virtualization products and their relationships. We began with a review of the Oracle Virtual Manager, a product that provides foundational virtualization capabilities by allowing multiple virtual machine images with a guest operating system to execute in isolation within a single physical server. We then moved on to an exploration of the capabilities of the JRockit and WebLogic Server Virtual Edition products. As we discussed, together these products allow for the execution of Java and WebLogic Server–based applications within an OVM environment without the need for a guest operating system. This allows for an improvement in performance and a higher virtualization density on OVM servers. We also covered the Oracle Virtual Assembly Builder products, which allow for the introspection of a physical environment into an assembly model consisting of appliances that can be remodeled and deployed as virtual machine instances within an OVM environment. Finally, we ended the chapter with a review of the Oracle Exalogic product, which promises to provide a solid hardware and software foundation for a virtualized Fusion Middleware environment.

Index

D

E

K

L

M

N

O

P

Q

R

S

T

U

V

W

X

Z

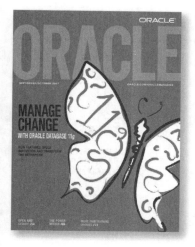

Want your own FREE subscription?

To receive a free subscription to *Oracle Magazine*, you must fill out the entire card, sign it, and date it (incomplete cards cannot be processed or acknowledged). You can also fax your application to +1.847.763.9638. **Or subscribe at our Web site at oracle.com/oraclemagazine**

○ **Yes, please send me a FREE subscription *Oracle Magazine*.** ○ No.

○ From time to time, Oracle Publishing allows our partners exclusive access to our e-mail addresses for special promotions and announcements. To be included in this program, please check this circle. If you do not wish to be included, you will only receive notices about your subscription via e-mail.

○ Oracle Publishing allows sharing of our postal mailing list with selected third parties. If you prefer your mailing address not to be included in this program, please check this circle.

If at any time you would like to be removed from either mailing list, please contact Customer Service at +1.847.763.9635 or send an e-mail to oracle@halldata.com. If you opt in to the sharing of information, Oracle may also provide you with e-mail related to Oracle products, services, and events. If you want to completely unsubscribe from any e-mail communication from Oracle, please send an e-mail to: unsubscribe@oracle-mail.com with the following in the subject line: REMOVE [your e-mail address]. For complete information on Oracle Publishing's privacy practices, please visit oracle.com/html/privacy/html

X

signature (required) date

name title

company e-mail address

street/p.o. box

city/state/zip or postal code telephone

country fax

Would you like to receive your free subscription in digital format instead of print if it becomes available? ○ **Yes** ○ **No**

YOU MUST ANSWER ALL 10 QUESTIONS BELOW.

① **WHAT IS THE PRIMARY BUSINESS ACTIVITY OF YOUR FIRM AT THIS LOCATION? (check one only)**

- □ 01 Aerospace and Defense Manufacturing
- □ 02 Application Service Provider
- □ 03 Automotive Manufacturing
- □ 04 Chemicals
- □ 05 Media and Entertainment
- □ 06 Construction/Engineering
- □ 07 Consumer Sector/Consumer Packaged Goods
- □ 08 Education
- □ 09 Financial Services/Insurance
- □ 10 Health Care
- □ 11 High Technology Manufacturing, OEM
- □ 12 Industrial Manufacturing
- □ 13 Independent Software Vendor
- □ 14 Life Sciences (biotech, pharmaceuticals)
- □ 15 Natural Resources
- □ 16 Oil and Gas
- □ 17 Professional Services
- □ 18 Public Sector (government)
- □ 19 Research
- □ 20 Retail/Wholesale/Distribution
- □ 21 Systems Integrator, VAR/VAD
- □ 22 Telecommunications
- □ 23 Travel and Transportation
- □ 24 Utilities (electric, gas, sanitation, water)
- □ 98 Other Business and Services ________

② **WHICH OF THE FOLLOWING BEST DESCRIBES YOUR PRIMARY JOB FUNCTION? (check one only)**

CORPORATE MANAGEMENT/STAFF

- □ 01 Executive Management (President, Chair, CEO, CFO, Owner, Partner, Principal)
- □ 02 Finance/Administrative Management (VP/Director/ Manager/Controller, Purchasing, Administration)
- □ 03 Sales/Marketing Management (VP/Director/Manager)
- □ 04 Computer Systems/Operations Management (CIO/VP/Director/Manager MIS/IS/IT, Ops)

IS/IT STAFF

- □ 05 Application Development/Programming Management
- □ 06 Application Development/Programming Staff
- □ 07 Consulting
- □ 08 DBA/Systems Administrator
- □ 09 Education/Training
- □ 10 Technical Support Director/Manager
- □ 11 Other Technical Management/Staff
- □ 98 Other

③ **WHAT IS YOUR CURRENT PRIMARY OPERATING PLATFORM (check all that apply)**

- □ 01 Digital Equipment Corp UNIX/VAX/VMS
- □ 02 HP UNIX
- □ 03 IBM AIX
- □ 04 IBM UNIX
- □ 05 Linux (Red Hat)
- □ 06 Linux (SUSE)
- □ 07 Linux (Oracle Enterprise)
- □ 08 Linux (other)
- □ 09 Macintosh
- □ 10 MVS
- □ 11 Netware
- □ 12 Network Computing
- □ 13 SCO UNIX
- □ 14 Sun Solaris/SunOS
- □ 15 Windows
- □ 16 Other UNIX
- □ 98 Other
- 99 □ None of the Above

④ **DO YOU EVALUATE, SPECIFY, RECOMMEND, OR AUTHORIZE THE PURCHASE OF ANY OF THE FOLLOWING? (check all that apply)**

- □ 01 Hardware
- □ 02 Business Applications (ERP, CRM, etc.)
- □ 03 Application Development Tools
- □ 04 Database Products
- □ 05 Internet or Intranet Products
- □ 06 Other Software
- □ 07 Middleware Products
- 99 □ None of the Above

⑤ **IN YOUR JOB, DO YOU USE OR PLAN TO PURCHASE ANY OF THE FOLLOWING PRODUCTS? (check all that apply)**

SOFTWARE

- □ 01 CAD/CAE/CAM
- □ 02 Collaboration Software
- □ 03 Communications
- □ 04 Database Management
- □ 05 File Management
- □ 06 Finance
- □ 07 Java
- □ 08 Multimedia Authoring
- □ 09 Networking
- □ 10 Programming
- □ 11 Project Management
- □ 12 Scientific and Engineering
- □ 13 Systems Management
- □ 14 Workflow

HARDWARE

- □ 15 Macintosh
- □ 16 Mainframe
- □ 17 Massively Parallel Processing
- □ 18 Minicomputer
- □ 19 Intel x86(32)
- □ 20 Intel x86(64)
- □ 21 Network Computer
- □ 22 Symmetric Multiprocessing
- □ 23 Workstation Services

SERVICES

- □ 24 Consulting
- □ 25 Education/Training
- □ 26 Maintenance
- □ 27 Online Database
- □ 28 Support
- □ 29 Technology-Based Training
- □ 30 Other
- 99 □ None of the Above

⑥ **WHAT IS YOUR COMPANY'S SIZE? (check one only)**

- □ 01 More than 25,000 Employees
- □ 02 10,001 to 25,000 Employees
- □ 03 5,001 to 10,000 Employees
- □ 04 1,001 to 5,000 Employees
- □ 05 101 to 1,000 Employees
- □ 06 Fewer than 100 Employees

⑦ **DURING THE NEXT 12 MONTHS, HOW MUCH DO YOU ANTICIPATE YOUR ORGANIZATION WILL SPEND ON COMPUTER HARDWARE, SOFTWARE, PERIPHERALS, AND SERVICES FOR YOUR LOCATION? (check one only)**

- □ 01 Less than $10,000
- □ 02 $10,000 to $49,999
- □ 03 $50,000 to $99,999
- □ 04 $100,000 to $499,999
- □ 05 $500,000 to $999,999
- □ 06 $1,000,000 and Over

⑧ **WHAT IS YOUR COMPANY'S YEARLY SALES REVENUE? (check one only)**

- □ 01 $500, 000, 000 and above
- □ 02 $100, 000, 000 to $500, 000, 000
- □ 03 $50, 000, 000 to $100, 000, 000
- □ 04 $5, 000, 000 to $50, 000, 000
- □ 05 $1, 000, 000 to $5, 000, 000

⑨ **WHAT LANGUAGES AND FRAMEWORKS DO YOU USE? (check all that apply)**

- □ 01 Ajax
- □ 02 C
- □ 03 C++
- □ 04 C#
- □ 05 Hibernate
- □ 06 J++/J#
- □ 07 Java
- □ 08 JSP
- □ 09 .NET
- □ 10 Perl
- □ 11 PHP
- □ 12 PL/SQL
- □ 13 Python
- □ 14 Ruby/Rails
- □ 15 Spring
- □ 16 Struts
- □ 17 SQL
- □ 18 Visual Basic
- □ 98 Other

⑩ **WHAT ORACLE PRODUCTS ARE IN USE AT YOUR SITE? (check all that apply)**

ORACLE DATABASE

- □ 01 Oracle Database 11*g*
- □ 02 Oracle Database 10*g*
- □ 03 Oracle9*i* Database
- □ 04 Oracle Embedded Database (Oracle Lite, Times Ten, Berkeley DB)
- □ 05 Other Oracle Database Release

ORACLE FUSION MIDDLEWARE

- □ 06 Oracle Application Server
- □ 07 Oracle Portal
- □ 08 Oracle Enterprise Manager
- □ 09 Oracle BPEL Process Manager
- □ 10 Oracle Identity Management
- □ 11 Oracle SOA Suite
- □ 12 Oracle Data Hubs

ORACLE DEVELOPMENT TOOLS

- □ 13 Oracle JDeveloper
- □ 14 Oracle Forms
- □ 15 Oracle Reports
- □ 16 Oracle Designer
- □ 17 Oracle Discoverer
- □ 18 Oracle BI Beans
- □ 19 Oracle Warehouse Builder
- □ 20 Oracle WebCenter
- □ 21 Oracle Application Express

ORACLE APPLICATIONS

- □ 22 Oracle E-Business Suite
- □ 23 PeopleSoft Enterprise
- □ 24 JD Edwards EnterpriseOne
- □ 25 JD Edwards World
- □ 26 Oracle Fusion
- □ 27 Hyperion
- □ 28 Siebel CRM

ORACLE SERVICES

- □ 28 Oracle E-Business Suite On Demand
- □ 29 Oracle Technology On Demand
- □ 30 Siebel CRM On Demand
- □ 31 Oracle Consulting
- □ 32 Oracle Education
- □ 33 Oracle Support
- □ 98 Other
- 99 □ None of the Above